THE BLACK PACIFIC NARRATIVE

RE-MAPPING THE TRANSNATIONAL
A Dartmouth Series in American Studies

SERIES EDITOR
Donald E. Pease
Avalon Foundation Chair of Humanities
Founding Director of the Futures of American Studies Institute
Dartmouth College

The emergence of Transnational American Studies in the wake of the Cold War marks the most significant reconfiguration of American Studies since its inception. The shock waves generated by a newly globalized world order demanded an understanding of America's embeddedness within global and local processes rather than scholarly reaffirmations of its splendid isolation. The series Re-Mapping the Transnational seeks to foster the cross-national dialogues needed to sustain the vitality of this emergent field. To advance a truly comparativist understanding of this scholarly endeavor, Dartmouth College Press welcomes monographs from scholars both inside and outside the United States.

For a complete list of books available in this series, see www.upne.com.

Etsuko Taketani, *The Black Pacific Narrative: Geographic Imaginings of Race and Empire between the World Wars*

William V. Spanos, *Shock and Awe: American Exceptionalism and the Imperatives of the Spectacle in Mark Twain's* A Connecticut Yankee in King Arthur's Court

Laura Bieger, Ramón Saldívar, and Johannes Voelz, editors, *The Imaginary and Its Worlds: American Studies after the Transnational Turn*

Paul A. Bové, *A More Conservative Place: Intellectual Culture in the Bush Era*

John Muthyala, *Dwelling in American: Dissent, Empire, and Globalization*

Winfried Fluck, Donald E. Pease, and John Carlos Rowe, editors, *Re-Framing the Transnational Turn in American Studies*

Lene M. Johannessen, *Horizons of Enchantment: Essays in the American Imaginary*

John Carlos Rowe, *Afterlives of Modernism: Liberalism, Transnationalism, and Political Critique*

Anthony Bogues, *Empire of Liberty: Power, Desire, and Freedom*

Etsuko Taketani

THE BLACK PACIFIC NARRATIVE

Geographic Imaginings of
Race and Empire between
the World Wars

DARTMOUTH COLLEGE PRESS
HANOVER, NEW HAMPSHIRE

Dartmouth College Press
An imprint of University Press of New England
www.upne.com
© 2014 Trustees of Dartmouth College
All rights reserved
Manufactured in the United States of America
Typeset in Sabon by Westchester Publishing Services

For permission to reproduce any of the material in this book, contact Permissions, University Press of New England, One Court Street, Suite 250, Lebanon NH 03766; or visit www.upne.com

Cloth ISBN: 978-1-61168-612-8
Paper ISBN: 678-1-61168-613-5
Ebook ISBN: 978-1-61168-614-2

Library of Congress Cataloging-in-Publication Data available upon request

5 4 3 2 1

For my beloved mother, Chieko Hosokawa Naruse, and in loving memory of my father, Yukio Naruse (1932–2013), and my brother, Takashi Naruse (1963–2013)

CONTENTS

Acknowledgments xi

Introduction 1

1 The Cartography of the Black Pacific: James Weldon Johnson's *Along This Way* 32

2 Colored Empires in the 1930s: Black Internationalism, the US Black Press, and George S. Schuyler 58

3 The Swing and the Sword in the Black *Mikados*: An Afro-Japanese Nexus in the US (White) Pacific Imagination 86

4 "Spies and Spiders": Langston Hughes and the Transpacific Intelligence Dragnet 116

5 The Manchurian Philosopher: W. E. B. Du Bois in the Eurasian Pacific 148

Epilogue 185

Notes 199
Bibliography 241
Index 257

ACKNOWLEDGMENTS

I could not have written this book without the generous support of the institutions on both sides of the Pacific that had faith in my project. My thanks go to the University of Tsukuba, my home institution. The Japan Foundation's Abe fellowship enabled me to start work on this project in the United States in the academic year 2003–2004, when I was affiliated with the University of Maryland, College Park. Along the way, this project was supported, in part, by a research grant in the humanities from the Mitsubishi Foundation and two Grants-in-Aid for Scientific Research from the Japan Society for the Promotion of Science. A research grant from the Fulbright Scholar Program allowed me to complete a first draft of the manuscript in Hawai'i in the mid-Pacific in 2011, when the University of Hawai'i at Manoa welcomed me as a visiting researcher.

I have been blessed with friends and colleagues who have been generous with their time, ideas, and advice. I am forever indebted to my mentor, Robert S. Levine, who has guided me through my career for two decades. I am particularly grateful to Carolyn Karcher, whose scholarly example I have adopted as my own, for having sustained me when my project was misunderstood and misrepresented. Only someone as truly culturally bilingual as Carolyn, who was brought up in Japan during and after the US military occupation, could understand why I wanted to write this book, and without Martin Karcher's encouragement, I doubt that this book would exist at all. I had only a vague idea of my project in August 2002, when Carolyn and Martin invited me to dinner at their house in Washington, DC. Martin, listening to my rambles about my project, said, "Fascinating!" This pushed me to pursue the project. Cynthia Franklin graciously agreed to be my sponsor while I was in Hawai'i on a Fulbright grant and gave me extensive feedback at a crucial stage in the project. I have also benefited from the excellent advice of Michael Keezing, who, over the years, provided feedback on my chapters in ways that taught me to become a better writer. I thank Jonathan Auerbach for his brutally honest, constructive comments. I have been fortunate to have wonderful colleagues at the University of Tsukuba. There are too many to thank individually, but Motoko Nakada and Eriko Yamaguchi deserve special thanks for their camaraderie and personal kindnesses.

At the research stage of this project, many archivists and librarians across the Pacific helped me find the materials on which this project is based. I thank the staff members at Bancroft Library, University of California, Berkeley; Beinecke Rare Book and Manuscript Library, Yale University; Free Library of Philadelphia; Huntington Library; Japan Foundation Information Center Library, Tokyo; Library of Congress; Moorland-Spingarn Research Center, Howard University; National Diet Library, Tokyo; New York Public Library for the Performing Arts; Schomburg Center for Research in Black Culture, New York; Syracuse University Library; and the University of Hawai'i Library at Manoa. I express my sincere appreciation for the professional research provided by Susan Strange at the National Archives and Records Administration, which has been integral to this project. I am also indebted to the librarians at the Interlibrary Loan Department of the University of Tsukuba for facilitating the arrival of materials from abroad. I thank my graduate student research assistants, Chiafung Schuemann-Lin and Zhang Xiaoqing, for identifying and translating Chinese sources, and Noriko Suzuki for tracking down prewar Japanese newspaper articles at the National Diet Library in Tokyo.

My ideas have been significantly shaped by the responses that I received to papers presented at the Modern Language Association, the American Literature Society of Japan, and the Multi-Ethnic Studies Association, and to articles published in the following journals. An earlier version of chapter 1 was first published in *American Quarterly* 59, no. 1 (March 2007): 79–106, copyright © 2007 The American Studies Association and reprinted with permission by Johns Hopkins University Press. A different version of chapter 2 appeared in *American Literature* 82, no. 1 (March 2010): 121–49, copyright © 2010 Duke University Press and reprinted with permission by Duke University Press. I thank the editors and anonymous readers for their helpful suggestions.

Richard Pult of the University Press of New England/Dartmouth College Press has been a very supportive editor. I am grateful to series editor Donald Pease for championing my project. My work also owes a great deal to anonymous readers at the University Press of New England/Dartmouth College Press and the University of Georgia Press, and Bill V. Mullen, whose detailed comments have made this a better book. I would also like to extend thanks to production editor Jessica Stevens and to Naomi Burns for her skillful copyediting. My thanks as well to Joanne Sprott for her fine work on the index.

I completed the final manuscript in one of the deepest valleys in my life, with the successive losses of my father and my brother. I am heartbroken that my mother is in a persistent vegetative state, awake but not aware, yet I am hoping for a miracle. To my sister, Keiko Okugawa, thanks for keeping me sane. Though long lost, my grandmother, Yoshii Endo Naruse; my aunt, Toshiko Naruse; and my uncle, Hirozumi Naruse, a telecommunications engineer who died at the age of twenty-two, far from home on the island of Luzon in the Philippines during the final months of the Pacific War, haunt the pages of my book.

Finally, I give enormous thanks and hugs to my twin daughters, Myra and Eura, for bringing immeasurable sweetness and richness to my life, and to my colleague and husband, Yoichiro Miyamoto, to whom I owe deep love and gratitude. There are not enough words to describe how grateful I am to you for who you are. I could never say how much you mean to me.

THE BLACK PACIFIC NARRATIVE

INTRODUCTION

Pearl Harbor. Hell, ain't nobody told the white man to come to Hawaii. Had no business having his ships there. All these other niggers was sorry when the Japanese hit those ships, those fools. Me and my friends was glad and we said so.
—Ishmael Reed, *Japanese by Spring* (1993)

THE IMAGES THAT CONSTITUTE America's historical memory of the Japanese military strike on Pearl Harbor on December 7, 1941—primarily the battleship USS *Arizona*, the Japanese fighter aircraft Mitsubishi Zero, and African American "mess attendant" Doris Miller—originate in the past, but they live on today in the plethora of books, films, television programs, websites, and other media through which American patriotism and faith in democracy are transmitted. Yet representations of Pearl Harbor in African American literature, as in my epigraph from Ishmael Reed's *Japanese by Spring*, have at times unsettled the meaning of memories of the attack that have become part of the American national identity. Although iconic in America's historical memory, "Pearl Harbor," as it functions in the black imagination, has by extension long complicated our understanding of the significance of the Pacific War, or the Pacific theater of World War II, to African Americans.

A vivid indicator of the valence of Pearl Harbor memories in the American mainstream may be found in allusions to the episode made in the media and elsewhere in the immediate wake of the 9/11 attacks. As images of planes crashing into the World Trade Center and the Pentagon appeared on television and in the newspapers, references to Pearl Harbor evoked the potent emotions of anger and rage with which Americans reacted to the "surprise attack" sixty years before. An editorial in the *Washington Post* seized on the analogy between 9/11 and Pearl Harbor by declaring, "What President Franklin D. Roosevelt said after Dec. 7 in Pearl Harbor, 'a date which will live in infamy,' applies to Sept. 11 just as well."[1] Newspapers across the country ran banner headlines reading "Day of Infamy" or simply "Infamy," and "many Americans seemed actually to 'experience' the attacks through the memories that the Pearl

Harbor–hyped summer of 2001 had helped forge," as historian Emily S. Rosenberg observes.[2] The media stretched the analogy between 9/11 and Pearl Harbor even to the point of associating the fanaticism of the Al Qaeda–affiliated hijackers with the Japanese soldiers of the Pacific War, with some commentators dubbing the hijackers "kamikaze" terrorists.[3] The "kamikaze" in this formulation refers to Japanese pilots charged in the final year of the Pacific War—and hence, with only figurative, rather than historical, relevance to Pearl Harbor—with the suicidal mission of crashing their aircraft into enemy targets, especially ships. In concert with such associations in the mainstream, President George W. Bush dictated a diary entry on the night of 9/11 that read, "The Pearl Harbor of the 21st century took place today."[4]

That African Americans may have reacted to 9/11 differently from the rest of the nation emerged during the 2008 presidential election, when the story of the Reverend Jeremiah Wright's 9/11 sermon flooded the media. Interpreting the 9/11 attacks of 2001 in the shadow of Pacific War memories, Rev. Wright, pastor and mentor to Barack Obama, sought meaning not in Pearl Harbor but in Hiroshima and Nagasaki—the ground zeros of the nuclear holocaust whereby the United States ended the Pacific War. "We bombed Hiroshima, we bombed Nagasaki, and we nuked far more than the thousands in New York and the Pentagon, and we never batted an eye," Rev. Wright said in a sermon at the Trinity United Church of Christ, Chicago, on September 16, 2001. Quoting Malcolm X, he told his congregation that "America's chickens are coming home to roost," implying that America had brought 9/11 upon itself.[5] On the same day, Minister Louis Farrakhan of the Nation of Islam, at a press conference at Mosque Maryam, Chicago, responded to the possibility of America's enacting new laws to combat terrorism: "I don't know what that means, but I hope it doesn't mean ultimately a repeat of what happened in 1941"—that is, after Pearl Harbor and the declaration of war—"when Japanese Americans were herded into concentration camps or in the movie '*The Siege,*' when Muslims were rounded up and put into concentration camps."[6] Evidently, Rev. Wright and Minister Farrakhan do not "remember Pearl Harbor" in a way that accords with the cultural memory of the American mainstream.

To be sure, such countercultural memories are far from prevalent among African Americans. The most frequently referenced memories of World War II in black America are perhaps those of Doris Miller firing a machine gun against Japanese planes at Pearl Harbor, and the "Double V" campaign against both fascism abroad and racism at home that the nation's largest black newspaper, the *Pittsburgh Courier*, launched in the aftermath of Pearl Harbor. When Barack Obama delivered his victory speech in Chicago following his election to the presidency on November 4, 2008, he alluded to Pearl Harbor through the experience of Ann Nixon Cooper, a 106-year-old black woman, in describing the history of struggle and progress that had culminated in his victory—a day on which, as he put it, "change has come to America": "When the bombs fell on our harbor and tyranny threatened the world, [Cooper] was there to witness a generation rise to greatness and a democracy was saved. Yes, we can."[7] Obama, the first African American president and the first to be born in Hawai'i, thus endorsed the mainstream American memory of World War II as a fight to save democracy.

Notwithstanding black cultural memories of World War II as a "good war," however, the questions remain of how and why countermemories such as Rev. Wright's and Minister Farrakhan's took shape. From where—from what reservoir of black American memories of the Pacific War—are they drawn, following 9/11? I am interested, in particular, in African American literature and letters as media that ensured (and still ensure) the viability of radical alternative black narratives of the Pacific. To students of African American literature, the seemingly pro-Axis sentiment reflected in the war memories of Wright and Farrakhan is not particularly surprising. Ernest J. Gaines's *Autobiography of Miss Jane Pittman* (1971)—a novel that ironically might have inspired Obama's use of the viewpoint of 106-year-old Cooper—depicts the African American experience from slavery times to the civil rights movement through the eyes of 110-year-old Jane Pittman, who recalls black soldiers recounting their Pacific combat experiences thus: "The japs wasn't like the white people said they was. They was colored just like us, and they didn't want kill us, they just wanted to kill the white soldiers. If the colored soldiers was marching in front, the japs would shoot over the colored soldiers head just to get to the white boys. If the colored soldiers was marching in the back, the japs would drop the bombs shorter. It was this that made them integrate that Army and nothing else."[8] In Gaines's novel, the memories of black veterans thus "reveal" that the Japanese aimed to kill only the white soldiers in the Pacific War and that it was this racial selectivity that led the US Army to end segregation in the armed forces—a major advance in civil and economic rights normatively ascribed to some progressive aspect of American democracy.

Alternative black memories of the Pacific are also, and even more distinctly, inscribed in John Oliver Killens's *And Then We Heard the Thunder*

(1962), a Pulitzer Prize–nominated novel based on Killens's firsthand experience serving in an amphibian unit in the Philippines during the war. In Reed's *Japanese by Spring*, protagonist Benjamin "Chappie" Puttbutt, a junior professor of English, refers to Killens's work as "the best novel about World War II written by an American."[9] As *Japanese by Spring* contains alternative black memories conveyed from an elderly black viewpoint, in this case that of the protagonist's pro-Japanese grandfather, *And Then We Heard the Thunder* invokes memories that radically diverge from most accounts of World War II. The perspective of one character, an old GI nicknamed "General" Grant, who is a black nationalist from Harlem and Trinidad, starkly contrasts with those of other black soldiers in his outfit, who rehearse the familiar rhetoric of Pearl Harbor—"infamy" and "the unprovoked attack"—that President Franklin D. Roosevelt established in his address to Congress on December 8, 1941. Grant instead avers that "the white mawn in Washington" and the US Navy in Hawai'i "getting ready to attack the Japanese mainland" provoked Pearl Harbor and that the Japanese (whom the soldiers refer to collectively as Tojo) are "fighting for your [his fellow black soldiers'] freedom and your dignity." Through the racial prism of the novel, the Pacific theater of World War II presents an eerily warped spectacle. For example, as Grant awaits Japan's invasion of the Philippines and the arrival of the enemy Japanese planes, he emerges from his tent to wave to the sky and scream, "Gwan, Tojo! Gwan, Tojo! Fly your ass off! Fly your ass off! Fly, black man! Fly! Fly! Fly!" The pathetic sight of Grant's wishful identification with the enemy moves the protagonist Solomon Saunders, a draftee from Harlem, to tears. But Saunders's own actions on the battlefield offer another tableau of black-Japanese affinity. In hand-to-hand combat, Saunders stabs a Japanese soldier with a dagger over and over again. Seeing that "the man's chest was a dark bloody geyser gushing blood, his pleading eyes his desperate eyes," a nauseated and tearful Saunders cries, "I don't hate you, Tojo, damn you. I don't hate you! I don't even know you—damn you!" The black soldier then falls "forward on top of this very very dead young stranger from the islands of Japan, and all was peace and all was quiet, and brotherhood and all that crap."[10]

In his essay collection *Black Man's Burden* (1965), published three years after *And Then We Heard the Thunder*, Killens remembers the ending of the Pacific War in Hiroshima and Nagasaki as acts of American violence in which "we" nuked hundreds of thousands of civilians in Japan and about which "our ex-President [Truman] apparently feels no deep remorse"—criticism that Wright's sermon about 9/11 seems to echo. While Hiroshima and Nagasaki bear multiple meanings, what Killens commits to memory in *Black Man's Burden* is black anger rooted in the sense that the atomic bombs were dropped on civilians in Japan *because* they were "colored," as "most colored people are convinced." In 1945, Killens was a soldier in the Philippines, preparing for the invasion of the Japanese homeland. The men in his outfit were elated when they first heard news of the atomic bombings and realized that the war was over, for, as Killens put it, "many of us would have discolored the immaculate beaches of Japan with our patriotic blood." However, when the soldiers' initial joy faded, "sober reflection" and even anger set in. Killens recalls one of his fellow soldiers saying, "The thing they should do now is dump the rest of those fucking bombs in the middle of the Pacific, destroy the formula, then round up all the bloody scientists who know anything about that formula and blow their fucking brains out!"[11] The black soldier's anger at Hiroshima and Nagasaki was directed specifically at the genocidal character of the bombings, which reflected the character of American violence against African Americans. Some in black America made this association explicitly; when "a poll taken in five Pacific Northwest cities showed that the 'men on the street' favored dropping more atomic bombs on Japan by a ratio of 12 to 1" (rather than dumping the rest of the bombs in the Pacific and destroying the formula as Killens's fellow soldier suggested), the *Chicago Defender*, a leading black weekly, speculated in its edition of September 15, 1945, "Perhaps the people of the Northwest participating in this poll have the same prejudices against the Japanese that Southerners have against Negroes. This may account for their insane feelings."[12]

Memories of the Pacific War in African American literature have given rise even to fictional representations of the unspeakable desire that some black men may have had to join the Japanese army. In *Lonely Crusade* (1947), a novel written by Chester Himes, the protagonist Lee Gordon is an unemployed African American graduate of UCLA whose frustration with life in Jim Crow America gives rise to his "secret admiration for Japan." In an early chapter in the novel, when unidentified planes fly into Los Angeles from the Pacific one night in 1942 and drive the white residents "craven," Gordon runs out into the yard and cries exultantly, "They're here! Oh, God-dammit, they're coming! Come on, you little bad bastards! Come on and take this city!" In the belief that "if Americans did not want him the Japanese did," Gordon awaits the arrival of the Japanese in what he views as the race war of World War II "so he could join them and lead them on to victory." This hope is framed in the narrative as "the wishful yearning of the disinherited" in America.[13]

Gordon's sentiment, if in naive form, resembles that of Malcolm X, minister and spokesman for the Nation of Islam, when faced with induction into the US Army. In 1943, Malcolm, then a street hustler in Harlem, claimed that only three things scared him: "jail, a job, and the Army." After receiving notice of his induction from the draft board, as he recalls in his autobiography (1964), he circulated the rumor that he "was frantic to join . . . the Japanese Army" in an attempt to fool the draft board and obtain 4-F (not acceptable for military service) status.[14] Though feigned, Malcolm's pro-Japanese desire was a "threat" that "carried weight" in wartime America, as critic George Lipsitz observes: the desire "played on the paranoia of White supremacy by posing the possibility of a transnational alliance among people of color."[15] Indeed, such paranoia proved powerful enough to fuel the success of Mississippi congressman John E. Rankin's bid for the internment of Japanese Americans during the war. Having built a reputation as a racial segregationist, Rankin galvanized anti-Japanese American sentiment with the rallying cry, "once a Jap, always a Jap." In February 1942, Rankin claimed before the US House of Representatives that Japanese fifth columnists were stirring unrest "among the Negroes in Harlem" so successfully that New York "city authorities" had "entirely lost control." Unless put into "concentration camps," Rankin warned (based on a news item from Tokyo) that those of Japanese ancestry in America would incite "20,000,000 Negroes" and others to "rise in revolt and create chaos."[16] Rankin thus gave voice to the conflation of antiblack racism and wartime anti-Japanese sentiment that Malcolm X played on in trying to evade the draft, and to which Farrakhan of the Nation of Islam alluded in his response to 9/11.

Such alternative memories of the war constitute part of the narrative of what I call the "black Pacific," namely, the literary and cultural production of African American narratives of the Pacific as it gained geopolitical importance in the twentieth century and eventually became a major theater of World War II. In crucial though often unexamined ways, African American literature represents the formation of the black Pacific, projecting a sense of belonging in a world that extends beyond US borders and the world's black belts. In the twentieth century, the Pacific was no longer simply "just there" as America's frontier but had significantly evolved into an international community, known as the "Pacific Community," reflecting a vision of a hemispheric regional order initiated and led by the United States.[17] The black Pacific, in my operative definition, is a sort of "imagined community,"[18] a community imagined contrapuntally to this regional order in the making, in which a sense of belonging is manufactured by the performance of black narratives that invent a shared history, one that African Americans imagine they share with the colored peoples of the Pacific Rim, especially in Asia. As such, the black Pacific is more than a literary representation or construction of a given community, or a vision of an alternative utopic community that the political art of black narratives brings into existence. It is vitally implicated in the material process of regional and international ordering. The black Pacific, as I hope to show in this volume, reframes our current spatial understanding of African American literature and letters, bringing to light the alterity of the black past that is radically "unpredictable" (to borrow historian Lawrence W. Levine's term).[19] This is a past that is contested terrain and that shapes present (and future) international and interracial relations in an unpredictable manner.

Pacific Mapping

Rereading African American literature from the time between the world wars, particularly writers and culture makers usually associated with the Harlem Renaissance, in the context of the Pacific hemisphere enables us to move beyond the frame of the nation-state and the ideological platforms of black nationalism and Pan-Africanism, as well as beyond US-bounded dynamics between African Americans and Asian Americans.[20] Although seldom discussed in the Pacific context, it is significant that the cultural movement known as the Harlem Renaissance developed at a time when the United States was establishing a burgeoning bioceanic empire.

The United States was a latecomer as a Pacific power, joining the great game of expansion in the Pacific—hitherto fought among seasoned European players such as Great Britain, France, Germany, the Netherlands, Portugal, and Spain—only in the 1890s. It is generally acknowledged that the milestone was the Spanish-American War of 1898, a brief but decisive war that resulted in US acquisition of the remnants of the Spanish Empire in the Pacific as well as in the Caribbean, namely, the Philippines, Guam, Cuba, and Puerto Rico. One important by-product of the Spanish-American War was the US annexation of Hawai'i, an archipelago that proved strategically important in the Pacific theater of war. Congress passed a joint resolution annexing Hawai'i to the United States in 1898 and provided a territorial government in 1900. Guam and the Philippines were classified as US "unincorporated territories," and governments were accordingly established in 1899 and 1902, respectively.

The United States first articulated the "Open Door"—which would, just like the Monroe Doctrine in Latin America, become the official US foreign policy toward the Far East—at the turn of the century. Through a series of Secretary of State John Hay's notes (1899–1900) to the major world powers—Britain, France, Germany, Italy, Japan, and Russia—that were marking out spheres of influence in the Chinese Empire, the United States aimed to secure international agreement to a principle that all should have free and equal access to trade with China. In 1900, the United States took part in military action in China to suppress a peasant uprising known as the Boxer Rebellion. Joining an international force from Austria-Hungary, Britain, France, Germany, Italy, Japan, and Russia to protect foreign interests, the United States quashed the uprising by dispatching American troops from one of its new Pacific island holdings: the Philippines.

The notion of the Pacific as an American sphere, and the idea of the "Pacific Age," took form in the United States at the beginning of the twentieth century under the Theodore Roosevelt administration (1901–1909), which expanded the American navy based on the theory of naval historian Alfred Thayer Mahan that sea power was the key to success in international politics.[21] To build a waterway for naval ships to pass between the two oceans, Roosevelt began the construction of a transisthmian canal in Panama in 1904. He abandoned a planned route across Nicaragua, because Panama had recently separated from Columbia to become an independent state, through the United States providing funds and a naval blockade in support of the Panamanian revolution. By connecting the Atlantic to the Pacific via the Caribbean, the interoceanic canal completed in 1914 brought spatial reorientation to America's worldview. Previously, ships sailing from the Eastern Seaboard took the long traditional route along the Atlantic, around Africa's Cape of Good Hope, through the Indian Ocean, and then to Asia and the Pacific—the route taken by Commodore Matthew Perry on his 1853 expedition to Japan, or Captain Ahab on his hunt for the white sperm whale in Herman Melville's *Moby-Dick* (1851). Ships could go in the opposite direction but first had to navigate southward in the Atlantic around Cape Horn at the tip of South America, which was in fact the only way for US battleships during the Spanish-American War. The Panama Canal joined the insular territories acquired after 1898—or what Lanny Thompson calls the "imperial archipelago," scattered throughout the Pacific and the Caribbean—to the United States. The canal across the isthmus of Central America and the imperial archipelago thus secured the position of the United States as a bioceanic empire.[22]

What I have termed the black Pacific belongs primarily, if not exclusively, to a distinct cultural moment in which the notion of a Pacific Community—which historian Tomoko Akami describes as a vision of a hemispheric regional order initiated and led by the United States—arose to internationalize the Pacific in the 1920s, the decade that also ushered in the Harlem Renaissance.[23] This vision was first expressed at the Washington Naval Conference of 1921–1922, an international conference called by the Warren G. Harding administration, and subsequently propagated by a nongovernmental organization, the Institute of Pacific Relations (IPR), founded in Honolulu, US Territory of Hawai'i, in 1925. At this time, the Pacific area was predominantly composed not of modern nation-states, as was Europe, but of the colonies, spheres of influence, and League of Nations mandates of the Japanese and Western maritime empires as they emerged from World War I. The modern concept of an American-led Pacific regionalism, independent of European politics, gave rise to a nascent Pacific-centered perspective on the world, transforming the region from the periphery of Europe to a central stage in international politics—a shift that is symbolized by a map entitled "The Pacific Region" in the proceedings of the second biennial conference of the IPR in 1927 (figure 0.1).[24] Drawn using Goode's homolosine equal-area projection, which challenged the distortions perpetuated by the long-accepted Mercator projection,[25] this map represented a Pacific region comprised of Pacific Rim countries. It placed Siberia/Soviet Russia and Asian countries such as China and Japan and the Philippines on the western shores; the United States and Latin American countries such as Mexico and Nicaragua on the eastern shores; and the Hawaiian archipelago in the middle. I argue that this shift in social cognitive mapping—or a new spatial ordering of the world—had a significant bearing on the terrains of black culture and black internationalism in the United States during this period.

The formation of the black Pacific can be read in relation to this making of a Pacific Community that began with American efforts to internationalize the Pacific and to institute a modern regional order. As I discuss below, this was an order that would ultimately be challenged by the Pacific War—a war that island Japan and "island" America fought for Pacific regional hegemony.[26]

Black Internationalism

Most accounts of African American literature during the Harlem Renaissance era have little to say about a Pacific Community. This is not entirely

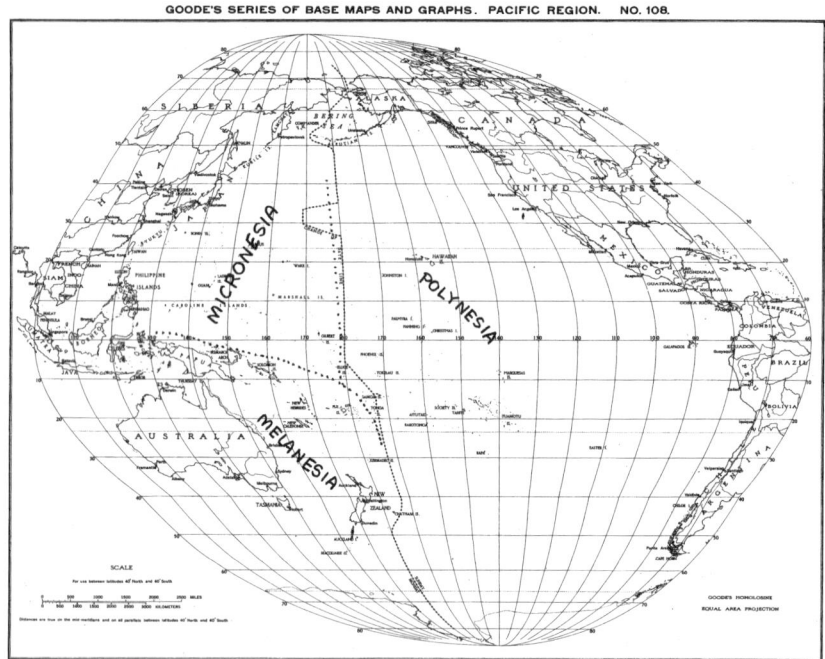

0.1. Goode's homolosine projection map of "The Pacific Region." *Photograph courtesy of the University of Chicago Library. The map was reproduced in* Institute of Pacific Relations, Problems of the Pacific: Proceedings of the Second Conference of the Institute of Pacific Relations, Honolulu, Hawaii, July 15 to 29, 1927, ed. J. B. Condliffe (Chicago: University of Chicago Press, 1928).

surprising, given that the Renaissance was a national cultural phenomenon and one centered not in cities along the Pacific Rim but in Harlem and, to a lesser degree, other urban centers of the North, most notably Chicago. Yet having drawn blacks from throughout the African diaspora in the Atlantic world, including the West Indies and even Africa, Harlem had become the race capital of modern black culture. Notwithstanding the emphasis of much of the scholarship on African American literature of the period on US-bounded themes, recent theoretical work has often placed black internationalism at the center of analysis. The discourses of this internationalism drew on, contested, appropriated, and transformed the expressions of the political ideologies and practices widely circulated during the period, such as liberal or Wilsonian internationalism as embodied in the League of Nations, which supposed an international community of sovereign states; socialist internationalism on the basis of a class solidarity of the proletariat as envisioned by the Communist International (Comintern), which called for a revolutionary overthrow of liberal, capitalist, and imperial governments around the globe; black nationalism and Pan-Africanism; and "the globe-carving discourse of European colonialism."[27]

However, the geographic frame wherein this recent work has addressed black internationalism has mainly been the oceanic frame offered in Paul Gilroy's *Black Atlantic* (1993), or the circum-Atlantic regional frame bounded by Europe, Africa, and the Americas. In *The Practice of Diaspora*, for instance, Brent Hayes Edwards argues that nearly all major literary figures identified with the Harlem Renaissance became mobile during and after World War I, and along with many early French-speaking Antillean and African intellectuals, found in metropolitan Paris a key site at which to "link up" with people of African descent, resulting in US-Francophone conjunctures that involved exchange and translation. Edwards argues that "the cultures of black internationalism can be seen only *in translation*," in a process of linking or connecting across gaps, or "décalage," by which he means "the kernel of precisely that which cannot be transferred or exchanged."[28]

Also in the black Atlantic frame, Michelle Ann Stephens, in *Black Empire*, views the black internationalism that radical Anglophone Caribbean emigrants created in the twentieth century as a central influence on the New Negro movement. Stephens suggests that "empire ... provided the material conditions for black solidarities to emerge across nation, language, gender, and even class" and that Caribbean radicals in Harlem, most prominently Marcus Garvey, inhabited a black transatlantic space and projected a vision of a global black community, "resisting empire and carrying its tropes along in their wake."[29]

Kate A. Baldwin, in *Beyond the Color Line and the Iron Curtain*, proposes extending the terrain of black internationalism beyond Gilroy's mapping of the black Atlantic, "moving it beyond Anglophone archipelagoes and resisting the continental confines of Europe-Africa-US triangulation" to include the Soviet Union and the Comintern, which influenced Harlem Renaissance writers such as Claude McKay and Langston Hughes. However, Baldwin's analysis, critically, must be regarded as Atlantic-centric (a perspective often understood as synonymous with "global"), in that she seeks to demonstrate how the frame of the Soviet Union, with its vexed position vis-à-vis Europe, modifies and extends the black Atlantic model.³⁰

While I share the interest reflected in such recent work on black internationalism, I aim in this study to recast black internationalism geographically, in light of America's development into a bioceanic empire, by examining the African American narratives of the internationalized Pacific between the world wars. These were narratives that decentered, rather than extended, the Atlantic-centric (read "global") narratives of black internationalism.

The black Pacific, as I have suggested, was primarily an idea, an imagined community, forged by geographic imaginings of African American narratives. However, as it manufactured feelings of African Americans' connectedness to foreign (colored) nationals and colonial subjects in the Pacific Rim, especially Asia—building the emotive foundation for the organization of material internationalist practices—the black Pacific was not just imagined. It was also counterimagined, as it was by US government and intelligence agencies, as a form of internationalism that threatened home security and contested America's national interest in the Pacific regional order. To illustrate this function of surveillance that makes the black Pacific legible, I begin with the Federal Bureau of Investigation (FBI)—a "fact-gathering" agency that in its attempt to suppress "subversive" black narratives became an avid (sometimes even imaginative) reader of them—and in particular its files on Marcus Garvey, which tracked the routes that Garvey and the Garvey movement navigated for black internationalism well beyond the black Atlantic context explored by Stephens.³¹

To understand the significance of the FBI investigation that produced the black Pacific as an object of surveillance, let us nonetheless consider Stephens's argument further. A profoundly inspiring figure of the Harlem Renaissance who influenced every subsequent generation of African American writers, Garvey has traditionally been discussed in terms of the history of the Back-to-Africa movements and black nationalism, but Stephens has revised our picture of Garvey from a circum-Atlantic perspective, as mentioned above. Stephens argues that Garvey "created a global vision of the race that drew on transatlantic histories of movement" and that the Black Star Line Steamship Corporation, one of Garvey's pet projects, was a powerful symbol of that vision. Garvey's fleet of ships, according to Stephens, was important not so much "in the nationalist search for a territorial homeland—back to Africa—but as the vehicles to facilitate a black transnational dream of free movement in modernity."³²

Yet Stephens's transatlantic reading of the symbolism of the Black Star Line is significantly complicated by FBI files recording another pathway that Garvey navigated—or rather could have navigated—for his race program. In 1920, a special agent of the Bureau of Investigation (a precursor to the FBI) in New York was assessing whether "any Japanese are behind" the Garvey movement. A November 1920 report reveals that Garvey allegedly admitted to this agent, who had cultivated Garvey's friendship for intelligence purposes, that the first Black Star Line ship, the *Yarmouth*, was "simply purchased in order to better stir up the Negroes in all parts of the world to invest and [to inspire in them] a hatred of the white race," which would "bring about an upheaval and finally racial equality." Garvey apparently told the agent that "he had had a conference with two Japanese a few months ago in the hope of interesting them in his scheme, especially in the purchasing of ships from them."[33] It may not have been true that Garvey had been trying to draw the Japanese into his ocean-liner scheme, but it certainly could have been. What I want to draw attention to here is the ways in which the black Pacific entered the domain of the thinkable, the imaginable, in the national security discourse.

Other intelligence agencies, including the Office of Naval Intelligence (ONI) and the Military Intelligence Division (MID) of the army, shared the FBI's suspicion of a Garvey-Japanese connection. The ONI monitored the activities of Garvey's Universal Negro Improvement Association (UNIA) on the West Coast, closely monitoring the organization's suspected contacts with Japanese agents as they pursued a clandestine program of rousing and spreading racial hatred of the black race for the white.[34] According to a report that the MID prepared on the subject of "Japanese Racial Agitation among American Negroes" (April 15, 1942), "in 1918, Garvey stated before a mass meeting in New York City that the next war would be between Negroes and the Whites, and that with Japan's assistance, the Negro would win." The MID included the UNIA among "Japanese-Negro Front Organizations" operating in the United States.[35]

During the Pacific War, the FBI launched a nationwide investigation of black internationalism in search of the origins and interconnections of black organizations fomenting pro-Japanese sentiment among African Americans. Robert A. Hill remarks that the resulting FBI study, *Survey of Racial Conditions in the United States* (*RACON*, 1943), pointed to "the central significance of Garvey's UNIA as the progenitor as well as incubator of the welter of new nationalist formations that sprang up in the U.S. in the 1930s, all of which absorbed and adapted UNIA principles of racial independence, African redemption and colonization, and Afro-Asiatic racial solidarity."[36] In the wake of Pearl Harbor, according to historian Ernest Allen Jr., the FBI arrested some 125 African Americans on charges of draft evasion, sedition, and most seriously, pro-Japanese espionage that constituted a grave threat to state security. Among those arrested were Elijah Muhammad of the Nation of Islam, Mittie Maud Lena Gordon of the Peace Movement of Ethiopia, Stokely Delmar Hart of the Brotherhood of Liberty for the Black People of America, Robert O. Jordan (also known as Leonard Robert Jordan) of the Ethiopian Pacific Movement, and David D. Erwin and General Lee Butler of the Pacific Movement of the Eastern World.[37] These were all members of the inner circles of "the crack-pot negro organizations" whose "fountainhead . . . is the Universal Negro Improvement Association founded by Marcus Garvey, a West Indian negro," in the language of the *RACON* report.[38]

These arrested leaders, according to the report, made seditious speeches. In May 1942, Gordon allegedly declared to an audience of four hundred people in Chicago that "on December 7, 1941, one billion black people struck for freedom." Hart stated in a meeting that his "prayers to Tojo" (whom he had referred to as "the savior of the American negroes" at another meeting) "were answered by the bombing of Pearl Harbor."[39] In New York, Jordan apparently urged his audiences "not to remember Pearl Harbor but to remember Africa."[40] (Similarly, James R. Stewart, who succeeded as president-general of UNIA after Garvey's death in 1940, made a speech in Ohio in February 1942, in which he stated, "We will remember Missouri and then Pearl Harbor" and "To hell with Pearl Harbor."[41]) The FBI study of World War II black movements thus produces as an object of surveillance a strand of black internationalism that originates in Garvey's UNIA and branches along transpacific vectors in the interwar years to emerge in alleged black-Japanese front organizations during the Pacific War.

In putting a spotlight on this different pathway that black internationalism as recorded by government and intelligence archives may have navigated—a strand that is obscured in Atlantic-based literary studies of the Harlem Renaissance—I do not, however, propose to replace the spatial template of Gilroy's "black Atlantic" with what I have termed the "black Pacific." I aim rather to draw attention to a shift in geographic imaginings that transpired in (African) American culture as the United States evolved into a bioceanic empire that would fight World War II as a two-ocean war. The army's MID perceived this shift in race geopolitics in its aforementioned 1942 report, "Japanese Racial Agitation among American Negroes." The MID concluded that "the British West Indies is the most common point of origin of the organizers and agitators who arouse the Negro organizations" to the point of vulnerability to Japanese agents, thereby suggesting that the Anglophone Caribbean no longer lay within a specifically transatlantic history but was a constituent of the transpacific georacial imagination.[42] (Killens's monumental Pacific War novel *And Then We Heard the Thunder* reflects this view as well, in the character of "General" Grant, a black nationalist from Trinidad who is brazenly "pro-Japanese," as noted above.[43])

A grasp of the hemispheric shift in the political geography of race in the twentieth century led the FBI to suspect that what happened in the islands of the Caribbean as it affected black America was connected with foreign influence or sabotage emanating from the islands of Japan in the Pacific.[44] To illustrate this, the *RACON* report cites a Japanese novella "entitled 'Michibeisen [sic] Miraiki' (Forecast of Future American Japanese War) written by Lieutenant Commander Kyosuke Fukunaga and prefaced by Admiral Kanji Kato, both of the Imperial Japanese Navy, [and] published as a supplement to the Japanese magazine 'Hinode' on November 28, 1933."[45] In January 1934, 1,250 copies of the book had been seized by American customs officials in Honolulu, in the US Territory of Hawai'i. Subsequently, the *Washington Herald* (Washington, DC) published an English translation of the book in four installments from January 15 to 18, 1934, by way of warning the American audience.[46] A story about an imaginary Pacific war, *Nichibeisen Miraiki* begins with a surprise attack by the Japanese destroyer *Nara* on the USS *Houston*, flagship of the US Asiatic Fleet, at anchor at Shanghai Harbor in China, and ends with Japan's triumph, which is commemorated by the erection of a bronze statue of the captain of the *Nara* in Japanese-occupied Hawai'i.[47] The FBI took a particular interest in the novella's depiction of the Japanese "utilizing negroes against the United States." In the course of the narrative, an African American "mess boy" blows up the USS *Oklahoma* as it is passing through the Panama Canal, the conduit that joins the Atlantic and the Pacific via the Caribbean. The *RACON* report describes this episode as follows: "One incident relates that a negro mess boy, won over by the Japanese, procured information as to the time United States warships would pass through the Panama Canal after the commencement of hostilities between the United States and Japan. This negro mess boy leaves the fleet at Havana after planting a time bomb which resulted in the fictitious destruction of the Battleship Oklahoma while it was passing through the Canal lock."[48] In the realm of reality, the USS *Oklahoma* was sunk in the Japanese attack on Pearl Harbor.

Such "literature of the 'coming war in the Pacific,'" as historian and Japanologist Mark R. Peattie identifies it, constituted an aspect of the Japanese cultural scene between 1912 and 1933.[49] However, sabotage by African Americans, let me hasten to add, thematically formed no distinct subgenre as the FBI may have suspected it did; the black Pacific was in no way imagined reciprocally. Besides *Nichibeisen Miraiki, Nichibei Senso Yume Monogatari* (A Fantasy of the Japanese–United States War; 1921), by Lieutenant-General Kojiro Sato, a retired army officer, is, perhaps, the only other known example of Japanese future-war fiction that significantly includes episodes of sabotage by African Americans in an imaginary Pacific war. In this novel (which has never been translated into English), Japan launches a surprise attack on New York with the Mother Plane, an airship that carries smaller airships and munitions in its bay. The Japanese bomb the Brooklyn Bridge and occupy the Woolworth Building, then the highest skyscraper in the world, establishing a base from which to launch an offensive against the United States. Japan's war effort in the novel is supported by the character Marcus Garvey, who has concluded an agreement with the Japanese imperial government to support the invasion. When the Mother Plane lands, ten million black Americans led by Garvey rise in revolt against the United States with arms and ammunition supplied by Japan via the great airship.[50] Such a Garvey-Japanese alliance might not have seemed as preposterous a scenario to the government and intelligence agencies that monitored Garvey—the FBI, the ONI, and the MID—as it does to a modern readership. In 1923, two years after the publication of the book, the historical Garvey is known to have sent a cable to Emperor Yoshihito of Japan after a major earthquake struck Tokyo, killing over one hundred thousand people. In the cable, Garvey expressed condolences for the catastrophe on behalf of "the four hundred million Negroes of the world and the Universal Negro Improvement Association" and affirmed that "the Negro peoples looked to Japan as a friend in the cause of racial justice."[51]

The police-state surveillance of narratives of the black Pacific that emerged in the Harlem Renaissance indicates that the Renaissance was not simply a flowering of literature and culture comparable to, say, the American Renaissance—a term coined by F. O. Matthiessen in 1941, just before the United States entered World War II, to characterize the period of canonical white male writers Ralph Waldo Emerson, Henry David Thoreau, Nathaniel Hawthorne, Herman Melville, and Walt Whitman, whose "one common denominator ... was their devotion to the possibilities of democracy."[52] Rather, it was also a renaissance of black internationalism that can be read in relation to foreign affairs and policy processes between the world wars that reflected the new status of the United States as a bioceanic empire. Hence, I draw significantly in this volume on government and intelligence archives on African Americans, including records of the FBI, the MID, the Office of Facts and Figures, the Office of War Information, the State Department, the Shanghai Municipal Police (China), and the Ministry of Foreign Affairs (Japan)—in conversation with a diverse cast of African American literary and cultural texts including autobiographies, fiction, newspaper columns, memoirs, travel journals, and theatrical performances. Adopting an approach that mixes the archival and the interpretive, I seek in this book to recover the black Pacific produced by African American narratives, narratives that were significant enough in their time to warrant surveillance and suspicion, and hence are significant enough in our time to warrant modern scholarly attention and reappraisal.

The Pacific Community: Race, Empire, and Regionalism

The FBI's *RACON* report offers a peculiar prefiguring of my narrative of the black Pacific in beginning its account of a transpacific strand of black internationalism—or, from its reductive view, the black-Japanese alliance for subversion—with two events that predate my time frame (which is marked by the rise of a Pacific Community): the 1904–1905 Russo-Japanese War, for which the major theater was southern Manchuria, and the 1919 Paris Peace Conference following the end of World War I.[53] I draw attention to these events not to contest the bureau's periodization but rather, as I begin my discussion of the black Pacific, to speculate on the possibilities for reframing pre–Harlem Renaissance literature—and in particular, African American efforts to tell their stories of the Russo-Japanese War and the Paris Peace Conference—in a Pacific hemispheric context. My analysis here is framed by the question of what was at stake in the making of a regional order prior to the rise of a Pacific Community, that is, an American vision of modern regionalism, in the 1920s. Specifically, I want to call attention to how the ideas of race and "empire" entered into the geographic imaginings of the Pacific in 1904–1919.

Although Brent Edwards observes, and I agree, that "the 'New Negro' movement is at the same time a 'new' black internationalism,"[54] the trope of the New Negro in African American literature was historically coterminous with the emergent concept of the Pacific Age that was brought into American political discourse at the beginning of the twentieth century.

Consider, for instance, *A New Negro for a New Century* (1900), an anthology edited by Booker T. Washington and his fellow editors. As Henry Louis Gates Jr. remarks, this work includes "extended defenses of the combat performances of black soldiers ... [in] the Spanish-American War in general and ... the actions of 'Regulars in the Philippines' and 'Regulars in Cuba' more specifically." This "militaristic emphasis" in *A New Negro* was intended to "refut[e] claims made by Theodore Roosevelt in *Scribner's Magazine* in 1899 of the inherent racial weaknesses that would prevent black officers from commanding effectively, thus making mandatory, in subsequent wars, their [black soldiers] command by white officers," according to Gates.[55] However, it is instructive to note that the attempt by Washington and his colleagues to redefine the "Negro" race occurred in the context of the Spanish-American War, a war fought in both the Caribbean and the Pacific that resulted in the US seizure of a bioceanic empire, ushering in America's Pacific era.

The frame of a Pacific era then reveals the implications of the 1904–1905 Russo-Japanese War for the "New Negro" movement in African American literature. The Russo-Japanese War was an imperial war between the Russian Empire and the Japanese Empire over control of Manchuria and Korea in the Far East,[56] but the war—from a US perspective—changed both the strategic and racial landscape of the Pacific "with one stroke," according to historian Pekka Korhonen. Japan's annihilation of the Russian fleet occurred at a time when Great Britain, as a result of the Anglo-Japanese alliance of 1902, had reduced its military presence in the Pacific and the United States had only begun to expand its navy. Thus, Russia's loss of its fleet signaled Japan's emergence as the strongest maritime power in the region.[57] The Japanese victory was widely covered by war correspondents, including Jack London, who had just published *The Call of the Wild* (1903). In the (white) United States, the Japanese Empire's regional dominance was interpreted, accentuated by psychological shock, as a defeat of a European great power by a "colored," non-Western empire. London, whose career encompassed the Pacific after 1893, perceived it as a racial threat, a "yellow peril." The FBI's *RACON* report alleges that Japan began to "endeavor ... to assume the position as champion of the 'non-white' races ... soon after the Russian defeat by the Japanese in 1904–05."[58]

African American writers who paid attention viewed these Pacific events differently, reading in them the progress of the international "Negro" race. Such readings were based on an understanding of the Japanese as essentially Negro. In October 1905, the *Colored American Maga-*

zine, a magazine that Booker Washington had gained control of in 1904, carried an article entitled "The Ethnology of the Japanese Race" by Rev. James Marmaduke Boddy, then known as "the most noted scientific writer of the Negro race."[59] According to Boddy, the triumphs of the Japanese in the Russo-Japanese War—"the brilliant master strokes of the Japanese arms, under Generals Kuroki and Nodzu, and Field Marshal Oyama, and the unprecedented achievements of the Japanese naval forces, under the command of the brilliant Admiral Toga [sic]"—may "justly be regarded as the achievements of the Negro race." Boddy theorized that the physical characteristics of the Japanese associated them with "the Oceanic Negro," whose ethnology is "of an African origin." Hence, Boddy concludes, the Japanese must be "of an African origin, and therefore a part and parcel of the Negro race."[60]

Pauline E. Hopkins, African American novelist and journalist, and regular contributor to the *Voice of Negro* from 1905 onward, similarly internationalized the Negro race in a series of articles entitled "The Dark Races of the Twentieth Century." Hopkins claims that the Negritos of the Philippines, which had recently become an American possession, are "of the family of Ham." She also notes that the Russo-Japanese War, which "surpris[ed] the entire world," confounded scientists in "their attempt to classify the living races of their time" but that "silently God demonstrates His power and the truth of His words: 'Of one blood have I made all races of men to dwell upon the whole face of the earth.'" Hopkins thus situates the Japanese—dark conquerors of a great (white) empire—along with their Pacific neighbors within the international Negro or dark races.[61]

W. E. B. Du Bois, who proclaimed the problem of the twentieth century to be "the problem of the color-line" in his seminal *Souls of Black Folk* (1903),[62] saw the Russo-Japanese War in 1904–1905 as bearing crucial importance for the "awakening" of the darker races. In a 1906 article entitled "The Color Line Belts the World," Du Bois writes as follows: "For the first time in a thousand years a great white nation has measured arms with a colored nation and been found wanting. The Russo-Japanese War has marked an epoch. The magic of the word "white" is already broken, and the Color Line in civilization has been crossed in modern times as it was in the great past. The awakening of the yellow races is certain. That the awakening of the brown and black races will follow in time, no unprejudiced student of history can doubt."[63] Du Bois subsequently championed the rise of the Japanese Empire to power as a challenge to Western imperialism and became an outspoken defender of Japan—and its ascent, even into authoritarianism and militarism—in the 1930s (see chapter 5).

Like the Russo-Japanese War, the FBI's *RACON* report allocates the 1919 Paris Peace Conference a privileged position in the black-Japanese alliance for subversion. Yet, I suggest that to understand the significance of the conference requires a grasp of the realignment of the Pacific region within the post–World War I world order that it prescribed. As per the Treaty of Versailles, the conference redrew the political map of the Pacific, wiping off the German Empire and drawing in an expanded sphere of influence with the Japanese Empire. The treaty awarded Japan a League of Nations mandate (the trusteeship of former enemy territories) over former German colonies in the South Pacific north of the equator, the Marianas, Marshalls, and Carolines, and required Germany to renounce, in favor of Japan, all its rights and concessions in Shantung, China. In view of the issue of race that Japan presented, this sea change was perceived in the United States, a bioceanic empire in the making, as a threatening alteration to the Europe-centered cartography of a Pacific previously under white dominion. In *The Rising Tide of Color against White World–Supremacy* (1920), Lothrop Stoddard, a Harvard-educated political theorist, observes that an ever-expanding colored Japanese imperium had been "written plainly upon the map" for the past twenty-five years. Unless "some sort of provisional understanding" was reached "between the white world and renascent Asia," warns Stoddard, the world would "drift into a gigantic race-war—and genuine race-war means war to the knife."[64] Stoddard's views were widely known, and traces of their influences are discernible in American literary works of the period such as F. Scott Fitzgerald's *Great Gatsby* (1925), in which the white supremacist Tom Buchanan alludes to Stoddard's book as *The Rise of the Colored Empires* by "Goddard."[65]

The Paris Peace Conference featured in the formation of black internationalist ideologies and organizations. One notable move by the New Negro intelligentsia in Harlem was the founding of the International League of Darker Peoples (ILDP) in 1919, principal members of which included A. Philip Randolph and Marcus Garvey. The ILDP aimed to cross the boundaries of "narrow nationalistic provincialism" to embrace the broader "spirit of race internationalism," as *The World Forum*, the organization's journal, describes it. The organizers of the ILDP expressed this spirit of race internationalism at its inaugural conference in the home of the millionaire businesswoman Madam C. J. Walker, by adopting "the welcomed suggestion" of sending a floral bouquet to a Japanese delegation staying in New York en route to Paris for the Peace Conference "as a token of friendship and brotherhood." Subsequently, on January 7, 1919, Randolph, along with several other ILDP members, met at the Waldorf-Astoria Hotel with Shuroku Kuroiwa of the *Yorozu Choho*, a Tokyo newspaper, who was on his way to Paris to join the Japanese delegation. Randolph presented Kuroiwa with a "Memorandum of Peace Proposals" that the ILDP had drafted, including a proposal for "the abolition and prohibition of all economic, political and social discriminations, in all countries, based upon color, by international agreement."[66] In historian Yuichiro Onishi's account, the radical black intellectuals of the ILDP "helped construct the iconography of the Japanese as the New Negro of the Pacific."[67] In Paris, the Japanese delegation proposed a racial equality clause to be included in the covenant of the League of Nations. This proposal sparked a firestorm of debate in the League of Nations Commission. On April 11, 1919, at the fifteenth meeting of the commission, Baron Nobuaki Makino, the de facto delegation head, renewed the Japanese plea for the principle of equality and called for a vote to be taken upon it.[68] A majority, eleven out of seventeen, voted in favor. However, US president Woodrow Wilson then imposed from the chair a unanimity rule that blocked the proposal.

The League of Nations, an international body created to ensure a just and equitable postwar order, was thus "born, without a racial or national equality hair on its head."[69] Du Bois deemed the defeat of the Japanese proposal as "deplorable" and remarked that "Peace for us is not simply Peace from Wars like the past, but relief from the spectre of the Great War of Races."[70] Mary Church Terrell—who had met with Baron Makino in Paris and "discussed the attitude of the proud, white races toward the dark"—regretted that "at the Peace Conference in Paris 'the two most highly civilized and the most Christian nations' in the world [Great Britain and the United States] had denied racial equality to Japan which she had a right to demand." Terrell predicted, "You may talk about permanent peace till doomsday ... but the world will never have it till the dark races are given a square deal."[71] The FBI's *RACON* report observes that a noticeable development in "Japan's interest in the negroes in the United States" began in 1919, when Japan attended the Peace Conference as one of the five great powers that won World War I.[72]

Although the assumption in the FBI's *RACON* report that the Peace Conference helped move race internationalism along a transpacific vector—a movement that soon roused the bureau to undertake surveillance of "negro subversion"—reflects an element of the truth, the black Pacific to emerge out of the First World War's destruction of the nineteenth-century order of international relations, as I will be demonstrating in this volume, is a community imagined in a much more complex manner. This is partly because African American writers, in projecting the black Pacific, appropriated and transformed diverse postwar internationalist ideals. These ideals were not limited to the race internationalism that fostered Afro-Asian solidarity but included those that found expression in the League of Nations and the Comintern (born in Moscow in the same year as the league), as well as in nongovernmental organizations such as the IPR that promoted the concept of a Pacific Community. However, I argue that, more importantly, the imaginings of the black Pacific in the post–World War I order required a radical reconfiguration of the notion of "empire" as it related to the making of an international system in the region.

Empire is a highly elusive concept. As historian Dominic Lieven points out in his comparative study of empires entitled *Empire* (2000), empire is "a much older, more complicated and more diffuse concept than imperialism, which indeed the word 'empire' itself to a great extent encompasses." The term "empire," whose history stretches back two millennia to the Latin *imperium*, has over time evolved within the Latin Christian tradition but has also been applied to political systems well outside the Western tradition. In that process, it has acquired meanings and connotations that are highly polemical, although "the same word used in a different cultural context may give a wholly illusory sense of common reality."[73] Recently, Michael Hardt and Antonio Negri, in their influential work of the same name (2000), created the postmodern concept of Empire (with a capital *E*) to designate a new global form of sovereignty—"a *decentered* and *deterritorializing* apparatus of rule that progressively incorporates the entire global realm within its open, expanding frontiers." Hardt and Negri declare that Empire, operating beyond the nation-state (even the present-day United States as a superpower), is "not limited to any geographical region."[74]

The empires that come into play in the imaginings of the black Pacific, however, are precisely those involved in the production of a geographic region. In the Pacific, the Western European maritime empires (the model empire of this type is Great Britain, with France and the Netherlands as lesser variations) engaged in a scramble for Pacific islands from the sixteenth century. With their primary focus on the islands within, the Pacific was an open frontier for those European maritime empires that became the world's leading industrial and financial powers by 1900. These empires, except for the German Empire, continued their hold over their overseas territories after the 1919 Peace Conference. Lieven observes that the more usual current definition of empire, which owes most to twentieth-century Marxist scholarship, is based on the models of those European maritime empires in which a clear distinction existed between their rich, white metropolitan nations, which enjoyed democratic civil rights, and their much poorer, nonwhite colonies beyond the oceans, which were subject to political domination and economic exploitation. This relation of wealth and power applies, as well, to what we now think of as the First and Third Worlds.[75] However, this framework of empire alone is not sufficient to apprehend and appreciate the making of a modern regionalism in the Pacific, contrapuntal to which the black Pacific was imagined.[76]

In a Pacific Rim context, the US policy of the Monroe Doctrine had traditionally served as a regional framework for the American continents since 1823, placing the Caribbean and Central America in the US sphere of influence. The Theodore Roosevelt administration articulated a corollary to the Monroe Doctrine in 1904, which enabled the United States to use military force to restore internal stability to Latin American nations. The League of Nations—though established as an international organization that supposed a community of sovereign nations—recognized the validity of the Monroe Doctrine under the designation of a "regional understanding" in its covenant (1919).[77] On the opposite shores of the Pacific, what appeared as regionalism in the nineteenth century had emerged from regional hegemonic systems instituted by modern and premodern empires, namely, the British, Chinese, and Russian. Major institutions of the British Empire in Asia were the treaty ports opened to foreign trade by unequal treaties, a system that replaced the traditional tributary trade system of the Ch'ing (Manchu) Dynasty of China (1644–1912), which had developed an organic network of relations between the imperial center and the periphery.[78] The British created an informal maritime empire in Asia based on a string of commercially and militarily strategic ports stretching from Penang and Singapore to Hong Kong, Amoy, and Shanghai, as well as along the Yangtze River and on the Yellow Sea coast. These ports fragmented the Sinocentric world of the Chinese Empire, whose strength and reach waxed and waned with its dynastic strengths, and reintegrated the region into a Westphalian international system, into which the Japanese Empire entered after the First Sino-Japanese War in 1895. In the subregion north of China, the Tsarist Russian Empire had consolidated its hold over its Eastern and Central Asian possessions through the building of railway lines, including the Trans-Siberian and the Chinese Eastern. The Russo-Japanese War—Japan's initial drive in continental Asia, resulting in its gaining control of the southernmost section of the South Manchuria branch of the Chinese Eastern—was an attempt to challenge the Russian Empire as a regional hegemon in Northeast Asia.[79]

By 1919, Asian hegemonic systems had undergone structural transformations. The Chinese Revolution of 1911 overthrew the Ch'ing Dynasty, establishing the Republic of China and bringing an end to over two thousand years of Imperial China but not to the long-established Sinocentric world, of which Japanese imperialism aspired to be "the middle"—an aspiration that would be expressed by Japan's Greater East Asia Co-Prosperity Sphere in the 1940s.[80] The Russian Revolution of 1917 destroyed the Tsarist Russian Empire, which led to the 1922 creation of the Soviet Union, a socialist state that cannot be described as an empire in the Leninist definition of imperialism but that was nonetheless "the successor" to the Tsarist Empire "in territorial terms" and that considered it had inherited the Tsarist Russian sphere of influence in Manchuria, China.[81] The British Empire, on the other hand, anticipated the slow demise of the treaty ports system in Asia in the face of Chinese nationalism.[82]

It is in this transformative phase that the United States, a burgeoning bioceanic empire, in 1921–1922 called an international conference outside the auspices of the League of Nations, inviting nine nations (the United States, Britain, Japan, France, Italy, Belgium, the Netherlands, Portugal, and China, but excluding Soviet Russia) with interests in the Pacific region. Based on a multilateral framework of cooperation between powers, the conference concluded three major treaties: the Four Power Treaty on the Pacific that resulted in the dissolution of the Anglo-Japanese alliance of 1902; the Nine Power Treaty on the internationalization of the US Open Door policy in China; and the Five Power Treaty on naval disarmament. The conference also instituted the Washington system, which embraced the principles of a new diplomacy in the Pacific, this being a region where the international order based on the League of Nations, as historian Naoko Shimazu notes, was already "*de facto* obsolete . . . due to the failure of the United States to ratify the Treaty of Versailles."[83] In addition to the multilateral agreements, a bilateral treaty was signed between Japan and China, providing for return of the control of the Shantung province to China that the Treaty of Versailles had transferred from Germany to Japan in 1919. The United States thus initiated a vision of a

Pacific Community, a modern regionalism led by the United States, which was beginning to leave its mark on the international relations in the Pacific hemisphere, beyond its territories and sphere of influence, interacting with and countering regional pressures and establishing a course of action that paved the way to the post-1945 US informal empire that was no longer regional but global.

The formation of the black Pacific reflects these complex narratives of "empire" in post–World War I international relations, as two contrastive responses from Randolph and James Weldon Johnson suggest. Randolph, whom the ILDP delegated to work with the Japanese in addressing the race issue at the Paris Peace Conference, brought a class-based analysis of imperialism to bear on the attempt of the Japanese to secure their empire in the Pacific. Randolph and his coeditor Chandler Owen published an editorial, entitled "Japan and the Race Issue," in the *Messenger* (the socialist journal that they proudly called "the only radical Negro magazine in America") in which they offered a "word of warning . . . to the unsuspecting and to those not thoroughly versed in social science." According to the editorial, Japan's statesmen were "no different from Woodrow Wilson" and were "not in the least concerned about race or color prejudice"; indeed, they oppressed the Koreans under their rule, forced "hard bargains upon unfortunate China," and cared nothing even for the Japanese people. Randolph claimed that Japanese diplomats' "real conflict" with Great Britain and the United States at the peace tables was "commercial and industrial"—not the race issue that they raised in the proposal for a racial equality clause, which was simply "psychological."[84] As Barbara Foley observes, Randolph insistently dubbed Japan an imperialist whose growing status as a world power "did nothing for the Japanese working class or the Asian peoples subjugated under the Japanese Empire."[85] The rise of the Empire of Japan in the Pacific constituted what Randolph understood as imperialism, an understanding based on the models of the classic European maritime empires, of which Japan was a lesser variation on the same theme or an epigone.

In contrast, Johnson, my subject in chapter 1, construed the expanding Japanese imperium in the Pacific in the context of League of Nations internationalism. In an editorial in the *New York Age*, Johnson acknowledged that the award of German concessions in Shantung to Japan, rather than their return to Chinese sovereignty, "does violate the principle of 'self-determination' so far as China is concerned" but claimed, "We feel that on the whole it is better for China to be dominated by Japan than to be dominated by some European government." Within the given structures and strictures of Wilsonian internationalism of 1919, which supposed a community of sovereign nation-states but did not replace great power politics, Johnson wrote, "We want to see Japan grab as much as she possibly can."[86] However, Johnson also understood the rise of the Japanese Empire, significantly, in the context of regionalism, or the "regional understanding," that the League of Nations would credit in the specific case of the US Monroe Doctrine. Johnson thus suggested in the same column, "We should like to see Japan relatively as powerful in the Orient as the United States is in the western continent. We should like to see an Asiatic Monroe Doctrine with Japan as its interpreter and administrator."[87]

However, Johnson's black liberal internationalist understanding of the Pacific regionalism was problematized in 1931, when Japan forcefully occupied Manchuria and justified its violence by pointing to the US Marine occupation of Nicaragua that Johnson himself had helped administer as the chief civilian American official in the Pacific port city of Corinto in 1912—an occupation that was implemented with the Monroe Doctrine as a US regional policy in Latin America. The complex field of forces in the making of a regional order in the Pacific thus trapped Johnson as they worked themselves out, even as they circumscribed the black internationalism to which they gave shape. In chapter 1, I shall read Johnson's autobiography, *Along This Way* (1933), as a text that addresses this material process of the spatial ordering in the Pacific as it involves the construction of the self—a text forming a genre that I call the "black Pacific narrative."

The Black Pacific Narrative

In this volume, the black Pacific narrative refers to the literary and cultural production of African American narratives of the Pacific space as an imagined community whose geography does not always overlap with a Pacific Community, the latter being tied to a construction of bounded space as a region. It intervenes in the Atlantic-centered worldview, which was perpetuated by the long-accepted Mercator projection as the standard projection for maritime navigation since the sixteenth century that "had in fact come to be taken *for* the world" in the United States, according to historian Susan Schulten.[88] The authors and culture makers that I consider in this volume chart the Pacific space in different (and sometimes even conflicting) configurations whose borders are more in flux than fixed. They produce a geographic framework of an east-west vector that laterally links Latin America and East Asia on the Pacific Rim, rather than just the north-south vector of the Atlantic Americas (chapter 1), a merging of black Atlantic and black Pacific imaginaries (chapter 2), an imperial vision of a Pacific Community on the home front (chapter 3), and actual travel narratives tracing Pacific itineraries (chapters 4 and 5).

As such, the black Pacific narrative does not necessarily form part of what Bill V. Mullen has termed "Afro-Orientalism" or Afro-Asian solidarity.[89] Mullen defines Afro-Orientalism—building on theories of Orientalism elaborated by Edward Said—as "a counterdiscourse that at times shares with its dominant namesake certain features but primarily constitutes an independent critical trajectory of thought on the practice and ideological weight of Orientalism in the Western world."[90] The spatial ordering of the world that is divided into East and West, the Orient and the Occident, enabling the set of beliefs known as Orientalism, is a resilient paradigm that continues to exert a profound influence on scholarly and popular perceptions of the world as it is informed by the Eurocentric codification of the Mercator projection (which historian and Islamicist Marshall G. S. Hodgson calls the "Jim Crow projection"[91]). And it is this view of the world in which the black Pacific narrative critically intervenes.

As my principal subjects in this study, I have chosen writers and culture makers—James Weldon Johnson, George S. Schuyler, the black Federal Theatre Project, Langston Hughes, W. E. B. Du Bois, and Walter White—who afford significant points of entry to a critical understanding of the stakes of the black Pacific narrative. My choice of these producers of Pacific narratives follows from my archival work, as well as my theoretical positioning, but I should acknowledge that my subjects are predominantly male and that this necessarily imposes limits on the perspectives that my study can present. I have resisted the temptation to include Harlem Renaissance women writers such as Nella Larsen and Zora Neale Hurston in this book, but I was intrigued by the signifying icons of collectible orientalism (such as a blue Chinese carpet, blue Chinese jars, and a Chinese red dressing gown) in the African American domesticity depicted in Larsen's *Quicksand*, as well as by the "ridiculous Japanese print on the wall across the room," a possible emblem of deviant (lesbian) desire, on which the protagonist Irene Redfield focuses at the end of Larsen's *Passing*.[92] Beyond their function in the black Pacific geographic imagination, things Japanese in the Harlem Renaissance may also have served as a matrix within which to represent unspeakable nonnormative sexuality. Richard Bruce Nugent, the openly gay writer of the Harlem Renaissance, thus explored same-sex (father/son) incest through his half-Japanese protagonist and narrator, Kondo Gale, a male geisha who longed for a white American father in Nugent's unpublished novel *Geisha Man*. I also find interesting Hurston's use of the metaphor "the Empress of Japan" in reference to the protagonist Janie in *Their Eyes Were Watching God* as well as what Hurston had to say about Japan and China in her autobiography, *Dust Tracks on a Road*, and in her pre-1945 letters. However, references to Japan and China alone do not constitute a black Pacific narrative, which is, after all, about a shift in social cognitive mapping, a mapping heretofore exclusively based on the (black) Atlantic-centered codification of the modern world. That said, the relative absence of African American women writers in the production of black Pacific narratives constitutes grounds not for dismissal but rather for future engagement.

At this point, I would suggest that the domination of Pacific narratives by men may well reflect the history of geographic knowledge that was often a function of state power and that had consequences for what accounts as legitimate knowledge and who can produce such knowledge. In the dominant narratives of geography, women continued to be marginalized both as subjects and as authors of geographical knowledge. Although my focus in the current study is on those figures who best serve my project of charting—via black Pacific narratives—new geographies of African American literature and culture, they may not be necessarily feminist geographies.

This volume is organized into six thematic chapters. In chapter 1, "The Cartography of the Black Pacific: James Weldon Johnson's *Along This Way*," I offer an examination of tensions in Johnson's complex internationalism by way of complicating our assumptions regarding the (black) Pacific—a stratagem to frame the critical project that follows. In 1929, Johnson arrived in Japan as the first African American delegate to the IPR, a nongovernmental organization that advocated the concept of the Pacific Community, envisaging a Pacific-centered perspective on the world. A corollary of this stance was US maneuvering in the Caribbean and Central America and in Asia as mutually constitutive of the affairs of the Pacific. A grasp of this paradigm shift is crucial to understanding the route that Johnson navigates for (black) internationalism in *Along This Way*. Johnson's is a route that reaches beyond US borders, the Caribbean, and Europe, to embrace the Pacific in the penultimate chapter, and in the process, it locates on a continuum two otherwise seemingly distinct memories of the Pacific Rim nations of Nicaragua and

Japan. This chapter discusses how Johnson engages the convoluted relationship that evolved between modern regionalism, internationalism, and imperialism, and seeks to draft an alternative black Pacific geography as it involves the construction of a black subject in *Along This Way*.

Chapter 2, "Colored Empires in the 1930s: Black Internationalism, the US Black Press, and George S. Schuyler," explores how George S. Schuyler's serial fiction, *Black Empire* (1936–1938), critically engages the fantasy of a colored empire that emerged as an imaginable political system during the Ethiopian crisis. I reread the Second Italo-Ethiopian War (1935–1936), Italy's assault on Africa's only remaining stronghold of independent black civilization, as a decisive moment in the formation of that fantasy organized around the dyad of the Ethiopian and Japanese Empires beyond oceanic divides. Both the US black press and the Italian fascist press engaged this scenario at the essentially indissoluble levels of both material life and cultural fantasy that the modern news media enabled. In this chapter, I examine how *Black Empire* plays on the concept of empire, mirroring and seeking to resolve the tensions between the different forms of empire of the 1930s—European, Japanese, Ethiopian, US, and Soviet—in its schema of empires at war. Furthermore, through an analysis of a series of unpublished articles entitled "Japan and the Negro" (1937), I want to illuminate Schuyler's postempire black Pacific narrative.

In chapter 3, "The Swing and the Sword in the Black *Mikados*: An Afro-Japanese Nexus in the US (White) Pacific Imagination," I turn from African American literature to a project of illuminating the US imperial vision of a Pacific Community presented by the New Deal–era Federal Theatre and Broadway with the adaptations of Gilbert and Sullivan's imperial-Japanese-themed operetta *The Mikado*. The Federal Theatre's *Swing Mikado* (1938), produced by the Chicago Negro unit, moved the action of the operetta from medieval Japan to a coral island in the South Seas—a setting that represented aspects of US regional imperialism and its rival, the Japanese Empire. In examining the Federal Theatre's geographic imaginings of the Pacific space, I provide a critique of antiracist impulse that coexisted with broader containment strategies and of *The Swing Mikado*'s role as a cultural container of a black Pacific imaginary. By analyzing *The Hot Mikado* (1939), which starred tap dancer Bill "Bojangles" Robinson in the role of the emperor of Japan, this chapter also shows how the centrality of Robinson's performance shifted the thematic emphasis of *The Mikado* to the Japanese emperor, a hitherto minor character in both Gilbert and Sullivan's original and in the competing *The*

Swing Mikado, and explores Robinson's satiric takes on American domestic political culture.

In chapter 4, "'Spies and Spiders': Langston Hughes and the Transpacific Intelligence Dragnet," I retrace the underground (and surface) routes that Hughes took in navigating, and at times slipping right through, the theater of intelligence dragnets during his 1933 trip to Asia. The section of Hughes's memoir, *I Wonder as I Wander* (1956), entitled "Spies and Spiders" is more than the wanderlust-inspired story of a poet's experience of being harassed by the Japanese police. As he recounts in the memoir, having freshly arrived from Moscow in East Asia in June 1933, Hughes found himself a focus of Japanese authorities' anticommunist paranoia, which resulted in his expulsion from the country on suspicion of being a Soviet spy. I compare facts gleaned from archival research with Hughes's retrospective account of his experience of being harassed by police in his memoir, published during the McCarthy era. Hughes's memoir, as I hope to show, affords significant insight into the intelligence dragnets created by multiple states in the Pacific Community before World War II and after. I discuss how *I Wonder as I Wander* committed to public memory the secret war on dissent under the fascism and communism emergent in the 1930s, revealing it as a force that eerily shaped the international Cold War blueprint in Asia.

Chapter 5, "The Manchurian Philosopher: W. E. B. Du Bois in the Eurasian Pacific," presents the hitherto ignored responses of W. E. B. Du Bois to Manchukuo (1932–1945)—a (puppet) empire on the Pacific Rim with demarcated territory bordering the Soviet Union, China, and Japan that disappeared into history at the end of World War II. Du Bois's responses cause us to rethink the Asian arc of his internationalism. I closely read a chapter entitled "I Gird the Globe" in his unpublished, book-length manuscript "Russia and America" and dispatches that he sent to the *Pittsburgh Courier* from Manchuria that record Du Bois's 1936 travel itinerary across the Eurasian continent from Germany via Soviet Russia to Manchukuo. Du Bois's Manchurian narrative makes a strong case for the liberal and anticapitalist empire, which he thought he was witnessing in Manchuria. This chapter also demonstrates that Du Bois's encounter with Yosuke Matsuoka, Japanese diplomat and president of the South Manchuria Railway Company, was a defining experience that inspired him to imagine the black Eurasian Pacific, in which his symbiotic sympathies both for Soviet Russia and socialism and for the Japanese Empire resonated.

In the epilogue, I briefly discuss the role of the black Pacific narrative in World War II, which the United States fought as a two-ocean war, by examining a largely neglected aspect of Walter White's black internationalism. Through an analysis of White's "Pacific Charter" and his actual travels to and through the Pacific, I consider the vision of a future black Pacific that White projected, departing from the Atlantic Charter, which became a founding text of the United Nations.

[1]

THE CARTOGRAPHY OF THE BLACK PACIFIC:
JAMES WELDON JOHNSON'S *ALONG THIS WAY*

At length, one day he said to me: "Well, get ready for a long trip; we are going to Egypt, and then to Japan."
— James Weldon Johnson, *The Autobiography of an Ex-Coloured Man* (1912)

CROSSING THE PACIFIC OCEAN on the Dollar Steamship Line from Seattle in October 1929, James Weldon Johnson—the black novelist, poet, songwriter, journalist, civil rights activist, and diplomat known as the "Renaissance man" of the Harlem Renaissance—tells of witnessing a rupture in the familiar spatial-temporal frame of the world that he had long taken for granted. Johnson describes how the passengers "went through the curious experience of losing a whole day" in the middle of the Pacific, going to bed Friday night, waking up Sunday morning and thus skipping Saturday entirely. "This happens on crossing the 180th meridian going west," he writes, referring to the international dateline, an imaginary north-south line drawn through the Pacific, where the passengers crossed the line while the ship sailed seamlessly over a vast expanse of waters.[1] The Pacific was divided by the imaginary, though internationally agreed, north-south line that demarcates the eastern and western hemispheres and demarcates one calendar day from the next. Against this backdrop of the spatial-temporal ordering of the world, Johnson's autobiography, *Along This Way* (1933), produces a black Pacific narrative that imagines a geographic framework that links Latin America and Asia laterally on the Pacific Rim, along with a corollary, reoriented view of the Atlantic Americas.

This chapter argues that Johnson's *Along This Way* charts a black Pacific geography that strives to resolve the tensions between the developing regional hegemonic systems in Central America and East Asia because it involves the construction of the African American self. As his autobiography describes, Johnson, a fluent Spanish speaker, secured a position with the US consular service under President Theodore Roosevelt in 1906, and then served in Venezuela and Nicaragua. In Nicaragua, political exigencies and opportunism led to Johnson's participating in the implementation of Big Stick diplomacy in Latin America, under the Roosevelt Corollary to the Monroe Doctrine as US international policy in the region. This event, as Johnson writes, was later cited as a precedent for "colored" Japan to justify both its occupation of Manchuria in China to create the puppet state Manchukuo and its attempt to reintegrate, or rather to invent, the area north of the Great Wall of China as a bounded region under Japanese hegemony. With its movement along both east-west and north-south vectors, African American diplomat Johnson's internationalism ironically emerges in *Along This Way* as contiguous and continuous with imperial and imperialist modes that traverse color lines, geographical divides, and political systems in the Pacific region, in which a black subject is trapped.

Johnson and the Institute of Pacific Relations

In the fall of 1929, Johnson took a leave of absence from the National Association for the Advancement of Colored People (NAACP), where he had served as the first black executive secretary since 1920, and sailed away to the Far East. As recounted in the penultimate chapter (chapter 37) of *Along This Way*,[2] the ship carrying Johnson docked on the morning of October 18 in the harbor of Yokohama, where a tumultuous crowd of newspaper reporters greeted Johnson, who was in Japan as a delegate to the third biennial conference of the Institute of Pacific Relations (IPR, 1925–1961).[3] The next day, the news of Johnson's VIP arrival in the headlines of the Japanese and English-language dailies in Japan startled readers into an anxious sense that African Americans were emerging as integral members of the Pacific Community.

Founded in Honolulu, in the US Territory of Hawai'i, the IPR was a nongovernmental organization that grew out of—and was intended to respond to—the imperative for a modern regional order in the Pacific where the international order based on the League of Nations was already "*de facto* obsolete ... due to the failure of the United States to ratify the Treaty of Versailles."[4] The mission of the IPR was to create a Pacific Community by "study[ing] the conditions of the Pacific peoples with a view to the improvement of their mutual relations." Membership in the organization was open to nations lying within or bordering on the Pacific, as well as imperial powers possessing dominions, colonies, dependencies, territories, and mandates in the region, including the European maritime empires such as Great Britain, France, and the Netherlands.[5] It dealt with a wide range of "Pacific problems," including Philippine independence, the "racial fears" underlying policies to maintain white privilege in the United States and Australia, Japan's subjugation of Korea, and American gunboats in Chinese waters.[6] Institutionalizing Wilsonian internationalism—a discourse that promoted and was promoted by liberal democracy—in the Pacific, the IPR envisaged a Pacific-centered perspective on the world, posing a challenge to the Eurocentric bias of the League of Nations. A grasp of the conception of a new world order was reflected in the emergent conviction among IPR members that the Pacific was to be "the stage where shall meet all the races and cultures of the world."[7]

Of particular interest, for the purposes of this chapter, is that in its formative years, the IPR reframed and reoriented the causes and effects of US regional policy in Central America as "conflicts of the Pacific." A statement from the organization asserted, "The attitude and dealings of the United States with Mexico and the Caribbean peoples is a cause of fear and resentment not only there but elsewhere about the Pacific."[8] The IPR demarcated the Pacific region as comprising the United States and Mexico and the Caribbean on the eastern shores, and Asian countries on the western shores. This paradigm shift sets the terms for the black Pacific geography that *Along This Way* charts, as I discuss below.

The reader of his autobiography might assume that the IPR's selection of Johnson as a conference delegate was a matter of course. However, Johnson was not on the original list of delegates drawn up by the American Council of the IPR. A "confidential" list of the American Council, "Present Status of American Membership in the Kyoto Conference" (May 23, 1929), did not include Johnson (or for that matter, any African Americans), nor did a supplementary "confidential list of Americans who are going to Kyoto" (June 3, 1929).[9] Yet in his autobiography, Johnson recalls Edward C. Carter, secretary-treasurer of the American Council, asking him in the summer of 1929 if he would go to Japan as a US delegate to the third biennial conference of the IPR. Johnson had heard little about the IPR and wondered with reason "what motives the gods in the guise of ... Mr. Carter might have in bringing me ... such [a] boon."[10] In fact, the "informal" invitation was extended to Johnson in a letter from Carter as late as August 7.[11] Evidently, Johnson's name was hastily added to the list of all-white American delegates at the last minute.[12]

This image of African Americanness in representations of the Pacific Community was unprecedented. A proposal to include "a Negro of distinction" in the US delegation made in 1927 had been opposed on the grounds that "the American Negro is not implicated in the relations between the United States and the Orient." One member of the American delegate committee feared that "the Orientals would think that they were being regarded as on the same level as Negroes if the American group thought that the White-Negro experience would be of any value in considering white-yellow relationships."[13] The committee failed here to recognize African Americans as an intimate alterity marking the limit of a Pacific communal vision structured dichotomously along the color lines of white and Asian. In a new turn, at the meeting of the American Council in May 1929, Charles F. Loomis, a conference program member of the IPR's International Secretariat in Honolulu, announced that "the Japanese personally expressed the desire in 1927 that the Americans bring a Negro." G. S. Phelps, senior secretary of the Japan YMCA, supported Loomis, saying that the inclusion of an African American would greatly please Japan, the host country of the 1929 conference. As to why this should be so, he submitted the following observation: several African Americans had recently visited Japan, and there was a "very apparent feeling of understanding between the two peoples." The American Council then debated whether it could include an African American to its advantage. Finally, one member asked whether the American group was "ready to recognize ... equality of participation in the facing of common problems" in the Pacific Community. This member argued that if so, "by including a Negro they would establish a precedent and a principle."[14] These remarks clinched the argument.

Regardless of the intended effects of deploying blackness, the inclusion of Johnson in the American delegation signified a turning point in Pacific relations at which the potential emerged for the interests of "Negroes" and "Orientals" to converge in the making of the Pacific Community. In the United States, black weeklies such as the *New York Age* and the Baltimore *Afro-American* reported Johnson's departure for the IPR conference on their front pages.[15] Japan's press coverage of Johnson's arrival seemed orchestrated to make him a star. The *Tokyo Asahi Shimbun*, a leading Japanese daily, carried a photograph of Johnson.[16] His arrival in Japan made the front pages of the English dailies, the *Japan Advertiser* and the *Japan Times & Mail*.[17] In *The Osaka Mainichi & the Tokyo Nichi Nichi*, he was acclaimed as "a world figure" who had "devoted his past 20 years or so to the emancipation of non-white races of the world."[18] The day after his arrival in Japan, while walking in the Ginza (which he styled "the Fifth Avenue of Tokyo"), Johnson was treated as a celebrity;

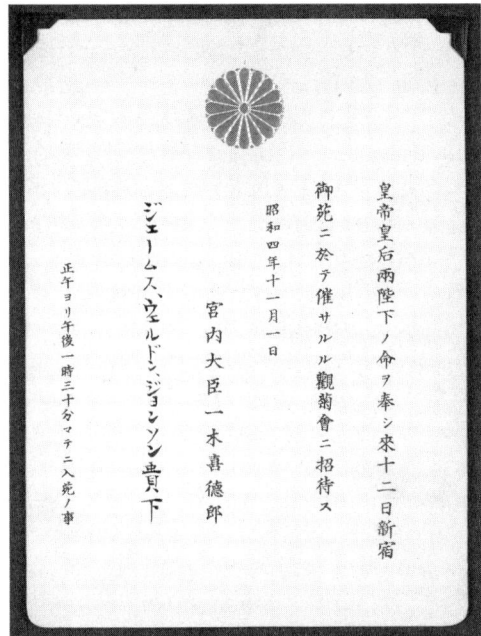

1.1. Letter of invitation to the emperor's garden party, addressed to James Weldon Johnson, dated November 1, 1929. *Photograph courtesy of Yale Collection of American Literature, Beinecke Rare Book and Manuscript Library, Yale University.*

in a letter to his wife, Grace Nail, Johnson wrote, "I've found myself recognized, even here in Tokyo."[19]

Perhaps no episode better represents the honor accorded to Johnson than his attendance at a garden party hosted by Hirohito, emperor of Japan. Johnson recalls in *Along This Way* that "the invitations [to the party], bearing the Imperial golden, sixteen-petaled chrysanthemum, caused a flutter of excitement" (*ATW*, 404; see figure 1.1). Among the nine thousand guests who attended the party were members of the Japanese cabinet, high-ranking officers of the army and navy, and international delegates to the World Engineering Congress and to the IPR. Mrs. Woodrow Wilson was also present.[20] Johnson was the first African American to be invited to one of the emperor's garden parties.[21] Standing directly opposite Japan's cabinet members and foreign diplomats, Johnson watched Hirohito, "dressed in a khaki military uniform" (*ATW*, 405), pass in a solemn parade with his retinue to the strains of the "Kimigayo" (His Majesty's Reign), the de facto national anthem of the Empire of Japan.[22]

In retrospect, Johnson had written over a decade earlier in a *New York Age* editorial that Japan was "perhaps the greatest hope for the colored races of the world."[23] Having recently attended the annual dinner of the

Japan Society in New York, where Viscount Kikujiro Ishii, the Japanese ambassador to the United States, made a speech calling for a racial equality clause in the proposed covenant of the League of Nations,[24] Johnson concluded in this *New York Age* editorial, "We should like to see Japan relatively as powerful in the Orient as the United States is in the western continent. We should like to see an Asiatic Monroe Doctrine with Japan as its interpreter and administrator." Johnson granted that Japan's regional ascendancy entailed the domination of other neighboring countries, but he argued that "it is better for China to be dominated by Japan than to be dominated by some European government"[25]—that is, for the region to be reintegrated as Asian and to remain a distinct sphere, independent of future Western colonization and interference. In 1929, Johnson went further, drawing the "Negro question" into Japan's orbit in the Pacific. The *Tokyo Asahi Shimbun* quoted Johnson as saying, upon his arrival in Japan, that as a representative of the Negro race, "he would give vent to the real feelings" of those who suffered racism, in the hope of making common cause with the "Japanese people, the [most] advanced among the colored races."[26] It is possible that Johnson was just being diplomatic, but Japanese readers evidently took his words to heart. Johnson found himself regarded as an ally of the Japanese; in Kyoto, he received a letter (written in shaky English, reminding Johnson of Wallace Irwin's *Letters of a Japanese Boy*) from a Japanese boy "welcoming [him] to Japan" and entreating Johnson to let him join the NAACP.[27] To work for "black race agitation," wrote the boy, would make him feel "extremely satisfied," and he offered the best of reasons for believing this to be the case: "Reason why, I am a Japanese" (*ATW*, 401). In addition, Johnson "received an offer from a Japanese firm to do a book—a book on Race as an international question."[28]

The third biennial conference of the IPR, which opened in Kyoto on October 28, proclaimed a "new Pacific era" in which "the peoples of the Pacific have become the captains of their own destinies."[29] The United States, Great Britain, Canada, China, Japan, Australia, New Zealand, the Philippines, and Hawai'i sent delegations to the third biennial IPR conference. France, the Netherlands, the Soviet Union, Mexico, the League of Nations, and the International Labor Organization dispatched observers. The chairman of the conference was Dr. Inazo Nitobe, author of *Bushido* and one of the undersecretaries-general of the League of Nations from 1920 to 1926; Johnson refers to him as "the distinguished Japanese statesman" in *Along This Way* (*ATW*, 396). Nitobe delivered the opening address, urging those present to cultivate an "international mind" and to "find a common ground for the old and the new races to join hands."[30] A message from Japanese premier Hamaguchi was read to the conference. It declared that his government was "pledged to curtail our national armaments so far as may be consistent with the safety of the realm and to cultivate the most amicable relations between Japan and the rest of the world."[31] Among those sending messages from overseas was President Herbert Hoover, whose telegraph from Washington (October 25, 1929) expressed his confidence in the approach of the IPR as "one of the most effective methods of securing peace and friendly relations" in the Pacific.[32] Its short history notwithstanding, the IPR was clearly seen to be having an impact upon the post–World War I international order in the region.

Johnson attended IPR round table discussions, where he contributed whenever and as much as he could. Topics discussed included the Machine Age and traditional culture, China's foreign relations, the problems of Manchuria, and diplomatic relations in the Pacific.[33] Not only did he learn a great deal about Asia, but he also exchanged views on US actions in the Caribbean and Mexico. He was vocal at a round table on "diplomatic relations in the Pacific," where he claimed that US Marines went to Nicaragua because the United States felt "obligated to make safe the Panama Canal" and "can't let other nation[s] or people dig [a] rival canal through Nicaragua"—thus endorsing the Monroe Doctrine and the Roosevelt Corollary as US regional policies on the eastern shores of the Pacific Rim.[34] Johnson spent an enormous amount of time reading papers relating to round table discussions; his hotel room was so full of books and pamphlets that it looked "like a store room of the N.Y. Public Library."[35] Such was his commitment that Johnson joined with others including Yusuke Tsurumi, member of the Japanese House of Representatives, to organize an "informal" IPR conference immediately after the formal one came to a close on November 9, to discuss and exchange views on "Race Prejudice and International Relations."[36]

Johnson wrote from Japan in a letter to his wife, "This conference has been a great thing for me. Not only as a relief from my work, but it has given me a worldwide view of many things, even of the Negro question."[37] The conference's promotion of a Pacific Community inclusive of African American members and its internationalizing of the Negro question for Johnson helped foster an awareness of a "universality of the race and color problem" that traversed the hemispheric dividing line that had previously separated the Americas and Asia on the Pacific Rim. "Negroes in the United States are prone, and naturally, to believe that their problem is *the* problem," says Johnson in *Along This Way*. "The fact is, there is a race and color problem wherever the white man deals with darker races" (*ATW*, 398).[38] Yet the conference also gave him an anxious inkling of a new form of imperialism operating in the Pacific Community—imperialism that is reenacted in *Along This Way*, as I discuss below. After all, the community was a compromised one because its political objectives were highly constrained by the interests of great powers that were present. The liberal internationalist politics of the IPR supported Pacific peoples such as those in the Philippines, Korea, China, Mexico, and the Caribbean but did not challenge the imperial (European, US, and Japanese) status quo in the Pacific regional order. It thus necessarily contained contradictions. In *Along This Way*, Johnson reproduces these contradictions; Johnson emerges as both supportive of a self-determining and free Haiti in the Caribbean but as uncritical of the US imperial framework in relation to Nicaragua. Thus, as David Levering Lewis has pointed out in his seminal study *When Harlem Was in Vogue*, Johnson in his autobiography problematically teeters between imperialism and anti-imperialism, as an "exposer of American imperialism in Haiti" who nonetheless "justif[ies] his role" in the US military intervention in the Nicaraguan revolution.[39]

The shifting positionality that Johnson occupies relative to imperialism has long made his critics uncomfortable; he has been characterized as "a racial 'hypocrite.'" To resolve this discomfort, Lewis has suggested that "from the viewpoint of class consciousness," any inconsistency on Johnson's part that is problematic from a racial point of view is "either nonexistent or of minimal consequence." He thus attempted to explain the negative implications of the proclivity (if any) of Johnson, a diplomat, to participate in the production of proimperialist narratives of US operations in Nicaragua, from the perspective of class and professional positioning among African American intellectuals. In this chapter, I would prefer to confront it as an important, if discomfiting, aspect of Johnson's black Pacific geography in *Along This Way*. This is because, as Lewis observes, Johnson justifies US actions in Nicaragua as having been dictated "by the *Japanese* threat of a canal across the isthmus" (emphasis mine) in Central America.[40] The significance of Nicaragua in *Along This Way* may be determined not in terms of the Atlantic Americas so much as in terms of a modern Pacific regionalism that forged the Latin America–Asia nexus for which the IPR was the catalyst. More specifically, I will argue that Johnson's vision of colored solidarities against worldwide racism and Western imperialism that his attendance at the IPR may have advanced was significantly modified in the early 1930s, when two isolated events on the Pacific Rim—the US Marine occupation of Nicaragua and Japan's military occupation of Manchuria—came together to shape Johnson's understanding of the developing regional hegemonic systems in Central America and in East Asia.

(Black) Yankee Peril in Nicaragua

Nowhere in *Along This Way* does Johnson sound so unnervingly like an apologist for US imperialism as in chapter 26, in which he relates how he aided the 1912 armed intervention in Nicaragua as the chief US civilian official in Corinto, a port city on the Pacific. Johnson had been appointed consul to Nicaragua in 1909, when under the Big Stick policy, also known as the Roosevelt Corollary to the Monroe Doctrine, the intervention in question was beginning to police Latin American nations that had unstable governments. In this position, his chief duties seemed to be closely monitoring Nicaraguan affairs and reporting on them to the State Department in Washington (*ATW*, 258).

When a revolt broke out against President Adolfo Diaz and his US-backed conservative administration in July 1912, Diaz "called upon the United States to maintain him in the position in which it had placed him" (*ATW*, 276). Johnson accordingly opened the consulate to serve as a headquarters for the US Marines, stalled rebel forces demanding the port of Corinto, and held the port open for the arrival of US forces. Commander Warren J. Terhune of the USS *Annapolis* landed with one hundred bluejackets, and the collier *Justin* returned from Panama with over three hundred marines under the command of Major Smedley D. Butler (*ATW*, 276–77). The USS *California* arrived with Rear Admiral William H. H. Southerland. In due course, there was a fleet of eleven warships under the command of the admiral in the port (*ATW*, 286–87). In all, nearly three thousand marines and bluejackets took the field, ostensibly to protect American lives and property, and they succeeded in crushing the insurgents who had risen up in arms against the puppet regime headed by Diaz. Liberals in Nicaragua condemned the US invasion as proof of the "Yankee peril," and loud cries of "*Abajo los americanos!*" echoed in the streets of Corinto (*ATW*, 283). Governments of the isthmus countries, particularly El Salvador, protested the US actions in Nicaragua.[41] US Marines occupied Nicaragua for the ensuing twenty years, until the Hoover administration pulled troops out in 1933, the year of *Along This Way*'s publication (*ATW*, 288n1). Johnson, who played a key role in quashing the Nicaraguan "revolt," won recognition from Admiral Southerland, commander in chief of the Pacific Fleet, and received the same honors as the officers of the fleet (*ATW*, 287).

Understandably, many Nicaraguans chose not to forget the historical experience of the US intervention.[42] Exploited for the purposes of what the Taft administration had termed "dollar diplomacy," Nicaragua was "a virtual colony of the United States" for two decades.[43] Even in the United States, books attacking US foreign policy in Nicaragua appeared, mobilizing public sentiment against US imperialism.[44] Yet if the reader of *Along This Way* anticipates an apology from Johnson for his role in supporting the US invasion in 1912, he or she will be disappointed. Johnson does not acknowledge any injury done to Nicaraguans by US troops, nor does he express guilt for his active involvement in US imperialism.[45] While he strongly denounces the US invasion of Haiti, Johnson offers only a lame justification for the US intervention in Nicaragua: "In Nicaragua," Johnson writes in chapter 33, "the American forces were there in accordance with the wishes of the government; they were there to sustain that government in power" (*ATW*, 345). Yet the government in question was clearly a puppet of the White House and the magnates of Wall Street.

Johnson's defense of the invasion in *Along This Way* is puzzling, all the more so in light of his testimony on February 25, 1925, before a subcommittee of the Senate Foreign Relations Committee in Washington. Historian William E. Gibbs notes of Johnson that, as "a spokesman for his race and an avowed opponent of imperialism, he condemned . . . US intervention to protect business interests in Nicaragua."[46] Moreover, according to an NAACP press release several days later, Johnson, executive secretary of the NAACP, criticized the intervention in Nicaragua as "sheer hypocrisy." This press release quoted Johnson as testifying, "In Nicaragua . . . I was United States Consul from 1909 until 1913, that is from the time of the overthrow of [Nicaraguan president José Santos] Zelaya to the time of the taking over of control of the country by American military forces. . . . The chief reason for Zelaya's overthrow was not his being a dictator but because he was not sufficiently submissive to the American bankers. A government representing a minority of Nicaraguans but favorable to the American interests was installed and since 1912 has been sustained in power by American armed forces."[47] The *New York Times* (February 26, 1925) characterized Johnson's senate testimony as asserting the following: "While he was in Nicaragua a revolution fomented in the United States used American forces to support one faction against the other in the interests of American business men."[48] Johnson's testimony was later corroborated by Major Butler, one of the commanders of the US Marine invasion of Nicaragua appearing in Johnson's autobiography. Butler stated in 1935 that he had served as "a racketeer for capitalism," helping to "purify Nicaragua for the international banking house of Brown Brothers in 1909–1912."[49] In light of this testimony, the reader might ask, why did Johnson justify the US armed intervention in Nicaragua in *Along This Way*? Why did Johnson fail to recall in his 1933 autobiography that he had testified on US imperialism before a Senate subcommittee? Why did Johnson apologize in his autobiography for a US intervention that he had condemned in 1925?

These questions are not meant to suggest that Johnson was inconsistent but rather to call attention to the way in which he came to apprehend US actions in Nicaragua not so much in terms of the US capitalist economy, which was monopolistic and dominated by finance capital, as in terms of the modern regionalism that the United States instituted in Latin America (as part of the Pacific Community) through military dominance. Furthermore, I wish to bring attention to the way in which he accordingly came to terms with his own complicity in the very imperialism that he denounced. One can certainly argue, as does Gibbs, that Johnson had a selective memory that allowed him, in 1925, to overlook his personal memories of Nicaragua to bolster support for the anti-imperialist cause that he espoused as executive secretary of the NAACP. Gibbs observes that, in testifying before the Senate subcommittee in 1925, Johnson did not choose to recall that he had initially supported the US military intervention of 1912 and that "through this selective use of memory, he was able to remain on safe ground while he echoed the sentiments of the growing opposition to 'Big Stick' diplomacy."[50] However, *Along This Way* implicates him in so problematic a political project as the US Marines' occupation of Nicaragua and represents the black self as an accomplice in that operation. Yet by reenacting how he aided the US armed intervention in *Along This Way*, Johnson is not (shamelessly) justifying past actions that he once chose not to recall. Rather, I argue that Johnson is deliberately acknowledging the convoluted relationship that emerged between modern regionalism, internationalism, and imperialism, and the continuity between his position and one that he repudiates as evil—a continuity that he failed to acknowledge in 1925.

This convolution and continuity is a blank spot that I aim to fill in on our map of Johnson's black Pacific geography. It is tempting to read Johnson's Nicaragua within a familiar frame of reference such as "US imperialism in the Caribbean."[51] However, a broader Pacific context encompassing

East Asia is required to understand why Johnson's relations with the people of Nicaragua were no longer as innocuous by the time of his 1933 autobiography as they were in 1925, when "he was able to remain on safe ground." As Johnson narrates in *Along This Way*, he had to deal in 1912 with Nicaraguan revolutionaries "armed with a great array of books on international law" who objected to US interference in Nicaragua's internal affairs and demanded the surrender of the port of Corinto. Johnson knew that the revolutionaries "were in every respect right" and that from the point of view of international law, his cause was hopeless (*ATW*, 282). Nonetheless, to facilitate the United States' instituting a modern regional order in Latin America as hemispheric hegemon and police power, even in conflict with the rise of Nicaraguan nationalism, he used all his wiles to stall the rebels. Not only did he entertain the commissioners of the rebel force with a bountiful roast beef supper and beverages at the consulate but also, as a gesture of compliance (in fact, a ploy to gain time), he required them to secure from their leader instructions for, and authorization to deal with, the American consul. In a subsequent negotiation, Johnson initiated a discussion of the terms for the transfer of the port to the commissioners but requested ostensibly as a procedural matter that they obtain from their leader a signed statement that he would hold himself bound by the terms negotiated—this was "one more stroke to gain time," in Johnson's account (*ATW*, 286). "Ten nights out of bed, running on black coffee" (*ATW*, 285), Johnson gave full play to his diplomatic ability and succeeded in stalling the rebels until the USS *Denver* arrived with a force strong enough to enable him to turn down their demands. Johnson recalls, "I went to bed that night and slept soundly; and, of course, without any thought that I was having a hand in establishing a precedent that Japan was to cite to us twenty years later" (*ATW*, 286), that is, the precedent by which Japan defended the rightness of its military occupation of Manchuria to create the puppet state of Manchukuo in Northeast Asia.

It is quite possible that Johnson was here referring specifically to a news story that the *New York Times* carried in late 1932. On November 23, a story headlined "Japanese Attacks Policies of United States in Pamphlets Broadcast in Latin America" appeared on the front page of the newspaper. According to the *Times*, a pamphlet defending Japan's maneuvers in Manchuria was widely circulated in Latin American countries. It condemned the regional policy of the United States in regards to Latin American countries as "imperialistic" and "conquistatory." In complete contrast, Japan's policy in Manchuria was reportedly motivated by "self-defense," because the "disintegration" of the region or "its annexation by a foreign country" would endanger the security of Japan.[52] Indeed, in the Sino-Soviet war that had occurred shortly before and created a Manchurian crisis, Soviet troops mounted an operation in the region to support the Soviet claims to the disputed Chinese Eastern Railway. A year earlier, a report had also appeared on the front pages of South American newspapers of "Japan's retort that she has as much right to protect her interests in Manchuria as the United States in Nicaragua." This news was "spread over page 1 with large headlines, accompanied by photographic layouts and comments on the United States' policy of intervention," the *Times* reported.[53] In January 1933, the black weekly *New York Age*, where Johnson served as contributing editor from 1914 to 1923 after he resigned from the consular service, commented on "the cleverness of Japan in quoting precedents."[54]

To dismiss Japan's military occupation of Manchuria as a local Asian affair irrelevant to black culture in the United States seems hasty at best and belittles the scope of contemporary black internationalism at worst. The current perspective of history on the Manchurian Incident is quite unequivocal: in 1931, after a staged provocation at Mukden—dynamiting a section of railroad owned by Japan's South Manchuria Railway and accusing Chinese dissidents of the act—the Japanese military occupied Manchuria under a specious pretense of self-defense and subsequently incurred censure from the United States and the League of Nations that resulted in Japan's international isolation, paving the way for the attack on Pearl Harbor ten years later. This perspective seldom recognizes the degree to which black intellectuals who followed Asian affairs intervened in "world opinion" to argue against viewing the Japanese Empire as evil. This intervention complicated Johnson's positioning.

Johnson was clearly well informed about Manchuria. In *Along This Way*, he describes the IPR round table in which Yosuke Matsuoka (former vice president [1927–1929] of the South Manchuria Railway) and Shuhsi Hsu (professor of international law at Yenching University, Peking) crossed swords over Manchuria in an emotion-laden argument that threw into sharp relief the Japanese and the Chinese, darker races occupying an internally conflicted space in East Asia. Johnson writes,

> Once, on the part of the Japanese, the frankness was brutal but, in my opinion, revealed the truth of the situation. Yosuke Matsuoka, of the Japanese group, and former vice-president of the South Manchurian Railway, enraged, like a bull at the hands of the picador, by the lances of inter-

national law thrust into him by one of the doctors of philosophy of the Chinese group, burst out, "If Japan in the war with Russia had known of the secret treaty signed by Li Hung Chang and Libanov, there would today be no Manchurian problem; Japan would have taken South Manchuria and held it against Russia. She made her mistake in not taking it when nobody could have stopped her." (*ATW*, 399)[55]

Referring to the 1904–1905 Russo-Japanese War when Japan took control of Manchuria from Russia, Matsuoka ventured his opinion that if Japan had known during the war of the secret Sino-Russian treaty of alliance entered into in 1896 (which granted the Tsarist Russian government the right to construct a railway across northern Manchuria—enabling Russia to "sweep down Manchuria on its southward movement," resulting in the war), Japan would have annexed Manchuria outright after the war, rather than returning it to China as it had done.[56] Johnson recalls that Matsuoka's "words were equivalent to a prediction of what happened this year, 1933, when nobody *could* stop [Japan]" (*ATW*, 399).

From the perspective of 1933, Johnson's experience at the IPR conference would certainly seem to have foreshadowed coming events, for subsequently Asian affairs had rapidly come to a serious pass. On September 18, 1931, less than two years after the conference, a Japanese force (known as the Kwantung Army) stationed along the Japanese-owned South Manchuria Railway invaded Manchuria without approval from the imperial government in Tokyo. In protest, Secretary of State Henry L. Stimson sent notes (January 7, 1932) to the governments of Japan and China announcing that the United States did not "intend to recognize" any situation, treaty, or agreement that might impair the treaty rights of the United States in China, including those that related to the Open Door policy, or that might be brought about by means contrary to the Kellogg-Briand Pact (also called the Pact of Paris), that is, by war.[57] The cornerstone of US Far Eastern policy, the Open Door in China, first enunciated by Secretary of State John Hay, had been reaffirmed as international law in the Nine Power Treaty at the Washington Conference in 1922—a conference that instituted a new, US-defined, international system in the Pacific region. The Kellogg-Briand Pact (1928) was a treaty providing for the renunciation of war as an instrument of national policy.

Unruffled by the Stimson Doctrine of nonrecognition, the Japanese Kwantung Army established a puppet state in Manchuria—a region that was the historical homeland of the Manchus, who founded the Ch'ing Dynasty of China (1644–1912)—by installing the last Manchu emperor, Pu Yi, as head of the regime. This led Stimson to take a still firmer stand on Japan.[58] In a speech delivered on August 8, 1932, to the Council on Foreign Relations in New York, Stimson reflected on the significance of the Kellogg-Briand Pact in the defense of which "the American government has been a leader." Stimson insisted that the pact did not allow any interpretations or qualifications on the part of the signatories—except for "the right of self-defense," which is the only limitation to the covenant against war. He called for worldwide "moral disapproval" of the "wrongdoer" Japan and warned that "a nation which sought to mask imperialistic policy under the guise of the defense of its nationals would soon be unmasked."[59] The United States, for one, ratified the pact with its own qualification that it would not prohibit military obligations arising from the Monroe Doctrine. Indeed, one of the questions raised in the IPR round table on "diplomatic relations in the Pacific" that Johnson attended was a "difference between war as [an] instrument of national policy and troops as such an instrument," because as IPR delegates observed, the United States had used and was using troops to carry out a national policy in Nicaragua.[60]

Still unrestrained, the Japanese government formally recognized Manchukuo in September 1932, thus setting itself on a course toward confrontation with the League of Nations, which would attempt to intervene in the Sino-Japanese dispute over Manchuria. In December, under the front-page headline "Japan Tells League It Cannot Stop Her," the *New York Times* reported that Matsuoka, now chief of the Japanese League of Nations delegation in Geneva, had declared that Japan would not be deflected even by "the severest sanctions."[61]

In all likelihood, Japan's defiance was startling, even shocking, to many Americans. Matsuoka's speech (December 8, 1932) to the league must have been particularly dumbfounding. In this speech, he portrayed Japan's defiant isolationism as the martyrdom of a latter-day Jesus: "Humanity crucified Jesus of Nazareth two thousand years ago. And to-day? Can any of you assure me that the so-called world opinion can make no mistake? We Japanese feel that we are now put on trial. Some of the people in Europe and America may wish even to crucify Japan in the twentieth century. Gentlemen, Japan stands ready to be crucified! But we do believe, and firmly believe, that, in a very few years, world opinion will be changed and that we also shall be understood by the world as Jesus of Nazareth was."[62]

Matsuoka's message was pathetically self-aggrandizing but blunt: Japan was fighting alone to save the Far East, and she was in the right. A cartoon in the December 10, 1932, issue of the *New York World-Telegram* offered a pointed satire of the self-righteousness of Matsuoka's speech. In the cartoon, a Japanese soldier thumbs his nose at a door marked "The League of Nations" and says, "65 million Japanese can't be wrong."[63] In response, another *New York World-Telegram* cartoon (January 18, 1933) showed Uncle Sam, backed up by a young woman labeled "League of Nations," sternly lecturing an obdurate Japanese soldier in Manchuria, saying, "A treaty is a treaty, my friend."[64]

When the League of Nations Assembly passed a resolution condemning Japan on February 24, 1933, Matsuoka defiantly walked out of the assembly hall with his delegation. On a stop in London on his way home, Matsuoka was jeered by a crowd shouting "Shame!" and "Japan is a nation of bandits."[65] Matsuoka arrived for a visit to New York on March 24 to be greeted by a mass of demonstrators—"Chinese, Communists and Chinese sympathizers"—displaying "placards denouncing 'Japanese imperialism'" and "a chorus of boos and 'Down with Japan.'"[66] In the United States, Matsuoka gave numerous press conferences and speeches, in New York, Boston, Washington, Chicago, Portland (Oregon), and San Francisco. Matsuoka's "busy schedule indicates that he had certainly not given up on" Japan's cooperative diplomacy in international relations, as historian Sandra Wilson has observed.[67] In front of newspaper reporters in New York, he said, "We cannot allow any people hostile to us to be intriguing or actually carry on any kind of warfare in Manchuria.... Suppose some hostile power was carrying on a campaign against you at the Panama Canal or in the Caribbean Sea. What would you do?"[68] However, the February 25, 1933, issue of the *New York World-Telegram* included a cartoon in which a lonely Japanese soldier stood looking out over the Pacific Ocean on a rock labeled "Moral Isolation."[69] The whole world, it seemed, was condemning Japan.

Yet the black Pacific, an imagined community produced by African American narratives, was not necessarily a space of alienation. As David Levering Lewis writes, "American Negroes who paid attention ... rushed to defend Japan and largely continued doing so even after, formally branded an aggressor, she self-righteously withdrew from the League of Nations."[70] Perhaps the most sensational counternarrative in this vein was the argument pursued in the *Chicago Defender* that Japan's aggrandizement was her "manifest destiny." The *Defender* contended that although "the brag division of the American press, wordy and dark, paints Japan as the Germany of the East, at war against civilization," Japan was really "at war against the uncivilized prejudices of the presumptions of superiority based on color." It was Japan's "manifest destiny" to shake

China "from slumber and to its feet" and "wipe contempt from the brow of color," the *Defender* argued; Japan was chastising China, "itself of kindred vein with Japan" but "unable to protect itself against the scoundrelism of western diplomacy."[71] This view was later taken up bombastically by the Baltimore *Afro-American*: along with a cartoon showing Japan "kicking China in the pants to make it stand up straight and be a man," the *Afro-American* declared that "the Chinese have become a kind of 'Uncle Tom' of Asia."[72]

One of the more outspoken and persistent defenders of Japan was W. E. B. Du Bois, writing in the official organ of the NAACP, *Crisis*. As Lewis observes with regret, "Typically, Du Bois would shave the edges of responsible opinion repeatedly when writing about the Japanese, all but welcoming explicitly what the Kaiser and Teddy Roosevelt had called the 'Yellow Peril,' and virtually anointing the Empire of the Rising Sun as the lodestar of all the 'darker races.'"[73] However, Du Bois's commentaries on the Japanese Empire are remarkable for how they tease out the continuity between one position and another that is repudiated as evil—a continuity often disregarded from our often Manichean perspective—by relating US and Japanese imperialism, particularly in regard to Latin America and Asia. Thus, Du Bois acidly observed to *Crisis* readers in December 1931, "The United States (which stole a large part of Mexico, invaded Nicaragua and Santo Domingo and raped Haiti, annexed the Philippines and Porto Rico and dominates Cuba, because of her economic interests and investments) is now explaining the Golden Rule to Japan."[74] In April 1932, he wrote, "What we call the Hypocrisy of Hypocrisies" is to see the European maritime empires, England and France, and "the United States (with [its actions in] Hawaii, the Philippines, Nicaragua, Porto Rico and Haiti), all crying 'Shame!' to Japan, whom they forced to choose between militarism or suicide."[75]

William N. Jones, writing in the *Afro-American*, also wondered "what the United States would have thought if Japan had raised a howl when we sent marines and the American Flag into Nicaragua to protect American dollars as Japan is now doing to protect the Japanese yen?"[76] Jones's commentary was apparently directed at Stimson, author of the recently published *American Policy in Nicaragua* (1927), who reproached Japan after having allowed the continuing presence of US Marines in Nicaragua as special emissary to that country in 1927, when the United States again landed thousands of marines to prop up the Diaz regime.[77] Pursuing a similar argument, William Pickens, field secretary for the NAACP and contributing editor for the Associated Negro Press, remarked that "if we were taking Haiti or Nicaragua . . . how much 'nerve' we would have thought the Japanese to show if they had sent word from Asia to tell us what to do in America!"⁷⁸

In Du Bois's eye, the United States, "with [its] hands red with blood and [its] pockets full of loot," was "hitting Japan on the wrist and crying, 'naughty, naughty!'"⁷⁹ In December 1933, the *Crisis* thus printed the following poem, entitled "The Naughty Japanee," which the periodical explained was "copied from a recent publication" in Manchukuo, "the newly born colored nation."

> I AM bad
> All others good;
> . . . .
> Benevolent the pious hand of Sam;
> Europe for his loans is full of praise;
> Hawaii, Haiti, blacks in Alabam,
> Bless his rule that brings delirious days.
> Ugh! I am bad
> All others good;
> O wherefore should this be?
> Faultless are the empires
> —Except the Japanee.⁸⁰

Ironically lamenting Japan's moral isolation, this poem satirizes the double standard of "empire" that Uncle Sam applied to himself and the Japanese. No elaborate explanation of the contradictory nature of the polemic of the US and European maritime empires against the Japanese Empire was necessary. The August 1932 issue of the *Crisis* thus carried a cartoon that showed Uncle Sam in Haiti, John Bull in India, and a French man in Africa, firing a fusillade of cries of "GET OUT!" "GET OUT OF THERE!" "GO HOME!" at a Japanese soldier in Manchuria. Undaunted, the soldier had only this to say: "THE SAME TO YOU!" (figure 1.2).⁸¹

Strictly speaking, the *Crisis* cartoon did not distinguish which empire was good and which evil. The point was rather, as Du Bois observed, that "the European and American pots are standing around making remarks on the color of the Japanese kettle."⁸² Yet for Du Bois and other blacks, speaking critically about a colored imperium did not come naturally. Pickens, for instance, seemed to praise the Japanese seizure of Manchuria in an article published in March 1932, writing, "'White Supremacy' was slain in Manchuria. . . . The Japanese killed it."⁸³ Although "we hate war," the NAACP field secretary declared, "we like Japan and Japanese."⁸⁴

1.2. Cartoon showing a defiant Japanese soldier in Manchuria. From the August 1932 issue of *Crisis*. Used with permission from the Crisis Publishing Co., Inc., the publisher of the magazine of the National Association for the Advancement of Colored People.

According to Jones, writing in the *Afro-American*, "The little brown men of Nippon are taking the weapons of western world exploitation and are beating the Westerners at their own game."[85] Pickens poked fun at Stimson, calling him "Wrong-Horse Harry,"[86] and Du Bois pilloried him as a double-dealer and a "blood-sucking, imperial tyrant." As Du Bois saw it, it was not Japan but Stimson, in cahoots with the British prime minister Ramsay MacDonald, and Premier Edouard Herriot of France, who was to be unmasked. Sending Japan and China "a word from twelve little black millions who live in the midst of western culture and know it," Du Bois cried out in the *Crisis*: "Unmask them, Asia; tear apart their double faces and double tongues and unite in peace."[87] Over a decade earlier, Johnson had ventured a similar opinion, writing in the *New York Age* that "if other nations are going to be allowed to hold and dominate parts of China, we are in favor of seeing Japan do the same thing." Acknowledging the continuum between nonwhite and white imperialism, Johnson hoped that "perhaps the sight of Japan engaging in the same game as the other great powers of the world will wake them up to the wickedness of the whole business."[88] Accordingly, it is ironic that Johnson, who put down the Nicaraguan rebellion and "went to bed . . . and slept soundly" in 1912 (*ATW*, 286), woke up to find himself located on the same continuum twenty years later.

When US and Japanese imperialism resonated in the early 1930s (despite their difference in polity as a "democracy" and a constitutional monarchy), the significance of the memory of Nicaragua that Johnson presents in his autobiography was not what it used to be. The US occupation of Nicaragua had been constituted as a point of reference for Japan's occupation of Manchuria. Thus, Johnson's *Along This Way* is informed by a weird inversion of historical causality in the black Pacific. It is not so much that an African American embraced Japanese imperialism (as George Lipsitz observes in his discussion of the black Pacific[89]) but that the US intervention in Nicaragua, in which Johnson "ha[d] a hand," had become "a precedent" that the Japanese Empire appropriated and emulated in Northeast Asia (*ATW*, 286). My claim is not that the historical Johnson, black US diplomat in Nicaragua, was an originator of the nonwhite imperialism that culminated in Japan's endeavor in Manchuria. Rather, my point is that Johnson's complex positionality with regard to imperialism, as represented in *Along This Way*, cannot be approached without an understanding of the Nicaragua-Manchuria nexus that was forged in the black Pacific. In contesting the ideological forces of the black Pacific that implicate him at the international crossroads of US and Japanese imperialism, Johnson in *Along This Way*, as I discuss below, revisits his past actions in Nicaragua even as they continued to shape the present and future of the Pacific Community and seeks to draft an alternative black Pacific geography.

Act of Memory

Johnson's drafting of an alternative black Pacific in *Along This Way* is a complex undertaking. What agency could Johnson exercise as he was caught in the intersection between the geopolitical realities of a new imperialism practiced by the United States in Nicaragua and Japan in Manchuria—a predicament that ultimately called into question the possibilities of agency that "resistance" implied?

In seeking to intervene in the ideological flows of the black Pacific that seemed so resolutely to defend the Japanese Empire by fabricating Nicaragua retroactively as a template for colored imperialism in Manchuria, Johnson in *Along This Way* ushers in yet another usable past: "the Japanese threat of a canal across the isthmus." Concluding his Nicaragua chapter, Johnson writes, "Only a year or so before the 1909 revolution, [Nicaraguan president] Zelaya was endeavoring to open secret negotiations with Japan for the acquisition of the Nicaragua route, and a copy of his letter broaching the matter was in the hands of the State Department" (*ATW*, 288). This evidence indicated the possibility that Nicaragua's foreign alignment would have posed security threats to the United States. Pointing to secret negotiations between Zelaya and Japan that preceded and precipitated the American intervention in Nicaragua in 1909, Johnson urges the reader to "go deeper" than "concessions and loans" and to discern the "fundamental policy" of "the State and Navy Departments," that is, to ensure "the security of the United States" (*ATW*, 288–89).[90] As Johnson claims, this policy held that security "depended upon controlling an inter-oceanic canal across Central America," and "even with the American ownership of the Panama Canal," it was still contingent upon "domination of the very possible route across Nicaragua" (*ATW*, 288).

Johnson asserts that the control of the interoceanic canal was imperative for the security of the United States. Indeed, the strategic landscape of the Pacific was drastically changed with the 1914 opening of the Panama Canal, a conduit that links the Atlantic and the Pacific via the Caribbean, because it enabled the United States to move its warships to the Pacific without exposing the Atlantic coast to undue danger of an attack from Europe. The canal impeded Japan—then the strongest Pacific naval power after its defeat of the Russian navy in 1904–1905—from pursuing a maritime empire, as historian Pekka Korhonen observes. With the opening of the canal, the days of Japanese naval superiority were coming to an end.[91]

Johnson was surely right that Japan's acquisition of a canal concession in Nicaragua would have raised "the possibility and fear of war between the United States and any other great power" such as Japan (*ATW*, 289). Johnson recounts that a letter from Zelaya's minister of foreign affairs to the Nicaraguan minister in Paris (dated April 29, 1908) was discovered that proposed overtures to Japan concerning a canal route.[92] According to the *New York Times* (May 18, 1909), the official newspaper of the Nicaraguan government "advocate[d] an alliance with Japan, and urge[d] the dispatch of a commission to Tokio to draw up the articles, and offer Japan the right to construct a canal through Nicaraguan territory," in order to counter America's "imperialistic advance."[93] There were thus clear signs of an emerging rapprochement between the two Pacific Rim nations, Nicaragua and Japan. With this secret international alliance as justification for the US intervention in Nicaragua that Johnson assisted, his 1933 narrative manages to counter the black Pacific discourse that seemed so resolutely to support the Japanese Empire in justifying its occupation of Manchuria, by pointing to the US occupation of Nicaragua.

However, herein lies a paradox: Johnson's revisionist historical account works to augment (as much as to undercut) proimperialist apologies. In the Nicaragua chapter (chapter 26) of *Along This Way*, Johnson seems to legitimize US imperialism in Nicaragua as being in the interest of "the security of the United States" (*ATW*, 288). In a subsequent chapter on the IPR conference in Japan (chapter 37), the reader witnesses Johnson's depiction of Matsuoka deploying the same logic that Johnson himself uses in the Nicaragua chapter: referring to a "secret treaty" between the Chinese and Russian Empires in 1896 that granted the Tsarist Russian government the right to construct a railway, if not a canal, across northern Manchuria. Matsuoka justified Japan's seizure of Manchuria as vital to its strategic defense in relation to Russia/the Soviet Union (*ATW*, 399). Insofar as Johnson seeks to counter the ideological flows of imperialism in the Pacific Community, he is effective in resituating (rather than undoing) the discursive imbrications of US empire building in Central America and Japanese empire building in Northeast Asia.

How then should Nicaragua be remembered? This question is central to my argument, because ultimately I am trying to locate Johnson's agency in his act of memory in articulating a black (ethical) approach to modern regionalism in the Pacific, in which puppet regimes or puppet states of the regional hegemons in the Americas and Asia were implicated in the relationship between race and imperialism.[94] Johnson's chapter on Nicaragua, unlike that on Haiti, is disturbing because Johnson emerges as a black representative of an imperial government; the chapter reenacts the support that he provided as a US consul to represent the interests of his government in its exercise of international policing power that disfigured the sovereign state of Nicaragua into a puppet and later provided a pretext for "colored" Japan in its military occupation of Manchuria.

This is in no way to suggest that Johnson's relationship with the Nicaraguans was one of nonwhite colonialism; such a notion is insupportable. Conceding that Johnson was of an imperialist constituency in Nicaragua in 1912, it would nonetheless be erroneous to define his agency as nonwhite colonialism because the power that he assumed in Nicaragua was not predicated upon his being black but upon his infatuation with the state.[95] It worked because it enabled Johnson—despite the same state's marginalization of minorities, himself included—to derive a new sense of a self-worth and power. Johnson fulfilled this sense through the act of participating in the state's attempt to create and perpetuate Nicaragua's puppet regime; indeed, it would seem that if America had been made to fail, he would have failed with the state. When he had a hand in the successful US armed intervention in Nicaragua, Johnson thus wrote to his wife: "I'm proud of the fight I put up.... I had many delicate cards to play, it took patience and time to finish the game, but it's finished now and I either win or lose—but I believe I've won.... I want to win the *recognition* of the [State] Department, and I want to win it on *my* merits" (emphasis in original).⁹⁶

In revisiting the US Marine occupation of Nicaragua, Johnson does not focus on the relationship between himself and the State Department but instead reenacts the international system of regional hegemons and their puppet regimes at the personal and professional level between himself and Nicaraguan officials in power. For many people, the image of Johnson as an able US civilian official follows from his adroit dealings with the rebels of the 1912 Nicaraguan revolution. As described in *Along This Way*, even a young Southern officer was so impressed by the diplomatic skill that the black consul displayed during the crisis that he approached Johnson and wrung his hand. The officer, Johnson recalls, "appeared to be proud that we were both Americans" (*ATW*, 286). Powerful as this image may be, it is nonetheless delimited in *Along This Way* by Johnson's countermemory of Nicaraguans—not so much of those nationalists or rebels quashed by the US Marines acting as international police as of the neocolonial elites surrounding the puppet regime who were complicit with the US government in crushing the rebels. It might be assumed that these elites consented to, and benefited from, the intervention of the United States, and with their explicit consent, international relations between the United States and the Nicaraguan regime in power seem legitimate and even democratic. However, Johnson is haunted in *Along This Way* by memories of the deep-seated resentment, anger, and pain that such Nicaraguan elites experienced, as did Johnson himself, even as they became international collaborators in preserving order in Nicaragua.

Johnson's bayonet-backed diplomacy with Nicaraguan officials is the least examined aspect of the black consul's foreign service career, but it is the aspect most central to a consideration of the black Pacific geography that Johnson charts in *Along This Way*. Johnson characterizes his experiences with the Nicaraguan rebels as an "opéra bouffe" in which he "was merely playing a part, a rather ridiculous part" (*ATW*, 285). In contrast to Johnson's experiences with Nicaraguan nationalist rebels, intense personal and collective hurt and animosity infuse his memories of encounters with Nicaraguan governmental forces, and in particular with General Toribio Tijerino, with whom Johnson had to cooperate to sustain the regime in power. As Johnson describes it, the black American consul and the general, acting as the proxy of the president of Nicaragua, came into conflict in a struggle for sovereignty despite the common interests that united them as international collaborators. Resentful of Johnson's assumed authority over Nicaraguan territory, Tijerino attempted to take military control of Corinto, sending word that he had installed himself as "the chief local authority at the port." Thereupon, US Lieutenant Lewis immediately placed the Nicaraguan general "under arrest" and marched him between six bluejackets to the American consulate (*ATW*, 279).

"The news spread like wildfire," Johnson recalls. In the ensuing scene, the Nicaraguan general was brought before Johnson, the American consul. "With a dramatic gesture," Tijerino surrendered his weapons and said, "Sir, I am your prisoner" (*ATW*, 279–80). Johnson offers the following description of the remainder of the scene, in which a colored internationalism (forged by a commonality of interests) emerges as tangential to, and contiguous with, the imperialism that Johnson, an African American, was seen to embody: "Then immediately [Tijerino] launched into an eloquent and incendiary speech, in a voice loud enough to reach the already excited crowd outside. He began by charging me with having placed under arrest the President of Nicaragua; the which was virtually true. He declared that he would protest to the Central American governments and to the world. . . . He called on patriotic Nicaraguans to resent the indignity to which he had been subjected. There were *vivas* from the crowd" (*ATW*, 280).

Anxious to be "rid of Tijerino," Johnson then agreed to a compromise requested by the general—that he be furnished with a train to return with his troops to Chinandega to see to the defense of the city (*ATW*, 279). "The entire plan, after all, worked out," Johnson reminisces, "for I never again laid eyes on Tijerino." In the battle for Chinandega, the Nicaraguan general "lost an eye" and "was captured and made a prisoner" by the rebel forces, a common enemy whom Johnson and Tijerino, international collaborators, were supposedly working together to quash (*ATW*, 281).

One can hardly overlook the emotional dimension of Johnson's memories of Tijerino and the puppet regime that he supported—a dimension so charged that it may seem inconsistent with the black consul's rationalized and rationalizing narrative of how the US intervention worked both for the Nicaraguan (puppet) state and for the United States.[97] I view this dimension of Johnson's memory as key to locating his agency in the articulation of a critical (and ethical) approach to the Pacific Community that became a new form of imperialism based on the principle of regional hegemony, of which both the United States and Japan are exemplars, and in the black Pacific imagined by African American narratives within this frame. Johnson's text speaks to the infrastructure of colored internationalism as it would be lived similarly in the puppet state of Manchukuo, where local elites putatively consented to, and benefited from, the emergent regional hegemon, the Japanese Empire. The creation of Manchukuo was Japan's plausible "'answer' to rising Chinese nationalism,"[98] and with the seeming consent of the peoples in Manchuria, the international alliance between Japan and Manchukuo kept up appearances as legitimate. However, as Edgar Snow, an American journalist in China, observed in *Far Eastern Front*, his account of the Japanese military occupation of Manchuria, published in the same year as *Along This Way*, "Curiously, the Chinese most bitter against Japanese rule are those making money from it." It was these local Chinese officials in government in Manchukuo—like Tijerino in Nicaragua—participating in sustaining the puppet regime who harbored "covert hatred and disgust with prevailing scenes" as they were, more than anybody else, "aware of their 'disgraceful position.'"[99]

By memorializing the pain, resentment, and anger felt by the Nicaraguan and the black American who despoiled one another's political ideals of equality, self-determination, and dignity, *Along This Way* thus works to address the infrastructure of colored internationalism in the black Pacific, revealing the material foundation of that infrastructure to be an infatuation with state power. By recalling taboo moments of the past (which he once chose not to recall) even as they shaped the present and future of the Pacific Community, Johnson in his autobiography takes on his own implication in, and accountability for, the imperialism that modern regionalism accommodated and even became.

Johnson's autobiography—after recounting his 1929 transpacific trip to the IPR conference in its penultimate chapter—ends with his resignation from the NAACP to take up a faculty position at Fisk University. Making a shift from activism to the academy, Johnson is relieved from "the stress and strain that had entered into so considerable a part of my life" and extols the "thrills . . . in the contemplative life" in which "there are also fields on which causes may be won" (*ATW*, 408–9). Johnson's black Pacific narrative in *Along This Way* was produced precisely in this reflective, critical space of contemplation, not in the pressured (necessarily compromised) space of action or diplomacy. In the closure of *Along This Way*, Johnson reimagines a national frame and declares: "If the Negro is made to fail, America fails with him" (*ATW*, 412).[100] Rejecting the infatuation with the state, his maxim is no longer "If America is made to fail, the

Negro [Johnson] fails with it." Thus, Johnson's autobiography does not just provide testimony to the predicament that the colored internationalism based on the hegemon puppet system in the Pacific Community presented to Johnson. It enables an insight into the construction of the black self as it is intricately implicated in the material process of the spatial ordering.

[2]

COLORED EMPIRES IN THE 1930S: BLACK INTERNATIONALISM, THE US BLACK PRESS, AND GEORGE S. SCHUYLER

> Today, the eyes of the white world, especially England, France, Italy and America, are once more focussed on this black empire, in consequence of the recent commercial treaty between Ethiopia and Japan; an alliance which might have tremendous and far-reaching importance, not only for Ethiopia, but for all *Black Africa*.
> —George Padmore, "Ethiopia Today: The Making of a Modern State" (1934)

IN THIS CHAPTER, I argue that the Second Italo-Ethiopian War (1935–1936) was crucial to the formation of the fantasy of a colored empire organized around the dyad of the Ethiopian and Japanese Empires, and that George S. Schuyler, America's most prominent black journalist of the Harlem Renaissance and right-wing conservative, critically engaged that fantasy through a merging of black Atlantic and black Pacific imaginaries. First in the chronological table of world affairs relevant to any theoretical argument about the black internationalism of the 1930s, Italy's invasion of Ethiopia on October 3, 1935, is generally acknowledged as a primal moment that galvanized African diasporic communities around a perceived Pan-African racial solidarity and anti-imperial activism in the circum-Atlantic world. Ethiopia had long figured prominently in the Pan-African discourse or Ethiopianism, a theological view of Africa's redemption deriving from the biblical verse (Psalms 68:31): "Princes shall come out of Egypt; Ethiopia shall soon stretch out forth her hands unto God." While in this religious tradition, the term "Ethiopia" referred to the whole continent of Africa south of Egypt, the Italo-Ethiopian War that showcased the globe-carving forces of Western imperialism in a gross and engrossing manner focused the attention of African Americans specifically on Ethiopia (formerly known as Abyssinia) as an ancient East African nation in a modern international political scenario. As historian Brenda Gayle Plummer has observed, the Italo-Ethiopian War like no other issue of the era "constituted a focus for anticolonialist and antiimperialist discourses."[1] In historian Penny M. Von Eschen's account, it opened "a new chapter in the organizational history of anticolonialism" by spurring the formation of numerous groups such as the Ethiopian World Federation. Von Eschen's own first chapter in *Race against Empire* thus begins with a discussion of the Ethiopian crisis.[2]

In this chapter, I am interested in complicating this historical narrative of the Italo-Ethiopian War, not to delegitimate African American antiimperial activism but to urge a rethink of the notion of "empire" as it functions in African American geographic imaginings that rework and resist established power relationships. Scholarly discourse on African American responses to the Ethiopian conflict often looks no further than anticolonial black campaigns against Mussolini's Italian Empire, or a neo-Roman Empire in the fascist worldview, that was to be built over contiguous territories to expand into Africa to gain access to the Atlantic and Indian Oceans. Such discourse leaves unexamined the symbolic valence that the polity of the Ethiopian Empire carried in the African American imagination, with a dynastic genealogy stretching back into antiquity, symbolized by Haile Selassie I,[3] who was descended from Menelik I, the son of King Solomon and the Queen of Sheba. I propose to recast the Ethiopian crisis as one of empire—a crisis that became a trigger point for black internationalism to move along both transatlantic and transpacific vectors. In campaigning against the Italian Empire that Mussolini dreamed of building, the African American public supported a black empire and its ruler, Ethiopian emperor Haile Selassie; and even as those calling African Americans to arms in defense of the Ethiopian imperial government worked to mobilize public opinion against Western imperialism, many (including Schuyler) invoked the Japanese Empire in the Pacific as a potential Ethiopian ally.

I suggest that the Ethiopian crisis was the material context in which the imaginings of a colored empire became possible in black internationalism as a polity that would bring diverse colored populations across oceanic divides under a new apex into a global collectivity. Schuyler's serial fiction *Black Empire* (1936–1938) reconnoiters this colored empire that emerged as an imaginable political system during the Ethiopian crisis—a system that Schuyler also calls the Black Internationale.[4] In Schuyler's fantastic narrative, the black genius and messiah Dr. Henry Belsidus masterminds a "Black Internationale" (BI) force that wipes the European colonial empires from the face of the earth and establishes or restores a black empire in Africa. This chapter discusses how *Black Empire* plays on the concept of empire—particularly an empire for the colored races—while retracing and seeking to revolve the tensions between the different forms of empire of the 1930s (European/Japanese/Ethiopian/US/Soviet) in its schema of empires at war. Furthermore, I wish to illuminate Schuyler's postempire black Pacific narrative through an analysis of a series of unpublished articles entitled "Japan and the Negro" (1937).

Schuyler and the Ethiopian Crisis

Written under the pseudonym Samuel I. Brooks, sixty-two installments of *Black Empire* were published as two serials in the *Pittsburgh Courier*, an African American weekly, between November 1936 and April 1938. The narrative of the first serial, "The Black Internationale," climaxes with Ethiopia's liberation from the Italian occupation force, and the second, "Black Empire," with the complete destruction of the Italian air base in Benghazi, Libya, the last stronghold of Mussolini's vanishing empire in Africa.

This fantastic prospect enthralled the readership of the *Courier*, and Schuyler's pulp fiction gained immense popularity. Such was the groundswell of enthusiasm for the serials that the circulation of the *Courier*—already increased by interest in its coverage of the war—skyrocketed from 40,920 in 1935 to 250,000 in 1937, making the *Courier* the nation's largest black weekly (only 20,000 readers of the paper were local Pittsburgh residents).[5] In their afterword to *Black Empire* published in book form in 1991, Robert A. Hill and R. Kent Rasmussen note that "Schuyler had an uncanny psychological ability to plumb the desires and fantasies of his black audience" (*BE*, afterword, 267). Significantly, Schuyler was also one of the most outspoken, militant voices supporting the Ethiopian cause in the African American community.

The story of Schuyler's emergence as the standard-bearer of the Ethiopia campaign is well known. In the summer of 1935, Ethiopia's survival in the face of fascist Italy was "the topic of angry debate in poolrooms, barber shops, and taverns" in Harlem.[6] Black Communists in Harlem tried to direct the emerging pro-Ethiopian sentiment into "'antifascist' rather than antiwhite channels" by stepping up an Ethiopian defense movement based on a carefully orchestrated interracialism, on black-white solidarity.[7] The National Association for the Advancement of Colored People (NAACP), led by Walter White, who in 1931 succeeded James Weldon Johnson as executive secretary, pressed the Franklin D. Roosevelt administration to oppose Italian aggression in Africa. In his poem,

"Call of Ethiopia" (1935), Langston Hughes called upon "all Africa to arise" for freedom "in answer to the call of Sheba's race."[8]

Schuyler was initially "skeptical" of such an outpouring of support for Ethiopia by black Americans (*BE*, afterword, 270). However, the New York–based writer and popular columnist for the *Courier* did not prove immune to Pan-African and anti-imperialist activism at both grassroots and institutional levels in the African American community; as Hill observes, "Schuyler underwent a sudden and remarkable political conversion."[9] In his *Courier* column, "Views and Reviews," Schuyler writes on July 27, 1935, that "the Ethiopian-Italian embroglio will very likely be the match that will touch off the world powder keg again"—a war by which "all the great exploiting powers of the world ... stand to lose everything" and "the exploited blacks and browns and yellows stand to gain much."[10] "Another World War will finish Europe," he predicts in his column of August 17, 1935, reasoning that while Europe "is engaged in committing hari-kari, the colored peoples everywhere, in all colonies, will revolt."[11] "As an old soldier," Schuyler fantasizes about "press[ing] a machine-gun trigger on the Italian hordes as they toiled over the Ethiopian terrain."[12] Schuyler's weekly columns during the period of the Ethiopian situation closely anticipate the theme of world revolution (that emerges as an international race war) in *Black Empire*.

Yet Hill's observation that Schuyler underwent a "sudden" conversion significantly implies a lack of clarity regarding Schuyler's motivations in joining the black internationalist cause. Hill and Rasmussen explain Schuyler's move in the summer of 1935 as follows: "As the black world waited through the anxious summer of 1935, watching the military and diplomatic maneuvering that every day tightened Italy's noose around the neck of Ethiopia, Schuyler initially adopted a skeptical attitude toward 'the clamor of Aframericans' to come to the aid of 'dear, old Ethiopia.' While such ventures appeared to him quite impractical, his criticism was directed far more against 'big imperialist powers' and their official impediments to western blacks' attempts to fight in Ethiopia. Ethiopia's bravery in the face of such bullying inspired him nonetheless to a sort of reverie of racial solidarity" (*BE*, afterword, 270).

At first glance, it seems that in Hill and Rasmussen's account, "the clamor of Aframericans" to contribute as much military support to Ethiopia as the US government would allow cumulatively reached a crescendo in the summer of 1935, at which time Schuyler was also touched by the situation of Ethiopia's brave but poorly equipped warriors as they confronted Mussolini's modern war machine, and that this converted him to racial solidarity in opposition to the fascist march. However, according to their logic, Schuyler's conversion was to a position, "a sort of reverie of racial solidarity," of which he was initially skeptical and which "appeared to him quite impractical."[13]

My question is, when and how exactly did reverie transform itself into anticolonial politics? An analysis of the *Pittsburgh Courier* and other black newspapers of the time exposes a contextual shift in which the reverie of racial solidarity in overthrowing—through Ethiopia—Western imperialism around the globe became more than an intransitive daydream. This happened when the alliance of the Ethiopian and Japanese Empires emerged as a possible scenario. On July 27, 1935, the *Courier* made the following front-page observation that the Italo-Ethiopian dispute had entered an unexpected phase: "Japan, 'dark-menace' of the fighting world and the most powerful nation of the Far East, may aid Ethiopia! . . . And as Japan's attitude became painfully clear to the western world, fear of another world war . . . a war between races . . . loomed in the offing."[14] This remark was prompted by Tokyo's disavowal of Italy's claim that Japanese ambassador Yotaro Sugimura had assured Mussolini that Japan had no intention of interfering in the coming Italo-Ethiopian conflict. This disavowal, the *Courier* reported, precipitated a furor in the Italian press, including the inflammatory charge that "Japan, in championing the Abyssinian cause, was setting herself up as a leader of Asiatic and African peoples against white civilization" and that "the Nipponese were dreaming of world conquest."[15] (The black weekly *New York Age* reported that the Italian press moreover "called upon the white races to present a united front against the colored races."[16]) With Japan entering the picture, the *Courier* anxiously concludes, "Another world war is inevitable"; "This time it appears to be a 'war of races' and nothing can stop it."[17]

The intensity of the Italian clamor for race war—reported in the black weekly *Courier* as resulting from Japan's apparent alignment with Ethiopia—is reflected in contemporary reports about the Italian press that appeared in the mainstream *New York Times*. According to a *Times* report from Rome on July 23–24, 1935, the Italian press (including Mussolini's own newspaper, *Il Popolo d'Italia*), angered en masse by Japan's new posture of friendliness toward Ethiopia, charged Japan with long harboring designs to "make that corner of Africa her base for a vast economic offensive against Europe."[18] As the Italian newspaper *Tevere* put it, Africa was "contiguous to Italy, the country of a white race and the champion of that race."[19] Yet "with impudence approaching temerity," the *Messaggero* observes, "Japan claims the right of tutelage over all colored men and does so in a tone that seems to herald an offensive against our civilization." "It is against this imposing, grandiose and almost apocalyptic background that the Italo-Ethiopian conflict must be viewed," the newspaper concludes. By gaining control over Ethiopia, Italy would in essence be "forestalling Japan."[20] Thus, the Italian press recast (and justified) the Italo-Ethiopian War. "One has the sensation," the *Tevere* provocatively declared, "of finally learning why so many races have been created with only one in the image and likeness of the Creator and why, among other variously colored ones, one is of the color of betrayal." Such inflammatory coverage of the war was "posted on walls throughout [Rome]," according to the *New York Times*. Fascist troops and police had to be deployed to guard the Japanese embassy from the threat of violence aroused by the anti-Japanese sentiment in the press.[21]

The supportive response from African Americans to the suggestion of Japan as Africa's new ally was as dramatic as the antagonism of the fascist Italian press. Japan's foreign minister in Tokyo received a telegram from a "Nationalist Negro Movement" organization in New York that read, "Blacks accalim [sic] Japan leader [of] colored world expect aid Ethiopia arms munitions."[22] For several weeks in July and August of 1935, Japan was on the front page of leading African American newspapers, in headlines such as "Japan Prepares to Aid Ethiopia," "Ethiopian, Italian Armies Face Each Other in Africa ... Hostilities Expected Any Minute as Emperor Turns to Japan," "Japanese Hit at Mussolini," "Japanese Scored by Italians: Attitude of Tokyo Called Hostile," and "Japan Looms as Bar to Italy,"[23] among others.

The fantasy of race war initiated in the Italian press by the Sugimura affair thus found corresponding canonical expression in the black US press, in which the *Pittsburgh Courier*, where Schuyler served as chief editorial writer and columnist, ranked foremost. In early August, the *Courier* carried a follow-up on the earlier report (quoted above) from Addis Ababa,[24] capital of Ethiopia, as its lead story, under the banner headline "JAPAN ARMING ETHIOPIA." It states, "Japan, mightiest military power of the Far East, is arming Ethiopia! This information, which is authentic, was given to the people of this country early Monday [August 5] and flashed to the four corners of the earth." Japan was supplying the Ethiopian Empire, the account continues, with "'a very large consignment' of arms and ammunition, with the express intention of 'speeding up modernization of the Ethiopian army.'" According to the *Courier* correspondent in Addis Ababa, "Japanese patriotic societies, public and newspapers have shown

2.1. "Tough Going," editorial cartoon. From the *Pittsburgh Courier*, August 10, 1935. *Used with permission from Pittsburgh Courier Archives.*

decided favoritism for Ethiopia in the present quarrel."[25] A cartoon on the *Courier*'s editorial page showed Mussolini standing with a lawn mower against the backdrop of a rising sun labeled "JAPAN," his efforts to mow over Ethiopia frustrated by a thick cover of Japanese swords sticking up from the ground (figure 2.1).[26]

In the *Chicago Defender*, the race war anticipated in the black and fascist Italian presses alike was envisioned as the fulfillment of the scriptural "prophecy of Armageddon." For the *Defender*, the Italo-Ethiopian War would consummate the prophecy of Daniel, which foretold a conflict between the King of the North and the King of the South (read Mussolini and Haile Selassie).[27] Daniel's reference to the "intervention of Eastern powers" prefigured Japan's military aid to the King of the South, who would win the final victory. The *Defender* of July 13 reported, under the scare headline "TROOPS MASS FOR WAR!," "Europe has now suddenly awakened to the realization of the fact that the Japanese navy has been carrying on deep-sea maneuveurs [sic] in the Red Sea within easy reach of Massua, port of Italian Eritrea, for several months," and "within a week's notice scores of these swift relentless cruisers from the third largest navy in the world, can dump tons of explosives under Mussolini's very nose in Africa." In the event of war, claims the *Defender*, "thousands of Japanese, most modernly equipped and highly trained soldiers of the world today, will go tramping through African hinterlands to the aid of their darker brothers on the lofty plateaus of Ethiopia."[28] "Nordic supremacy," the *Defender* predicts breathlessly, was "fast approaching its doom."[29]

The black cultural moment of such mediagenic war projections provided the context for Schuyler's "political conversion." This is not to suggest that Schuyler's newfound anticolonial activism centered on a conviction that black American and Japanese radicals would forge a united front in the event of world revolution to overthrow Western imperialism and fascism. Schuyler's Black Internationale is by no means aligned with the anticolonial movement of the (black) left, as I shall discuss. My point is that it is not possible to isolate the surge of the "reverie of racial solidarity" among African Americans in the summer of 1935—in which Schuyler shared—from the worldwide, and in particular the fascist, clamor for race war evoked by the emergent scenario of a unification between the Ethiopian and Japanese Empires.[30]

Emotional Geography of Empires

An intriguing, and to my mind significant, aspect of the circulation of the race war fantasy in the media is the credibility that the scenario thereby gained. In retrospect, one might wonder how such an improbable situation as the Japanese navy massing from the Pacific to the Red Sea, a seawater inlet of the Indian Ocean lying between Africa and Asia, to intervene on behalf of Ethiopia despite the distance gained any credibility at all. How was such a scenario—which ultimately informed the production of Schuyler's near-future fiction *Black Empire* (in which the BI soldiers are sent overseas to Africa, an offensive that begins with their "surprise attack" on Monrovia, Liberia [*BE*, 97])—passed off as a near-future likelihood in both the black and fascist presses?

The answer to this question lies in what may be termed the emotional geography of empires. To understand this geography from which the fantasy derived its power and resonance, let us turn to the news of a (seemingly odd) connection between Addis Ababa and Tokyo that broke in headlines around the world during the height of the Ethiopian crisis. When it emerged in July of 1935 that Japan might intervene in the Italo-Ethiopian conflict, the *Chicago Defender* carried two photographs under the umbrella title "Japanese Remember Shattered Romance." Over the caption "Objections of Mussolini to union of Japan and Ethiopia through marriage ... shattered the international planned romance," the photographs show an Ethiopian "prince" and a daughter of a member of the Japanese peerage whose marriage Il Duce had allegedly derailed the previous year.[31]

Announced in January 1934, the engagement of Lij Araya Abeba (a cousin of Haile Selassie) and "picture bride" Masako Kuroda (daughter of a Japanese viscount) was a symbol of the affective dimension added to the bilateral diplomatic and economic relationship—indeed of an unparalleled intimacy between the Ethiopian and Japanese Empires, often forgotten today, developing after the 1930 coronation of Ethiopian emperor Haile Selassie. In the words of Selassie's biographer Harold G. Marcus, "Tokyo and Addis Abeba were sentimental about each other."[32] The likeness of Ethiopia and Japan seemed indisputable from their mutual perspectives: both prided themselves on their uniquely ancient "unbroken lines" of sovereigns from founding dynasties. The Ethiopian emperor claimed lineal descent from King Solomon and the Queen of Sheba, who ruled in the tenth century BC, and the Japanese emperor claimed the oldest continuous hereditary monarchy, which began with the legendary Emperor Jimmu in the seventh century BC.[33] Selassie modeled his country's first constitution, which he promulgated in July 1931 to cap his modernization program, on Japan's Meiji Constitution (1889). Consisting of fifty-five articles that "enshrined the rule of law while acknowledging the emperor's ultimate power to delegate authority to other institutions such as a two-house parliament," Ethiopia's "Japanese-style constitution" was, in the words of Marcus, "a progressive statement that established a framework for a modern government."[34] In November 1931, in accordance with protocol and to cultivate a closer bilateral relationship, the Ethiopian emperor dispatched a special mission to Japan (which had sent an envoy representing the Japanese emperor to attend his coronation in Addis Ababa in the previous year) led by his foreign minister, Blatengeta Herui Wolde Selassie. In the Imperial Palace in Tokyo, Herui presented Emperor Hirohito with Haile Selassie's official letter and the Order of Solomon, first in order of precedence in the Imperial Orders of Ethiopia, to be awarded to the Japanese emperor. The empress of Japan was presented with the Order of the Queen of Sheba. Selassie's cousin, Araya Abeba, accompanied Herui's imperial embassy informally but was granted an audience with the Japanese emperor and empress.[35] Herui published "a glowing account of his experiences: *Mahdere Berhan Ha-Ager Japon* (The example of light, the country of Japan)" in Ethiopia in 1932.[36] It was translated and published in Japan in 1934.[37] In the economic sphere as well, Ethiopia and Japan were establishing closer cooperation. By the outbreak of the Ethiopian crisis, Japan had become Ethiopia's largest supplier of imports, including cotton goods that Japanese factories produced and sold at low prices.[38]

The international planned marriage was personally initiated by Araya Abeba. Impressed with Japanese women's gracefulness while in Japan, he decided that he wanted a Japanese bride. When the news that an Ethiopian prince was seeking a Japanese bride made the headline in the *Tokyo Asahi Shimbun* in May 1933, some two hundred adventurous girls from good families came forward as candidates; among them was Masako Kuroda. Subsequently, a Japanese lawyer, serving as an agent for Araya, narrowed the list to ten candidates and sent their photographs to Addis Ababa. From those, Araya selected Masako as his first choice. Araya bought land to build a Japanese-style house in Addis Ababa for his bride. In front of newspaper reporters in Tokyo in January 1934, Masako said that Japan would have to venture overseas, and she, although a woman, would lead in this trend, because she believed that women should also make efforts to move up in the world. She believed that this international marriage was a chance not to be missed. The difference of race did not matter, Masako answered; she was determined and felt sure of her life in Ethiopia because, more than anything else, Ethiopia was an empire just like that of Japan.[39]

I will not review the international response to news of the planned marriage of Araya and Masako here, except to point out that the wedding was canceled in the face of the fierce opposition it engendered. Many believed that fascist Italy, operating behind the scenes, effected the cancellation, and Italy's perceived involvement had significant implications for the way in which the Italo-Ethiopian War was projected and perceived. That Mussolini regarded the planned marriage as unsavory cannot be doubted. In a meeting with Japanese ambassador Sugimura in December 1934, Il Duce protested, "Japan is supplying arms and ammunition to Ethiopia, sending a crown princess, and a newspaper in Tokyo is vigorously advocating the maneuvering of Japanese-Ethiopian friendship."[40] For some (including Mussolini), the widely reported courtship of the international couple—although a personal matter because it was not really a royal marriage and involved no diplomatic arrangement between Ethiopia and Japan as was rumored—raised racial, economic, and political concerns, and it functioned as a gestural provocation for race war. As O. Tanin and E. Yohan allege in *When Japan Goes to War* (1936),

"Through the marriage of an Abyssinian prince to the daughter of a Japanese noble the Japanese were enabled to equip airdromes in Abyssinia and to receive a cotton concession there."[41]

The implications of the planned marriage—popularly understood as a dynastic marriage by which the antique monarchical states Ethiopia and Japan would unite to expand—were not lost on Schuyler. Contrasting imperialism and matrimonial diplomacy, or territorial conquest and sexual politics, he surmises in his *Courier* column of February 3, 1934, that the marriage would give Japan "a foothold on the continent of Africa." Schuyler predicts that "associated with Japan, the Ethiopian kingdom will doubtless become a power in Africa, albeit similar to Manchukoa [sic] and Korea"—a course of events that Great Britain, France, and Italy "will not like" as these European imperial powers "have had their eyes on Abyssinia for years." Ethiopia and Japan would unite to expand through an "inter-racial marriage"; and as Schuyler remarks in concluding his column, interracial marriage is perhaps not so "deplorable" as "some Negroes and most white folks would have us believe."[42]

The news that the marriage had been canceled through the intervention of a "certain power" widely believed to be Italy soon followed and confirmed for Schuyler that his reading of the marriage was correct.[43] Haile Selassie's own reminiscence of the Italian "rumour-mongering" is instructive in accounting for this universal belief in Italy's behind-the-scenes role. The emperor writes in his autobiography, "When [foreign minister Herui] returned [from Tokyo] having accomplished his mission, the Italians began spreading rumours in the newspapers to the effect that Ethiopia and Japan had concluded a separate secret treaty and, apart from this, Ethiopia had granted a concession of 3 million hectares of land to a Japanese company.... They published an even worse story in the press to the effect that the Crown Prince of Ethiopia was to marry a Japanese princess."[44] The emperor clearly held the view—which was widely shared—that the Addis Ababa–Tokyo nexus as it was portrayed in the fascist Italian press had fueled bitter feelings between Italy and Ethiopia.

The deep, bilateral historical roots of the tensions between Italy and Ethiopia notwithstanding, contemporaries thus made sense of the discord through the possible scenario of the union of the Ethiopian and Japanese Empires that this episode reflects—a union fantasized in the (hetero)sexual gender politics. In September 1934, when reports first emerged that Italy was sending soldiers and ammunition into the colonies of Somaliland and Eritrea (on the pretext of protecting its interests from Haile Selassie), the black press quickly sniffed out Italy's apprehensions over Japan as an underlying cause of its military actions. A *New York Age* editorial makes the inference that Japan's "penetration of Abyssinia" was at the root of Italy's actions, observing that the planned Ethio-Japanese marriage had recently been canceled due to "objections by Rome."[45] Along the same lines, the *Chicago Defender* editorializes, "the most important of all the reasons which occasion Italy's alarm has been caused by the manifest interest of Japan in the social and economic affairs of Abyssinia." The proposed marriage, according to the *Defender*, had the effect of arousing a suspicion in European circles that "back of this social amenity would be found a political understanding between the darker people of the Asiatic world."[46] Let us recall that it was the breaking off of the engagement—the "shattered romance"—that the *Defender* viewed as the final key indication that Japan would intervene militarily in the Italo-Ethiopian dispute in July 1935.

Established authorities on African affairs of the 1930s, including Schuyler's colleagues J. A. Rogers and George Padmore, also understood this Addis Ababa–Tokyo nexus as the source of the Ethiopian crisis. Writing in the February 1935 issue of the *Crisis*, the official organ of the NAACP, Rogers contends that in undertaking to arbitrate the dispute, "the League of Nations will be faced with the toughest nut in its history," for "if Geneva succeeds in cracking the outer shell it will find within a kernel of dynamite, namely Japan."[47] Padmore, also writing in the *Crisis* (May 1935), ascribes "much of Ethiopia's present difficulties" to "her friendly relations with Japan." According to Padmore's conspiracy theory, Britain and France had "assigned" Mussolini "the task to intervene in Ethiopia and break up the ties between herself and Japan before it is too late."[48]

Regardless of the direction in which one pursues this discourse, it is certain that the potential of a new spatial ordering by the dyad of the Ethiopian and Japanese Empires beyond oceanic divides emerged from the conflict as something that required policing—such that the proposed marriage of an Ethiopian to a Japanese, taken to signal new ties binding the destinies of African and Asian empires, was proscribed by a cluster of forces that included media slander, admonition through diplomatic channels, and threats of war. The Ethiopian crisis was never simply a consequence of the bilateral animosity between Italy and Ethiopia arising from Ethiopia's defeat of Italian forces in the Battle of Adowa in 1896. It occurred within, and reshaped, a matrix of media forces to generate the fantasy of empires at war in the 1930s: the (white) Italian Empire and the (black) Ethiopian Empire, the latter united by sexual politics with the Japanese

Empire. Schuyler and other black journalists, as well as the fascist Italian press, made sense of the situation in this milieu. In overlooking it, we risk missing crucial implications of the black internationalism that Schuyler imagined.

Black Empire

Produced in the mid-1930s, when demagoguery suffused the policy sphere in international relations, and when the media in fascist Italy, black America, and elsewhere foretold scenarios of race war, Schuyler's *Black Empire* closely engaged the war fantasies circulating in the media. Narrated in the first person by Carl Slater, ex-reporter for the *Harlem Blade*, *Black Empire* (a serial fiction that itself ran in the black weekly *Pittsburgh Courier*) presents a rendition of such a war, thereby both participating in and parodying the production of the mediagenic fantasy that it represented in the aftermath of the Italo-Ethiopian War.

Black Empire began in November 1936, several months after the end of the Italo-Ethiopian War, when it was no longer possible to save Ethiopia. Led by European imperial powers Great Britain and France, the League of Nations—of which both Ethiopia and Italy were members—proved ineffective in saving Ethiopia from the fascist sword; Mussolini utterly derided the league and asked derisively, "Has the League of Nations become the tribunal before which all the Negroes and uncivilised peoples, all the world's savages, can bring the great nations which have revolutionised and transformed humanity?"[49] The Soviet silence disappointed those who thought that the Soviet Union, an anti-imperialist model and champion of the rights of nonwhite peoples, would support Ethiopian justice. When Soviet delegate Maxim Litvinov failed to deliver his much-anticipated denunciation of Italian aggression at the league, Walter White, executive secretary of the NAACP, was outraged and sent him a cablegram, demanding an explanation of his reticence: "Has Russia abandoned its alleged opposition [to] imperialism and its much publicized defense [of] weaker peoples? Does your anti-imperialism stop at black nations?"[50] To contain Nazi Germany, a pact of friendship, neutrality, and nonaggression had been concluded between Italy and the Soviet Union in 1933, and their military contacts were preserved well after the Italo-Ethiopian War.[51] On May 2, 1936, Haile Selassic fled Ethiopia into exile as his nation fought on. A week later, in Rome, Mussolini proclaimed the Ethiopian Italian Empire and decreed that King Victor Emmanuel III of Italy be crowned emperor of Ethiopia.

Against this backdrop, *Black Empire* reenacts and continues the schema of empires at war and envisages an impending World War II from which the Black Empire emerges victorious. The symbolic valence that empires (including the Japanese Empire) carry in this fantasy resonates in the closing moments of *Black Empire*; the sweeping victory of the BI over the European imperial powers in World War II invokes "the fall of the Roman Empire, the defeat of Russia by Japan [that is, the defeat of the Tsarist Russian Empire by the Japanese Empire] or the Bolshevist revolution" that destroyed the tsarist autocracy and led to the creation of the Soviet Union (*BE*, 250), a paragon of the anti-imperialist state.

Indeed the Black Empire, destroying international imperialists, reads as a satiric blackface version of the Soviet Union (though the latter cannot be described as an empire by the Leninist definition of imperialism). As Hill and Rasmussen point out, the term Black Internationale "makes ironic use of communism as an international phenomenon" (*BE*, afterword, 295), or the Communist International (Comintern). In *Black Empire*, the BI is founded at the first world conference, held in Green County, New York. The delegates from fifty countries assemble to foment revolution, in which the exploited nonwhite peoples unite and free themselves from Western imperialists to achieve "Negro control of the world," that is, the dictatorship of the Negro (*BE*, 12, 25). This revolution is led by the African American Belsidus, whom Slater dubs the "bloodthirsty, fanatical revolutionist," and a vanguard of revolutionaries who form the "national cells" of the BI in Europe, Asia, Africa, South America, and the West Indies (*BE*, 18, 82). To finance the revolution, the organization creates "the B.I. farms" (*BE*, 100) that Hill and Rasmussen suggest are based on the Soviet model (*BE*, afterword, 296). They are a sort of collective or communal farm organized on a large scale and highly mechanized with technology (hydroponics) that is similar in description to "some in Russia" (*BE*, 49). The aim of the BI is to fight by "any and every means at our disposal," including armed force, for the overthrow of the international imperialists and creation of an international black empire, even as the Comintern envisioned an international Soviet republic (*BE*, 31).

There is much to offend in the anticolonial revolution of the BI. It is rife with the systematic use of violence that is directed more against civilian than military Western imperialists. In *Black Empire*, zero hour is set for a great revolt across the African continent that will be "a real showdown with the imperialists." A huge map of Africa displayed on a wall in Belsidus's headquarters in Liberia (which the BI captures in a surprise attack) marks every important town in electric lights "set to turn green if in our hands and red if remaining in the hands of the whites" (*BE*, 122, 124). In this Manichean framework of green or red, the exploited majority strikes back at the exploiting minority through the calculated use of bloodshed to cleanse Africa of the international imperialists. The BI air force attacks the West African colonial metropoles and seaports of Bingerville, Grand Bassam, Sekondi, Accra, Takoradi, Lagos, Freetown, Konakry (Conakry), Bathurst (Banjul), and Daker using high explosive and incendiary bombs, but the greater part of the "work" of destroying white civilization is willingly taken on by African natives. In the Belgian Congo, natives slaughter white men, women, and children at close quarters and with great brutality (*BE*, 128–29).[52] In the finale, in Italian East Africa, in concert with the BI air force that drops incendiary bombs on Italian barracks and supply stations in Addis Ababa, the Ethiopians on the ground massacre Italians (*BE*, 132).

In Schuyler's first *Black Empire* serial, the BI fulfills its destiny as "the greatest revolutionary organization the world had ever seen" (*BE*, 145). It destroys European colonial empires and brings about the establishment of a black empire in which the black race holds political and economic control. The BI immediately start a purging process, justified by the need to eliminate undesirable members of the black race who favor white rule and stir "counter-revolution." These are "ruthlessly purged and executed" by Belsidus (*BE*, 138). In the second world conference, this time in Liberia, Belsidus proclaims before nearly a thousand delegates from all parts of the world that he, as head of the BI, assumes leadership of "the new Empire of Africa": "Negroes are not yet used to freedom, and so for a time we must have dictatorship," declares Belsidus (*BE*, 139, 141). Belsidus thus consolidates his ironfisted reign and emerges as the black Stalin, or Mussolini. As John A. Williams observes in his foreword to *Black Empire*, "Dr. Belsidus, in the final analysis, is a dictator, a fascist, though his goals are established as moral ones" (*BE*, foreword, xiv).[53]

Although *Black Empire* can thus be read as a conservative deflection from what Schuyler saw as a hegemonic left and communist influence on black international thought, Schuyler's deployment of a "colored" internationale with the force of empire, as I have suggested, is closely related to the historical matrix of the Ethiopian crisis when an empire for the colored races emerged as an imaginable political system to fill a gap that neither liberal internationalism (as embodied in the League of Nations) nor Soviet internationalism could fill. Causing a spatial and temporal reorientation in the modern codification of the world, a colored empire—inspired by the scenario of the unification of Ethiopia and Japan—was a system that could bring diverse colored populations under a new imperial apex into a global collectivity.

Indeed, if any genius informs Belsidus's organizational scheme, it lies in his systematic reconstruction of a colored empire in a post-Ethiopian context. Without an imperial Ethiopia-Japan axis in the world of the story (having not materialized in the realm of reality), the black messiah Belsidus establishes the BI that replaces a nation-state and an international Soviet republic. Belsidus manipulates interracialism, black, brown, and yellow solidarity, to forge a colored internationalist organization, to trigger personal transformations, and to motivate collective action. Through an underground network of quasi-religious "Temples of Love," Belsidus takes advantage of a network-style integration of a colored community enabled by the mass media during the Ethiopian crisis. He reaches the colored populations "through their emotions" and commands them to love one another for solidarity—a love that "must include all black people, all brown people, all yellow people, for together these colored people are soon to rule the earth" (BE, 36, 65). The love practiced in the Temples of Love (built resembling the style of an Egyptian temple) is not modern "individual sex love," to borrow the words of Friedrich Engels; it is, rather, premodern and stretches back into antiquity, even into what Slater calls "primeval urges" (BE, 57, 62).

Belsidus similarly harnesses anger—a political anger that African Americans allowed themselves to experience and to express communally in public, in "poolrooms, barber shops, and taverns," during the Ethiopian crisis—to serve as the foundation for the imaginings and membership of the BI and to power the economy of solidarity. He assembles to work under him black scientists and engineers who "possess . . . hatred and resentment, that fuel which operates the juggernaut of conquest" of the white world (BE, 15). The revolutionary war that Belsidus instigates likewise ends not in the physical destruction of the systems of European colonial empires and America's racial-imperial hierarchy but rather in the terror that he produces in the white metropolitan core nations through violence. Belsidus prosecutes his scheme in the United States by inflaming hatred and terrorism among white Americans until it "roll[s] along under its own momentum" to their self-destruction (BE, 83). A war in Europe is precipitated by the "terroristic acts" of Belsidus's white European agent and "lover" Martha Gaskin; soldiers on the front and behind the lines die "like flies"; and air raids reduce civilians to "bestial fear and terror" (*BE*, 138, 183). White people kill each other off through racial "hari-kari" (or hara-kiri, a ritual suicide by disembowelment practiced by Japanese samurai), even as Schuyler fantasized in his aforementioned *Courier* column of August 17, 1935.

In "'That Just Kills Me': Black Militant Near-Future Fiction"—one of the first critical texts to trace "a distinguishable, though submerged, pattern of kill-the-white-folks futurist fiction in the African American literary tradition"—Kali Tal observes that Schuyler's work is "deeply uncomfortable for black and white critics alike, most of whom do not seem inclined to acknowledge that this level of hostility may exist."[54] Tal sees in Schuyler's hostile work a reflection of the social injustices that black people suffer. She approaches Schuyler's pulp fiction as what social scientist James C. Scott terms a "hidden transcript," or a discourse that takes place "offstage." It enacts the anger and reciprocal aggression denied in actual relations of domination.[55] In Tal's view, the reception of *Black Empire* by Schuyler's black audience suggests that "not only is the oppression of blacks still vigorous in the United States but that African Americans have stored up enough anger and hatred for white people" to embrace such a hostile vision.[56] The public enthusiasm for *Black Empire*, which outpaced Schuyler's own expectations and even control, may indicate that the emotionally charged hidden transcript at its heart reproduced a long-established discourse among black Americans that required only its expression in the form of pulp fiction in order to rapidly become a collective fantasy.

Yet *Black Empire* is more than an imagining of violent revolution in the tradition of the black militant near-future novel, that is, an imagining that draws its social appeal and energy from the shared hidden transcript nurtured by that tradition in the United States. It was also made possible by the emergence in the mid-1930s of a fantasy of empires at war. Capturing both the imperial and anticolonial imagination as it engaged the hope and threat of a colored empire, the fixation on race war reflected the reality portrayed in the media, which provided the mobilizing force to establish black internationalism even as it served different purposes in fascist Italy in relation to that country's invasion of Ethiopia. Schuyler's imperial fantasy in *Black Empire*, then, cannot be fully apprehended or appreciated outside the enabling context of this mediated (and mediagenic) rendering of empires at war ruled by a reciprocity ironically denied in colonial hierarchical relations.

Not often noted of *Black Empire* is how Schuyler plays on the notion of empire that became critically diffuse during the Ethiopian crisis and seeks to resolve the tensions between the different forms of empire in the 1930s. Serialized at a time when Ethiopia merged and mutated into the Ethiopian Italian Empire, or a neo-Roman Empire, *Black Empire* depicts the BI revolution as directed at the restoration of the ancient black empire that paradoxically lies in the future—a process that at the same time reveals the complexity that the word "empire" became. Aspiring to build "a great Negro nation in Africa" (*BE*, 15), the BI denies the polity of a republic for the black race; the Republic of Liberia is overthrown, and the president of Liberia is arrested. Belsidus functions internationally as "Provisional President" (*BE*, 114), but he abolishes republicanism in Liberia to establish a BI imperium, relocating the capital to Kakata, forty to fifty miles inland from Monrovia, which becomes "the Imperial capital" (*BE*, 214).[57] Assembling the paramount chiefs or native kings ruling in the areas outside Monrovia and its environs, Belsidus rises to the throne by installing himself as "the King of Kings" (emperor), a title that Haile Selassie and other Ethiopian rulers assumed (*BE*, 110–11). The BI's next step is to make a revolutionary war against the Western maritime empires that emerged four hundred years ago, represented by the British Empire, now "with a great empire at stake" (*BE*, 127). This war ends with the BI's "gain[ing] an empire"—an empire that is at once ancient and futuristic. At the "great imperial conference" to commemorate the victory, Belsidus defines this ending as a restoration, proclaiming upon its achievement that "Africa belongs once more to the Africans" (*BE*, 139–40). This restoration of black rule is symbolically coterminous with a regained Ethiopia, but the Black Empire, so the story goes, is a polity, ruled not by Haile Selassie restored to the throne but by Belsidus, who assumes sole and absolute power without hereditary ascension—hence, a dictator (like the black Stalin, or Mussolini, as discussed above).

This process of the black empire in the making is reprised in the second part of the *Black Empire* serial, in which the Second World War breaks out as a clash of empires from which the Black Empire emerges victorious. The Black Empire rises to "a new world power" whose "outlying districts" encompass America, Malaysia, and India (*BE*, 256). In the third (and final) world conference that is the denouement of the fictional serial, Belsidus derives the legitimacy of the Black Empire from the "consent" of its peoples as he says, "I shall lead you to a higher civilization than Europe has ever seen, with your consent" (*BE*, 258). Thus, the populations of the Black Empire are no longer subjects but have become citizens. Belsidus delivers the following address to delegates assembled from all parts of the colored world, telling them how they supposedly should feel and should not feel about themselves and about the white race: "You must not make the mistake of the white man and try to enslave others, for that is the beginning of every people's fall. You must banish race hatred from your hearts" (BE, 257). *Black Empire* thus closes with a vision of a colored empire as an imaginable political system that looks like a projection into the postcolonial future.

It is this subtle ground that the colored empire occupies and from which the articulation of something like a counter-discourse to Western imperialism becomes possible in a post-Ethiopian context. What I have proposed in this section is to reclaim this ground that Schuyler reconnoitered by clarifying the cultural work of the colored empire and the race war fantasy that it engenders. My attempt to mark and delimit the BI by a violent fantasy of empires at war, however, is admittedly a slippery project. Granted that the news of a rumored dynastic marriage that circulated in the international media during the Ethiopian crisis gave an illusion of common material ground on which the imaginings of a colored empire could emerge across nations beyond oceanic divides. However, the demise of the ancient Ethiopian Empire—and Japan, a (putatively) ancient monarchy that emerged into a quasi-fascist empire in the modern world—necessarily caused the signification of colored empire to mutate, as I discuss below.

The Postempire Black Pacific Narrative

For all its futuristic elements, Schuyler's pulp fiction *Black Empire* reads as a historical archive—specifically, an archive of the schema of empires at war that was prefigured in the international media during the Ethiopian crisis. Four months after completing his *Black Empire* serials, Schuyler published an article in the August 1938 issue of the *Crisis*, "The Rise of the Black Internationale," which he called his "most significant article" from the period.[58] In it, Schuyler heralded the historic rise of a real "Black Internationale of liberation"—"a community of interest of all colored peoples"—that encompassed "the sturdy and canny Nipponese."[59]

Schuyler's historical BI was by no means idiosyncratic as a form of post-Ethiopia black internationalism that accommodated, or continued to accommodate, the Japanese Empire as an ally of the African diaspora. Groups that similarly embraced Japan in the pre–World War II epoch included the Nation of Islam (NOI), the Ethiopian Pacific Movement (EPM), and the Peace Movement of Ethiopia, among other black organizations. The African American journalist Roi Ottley observes during the

Pacific War, in 1943, that "the [Negro] nationalist organizations, those groups which evolved from them, and the factors which kept them in motion . . . are the main sources of much . . . pro-Japanese sentiment."[60] Whether or not Ottley's assessment is correct, I provisionally align Schuyler's BI here, as a matter of interpretation, with these black nationalist organizations under the umbrella of a black internationalism that produced an imperial black Pacific narrative.

From the viewpoint of this black internationalism, the coming Second World War was not the "good war" of democracy over the fascism of normative memory but rather a total race war—such as that which the Italo-Ethiopian War in 1935 promised but failed to realize. The NOI, whose black nationalistic mythologies Henry Louis Gates Jr. compares with Schuyler's *Black Empire*,[61] offers an example of a black nationalist organization that regards Japan from a similar perspective. The NOI traces its origins to the enigmatic figure of Wallace D. Fard, who appeared in the black ghetto of Detroit in 1930 to found the organization, and to Elijah Muhammad, who led the sect after Fard's disappearance and relocated its headquarters to Chicago in 1934. The NOI—or the "Lost-Found Nation of Islam in the Wilderness of North America," as Fard originally called it—was a religious movement. Its aims were to resurrect "the original members of the Tribe of Shabazz from the Lost Nation of Asia," who were "the first founders of civilization of our Planet" but were denied self-knowledge through the institution of the Atlantic slave trade that exploited and dehumanized them, and to restore an ancient black Islamic empire that had a superior civilization.[62] In a full-length biography of Muhammad that draws on declassified Federal Bureau of Investigation (FBI) files, Karl Evanzz documents the esoteric teachings of the organization in its formative years, which are peppered with references to Japan. For example, Muhammad describes the Mother Plane—Ezekiel's wheel in the Holy Bible—as "built in Japan" to carry out the destruction of the white world.[63] In the years before Pearl Harbor, Muhammad repeatedly foretells of the impending destruction of the white world through an apocalypse in which "the Japanese will slaughter the white man." In a sweeping gesture of jihadist optimism, Muhammad tells his black Muslim audience that it was "Japan's duty to save you; they have been given the power by the Asiatic nation to save you in the West."[64] In September 1942, the FBI arrested Muhammad on charges of draft evasion and pro-Japanese espionage.

A more secular manifestation of the imperial black Pacific narrative was produced by the Harlem-based EPM headed by Robert O. Jordan (also known as Leonard Robert Jordan). The EPM was an organization "incorporated under the laws of the State of New York on September 18, 1935"—that is, during the Ethiopian crisis—and was "largely made up of British West Indian Negroes."[65] In the article entitled "Second Garvey Asks for United Black World," the *New York Amsterdam News*, an African American weekly, describes Jordan as a black nationalist who calls for "the colored world to close ranks against the duplicity and aggression of whites" just as Marcus Garvey aspired to unite a scattered race to found an empire. His headquarters in Harlem flew the flag of Ethiopia, "representing the black man's ambition for a sovereign government of his own," a sovereign polity that is represented by a black empire.[66] In May 1936, when Haile Selassie fled Ethiopia into exile and Mussolini declared the new Roman empire of Ethiopia and proclaimed King Victor Emmanuel emperor of Ethiopia, Jordan, in his capacity as president-general of the EPM, petitioned Japan's foreign minister in Tokyo to "help Ethiopia to RETAIN HER INDEPENDENCE from the outlaw government of Italy."[67] In another of his petitions six months later, Jordan writes, "We, the dark race of the Western Hemisphere, through the Ethiopian Pacific Movement Inc. . . . are putting our entire confidence in the Japanese people with the hopes that in the very near future we will be one hundred per cent united and when this [is] accomplished, we will desire very close relationship with the Japanese Government."[68] Jordan's Sunday-evening gatherings in Harlem attracted crowds of three to four hundred.[69] In these meetings, audiences heard the "Harlem Hitler," as he was called, claim that "Japan was to save the darker races."[70] In the wake of Pearl Harbor, Jordan reportedly declared at meetings of the EPM that "Japan will win, they will force the United States out of Asia and into the Atlantic Ocean."[71] He not only expected them to "chop foes' heads off," as the *New York Times* reports in 1942 but also called for having "President Roosevelt picking cotton, and Secretaries [Frank] Knox and [Henry] Stimson riding [him] around in rickshaws" when Japan crushed the United States in World War II.[72] Jordan was indicted in 1942 on charges of sedition and of "enlist[ing] the population of Harlem in a move to . . . help the Japanese establish a world empire for the 'dark races.'"[73]

The intensity of the black internationalist fantasies of a future cosmic or global race war in the pre–World War II period is unsettling. At the least, it is uncomfortable to acknowledge a link between black internationalism (which we associate with progressive, anticolonial politics) and empathy for the Japanese Empire (with all the negative associations accompanying such an emotion). However, on setting this discomfort aside, important questions emerge. What were the grounds of the appeal that empire—as opposed to democracy—held for American blacks in the prewar period? What possibilities were inherent in the mix of proempire sentiment and anticolonial politics that suffused black internationalism? What postcolonial moments were prefigured in so unlikely a context as empires at war? As I have argued, approaching such questions requires an understanding of the potential of new geographic imaginings for reworking and resisting established power relationships that the dyad of the Ethiopian and Japanese Empires made possible. However, here I am also interested in considering how this potential necessarily mutated after the demise of the ancient black Ethiopian Empire in 1936, when the imperial Ethiopia-Japan union evaporated to reveal the discontinuity and difference of the empires (despite the use of the same term "empire" in their different cultural contexts).

In a series of unpublished articles entitled "Japan and the Negro" (1937),[74] Schuyler writes, "Ethiopia was the acid test of Japan's love for the darker peoples." He observes that if Japan had "wanted to help Ethiopia she could have done so with arms, ammunition, planes and military instructors and Italy could not have stopped her." Yet with all the hyperventilated clamor for race war in the summer of 1935, the rumored military aid from Japan never materialized, and "the sad fact remains that Japan left Ethiopia to her fate."[75] Nevertheless, Schuyler, like Muhammad of the NOI, Jordan of the EPM, and other allegedly pro-Japanese black nationalists under FBI surveillance, seemed to continue to accommodate Japan in his BI.[76]

Schuyler certainly had personal contact with Japanese agents. On April 18, 1938, he attended dinner at the Nippon Club in New York along with other black guests including Walter White of the NAACP.[77] Among the Japanese agents in attendance was Yasuichi Hikida, and journalist Masao Dodo, who had recently spoken in Harlem in defense of Japan's military operations in China in the Second Sino-Japanese War that broke out in 1937. Dodo swayed the opinions of many African Americans in his audience, one of whom, Arthur Schomburg, a Harlem bibliophile, was reported to declare, "If Japan will help the darker people to gain equal opportunities, I am ready to shoulder arms for Japan now."[78] Four months earlier, the *Pittsburgh Courier* had refused to print Schuyler's "Japan and the Negro" series, which it had commissioned. Schuyler, alluding to strong undercurrents of pro-Japanese sentiment among black Americans, not only asserts in this series that "the majority of thinking Negroes favors Japan" but also maintains that Japanese victory in

Asia offered "an immense psychological satisfaction to the teeming millions of oppressed colored people the world over"[79]—an opinion that publisher Robert L. Vann found too contentiously pro-Japanese and "injudicious" to print.[80] In the same month, in an unsigned *Courier* editorial, Schuyler ventured that Japan's war humbled Western imperialists in China: "With Japanese troops parading in Shanghai last week, the white Powers definitely lost 'face.' England, France, the United States and the others were told who was boss in Asia, and they couldn't do anything about it. At least there is ONE part of the earth no longer ruled by white imperialists."[81]

Such pro-Japanese sentiment can be viewed as a residue—and a tenacious one at that—of the reverie of colored solidarities forged through the rapprochement of the Ethiopian and Japanese Empires. Yet from another perspective, such sentiment is precisely what Schuyler explicitly disavowed after the Italo-Ethiopian War. In "Japan and the Negro," he not only criticizes Japan for leaving "Ethiopia to her fate" but also condemns a Japanese (colored) imperialism that "enslaved millions in Manchuria, Korea, Formosa and Eastern China." Indeed, according to Schuyler, the Japanese "ruthlessly murdered, raped and tortured without let" the Chinese, who are "also a colored people," thus evincing, as he writes with evident sarcasm, "a mighty strange way to show affection for China."[82] While Schuyler clearly believed in the "good psychological effect" of the Japanese imperium in Asia on the diasporic, oppressed peoples of color under modern Western imperialism, he was simultaneously a harsh critic of a Japan that "has been like all the other aggressor nations, including the United States." Even as Japan took the place of Ethiopia on the terrain of Schuyler's historical BI ("Here is no . . . Haile Selassie to be strafed into submission after a short period of terror"), Schuyler warned against viewing the Japanese Empire as an ally of the African diaspora such as Muhammad, Jordan, and other black nationalists envisioned: "Colored people are barking up the wrong tree if they think that Japan is out to help anybody except Japan." "American Negroes," writes Schuyler, "need to get the notion out of their heads that some Saviour is going to come from abroad to help them or that they can even look outside our borders for aid."[83] This warning is reiterated in *Black Empire* by Belsidus: "No one would or could help the Negro except himself" (*BE*, 257). Obviously, Schuyler's BI contains contradictory currents. In "Japan and the Negro," he simultaneously criticizes and valorizes the notion of a colored empire. This contradiction also characterizes *Black Empire*, which at once critiques, while unnervingly echoing, imperial rhetoric. This is employed by Belsidus to mastermind a fictional BI over the course of the narrative.

The simplest and perhaps most important way to resolve this contradiction, at least in the case of Schuyler's post-Ethiopia BI, is to read *Black Empire* as a satire. Advocates of this approach, taken by literary critic John Cullen Gruesser, regard the fictional narrative as an important work of the critical imagination precisely because its satirical or parodic replication of Black Empire works to contest it affirmatively. By proving that the BI is fascist and hence "no better than (or just as bad as) a group of white fascists bent on establishing an empire for their own aggrandizement," Gruesser supports his argument that Schuyler "targets black oppression of black people" as couched in Marcus Garvey's scheme to found a black empire in Africa, and practiced in Liberia, where Americo-Liberian officials exploited the native African population.[84] This line of argument offers a reassuring account of Schuyler's discomforting apparent embrace of Japan in the terrain of his BI. The question of whether or not *Black Empire* is a satirical replication of colored empires in the 1930s that signify the Japanese imperium as much as Garvey's African empire and Liberia's racial-imperial hierarchy, to expose colored oppression of colored people, thus bears careful consideration.

There is good circumstantial evidence to support such a reading. In the autumn of 1937, in the midst of war news coming from the Far East that the Japanese had carried out aerial bombing raids against Shanghai, two ostensibly unrelated serials appeared at the head of the feature page of the *Courier*. In one of them, "Forum of Fact and Opinion," W. E. B. Du Bois unflinchingly defends the Japanese Empire at war in Asia, maintaining that "Japan fought China to save China from Europe, and fought Europe through China and tried to wade in blood toward Asiatic freedom."[85] Du Bois, during the Ethiopian crisis of 1935, had written on the interracial implications of the crisis by drawing attention to the "new distribution of world power" that Japan created in the world's race relations. The moral of the Italo-Ethiopian War, according to Du Bois, was that if a colored nation wished to sustain itself against white Europe, it needed to "appeal neither to religion nor culture but only to force."[86] Du Bois seemingly dismisses qualms about "killing the unarmed and innocent in order to reach the guilty" and is adamant in his defense of Japan's actions, alleging that "the same spirit that animates the 'white folks' nigger' in the United States" motivated China to "prefer . . . to be a coolie for England rather than acknowledge the only world leadership that did not mean color caste," namely, "the leadership of Japan."[87] Across the page from Du Bois's arguments for dismantling Western imperialist hegemony through the victory of the Japanese imperium in Asia appeared Schuyler's *Black Empire* serials. They imagined a spectacular climax to global racial-imperial oppression, in which the BI under the leadership of Belsidus invades European countries using weapons "far more dangerous than bombs." "After all, air bombs do not win wars," declares Belsidus, citing the example of Shanghai, which "continued to be held even after repeated heavy attacks from the air" by the Japanese (*BE*, 169). The BI force would therefore launch airborne germ warfare against European metropolises.

In view of this terrorism, one begins to understand the fine line upon which the Japanese Empire stands in Schuyler's notion of the post-Ethiopia BI. In the aforementioned *Crisis* essay, "The Rise of the Black Internationale" (which Hill and Rasmussen read as an "ideological companion piece" to *Black Empire* [*BE*, afterword, 279]), Schuyler observes how blacks in the United States see "erstwhile haughty whites cowering in the shell-holes of Shanghai, a British ambassador machine gunned on the road to Nanking and an American gunboat bombed to the bottom of the Yangste [*sic*] River without reprisal from a Caucasia become panic-stricken and paralyzed" through Japan's war in Asia.[88] Schuyler also explains how Japan's war becomes a race war that integrates politics and emotions at the affective level in "Japan and the Negro": "The white ruling class looks with fear and loathing as it sees the prospects of future robbery of other people [in Asia] going up in smoke, but it stands helpless, biting its finger nails in chagrin, trying to put a pleasant face upon it all. But that pleasant face isn't fooling the colored world. It knows that that ghastly smile masks stark terror.... It gives colored men and women everywhere who chafe under the white yoke renewed hope that what is transpiring in eastern Asia may spread to Malaysia, to India and to Africa."[89]

Schuyler defends the Japanese colored imperium because of its psychological impact on a white Western imperialist hegemony perpetuated in the name of prosperity, order, and peace. The race war that began in Asia, Schuyler predicts, in tandem with resistance in other parts of the darker world, would set the stage for the arrival of a "New Negro" who is "no longer ... terrorized" but "waits, and schemes and plans" to launch "a Black Internationale of liberation"[90]—a development that Belsidus rehearses in the realm of fiction. In *Black Empire*, the BI commands superior, futuristic military technologies such as biological and chemical weapons and electric ray machines to destroy the British Empire and other Western imperialist powers; thus, "the white countries became panic stricken," and "gone was the old haughty sureness" (BE, 253).

With colored empire, race war, and the overthrow of the international imperialists, one might well surmise that Du Bois's Japan and Schuyler's Belsidus, appearing together and side by side in the same weekly, were de facto embodiments of the same revolutionary agency (if a race war is called a revolutionary war). It is perhaps no coincidence that when the second *Black Empire* serial began its run in the fall of 1937, Ira F. Lewis, business manager of the *Courier*, solicited from Schuyler the series of articles that would become "Japan and the Negro." Lewis wrote to Schuyler, "The Negro is becoming interested in the foreign situation because somewhere beyond the physical horizon, he has visions of the Japanese becoming the new leader of the dark peoples."[91] Upon reading the first of the three installments of Schuyler's "Japan and the Negro," Lewis offers Schuyler his opinion that "the tocsin has been sounded, and the Japanese invasion of China and later India is but a beginning of the self-determination and self-assertion of the darker races lead [sic] by the Japanese."[92] One might speculate on the toll that the Japanese imperial army exacted in Asia on behalf of *Courier* staff and readers—especially in competition with Belsidus's military conquest of the African continent as it unfolded in Schuyler's pulp fiction. Thus, *Black Empire* can justifiably be read as a satirical replication of colored empires in the 1930s signifying the Japanese Empire, as much as Garvey's African empire and Liberia, that the "majority of thinking Negroes," including Du Bois and perhaps Schuyler himself, "favors." If this sounds too far-fetched, recall how Belsidus's empire, in hindsight, eerily anticipated Japan's design for the Greater East Asia Co-Prosperity Sphere, a bloc of Asian nations "liberated" from Western imperialist powers that in the end exposed the Japanese as no less overweening and often even more oppressive than white colonialists.

Building on Gruesser, the rendering of *Black Empire* that I have offered as a satire of colored oppression of colored people helps explain and exorcise the haunting presence of what is notionally suspect in Schuyler's BI. However, precisely because it is detached from the pro-Ethiopian matrix from which Schuyler's (and a collective) black internationalism developed in the mid-1930s, such an interpretive narrative eerily approximates the profascist propaganda employed to justify the Italo-Ethiopian War. The rhetoric of the Ethiopian imperium as "black oppression of black people," as in a satirical reading of *Black Empire*, is the very rhetoric that profascist apologists such as Baron Roman Procházka found most serviceable for their cause. In his libelous pamphlet *Abyssinia*

(1936), Procházka contends, "The opponents of Imperialism should bear in mind that the numerous non-Amharic native tribes in Ethiopia, and these constitute by far the greater part of the total population of the empire, are themselves the victims of *Abyssinian imperialism*. It is therefore utterly mistaken to represent the Abyssinian usurpers as being in any way oppressed and worthy of protection" (emphasis in original). In conclusion, Procházka writes, "The empire of the Negus had been built up by conquest and forcible annexation."[93] Thus did fascist propagandists depict the black empire as a political system of domination by the imperial center of multiethnic peoples on the periphery—a polity that is ruled without the consent of its native peoples, which Procházka terms Abyssinian imperialism.

It seems beyond question that Schuyler is to some extent mocking his readers' (and perhaps his own) naive faith in Black Empire—and their related view of the Japanese Empire as an ally—but there are clear limits to reading *Black Empire* as a satire of colored oppression of colored people. Rather, the issue at stake here is, as I have suggested, how Schuyler strove to resolve the concept of empire that became critically diffuse in the post-Ethiopian crisis.

The global scenario of race war, though imagined as a near-future likelihood in the black and fascist presses alike, was later advocated and lived out by only a handful of pro-Japanese black nationalist organizations, such as the aforementioned EPM, whose principal members were arrested by the FBI in 1942. Harlem's leading black weekly, the *New York Amsterdam Star-News*, commended the FBI's arrest of those members of the EPM who were "prostituting the fair name of Ethiopia." Indeed, according to the *Star-News*, the only "bona fide" Ethiopian organization in America was the Ethiopian World Federation[94]—an organization that, Von Eschen observes, opened "a new chapter in the organizational history of anticolonialism." However, the FBI saw only a thin line between the two organizations bearing the name of Ethiopia. The Ethiopian World Federation was founded by Malaku E. Bayen for organizing aid for Ethiopian refugees. However, the FBI reported that after the death of the founder, the Ethiopian prince Araya Abeba "rumored to have been affianced to Masako Kuroda" "is said to have attempted to take his place among the Negroes in New York City," thus suggesting the enduring valence of the rapprochement of the Ethiopian and Japanese Empires in the African American community.[95]

The scheme of empires at war, as was enacted (and satirized) in *Black Empire*, then, should not be consigned to historical oblivion. Merging black Atlantic and black Pacific imaginaries, Schuyler's near-futurist pulp fiction gave the signifying colored empire—both as the basis for an anticolonial politics and as a projection into a postcolonial future—full play. *Black Empire* thus affords a deeper understanding of what the black internationalism of the mid-1930s was fighting for in its violent fascination with empire.

[3]

THE SWING AND THE SWORD IN THE BLACK *MIKADOS*: AN AFRO-JAPANESE NEXUS IN THE US (WHITE) PACIFIC IMAGINATION

> If you want to know who we are,
> We are gentlemen of Japan:
> On many a vase and jar—
> On many a screen and fan,
> We figure in lively paint:
> Our attitude's queer and quaint—
> You're wrong if you think it ain't, oh!
> —Gilbert and Sullivan, *The Mikado;
> or, The Town of Titipu* (1885)

DURING THE NEW DEAL era of the 1930s in the United States, the government performed an important role as a cultural producer in directly delineating the imperial vision of a Pacific Community on the home front through the Federal Theatre Project (FTP), a state-sponsored public arts organization under the Works Progress Administration (WPA). The FTP created a Pacific narrative of particular significance with its production of *The Swing Mikado* (1938), which was a swing version of Gilbert and Sullivan's Japanese Empire–themed operetta, *The Mikado*. The Federal Theatre production moved its setting spatially and temporally from the genteel town of Titipu in medieval Japan to a coral island in the South Seas, which signifies at once the Japanese imperium in the Pacific and the US insular territories or "imperial archipelago" (to borrow from Lanny Thompson) in a manner reminiscent of the Philippines, Guam, or Hawai'i.

An operetta in two acts, Gilbert and Sullivan's *Mikado* offers a comical story of frustrated love and mistaken identity performed by British actors. It tells the story of wandering minstrel Nanki-Poo—in actuality, the son of the Mikado and the heir to the throne of Japan—fleeing his father's imperial court to avoid an arranged marriage to the elderly and unattractive Katisha only to find himself falling in love with the beautiful Yum-Yum, ward and betrothed of the tailor Ko-Ko, who has been newly appointed the lord high executioner. In despair over Yum-Yum, Nanki-Poo starts to hang himself. Ko-Ko pleads with him to wait and be his first victim in his line of duty, because he has received a message from the Mikado that unless an execution is carried out within a month, the town of Titipu will be reduced to the rank of a village, which would bring "irretrievable ruin." Nanki-Poo agrees on the condition that he be married to Yum-Yum for one month. When the Mikado and his entourage arrive in Titipu, the tenderhearted Ko-Ko, unable to actually perform his duties, forges an affidavit to the effect that Nanki-Poo, "Second Trombone," has been executed. But the Mikado and Katisha, his daughter-in-law-elect, discover that the slain man is his own son. The Mikado schedules the statutory punishment for compassing the death of the heir apparent for after luncheon. To avoid this horrible fate, Ko-Ko reluctantly agrees to marry Katisha, which is the only solution to the whole dilemma. In the finale, Nanki-Poo shows up with his bride Yum-Yum, and all is well because it ends well.

In contrast to the Savoy tradition of British actors playing white-masked oriental comic opera roles, the Federal Theatre's streamlined *Mikado* featured an all-black cast of African American actors—the Negro unit of the Chicago FTP employed through public assistance—in these roles in the South Sea island setting. The production thus posed a new black-Japanese nexus in the Pacific for national and popular consumption and created in its wake an unprecedented boom of *Mikado* productions across the United States. One of the most influential productions during this boom was producer Michael Todd's *Hot Mikado* (1939), which also featured an all-black cast but starred tap dancer extraordinaire Bill "Bojangles" Robinson in the role of the emperor of Japan. Robinson's starring performance as an Oriental potentate in *The Hot Mikado* made the radical conflation of African Americans and Japanese an even more salient image in Todd's production than in the FTP version and heightened its appeal as entertainment for the dominant (white) classes.

In this chapter, I turn from African American literature to a project of illuminating the US imperial vision of a Pacific Community presented by the New Deal–era Federal Theatre and Broadway. *The Swing Mikado*'s geographic imaginings of the Pacific space represented aspects of US regional imperialism and its rival the Japanese Empire, even as the South Sea island setting at the same time signified America's and Japan's colonial holdings. I will examine the FTP's liberal impulse, which coexisted with broader containment strategies, and will discuss the troubling Japanese signification of the opera that the Chicago Negro unit set in motion. This opera lampooned the Anglicized image of the "queer and quaint" Japanese in British imperial eyes. Furthermore, this chapter illuminates how Robinson's casting as the central character in *The Hot Mikado* shifted attention to the sadistic Japanese emperor, a hitherto minor character in both Gilbert and Sullivan's original and in the competing *Swing Mikado*. This enabled Robinson's satiric take on American domestic political culture. The black Pacific script of Africanized Japanese and their inhumane emperor in the New Deal era subsequently came to inform images of the Japanese Empire, as well as both militant Japanese and African Americans (and their nexus), in media-based programs of the Franklin D. Roosevelt administration during the Pacific War. Lurking beneath the emerging narrative of these programs was also a violent process of containing representations of the black Pacific under US cultural hegemony.

Great Britain's Comic Opera Diplomacy

"Blackening" the Savoy tradition of Gilbert and Sullivan's *Mikado*, the Federal Theatre's *Swing Mikado*, produced by the Chicago Negro unit, is rich with suggestions of transnational and racial crossovers. So was the original *Mikado*—in which British actors performed white-masked Japanese roles—similarly deriving its appeal to audiences from Orientalism and "racechange" (to borrow Susan Gubar's terminology).[1] The setting and characters come from Japan, but *The Mikado* should be appreciated as standing for what it is not: Gilbert and Sullivan's operetta mocks the English by proxy, not the Japanese whom it represents. I begin by discussing this problematic of the Japanese signification of *The Mikado* that *The Swing Mikado* inherited from Britain across the Atlantic.

The Mikado is perhaps surpassed only by Puccini's *Madame Butterfly* as the most popular internationally of the Japan-related musical and theatrical productions. However, unlike *Madame Butterfly*, which could cast Japanese performers in key roles, *The Mikado* historically proved to be unplayable, unadaptable, and even unwatchable by the "real" Japanese.[2] It occupied a peculiar and troubling space in international and transcultural politics. In fact, staging of *The Mikado* was banned in Japan during the pre–World War II era, and the ban was only lifted after Japan's unconditional surrender to the Allies and the conditional demise of the Japanese Empire. The first performance of *The Mikado* in Japan was staged in August 1946 by the US occupation forces to mark "the first anniversary of the end of the war in the Pacific." As one Japanese member of the audience commented, "If we had won the war, we never would have been able to see this."[3]

However, the genesis of *The Mikado* lay far from politics. Legend has it that dramatist William S. Gilbert was pacing up and down in his study, when an old Japanese sword happened to fall off its mounting on the wall and inspired the idea for *The Mikado*.[4] Whether or not this story is true, Japan certainly offered Gilbert topical subject matter. All things Japanese were in vogue in the 1880s, a time when Japan was "a kind of fashionable new toy to London society."[5] The enthusiasm for Japan led to, and was heightened by, the opening of the Japanese Village exhibition in Knightsbridge (referred to in *The Mikado* as the address of the residence of Nanki-Poo, the Mikado's son, when he is traveling in disguise as a musician) two months prior to the premiere of *The Mikado*.[6]

Like the Knightsbridge exhibition, the first run of *The Mikado* at the Savoy Theatre in London in 1885 was a carefully stage-managed affair. In mounting the opera, Gilbert took great care to ensure that everything Japanese was genuine. The Savoy sets and costumes were to be as authentic as possible to make them look like a traditional Japanese town at the time. Gilbert hired Japanese nationals who had been employed in the Knightsbridge exhibition to teach Japanese deportment to the D'Oyly Carte Opera Company during rehearsals. A Japanese tea girl took on the job of coaching the cast in walking the pigeon-toed, shuffling steps of ladies in kimono; in opening, spreading, waving, snapping, and closing of fans to indicate delight, anger, or coquetry; and the giggling and sibilant hissing of Japanese girls in mannerisms perpetuated in *Mikado* performances today.[7] Significantly, the first public production of *The Mikado* strove for a realism that aimed to fulfill its billing as a "Japanese opera."

Notwithstanding Gilbert's efforts to reproduce premodern Japan faithfully, the mimesis in *The Mikado* extended only to the mise-en-scène, according to Gilbert scholars. The characters are largely burlesqued, but Gilbert scholars have traditionally argued that the mockery is directed not at the Japanese characters but at the institutions, manners, and class pretensions of Victorian England. Despite the imperative against understanding Gilbert and Sullivan's masterpiece as literally a "Japanese opera" that follows from this argument, *The Mikado* does invite a reading as a satire of the "queer and quaint" Japanese. Indeed, the disclaimers of scholars and critics that "*The Mikado* is not about Japan" reflect not only the pervasiveness of such readings but also the troubling signification of the work itself.

I argue that the normative reading of *The Mikado* as a satire of British institutions was a political invention aimed at containing the Japanese signification of the opera, which became increasingly problematic at a time when the relationship between the British Empire and the Japanese Empire was changing in the Pacific region. Japan had made the transition from being a shogunate to a modern nation-state in a relatively quick time. The Japanese Empire had been promulgated in 1868. While in form it was modeled on Imperial Germany (Prussia), it was surmounted by the then mikado (Emperor Meiji) as emperor, "for to be anything less would be an admission of a status inferior to that of the leading European rulers."[8] Following its victory in a war with China (1894–1895), Japan entered the British-led system of treaty ports (opened to foreign trade by unequal treaties) in China, which was a major institution of the informal maritime British Empire in Asia. The conclusion of the Anglo-Japanese alliance in 1902 then made Japan a regional partner with Great Britain in the Pacific—an alliance that was renewed and extended in the wake of Japan's victory in a war with Russia (1904–1905). The new Anglo-Japanese relationship developed not only in military and governmental affairs but also in the realms of court diplomacy.[9] In 1906, King Edward VII sent a delegation to Japan to confer on the Japanese emperor the Order of the Garter, and in accordance with protocol, in the following year, Japan sent a reciprocal delegation to England led by royal prince Fushimi Sadanaru, to convey the emperor's gratitude for the Order of the Garter. It was at this point that the Lord Chamberlain, chief officer of the British royal household and licensor of plays, increasingly concerned over its possible effects on the evolving Anglo-Japanese relationship, decided to ban *The Mikado*.

The heated debate that ensued over the ban represented a barometer of the extent to which *The Mikado*'s Japaneseness was contested at the time of the official visit of the Japanese prince. No event bearing on Anglo-Japanese relations caused so great a tumult as this "comic opera diplomacy," as the *New York Times* called the ban from across the Atlantic.[10] The English public found the state action to be "ludicrous." Furthermore, the Lord Chamberlain had made England the "laughing stock" of the world in prohibiting *The Mikado* as offensive only after Japan proved itself worthy of respect by winning the Russo-Japanese War.[11] One member of Parliament asked, with evident sarcasm, whether Shakespeare's *Hamlet* should not also be prohibited, since it portrayed the king of Denmark as a murderer and was therefore liable to cause offense to Denmark, a friendly power.[12] The controversy ensued for six weeks, until Prince Fushimi left England and the home secretary lifted the ban.

This episode of the ban is important, for the ensuing controversy showed that *The Mikado* could, and did, evolve into a political trope for the Japanese Empire. Much of the controversy initiated in 1907 began on the premise that *The Mikado* was an opera about the Japanese Empire, and it revolved around the issue of whether the opera was therefore offensive to the Japanese imperial government. Some cited the cancellation of a proposed performance of *The Mikado* in Japan as proof of its offensiveness, while others cited as counterevidence the fact that *The Mikado* had once been performed in Japan, under the altered title *Three Little Maids from School* (although this production was staged in an extraterritorial area outside the jurisdiction of the emperor in nineteenth-century Japan before the unequal treaties that Japan had concluded with Great Britain were abolished).[13] Some insisted that *The Mikado* was "void of offense"—and that this was why the opera had been applauded for the twenty years it had been playing—while others proposed removing the cause of offense by changing either the title of the work or the country that it burlesqued.[14] There were also suspicions that Tokyo had engineered the ban. Gilbert, at least, believed this to be the case: "I learn from a friend, who had it direct from the King, that *the Japs* made the objection to *The Mikado*, and that it was at their instance it was suppressed." Gilbert further observes, "The rights in the piece do not revert to me for three years; by that time we shall probably be at war with Japan about India, and they will offer me a high price to permit it to be played"—which suggests that in its creator's view, *The Mikado* could equally be an instrument of foreign policy in times of war with Japan as in times of peace.[15]

The new position that emerged from the 1907 controversy—that *The Mikado* represents a kind of displaced England—originated with the critic G. K. Chesterton, who argued that "all the jokes in the play fit the English" and thus initiated Gilbert criticism as we know it today.[16] When word of the ban began to circulate, Chesterton at first approached the problem of offensiveness as an issue of aesthetics versus politics by asking, "Are we to suppress good literature even if some such country is in some such work treated in no very respectful way?"[17] At the height of the controversy, Chesterton reaffirmed his stance against state suppression of *The Mikado* in his *Illustrated London News* column of May 25, 1907. He began his column along the lines of his earlier approach, asserting,

"Even if 'The Mikado' did make outrageous fun of Japan, it ought not to have been suppressed on that account." However, later in the same column, Chesterton abruptly abandoned this argument for the now-familiar tack of dissociating the theme and characters of the opera from its mise-en-scène: *The Mikado* is not about Japan but about England. In Chesterton's view, it would be fallacious to consider *The Mikado* offensive to the Japanese because the play "is a satire on England," not on Japan. Pooh-Bah, a prime example of Gilbert's satire, is mocked "as an English aristocratic politician"; he is "a pretty effective satire upon our own oligarchy," not an "Oriental oligarchy." For Chesterton, the whole satire of *The Mikado* is thus "sustained on this principle" of displacement and self-mockery.[18]

Chesterton's view that the audience must attend to the function of the theme and characters of the opera to understand it properly has subsequently been adopted by critics to such an extent that it has become "commonplace to say that *The Mikado* isn't about Japan but about England," as Gayden Wren observes.[19] Yet Chesterton's reading was a politically motivated one in 1907, when the thematic dissociation of *The Mikado* from Japan was a diplomatic imperative. This suggests that the theme and characters of the opera could exercise state cultural and foreign policy in naming the Japanese Empire. In the next section, I discuss how the government-sponsored African American adaptation of *The Mikado* in the FTP's *Swing Mikado* transformed the opera into a potential trope for "colored" imperial Japan that reflected and reacted to US foreign relations with Japan on the brink of World War II by conveying intensely racial/racist overtones via the black-Japanese nexus in the Pacific.

The Swing Mikado *and the Federal Theatre's Vision of a Pacific Community*

The New Deal era was a significant watershed in black theater culture, as well as in the political thought of African Americans who had long remained loyal to the Republican Party of Abraham Lincoln. The Roosevelt administration of the 1930s was the first administration to acknowledge publicly the value of African Americans as citizens in a form that was both substantive and symbolic. The New Dealers made explicit the federal government's concern for African Americans by making stable employment available to African Americans who had experienced being the last to be hired and the first to be fired during the Great Depression, and who had consequently shifted their political allegiance to the Democratic

Party.[20] As part of Roosevelt's New Deal, the WPA created a collection of federally sponsored cultural programs, which historian Lauren Rebecca Sklaroff observes "represented an important strand of civil rights policy." The New Deal's cultural programs, marked by the dynamic intermingling of white and black liberals, "engendered a political landscape in which government officials and civil rights leaders probed the nature and meaning of black Americanness" during the Roosevelt era, according to Sklaroff.[21] Among the numerous African American writers supported by the WPA during the depression years were Zora Neale Hurston, Theodore Ward, Richard Wright, Langston Hughes, Shirley Graham (Du Bois), and Margaret Walker.

The FTP was created under the WPA in 1935, establishing sixteen Negro units within the FTP in cities across the United States. African American actors and professionals (supported through public assistance) played an integral part—if under white directors—in shaping the federally sponsored cultural program from its inception until its demise in June 1939.[22] For instance, the Harlem unit's *Macbeth* (1936, known as the "voodoo" *Macbeth*), directed by Orson Welles, was the first full-scale black professional production of Shakespeare in US theatrical history. It transplanted the story of *Macbeth* from feudal Scotland to nineteenth-century Haiti in the Caribbean and recast the witches as voodoo priestesses. The Harlem unit further enhanced the supernatural atmosphere of the mise-en-scène by incorporating a troupe of African drummers led by Asadata Dafora Horton, a native of Sierra Leone, then in the United States to perform *Kykunkor* (Witch Woman). The "voodoo" *Macbeth* opened on April 14, 1936, at the Lafayette Theatre in Harlem to near universal acclaim from both black and white audiences. After running through the summer, the production toured nationally in WPA theaters.[23]

Adopting the Harlem unit's approach to Shakespeare, the Chicago Negro unit "blackened" another Western classic from across the Atlantic with its production of *The Swing Mikado* (although the status of Gilbert and Sullivan's *Mikado* as a work of either high or popular culture was still undecided in the 1930s) and moved the setting from feudal Japan to a tropical island in the Pacific. The new production also featured five re-scored musical numbers from the original version, including "A Wandering Minstrel," "My Object All Sublime," and "The Flowers that Bloom in the Spring."

The popular and financial success of *The Swing Mikado* fueled a boom in *Mikado*-related productions across the United States. The spicy rhythms of *The Swing Mikado* first took audiences by storm in Chicago.

Its premiere on September 25, 1938, at the Great Northern Theatre broke all previous box-office records and led to a twenty-two-week run. After five months in Chicago, the WPA and FTP brought the production to Broadway, where it was met with great enthusiasm at its gala opening at the New Yorker on March 1, 1939. Members of the highest echelons of the New Deal administration, including first lady Eleanor Roosevelt, secretary of commerce Harry Hopkins (former WPA director), and Colonel Francis Clark Harrington (incumbent WPA director), and New York City mayor Fiorello Henry LaGuardia attended.[24] Their enthusiastic response publicly highlighted the government's sponsorship of this cultural production. Black reviewers also responded favorably, including Alain Locke, the preeminent African American aesthetician of the Harlem Renaissance who underscored the seminal significance of *The Swing Mikado*: "Because of its exotic character, it was perhaps pardonable for Broadway to have overlooked the suggestive novelties of *Kykunkor*, the African dance-ballet, but not to have seen in the *Swing Mikado* the new horizons of Negro musical comedy was, it seems to me, unpardonable."[25]

Three weeks later, New York was treated to a second all-black, swing version of the opera with the opening of Michael Todd's *Hot Mikado*, starring the great tap dancer Bill "Bojangles" Robinson in the title role. The audience at the March 23, 1939, premiere of *The Hot Mikado* included its own lineup of dignitaries, including Thomas E. Dewey, district attorney of New York County, who ran for governor of New York, and FBI director J. Edgar Hoover, who traveled from Washington for the occasion—a conservative turnout that indicates the salience of the political dimensions of the competing productions.[26]

As the spring of 1939 waxed, a fully fledged *Mikado* boom took hold in the United States. As one contemporary observer noted, it was "a banner year" for the Gilbert and Sullivan opera.[27] Four versions were produced in New York alone: in addition to *The Swing Mikado* and *The Hot Mikado*, the D'Oyly Carte Opera Company troupe—visiting Savoyards—mounted a traditional production, and a Technicolor film version of *The Mikado* was produced with several principals of the D'Oyly Carte troupe.[28] This New York *Mikado* boom, a "Mikadization of New York" as theater historian Allen Woll put it, also prompted a parody of the parody entitled "The Red Mikado," which, in *Time* magazine's words, "kids the Mikado epidemic."[29] "The Red Mikado" was a sketch in *Pins and Needles*, a revue produced by the International Ladies' Garment Workers' Union at Labor Stage Theatre, and featured Gilbert and Sullivan as angels descending from the clouds with banners that read, respectively, "Unfair to Sullivan" and "Unfair to Gilbert." The two are picketing in front of posters for such presumably forthcoming *Mikado* productions as the "*Strip Mikado*," the "*Flea Mikado*," and the "*Hollywood Mikado*"—to protest capitalist appropriation and exploitation of their masterpiece.[30]

On one level, this array of productions and adaptations of the opera that flared up in 1939 was simply part of the *Mikado* fever that had gripped the United States since Richard D'Oyly Carte first presented *The Mikado* to an American audience in 1885, at the Fifth Avenue Theatre in New York. This production had immediately proven a smash hit, inaugurating the first American craze for *The Mikado*. On one evening in 1886 alone, there were said to have been 170 separate stagings of *The Mikado* across the nation.[31] Fueled by the "racechange" at the heart of the appeal of the opera, the *Mikado* boom also inspired cross-racial parodies such as the blackface minstrel shows *The Mick-ah-do* and *The Black Mikado*, which some critics regard as antecedents to the black *Mikado* productions of the New Deal era.[32] In view of this history, the *Mikado* boom sparked by *The Swing Mikado* of the Chicago Negro unit may be understood both to have stemmed from and to have contributed to the enduring appeal of the English operetta to American audiences in its intersection with America's minstrel tradition.

However, on another level, the *Mikado* boom of the New Deal era was a singular cultural phenomenon that was initiated by the government (the WPA and the FTP) in pursuing a liberal politics through its cultural programs. Beyond the Federal Theatre's primary goal of providing employment to African American actors and professionals, the Negro units also aimed to create socially progressive art. Shirley Graham (Du Bois), for instance, made a breakthrough in musical theater in 1932 by mounting her opera entitled *Tom-Tom: An Epic of Music and the Negro*; it was the first all-black opera to be produced by an African American woman. She joined the Chicago FTP and helped to adapt Gilbert and Sullivan's *Mikado*.[33] Furthermore, the idea of putting "swing"—a popular mainstream music form of the 1930s—at the heart of *The Swing Mikado* originated in the Chicago Negro unit's improvisations. Harry Minturn, director of the Chicago FTP, happened to catch sight of some of the Negro unit's black cast members swinging and tap dancing to songs from *The Mikado* during a break in a music rehearsal for what the Chicago FTP had planned to be a traditional production of the opera. Seeing promise in the actors' improvisations, Minturn called in Gentry Warden (a member of the Negro Musician Union) to arrange swing versions of several of the songs. Based on the results, the production was reconceived into what came to be known as *The Swing Mikado*.[34]

In its revamp of a British classic, the swing Negro unit pursued strategies that were both forceful and subtle. Pivotally, director Minturn decided to shift the mise-en-scène of *The Mikado* from its time-honored setting in Titipu, which Gilbert and the Savoy tradition had conceived as a faithful mimesis of medieval Japan. While the conventional approach worked well enough with white actors, it would have been "incongruous," in Minturn's view, to cast the black members of the Negro unit "into a traditional 'Mikado' using all the hallowed Victorian costumes and stage-business that have invariably been employed from the time of the original production at the Savoy Theatre in London under the eyes of Gilbert and Sullivan fifty-odd years ago." Minturn's underlying assumption in drawing a racial distinction was that African Americans did not belong to the tradition of Western civilization, which was rather the cultural property of the white race. In considering how to avoid this "incongruity," Minturn imagined that if the setting were changed from the genteel town of Titipu (inhabited by English Japanese) to a South Sea island—Japan was, after all, an archipelago in the Pacific—"then there was some logic in it." Taking such poetic license seemed reasonable to Minturn because "the Japan of 'The Mikado' is not a real Japan, but a mythical barbarous island that Gilbert might just as well have called Zanzibar or Nyasaland" in Africa.[35] Reasoning thus, Minturn transposed the locale of Titipu to a coral South Sea island. The unspecific but "barbarous" tropical island setting, inhabited by dark-skinned, comical characters—remarkably suggestive of the US imperial view of their insular territories such as the Philippines, Guam, and Hawaiʻi, as Stephanie Leigh Batiste observes[36]—represented the Federal Theatre's geographic imaginings of a Pacific Community and its island members.

The Chicago Negro unit surrendered the realism of the mise-en-scène of *The Mikado*, which had mediated its function as the "Japanese opera" of Gilbert's conception. Nevertheless, from a historical point of view, the Federal Theatre version of Titipu dovetailed neatly with the reality of the contemporary Japanese imperium in the Pacific. In set designer Clive Rickabaugh's description, Titipu in *The Swing Mikado* was "a mythical Japanese island possession with a note of the South Seas"[37]; it referenced the reign of the Japanese Empire, whose colonial territories included chains of volcanic and coral islands in the South Seas such as the Marianas, Marshalls, and Carolines (although Guam remained under US control). Japan had acquired these by a League of Nations mandate in 1919

3.1. The Chicago Negro unit's *Swing Mikado* (1938). *Federal Theatre Project Collection, Library of Congress.*

and continued to hold them even after it withdrew from the League of Nations in 1933. In Rickabaugh's stage sets, Mount Fuji, an icon of Japan and a defining background in traditional productions of *The Mikado*, was conspicuously replaced by three volcanic cones. In this South Sea island setting, the performers of the Chicago Negro unit emerged as Japanese imperial subjects, significantly creating a black-Japanese conflation in the Pacific.

In the Federal Theatre version of *The Mikado*, set designer Rickabaugh was not the only white staff member whose aesthetic and racialist imagination informed the African-Japanese nexus on stage. John Pratt, the costume designer, resolved the "knotty problem of costuming by finding a striking meeting ground of African and Japanese motifs."[38] The familiar kimonos of the Savoy tradition made no sense in the new setting of a Pacific coral island; Pratt would need to invent costumes "to meet the requirements of various elements—African, Sothern [sic] Pacific, Japanese," as he recorded in his costume notes.[39] The resulting costumes resembled sarongs in elaborate colors. Pratt complemented these with handheld fans, the sine qua non in the Savoy tradition of *The Mikado*. The effect was further enhanced by props such as bamboo poles with streamers, tom-tom drums, feathers, wooden poles, and spears that indicated the "barbarous" conditions of Titipu (figure 3.1).

The gap between the Federal Theatre and Savoy versions of Titipu in *The Mikado* was immediately clear to the audience. To those familiar with the Savoy tradition, for whom Titipu was a repository of Victorian fantasies of the Far East, it would seem that in *The Swing Mikado*, "the Africans have invaded the genteel town."[40] *The Swing Mikado* shattered the image of the "queer and quaint" English Japanese both visually and aurally. When the curtain rose, the opening chorus—"We are gentlemen of Japan"—foreshadowed the "outbursts of animal revelry" that followed, as Brooks Atkinson, theater critic of the *New York Times*, remarked: "A wave of animal high jinks" coursed through the show, reaching a climax with "the roaring antics of the choruses swinging like frenetic savages, swaying and shaking, grinning with delight, their eyes dancing as madly as their feet."[41] The emperor of Japan (played by Edward Fraction) came on the stage wearing as garments of state not a kimono but "a flowing robe of red and yellow awning stripes" and a top hat studded with dilapidated pheasant feathers.[42] The town of Titipu carried "overtones of Japan, the Congo and Harlem."[43] "The male principals were," in the words of one white reviewer, "made up like comic artists' impressions of cannibals,"[44] and the members of the chorus were dressed "like coolies when they are supposed to be very stiff and proper gents," which seemed "silly" to another reviewer.[45] In their eyes, the aristocratic status of the English Japanese in the Savoy tradition was ridiculously replaced by Africanized Japanese in *The Swing Mikado*, which expressed instead, reflexively, the perceived cultural inferiority of Africans and Asians by invoking their savagery, their ultimate otherness ("cannibals"), and their low status as manual laborers or slaves ("coolies").

"Those sun-burned coral island Japs are not too easy on either the eyes or the imagination" declared theater critic Burns Mantle, who was obliged to enjoy the production of *The Swing Mikado* "most with [his] eyes closed two-thirds of the time."[46] Because of its radical aesthetic ingenuity, there was something fundamentally parodic—and shocking—in *The Swing Mikado*. The series of racist clichés that the white reviewers assembled reflected, beyond an antiblack slant, the efficacy of the Chicago Negro unit's travesty of the "hallowed" Victorian opera—a product of British imperialism and Orientalism. The Chicago Negro unit burlesqued not so much the Japanese whom they represented as the white-masked, comic-opera Japanese played by British actors in the Savoy tradition that they adapted. In her study of African American performances in the New Deal era, Stephanie Batiste observes, "Given the complexity of the role of Japan in black political thought, it makes a certain cultural sense that the African American performance of *The Swing Mikado* in 1938 failed to directly lampoon the Japanese." *The Swing Mikado*, Batiste suggests, could be "highly revolutionary as a statement against American racism and yet also radically conservative in its overlay of Japanese imperialism and belligerence upon blacks' sense of colored brotherhood in the embodiment of colonized Islanders."[47]

In view of this transatlantic parodic or satiric stance toward the Savoy version of *The Mikado*, it is not surprising that the Chicago Negro unit's *Swing Mikado* set in motion the troubling Japanese signification of the opera that seemed to have been contained since 1907. Some reviewers were resistant to the new vision of the Japanese that the Chicago Negro unit set before them; "Even though they wear sarongs instead of kimonos and light primitive camp fires instead of quaint Nipponese lanterns," one critic noted incredulously, "'The Swing Mikado' songsters insist—'If you want to know who we are, we are gentlemen of Japan!'" Yet, however great the discrepancy between Gilbert's English Japanese and those of the Chicago Negro unit, director Minturn "insists that 'if you scratch his South Sea islanders you will find full-fledged gentlemen of Japan.'"[48] Others regarded the Chicago Negro unit's colored Japanese to be more authentic than others. A theater critic for the *Wall Street Journal*, for instance, reported that "most of the cast ... looked more Japanese to this observer than certain other casts he has seen assembled for the work," observing the racial proximity of Japanese and African Americans to be closer than that of Japanese and English.[49]

To yet other reviewers, it would seem that in presenting the Japanese emperor as a "colored jitterbug" on a barbarous island, the Chicago Negro unit asserted more than poetic license, for the production was funded directly by the government. As an exercise in the presentation of a foreign head of state (the mikado) by the US government, *The Swing Mikado* was open to interpretation by contemporary audiences as an expression of Uncle Sam's official view of the Japanese imperial institution and its incumbent (Emperor Hirohito). Such an understanding may have framed *New York World-Telegram* critic Sidney B. Whipple's speculation on the site regarding the Federal Theatre's relocation of the setting: "Perhaps in respect for our little brown brothers in Tokyo, the producers set the scenes for fantasy in 'a coral island in the Pacific.'"[50] In Whipple's logic, the Japanese imperial government—"our little brown brothers in Tokyo"— had no grounds for being offended by the production, because the change of setting to an island in the South Seas precluded the possibility of understanding the Federal Theatre to be drawing racial parallels between

Japanese people and African American people. The *New York Times*, in an editorial focused on the potential of *The Swing Mikado* to give diplomatic offence, pursued a similar logic in defending the show: "The actual Japanese Mikado need not be bothered, because this drama is specifically located on 'a coral island in the Pacific.'" Given the change of setting, the editorial suggests, *The Swing Mikado* is about not Japan but rather an unspecified island in the South Seas. The editorial further observes that the Federal Theatre had also "take[n] the precaution to announce on its programs that 'the viewpoint expressed in the play is not necessarily that of the WPA or any other agency of the Government.'" Hence, the *Times* concludes, *The Swing Mikado* "does not commit the present National Administration to anything.... No 'apologetic statesman of a compromising kind' can feel hurt, for the State Department is not responsible for the description [that the production might seem to offer of the Japanese]."[51] The editorial thus implies that the US government had no reason to defund, much less to ban, the production of *The Swing Mikado* in light of its foreign diplomacy as its British counterpart had done in the case of its "comic opera diplomacy" of 1907.

Beyond these attempts, aimed at containing the Japanese signification of the Federal Theatre's show, the Chicago Negro unit's performance finally invited a reading that is a fantasy of the imperial vision of a Pacific Community, in which the Japanese are rendered innocuous islanders (like those in the US insular territories such as the Philippines, Guam, or Hawaiʻi). In 1938, the formation of a Pacific Community—first expressed by the Washington Treaties of 1922 that abrogated the aforementioned Anglo-Japanese alliance and instead established a multilateral framework of cooperation under American leadership—was faced with a difficult situation. The Japanese Empire had come up with its own new vision of regionalism, directly challenging the US Open Door policy in China. Within several weeks of the premiere of *The Swing Mikado* in Chicago, Japan had declared a new regional policy that aimed to replace the US-defined Washington system. On November 3, 1938, the birthday of the late Emperor Meiji, the Japanese government proclaimed a "New Order in East Asia," and Japan's premier, Prince Fumimaro Konoye, "delivered a radio address in which he blamed foreign [i.e., Western] power imperialism for disrupting peace in Asia."[52] Apparently, Japan was intent upon driving European and American imperial powers from the western shores of the Pacific. By March 1939, when the WPA brought *The Swing Mikado* to Broadway, Japan's intention to expand into Southeast Asia was clear. Japanese troops had moved down into the environs of Hong Kong and had occupied Hainan Island as a base for their drive into Southeast Asia and eventually into the Pacific.

Against this historical backdrop, Richard Watts Jr., a theater critic for the *New York Herald Tribune*, observed that the streamlined, all-black *Mikado* evoked "a nice thought" of Japan in the Pacific, a pleasurable exercise in fulfilling the wish that Japan was no more than "a merry and colorful South Sea island": "It is the pleasant contention of the newfangled 'Mikado' that Japan is in reality a merry and colorful South Sea island, peopled with fast-stepping and gaily garbed brownskins. It is a nice thought and would no doubt make for a more attractive page of modern Asiatic history. In this amiable Nippon you will find a silk-hatted emperor, a dusky harmony trio, some fine tap dancers and the truckingest chorus recently encountered in these parts."[53]

In appreciating the "amiable Nippon" that the Federal Theatre presented, Watts alludes to the actual Japan that was not so amiable. The "more attractive page" that Watts suggests could be written in "modern Asiatic history" similarly alludes—if not explicitly—to a string of unattractive recent incidents of Japanese aggression in Asia. Watts may well have had in mind Japan's invasion of Manchuria and establishment of the puppet state of Manchukuo, its full-scale war with China, and its bombing and sinking of the US Navy gunboat *Panay* in the Yangtze River, all of which challenged the international coordination of the Washington system in the Pacific. In Africanizing Gilbert's English Japanese, *The Swing Mikado* made the Japanese friendlier and sunnier, and hence less of a threat to US foreign policy and regional order in a Pacific Community.

In an article in the *Washington Post*, Watts firmly approves of the federally supported vision of the Japanese Empire in *The Swing Mikado*. In his assessment, the Federal Theatre's "conception of Japan as a merry South Sea Island, inhabited by dusky jitterbugs, is a pleasantly idyllic one, supplying one of the neatest bits of national wish-fulfillment imaginable" (though, as he laments, "If only they were right about it, how much more agreeable the recent course of Far Eastern history would be!"). In *The Swing Mikado*, the audience could indulge in an "attractive political dream" that the Japanese were innocuous "dusky jitterbugs" rather than a "yellow peril" menacing both the United States, an emerging regional hegemon in the South Seas, and the status quo of international relations in a Pacific Community.[54] In the end, as Shannon Steen insightfully observes, swing adaptations of *The Mikado* "domesticated Japanese imperial menace by projecting it onto the spectacle of happy black Americans, and simultaneously Americanized Japan by projecting the physical exhilaration of swing culture onto it."⁵⁵

The Federal Theatre created the imperial vision of a Pacific Community that simultaneously reflected and acted upon both the articulated liberal politics and the unarticulated racism that accompanied anti-Japanese sentiment. Despite what Batiste referred to as an element, at once revolutionary and conservative, expressed in the performance of the Chicago Negro unit playing the Japanese Empire that had a complex role in black political thought, the Federal Theatre's production performed its containment function in packaging a black-Japanese nexus in the socially acceptable format of *The Swing Mikado* for national and popular consumption.

Enter the "Harlemperor"

A commercial version of *The Swing Mikado*, *The Hot Mikado* capitalized on this black-Japanese nexus to achieve success in direct competition with the Federal Theatre production. Todd, a showman, had offered to take over the Federal Theatre's *Swing Mikado* as a private venture after its successful Chicago run, but when his offer was rejected, Todd decided to produce his own version. Unwilling to give up what had become a cash cow, the Federal Theatre itself brought its production to New York, where the private and government-sponsored productions competed head to head.⁵⁶

The Hot Mikado hit the jackpot, mainly due to Todd's ingenious casting of Bill "Bojangles" Robinson in the role of the emperor of Japan. The King of Tap and an honorary "Mayor of Harlem,"⁵⁷ Robinson was America's favorite entertainer at the time, dubbed by theater critic Brooks Atkinson "the Good-Will Ambassador from Harlem to the Western World."⁵⁸ Robinson had come to prominence during the 1930s in a series of films including *The Little Colonel* and *The Littlest Rebel*, in which he appeared with Shirley Temple. In these films, Robinson played old-fashioned Southern servant roles and danced with the white child star. The dance pairing of an African American male and a Caucasian girl—which would have been taboo if managed less deftly—proved to be a highlight of Robinson and Temple's movie performances. Such was the persona that Robinson established that FBI director Hoover, an avowed racist, traveled from Washington to see the star in the New York premiere of *The Hot Mikado*; Robinson was "a black Hoover could understand," as biographers Jim Haskins and N. R. Mitgang put it.[59] The black-Japanese nexus, repackaged for Broadway consumption in *The Hot Mikado*, was a production that even the chief of the FBI could enjoy (though wartime FBI special agents would surveil it).

To maximize its appeal to New York audiences, *The Hot Mikado* developed and stylized the Federal Theatre–created black Pacific. Abandoning the South Sea island setting of *The Swing Mikado*, the new production recreated Titipu as a streamlined town of Japan—itself an archipelago in the Pacific—rendered in Oriental abstractions and geometrical patterns, at once romantic and bizarre, with lamp shades made of dice and a Rising Sun flag redesigned with an image of Mount Fuji as the backdrop.[60] *The Hot Mikado* also featured spectacular stage effects that included a forty-foot cascade of soap bubbles that flowed down a canvas onto the bathing girls, an electrical storm, the talking moon that sang with Yum-Yum, and a volcano that erupted on Katisha's entrance in the finale of act I. All of these effects were devised by Nat Karson, who had designed sets and costumes for the "voodoo" *Macbeth*. The sets represented Japan but "what a Japan! A Japan as torrid as Fujiyama in eruption," as contemporary reviewer Robert Coleman described it.[61]

The spectacular Afro-Oriental ambience of the production set the stage for Robinson to establish his identity as "the latest ruler of Japan," beginning with his entry in full regalia in act II, amid fanfare and brigades of jitterbug girls and boys.[62] The costumes that Karson designed for *The Hot Mikado* were, as a drama critic for the *New York World-Telegram* commented, "a happy cross between Harlem and Tokyo," and Robinson's was no exception: gorgeously decked out in a diamond-encircled derby hat, gold uniform, and sparkling shoelaces, Robinson conveyed a fantastic conflation of the mayor of Harlem and the emperor of Japan.[63] In the eyes of contemporary (white) reviewers, he presented the image of "a gold-embossed Mayor of some Japanese Harlem," or the "Harlemperor of Japan."[64]

The black Pacific—through the persona of Robinson—would thus seem to have been entirely stylized and commodified for Broadway in *The Hot Mikado*. But in its casting of Robinson as the emperor, *The Hot Mikado* also revised the signification of *The Mikado* in critical respects, particularly in shifting the focus from the love entanglement at the center of Gilbert and Sullivan's operetta to the character of the Japanese emperor. Though a relatively minor character who appeared only in the second half of the play in Gilbert and Sullivan's 1885 original, in *The Hot Mikado*, the Japanese emperor is the central figure. As a contemporary critic commented, Robinson's Mikado was "practically the whole show"; he overshadowed all of the other characters, including Ko-Ko, Nanki-Poo, Pooh-Bah, Yum-Yum, and Katisha.[65] The centrality of Robinson to the production therefore rendered *The Hot Mikado* literally as the story of the Mikado, the absolute monarch of Japan.

In Gilbert and Sullivan's original comic operetta, Titipu is a society in which the behavior of its citizens is dictated by laws emanating from the Mikado, who demands obedience "from every kind of man."[66] The Mikado makes his long-delayed appearance only in act II, heralded by a procession singing "March of the Mikado's troops" ("Miya sama, miya sama . . ."), the one genuine Japanese-language song in the operetta. The Mikado then sings "My Object All Sublime," interpolating a "blood-curdling laugh between verses" that is "a feature of D'Oyly Carte Mikados"[67]:

> A more humane Mikado never
> Did in Japan exist,
> . . . .
> My object all sublime
> I shall achieve in time—
> To let the punishment fit the crime—
> The punishment fit the crime;
> And make each prisoner pent
> Unwillingly represent
> A source of innocent merriment!
> Of innocent merriment! (*Mikado*, 621, 623)

In this song, the Mikado relates how retributive justice is served in his domain. One of his decrees, reflecting the misogyny and racism of Victorian England, states, "The lady who dyes a chemical yellow / Or stains her grey hair puce, / Or pinches her figger, / Is blacked like a nigger / With permanent walnut juice." These were amended in productions from 1948 onward due to the objections of African Americans to the word "nigger." For the same reason, "the nigger serenader" in the Lord High Executioner Ko-Ko's "little list" song was also replaced with other material that year.[68] These expressions of antiblack racism in *The Mikado* were retained in the prewar, US government–sponsored *Swing Mikado*.

In Gilbert's original operetta, the Mikado is caricatured as a bloodthirsty, despotic Oriental monarch for whom capital punishment, carried out by decapitation, live burial, and boiling in oil, is a chief interest in life. Following the arrival of the Mikado in Titipu in act II of *The Mikado*,

Ko-Ko, the Lord High Executioner, provides the emperor with a grim portrayal of the execution he has supposedly just carried out. The executioner elatedly describes, in an entire song about decapitation ("The Criminal Cried"), how he decapitated a tough prisoner by "seiz[ing] him by his little pig-tail," and how the prisoner "squirmed and struggled, / And gurgled and guggled" when he "drew [his] snickersnee." The prisoner utters a death scream that Ko-Ko would never forget:

> Oh, never shall I
> Forget the cry,
> Or the shriek that shrieked he,
> As I gnashed my teeth,
> When from its sheath
> I drew my snickersnee! (*Mikado*, 627)

Pitti-Sing and Pooh-Bah join Ko-Ko's reenactment of the execution to help convince the Mikado of its cruelty, violence, and grotesqueness. Pitti-Sing testifies that the prisoner "whistled an air" as "the sabre true / Cut cleanly through / His cervical vertebræ!" (*Mikado*, 627). Pooh-Bah adds that the decapitated head, though dead, did not forget to pay "the deference due to" him, "a man of pedigree":

> Now though you'd have said that head was dead
> (For its owner dead was he),
> It stood on its neck, with a smile well-bred,
> And bowed three times to me! (*Mikado*, 629)

This story of the execution pleases the Mikado, who wishes that he had witnessed it personally.

Robinson had reportedly not seen the Gilbert and Sullivan version of *The Mikado* performed by the D'Oyly Carte Opera Company and "knew nothing of Gilbert and Sullivan" prior to attending the FTP Chicago Negro unit's *Swing Mikado*. In the FTP production, Robinson watched Edward Fraction, in the role of the Mikado, explaining his "object all sublime" in swing rhythm, leading Robinson to the dubious conclusion that "the Mikado of tradition [is] a mighty nice character."[69] Robinson brought all of his tap-dancing ingenuity and the gusto of his genial personality to the creation of his own Mikado, imparting an air of irresistible charisma to this otherwise unattractive character. Robinson's "My Object All Sublime" proved a showstopper with "eight encores" on its first night at the Broadhurst.[70] The drama critic John Mason Brown wrote, "Certainly a more humane Mikado never did in Japan exist than

Bojangles."⁷¹ Robinson's performance transformed the image of the African American emperor of Japan into a milder form of entertainment than the FTP version, in the process bringing the federally scripted black Pacific further under the control of the dominant (white) classes.

Nevertheless, I would like to suggest that Robinson's remaking of the character of the Mikado had a subversive dimension. Robinson conveyed noncompliance by altered lyrics and ad-libbing, practices that Gilbert had strictly forbidden and the FTP had kept to a minimum.⁷² One of the renditions of "My Object All Sublime" that Robinson sang, for instance, included topical allusions to contemporary black society in Harlem (of which he was an honorary mayor) as well as to its "criminals," including "The careless type of chewing gum people / Who spread their wads on the street," and "The fellow who peddles, / The counterfeit ticket / For Sweepstakes or a pool." Like Gilbert's Mikado, Robinson's Mikado could call for punishments that were sometimes violent, if silly ("The talkative barber who bends your ear, / While he barbecues you, with hot towels / Shall have a guy shove him, inside of an oven, / And bake him until he howls"). Yet at other times, his Mikado could pardon crimes, if venally, as when they related to numbers games, which Robinson loved ("chiselers, who are bankin' the numbers / Your nickels and dimes to rake, / Whenever I snarl 'em, / I'll run 'em from Harlem / Unless I gets half of the take"). In Robinson's kingdom, it is "the numbers" that "are sublime," as his parody of Gilbert's original verse makes clear:

> The numbers are sublime
> You will have to play 'em in time
> To make the punishment fit the crime
> The punishment fit the crime
> And make each prisoner pent
> Unwillingly represent
> A source of innocent merriment!
> Of innocent merriment.⁷³

Robinson's version of the song thus provided humorous commentary on Harlem by burlesquing the caricatures of blackness embedded in both the fixed lyrics of Gilbert and Sullivan's 1885 original and in the Federal Theatre's *Swing Mikado*.

Robinson also took a political turn on "My Object All Sublime" by playfully invoking a black New Deal vision for Harlem (black America) with Robinson and Joe Louis as premier and vice premier, and with satiric reference to Franklin D. Roosevelt as president for life/dictator.

Employing his own black slang coinage "copicedic" (or "copacetic") for satisfactory, Robinson sings,

> Whenever I find things, are not copicedic,
> In this domain of mine,
> I'll double the taxes, and frame up an axis,
> Between me, and Father Divine,
> . . . .
> Joe Louis is gotta,
> Be the Vice Mikado
> If I choose to take a third term.[74]

The plans of Robinson's Mikado to consolidate his domain—by "fram[ing] up an axis" with Father Divine (an African American spiritual leader who claimed to be God) and, if he "choose[s] to take a third term," to have Joe Louis (the African American world heavyweight champion) as vice mikado—link key political actors in the black Pacific. With Robinson in the role of a despotic (and colored) emperor of Japan, his use of the word "axis" here evokes the Axis powers of the Kingdom of Italy and the Third Reich, and their white dictators. His topical reference to FDR's third term, and contemporary fears of his assuming the role of president for life/dictator (Hitler's ascension to power preceded FDR's inauguration by barely a month) folds FDR into this allusion to the world's white dictatorships.

Such a couched allusion was also evident in the altered lines of *The Hot Mikado*'s Pooh-Bah, or the Lord High Everything Else, played by Maurice Ellis. In the original *Mikado*, Pooh-Bah is a pompous official who holds many offices—"First Lord of the Treasury, Lord Chief Justice, Commander-in-Chief, Lord High Admiral, Master of the Buckhounds, Groom of the Back Stairs, Archbishop of Titipu, and Lord Mayor, both acting and elect, all rolled into one" (*Mikado*, 567)—an arrangement that satirizes English titles and institutions. In *The Hot Mikado*, Pooh-Bah, in addition to the offices of state that Gilbert gave the character in 1885, assumes a new post, "Minister of Propaganda and Unenlightenment." This parody of Nazi Germany's Reich Ministry of Public Enlightenment and Propaganda (headed by Joseph Goebbels) led a *New York Post* reviewer to comment, "You can't get away from Hitler even by attending a Harlem version of Gilbert and Sullivan."[75]

In its parodic treatment of the dictatorship that is the Mikado's reign, finally, *The Hot Mikado* also evoked the Japanese Empire in the minds of some audience members. Playing as parody does on the audience's prior

3.2. Michael Todd's *Hot Mikado* (1939), starring Bill "Bojangles" Robinson in the role of the emperor of Japan. *Vandamm Studio/©The New York Public Library.*

knowledge of what it ostensibly mocks, *The Hot Mikado* furnished a fantasy of the Japanese invasion of Manchuria, transformed—as drama critic John Mason Brown quipped—into an "innocent merriment." When Robinson's Mikado arrived in the second act, Brown writes, the emperor seemed to be "invad[ing] Titipu as if it were Manchukuo."[76] Yet Robinson, preceded not by troops but by "gigantic guards carrying shields bearing his grinning puss," delivered the "dancing dynamite" rather than the horrors of war (figure 3.2); he "only so agreeably" invades Titipu (Manchukuo) that "it does not seem to be an occupation at all."[77] Brown concludes, "As the potentate of Oriental potentates, Bojangles has only to emerge as an end man in a Minstrel Show to turn his conquered province into an annex to the Cotton Club."[78]

For others, including a cartoonist for the *Chicago Daily News*, the "tap-dancing dream" of Robinson in *The Hot Mikado* only brought home the grim reality of the Japanese Empire as its negative.[79] Following a performance of *The Hot Mikado*, which was then on tour, at the Auditorium Theatre in Chicago, the *Daily News* of January 29, 1940, published an editorial cartoon entitled "Hot Mikado." The cartoon depicted a bespectacled Japanese mikado, with a likeness closer to Emperor Hirohito than to Robinson, in the role of the "Hot Mikado" (figure 3.3).⁸⁰ In the cartoon, the mikado sits atop Mount Fuji. His buttocks cover the crater, but nonetheless clouds of volcanic smoke labeled "Chinese Incident," "US Relations," "Economic Situation," and "British Relations" continue to vent around him. The cartoon suggests that Mount Fuji, representing Japan under pressure from these explosive problems, is about to erupt, and in *The Hot Mikado*, indeed it does through a stage device designed by Karson. Published immediately after America's abrogation of the 1911 Japanese-American commercial treaty, the "Hot Mikado" cartoon was a caricature of the disliked Japanese emperor (and a replacement for the well-liked "Harlemperor" played by Robinson), whom the Roosevelt administration was taking steps to confront in the Pacific. The abrogation of the treaty on January 26, 1941, freed the US government to impose economic sanctions on Japan for violating the US Open Door policy in China, as well as to increase pressure on the Japanese economy to hinder Japan's further advance into Southeast Asia.

The *Daily News* depiction of Hirohito in the role of the Hot Mikado appeared when Japanese-American relations were deteriorating rapidly into a drift toward war. Perhaps unsurprisingly at the time, it struck the Japanese consulate general in Chicago as a foreign diplomatic affront to Japan's revered imperial institution. The consulate protested to the *Daily News* against this "satirical use of the likeness of the ruler" of Japan—"a friendly nation"—whom the Japanese "regard . . . with especial reverence." In response, the *Daily News* editor replied that he would ask his cartoonists "to refrain, in future, from depicting the Japanese emperor in person, whenever they find that some other Japanese figure would serve their purpose as well." Declassified prewar files of the Japanese Ministry of Foreign Affairs indicate that this consulate general forwarded copies of the cartoon and his communications with the editor to the Foreign Office in Tokyo as well as to the Japanese ambassador and consuls throughout the United States, warning that similar cases of lèse-majesté could arise.⁸¹

Yet historical events set the conditions for negative images to prevail in representations of the mikado and redirection of the function of *The Mikado*. Abrogation of the treaty by the United States paved the way for retaliatory measures against Japan, enabling the Roosevelt administration to embargo exports of essential materials to the Japanese military—a key factor in Japan's decision to attack Pearl Harbor.

[110]   THE BLACK PACIFIC NARRATIVE

3.3. "Hot Mikado," editorial cartoon. From the *Chicago Daily News* of January 29, 1940. *Frame 0516, Ref. B02030592500, Japan Center for Asian Historical Records, National Archives of Japan, Tokyo.*

The Mikado *in the Pacific Theater*

The black Pacific script that the Federal Theatre drafted and Broadway revised in the New Deal era—a script of Africanized Japanese and their (in)humane emperor—did not end with Pearl Harbor but rather gave rise to further, darker iterations in wartime cultural programs under the Roosevelt administration. In the outpouring of war-inflamed hatred that followed Pearl Harbor, benign images of Japanese buffoonery from *The Mikado* held little appeal.[82] Charged with negative emotional valence, the Africanized imagery of the Japanese that emerged from the New Deal era versions of *The Mikado* proved a potent propaganda vehicle for the Pacific War.

For example, a segment entitled "A Lesson in Japanese" on the radio program *Treasury Star Parade* (1942–1943) depicted Japanese soldiers as modern samurai warriors reenacting the sadistic drama of cruelty and death from *The Mikado*. Sponsored by the Treasury Department and produced in cooperation with the entertainment industry, *Treasury Star Parade* was distributed to radio stations as a public service to promote the sale of war bonds and stamps.[83] "A Lesson in Japanese" was hosted and narrated by Frederic March, who in 1932 was awarded the Academy Award for Best Actor for his role in the horror movie *Dr. Jekyll and Mr. Hyde*. In a manner suggestive of a horror drama, March advised listeners to see the Japanese, "our enemy—*your* enemy in the *Pacific*," in a true light, for it is "no good to swing this way and that way, at something unseen and unknown." In March's view, Americans had previously "had the Japanese in a quaint little picture"—that is, "until *they* framed *us* at Pearl Harbor, on December seventh, nineteen hundred and forty one!" Backed up by David Broekman and his orchestra and chorus performing the Gilbert and Sullivan tune from *The Mikado*, "If You Want to Know Who We Are," March then declares, "Gilbert and Sullivan's 1885 'Mikado' got to the center of the stage . . . with music, lively, gracious music," but it is with the sounds of bombing planes and machine guns, according to March, that "the MIKADO of 1942, who is called Hirohito—and sometimes HIRO-HITLER—got to the center of the stage." The government-sponsored radio program broadcast to millions of listeners performances of the horrors of war. These were atrocities enacted in the name of "Bushido," the feudal samurai code of conduct, perpetrated in the jungles of the Pacific by "brown" Japanese, or as March called them, "monkeys."[84] Such imagery represented a clear break from the Savoy tradition of "quaint" English Japanese burlesquing English institutions, manners, and class pretensions.

The Africanized imagery of *The Mikado* was also used to frame the retributive justice—or punishment—that the US government aimed to bring upon the Japanese for what President Roosevelt condemned as their "diabolical crimes," as an incident early in the war suggests. In April 1943, Roosevelt announced in a statement released by the White House that the Japanese government had executed some of the eight captured American aviators who had taken part in the Doolittle raid over Tokyo one year previously. The president denounced the executions as "barbarous," which he expressed with "a feeling of deepest horror, which . . . will be shared with all civilized peoples." The text of the US government's protest to Tokyo—which Roosevelt instructed the Department of State to make public—not only denounced the "murder" of the American airmen in violation of the Geneva Convention governing the humane treatment of prisoners of war but also warned that "the American Government will visit upon the officers of the Japanese Government responsible for such uncivilized and inhumane acts the punishment they deserve."[85] A *New York Times* cartoon, which took its caption, "Let the Punishment Fit the Crime," from the Gilbert and Sullivan operetta, offered a visual representation of the government's intention of subjecting Japanese war criminals to capital punishment. To convey condemnation of the Japanese executioners, and to portray their punishment as just, the cartoon showed a hand labeled "Civilization" pointing a revolver at the head of a menacing black ape labeled "Murderers of American Flyers." This simian image of the Japanese, peculiarly Africanized in the discursive matrix of *The Mikado*, reveals the representational violence couched in the black Pacific script that the Federal Theatre created by conflating antiblack racism with anti-Japanese sentiment.[86]

What Batiste referred to as at once a revolutionary and conservative element in the performance of the Chicago Negro unit playing the Japanese Empire in colored brotherhood, on the other hand, was deliberately contained in media-based programs of the Roosevelt administration. The US Department of War's orientation film *The Negro Soldier* (1944)—produced by Frank Capra and written by the African American screenwriter Carlton Moss (who also plays the role of a preacher giving a sermon in the film)—is one of the few wartime films that featured black soldiers fighting the Japanese in the Pacific theater. *The Negro Soldier* depicts an anonymous black sailor firing at the invading Japanese planes over Pearl Harbor, then falling to Japanese bullets, in a staged re-creation of the battle. The sailor was modeled on Doris Miller, a navy "mess attendant" who manned an antiaircraft gun at Pearl Harbor despite having no prior training in the use of the weapon. While it promoted Miller as an icon of black American patriotism, the government film also used his story to warn against the possibility of a transnational alliance between blacks and Japanese. The narrator/preacher (Carlton Moss) thus says, "There are those who will still tell you that Japan is the savior of the colored races."[87] It was such a subversive black Pacific script that liberal wartime cultural programs aimed to foreclose.

The Roosevelt administration's preoccupation with this script is reflected in a federal study to assess African American attitudes toward World War II. The Office of Facts and Figures, a government propaganda/information agency under the direction of Archibald MacLeish, the poet and librarian of Congress, conducted the study, "The Negro Looks at the War," in New York City in April–May of 1942. Participants in the study were divided into two groups, one of which was assigned to colored interviewers and the other to white interviewers. The key question posed to participants was the following: "Just supposing Japan did come over here to rule this country, do you think the Negroes would be treated better, or worse, or about the same as they are now?" Responses to this question indicated a significant lack of concern among African Americans about the possibility of an enemy victory. Eighteen percent of participants interviewed by colored interviewers responded that Negroes would be treated "better" under the Japanese government. The result dropped to 8 percent for participants in the group interviewed by whites, but as the researchers observed, it was "significant that even eight per cent would disclose to White interviewers that they would prefer Japanese rule."[88] While the African American participants as a whole voiced "a fundamental loyalty to the United States Government and to democratic ideals," some had low expectations for their prospects in a victorious postwar America.[89] Overall, the study confirmed government officials' fears of a lack of black identification with the war effort.[90]

The seminal World War II combat film *Bataan* (1943), produced by MGM in collaboration with the Office of War Information (OWI)'s Bureau of Motion Pictures, then significantly redrafts this black Pacific script of a black-Japanese alliance in its essential function as counterpropaganda. As the first World War II movie to represent a multiracial military patrol unit, *Bataan* reflected the liberal policy that the OWI was charged with implementing through Hollywood movies. The racially integrated platoon of thirteen men in *Bataan* included the black soldier Wesley Epps (played by the African American actor and opera singer Kenneth Spencer) on terms of equality, breaking with the traditional subservient or comical racial/racist stereotypes of the Hollywood industry to usher in a new image of African Americans. The National Association for the Advancement of Colored People recognized *Bataan* as an epoch-making film and awarded a scroll to MGM.[91]

Employing Epps as a cinematic symbol of the American nation as a multiracial democracy, *Bataan* stresses the African American soldier's patriotism and blackness: he appears shirtless (exposing his black body) and is often heard humming "St. Louis Blues" (a signifier of black culture), and he fights the Japanese enemy, the real racial and cultural other in the Pacific. Epps, as well as the other soldiers, dies a sacrificial death, as does the anonymous black sailor in *The Negro Soldier*, for the American nation. As Sergeant Bill Dane (Robert Taylor) remarks, "It don't [*sic*] matter where a man dies as long as he dies for freedom." The location of a man's death may not matter in the creed of the film, but the means of his death is an important concern in *Bataan*. The Japanese army has "everything it takes to make modern war," including planes, trucks, tanks, artillery, and searchlights.[92] However, in rendering the jungle battle in the Philippines—a battle waged outside of the rules of civilized warfare—the film employs the samurai sword, a relic of medieval Japan, as an icon of Japanese aggressiveness.

Bataan emerges as a Hollywood film highly concerned with the Japanese other in the Pacific theater and thus becomes an eerie sequel to the US government-sponsored entertainment *The Swing Mikado*—even in its preservation of the central trope of swing music. In an early scene in the film, viewers hear swing music from a portable radio in the patrol's foxhole. A Latino private in this scene, Felix Ramirez (Desi Arnaz)—or "Jitterbug kid," as Sergeant Dane calls him—tunes in to a radio station broadcasting swing music. When Dane exclaims disbelievingly, "Don't tell me that's a Jap jive!" Ramirez responds, "No Sarge, no. That's good old America. That's USA." Ramirez the Jitterbug kid later dies of malaria, "shakin' himself to death."

In a scene later in the film, after the few remaining soldiers have succeeded in repelling a massive frontal attack, the soldier Leonard Purckett (Robert Walker) turns on the same portable radio to relax. However, instead of swing music, the voice of a Japanese man emerges from the radio urging the American soldiers to surrender, promising their humane treatment as prisoners of war. "You will be treated kindly, with chivalry, according to the rules of Japanese Bushido," the voice promises. "Bushido! Bushwah! You stink!" Purckett cries out as he climbs to his feet—only to be shot and killed.

This Bushido-themed Hollywood entertainment reserves the cruelest death in battle, which represents a kind of capital punishment at the hands of the Japanese, for the African American Epps. In a manner reminiscent of the decapitation scene in *The Swing Mikado* in which the Lord High Executioner Ko-Ko wields a "snickersnee" to stage a fictive decapitation of the black Mikado's son, in *Bataan*, a Japanese officer swings a samurai sword to perform an actual, brutal decapitation of Epps. In the hand-to-hand combat sequence near the film's end, he dies screaming as a Japanese officer rushes forward. The scene stops as the sword hits him squarely in the back of the neck, as in a beheading (but just before his head falls off and blood spurts out)—a "breathtaking" scene that film critic Jeanine Basinger has called "one of the most graphic and violent killings of the pre-sixties period of film history."[93]

In *Bataan*, Epps's decapitation offers a spectacle not for the pleasure of the Mikado, who plays no role in the diegesis, but rather, it would seem, for the (sadistic) pleasure of the audience. In this regard, film critic Brian Locke suggests that "for the sake of the white audience, the film must punish Epps [an African American integrated into the military] for rising above his station." Locke furthermore maintains that in *Bataan*, the racism of American society is partly "displaced" onto the Japanese, the foreign, common enemy in whose degenerate character it can be seen reflected. The "racist" Japanese in the film not only decapitate Epps but also lynch a Filipino soldier, Yankee Salazar (J. Alex Havier), whose mutilated body is found hanging by the neck, swinging slowly from a tree—iconography that references the lynching of African Americans in the southern United States of America. In Locke's argument, the film's punishment of Epps (and Salazar, a Filipino stand-in for an African American) functions as a warning against the potential "alliance between black and Japanese" that the Roosevelt administration "feared."[94]

Epps is subjected in *Bataan* to the capital punishment at the heart of the representation of the Japanese in both the original and black *Mikado*. In this post–Pearl Harbor sequel to *The Swing Mikado*, however, Epps's beheading is not only dictated by the unseen mikado (or by Uncle Sam, as Locke argues) but also driven by the imperative that, as America's representative black patriot, he severs himself violently from the cross-racial image conflation of blacks and Japanese that the FTP's *The Swing Mikado* popularized and legitimated in American culture. As *Bataan* demonstrates, the black Pacific script produced by the Federal Theatre perhaps did not vanish with its repression after Pearl Harbor but returned in mutated form to mediate racial realignments in America's geographic imaginings of the Pacific. Media-based programs of the Roosevelt administration thus played a significant role as cultural containers of a black Pacific imaginary.

[4]

"SPIES AND SPIDERS": LANGSTON HUGHES AND THE TRANSPACIFIC INTELLIGENCE DRAGNET

> Japan . . . was the hired gunman of Anglo-Saxondom . . . checkmating Russia.
> —George S. Schuyler, "The Caucasian Problem" (1944)

ACCORDING TO KATE BALDWIN in *Beyond the Color Line and the Iron Curtain*, the currently fashionable concept of black transnationalism, the "black Atlantic," entails the parochialism of excluding the Soviet Union from its critical terrain. Rather than approaching black American interest in the Soviet Union (to whatever extent it existed) as essentially the infiltration of black America by an ideology, Baldwin identifies the African American "experience" of the Soviet Union, as elaborated in the works of Langston Hughes, W. E. B. Du Bois, Claude McKay, and Paul Robeson, as crucial to the formation of a black Atlantic. In Baldwin's view, the terms "the Soviet Union" (as terra firma) and "communism" (as ideology) are not to be understood as interchangeable but rather as having different casts. To disconnect the terms is thus to reconsider black internationalism not just as a discourse but also as a product of the travels of both the ideology and black writers (whether as communists, fellow travelers, or just tourists) who crossed the Atlantic, into and out of the Eurasian Soviet Union, traversing borders that divide and connect East and West as much as they do white and colored. Retracing the transatlantic routes of African American writers who traveled extensively in the Soviet Union, Baldwin redraws the borders of a black Atlantic in which black internationalism, true to its Marxist philosophy, emerges as "a dynamic mix of antiracism, anticolonialism, social democracy, and international socialism."[1]

Baldwin's study may be seen as a provocation; it provides the theoretical beginnings for my own exploration of the influence of the Soviet Union on the black Pacific. As terra firma, the Soviet Union—the successor to the Tsarist Empire in territorial terms—was a Pacific power, bordering on the Republic of China and the Empire of Japan. Siberia, an extensive geographical region dominated by the Russians, stretched to the Pacific Ocean. As ideology, Soviet Communism—specifically, the Communist International agency known as the Comintern (1919–1943), a Soviet-sponsored agency responsible for coordinating the proletarian revolutionary overthrow of capitalism worldwide—represented both an imperative and a threat in East Asia. How then must the terrain of the black Pacific be redefined to encompass the Soviet Union? Would a Soviet-allied black American internationalism, particularly one that traverses the East-West divide, retain what Baldwin terms "a dynamic mix of anti-racism, anticolonialism, social democracy, and international socialism" as its character, whether crossing the Atlantic or Pacific? What light would such a Soviet influence cast on the development of black socialist internationalism in the Pacific region in the 1930s, when shifting alliances among the members of the Pacific Community—the Soviet Union, the United States, Great Britain, China, and Japan—rendered the international scene increasingly fluid and unstable? In other words, is the black Pacific still a "radical" or subversive formation?

In this chapter, I approach these questions by examining a transpacific route that Hughes navigated toward Soviet-allied internationalism. Hughes was known in his time as a radical of the black left. He was not a card-carrying member of the Communist Party of the United States of America (CPUSA), but his ties to the party were substantial. He was president of a communist organization, the League of Struggle for Negro Rights, and he was published most frequently during the first half of the 1930s by the CPUSA-influenced *New Masses*.[2] In 1932, Hughes traveled to the Soviet Union, crossing the Atlantic on the *Bremen* from New York, with a group of twenty-two African Americans to make *Black and White*, a motion picture about US race relations proposed by the Soviet authorities and backed by the leading black American communist, James W. Ford. When the film project collapsed, Hughes elected to stay in the Soviet Union, where he wrote and published several revolutionary poems, including "Good Morning Revolution" and "Goodbye Christ."[3] In the end, he spent a total of twelve months in the Soviet Union, touring extensively in Soviet Central Asia—a journey that Baldwin sees as the impetus behind Hughes's conceptualization of black internationalism. I take up the story of Hughes's transatlantic journey to the Soviet Union where Baldwin leaves off. In retracing his route, it must not be overlooked that Hughes's journey in 1932–1933 did not end in the Soviet Union, for it is significant that rather than doubling back across the Atlantic, he traveled further east, returning to the United States by crossing the Pacific. That is, neither Hughes's journey nor his Soviet-allied internationalism came full circle within the ambit of black Atlantic culture but rather unfolded in a broader context within which they should be reconsidered.

Hughes's wide travels in the world of the Pacific transpired under the gaze of state security forces. As he recounts in the section of *I Wonder as I Wander* (1956) entitled "Spies and Spiders," having freshly arrived in East Asia in June 1933 after a year in the Soviet Union, Hughes found himself a focus of Japanese authorities' anticommunist paranoia, which resulted in his expulsion from the country. His expulsion immediately became an international scandal; newspapers across the Pacific reported it under headlines such as "J. L. Hughes Will Depart after Questioning as to Communism," "American Negro Poet Deported by Japan as Red," "American Writer Questioned ... as Red Suspect," "Japan Ousts Negro for 'Red' Leanings," and "Hughes Refused Entry in Japan as 'Red,'" among others.[4] Hughes makes the following observation about his humiliating experience: "I, a colored man, had lately been all around the world, but *only* in Japan, a colored country, had I been subjected to police interrogation and told to go home and not return again. The word 'Fascist' was just coming into general usage then. When I got to Honolulu, I said in a newspaper interview that in my opinion Japan was a Fascist country."[5] In a press interview that appeared in the *Honolulu Star-Bulletin* shortly after his arrival in Honolulu, in US Territory of Hawai'i, Hughes is quoted as saying, "Japan's present regime ... may be compared in some degree with the Hitler group in Germany"—a trenchant criticism that the newspaper carried on its front page (August 3, 1933) along with a photo of Hughes, under a headline that characterized him as the "Negro author ... tossed out by Japanese."[6] Yet two decades later, even as he was composing his memoir about these events, Hughes suffered through another ordeal resulting from anticommunist fervor, this time in the United States at the hands of Joseph McCarthy and, more portentously, General Douglas MacArthur, supreme commander for the Allied powers in American-occupied postwar Japan. Published during the Cold War era, Hughes's memoir, as I hope to show, affords significant insight into the intelligence dragnets created by multiple states before World War II and after, a theater of secret war on dissent that was not confined to a national scope.

Hughes's testimony before McCarthy's subcommittee during the reign of McCarthyist terror that attempted to silence dissent is a story familiar to scholars. On March 21, 1953, Hughes was served with a subpoena to appear the following week before the Senate Permanent Subcommittee on Investigation and was subsequently questioned by McCarthy and his chief counsel, Roy Cohn, who had helped to prosecute Julius and Ethel Rosenberg in 1951 for passing atomic secrets to the Soviet Union (resulting in their conviction and execution). Less well known is the poet's ensnarement in a red-baiting smear campaign conducted by the American occupying forces in postwar Japan. Over the course of this campaign, MacArthur used confiscated Japanese police and court records to produce intelligence reports on the Soviet spymaster, Richard Sorge, and his ring. MacArthur's reports unsettled the American nation with their revelations—such as their naming of Agnes Smedley, a radical writer and Hughes's friend, as both a principal member of the Sorge spy ring and an American "traitor" who was undermining the war against communism in Asia, a charge with repercussions that eventually extended to Hughes. Thus, in US-occupied postwar Japan, by exposing these archived reports, MacArthur resurrected charges of Soviet espionage that had been leveled against Hughes in the 1930s.

"Spies and Spiders" is more than a narrative of the black Pacific that describes a wanderlust-inspired encounter with a colored "Fascist country."[7] MacArthur's actions and the climate of civil-liberties abuses in the McCarthy era notably influenced Hughes's retrospective narrative of his experience in Asia. He not only muted his sympathy for communism but also omitted several important particulars about his travels from the published version of *I Wonder as I Wander*, which this chapter attempts to recover through archival work on early drafts of the memoir, a pocket diary Hughes kept while in Asia, and records on Hughes amassed by the Shanghai Municipal Police (SMP) and the US State Department. In examining the black Pacific that Hughes charted, I retrace the underground (and surface) routes that the poet took in navigating, and at times slipping right through, the intelligence dragnets and discuss how *I Wonder as I Wander* committed to public memory the secret war on dissent in the 1930s, revealing it as a force that eerily shaped the international blueprint for the Cold War.

Hughes Goes to Tokyo

Hughes's Asian travels were from the start constrained by—and contingent upon—the political situation in the Far East. According to his memoir, Hughes dreamed of seeing the ancient city of Peking, China, on his way back to the United States from Moscow, and made plans to do so by rail. However, just as he was about to leave, the *Moscow Daily News* (June 2, 1933) reported that the Japanese had closed the Pogranichnaya junction connecting the Chinese Eastern and the Trans-Siberian rail lines that he would have used. Hughes was informed at Intourist that he could no longer obtain a ticket to Peking with connections via the Chinese Eastern rail line. It augured ill for Hughes that the Japanese had cut the Chinese Eastern line just before his departure; as he recalls with chagrin, "It had taken three months to achieve the point where I could leave Moscow for China—now the Japanese had cut the railroad!" (*IWAIW*, 226).

This incident bespeaks the political context in which Hughes had to pursue his Asian travels in 1933. The outbreak of the Manchurian Incident, the subsequent Japanese military occupation of Manchuria, and the founding of the puppet state of Manchukuo that precipitated Japan's withdrawal from the League of Nations had seriously affected Japanese-Soviet relations. Following its victory in the Russo-Japanese War, Japan had gained control of the southernmost section of the South Manchuria branch of the Chinese Eastern from Russia and founded the South Manchuria Railway in 1906. In northern Manchuria, a region that Japan brought under its armed control after the Manchurian Incident, the Soviet Union's influence had been established by means of its administration of the Chinese Eastern Railway. The Soviets considered themselves to have inherited the Tsarist Russian sphere of influence. The breaking of the connection between the Chinese Eastern and the Trans-Siberian lines that Hughes describes in *I Wonder as I Wander* was just one in a series of incidents that the Japanese Empire engineered to replace the Soviet Union as the dominant foreign power in Manchuria and the regional hegemon in Northeast Asia.

With the overland route closed, Hughes's best alternative for traveling to China from the Soviet Union was by sea, although this would entail a long detour via Japan. He therefore obtained a Trans-Siberian ticket from Moscow to Vladivostok in the Soviet Far East, "plus difficult Foreign Office permissions to pass through that highly guarded military port" with its fortress edging the water, and much of the town "marked off limits" to tourists (*IWAIW*, 227, 235). In response to the Manchurian Incident and subsequent developments, Moscow had reinforced its Special Far Eastern Army and constructed fortified points along the entire Manchurian-Soviet border. It also established its naval forces in the Far East in 1932 (renamed the Pacific Fleet in 1935).[8] To Hughes, arriving eastbound from Moscow, Vladivostok "looked like the last outpost of a shabby frontier" (*IWAIW*, 234), yet it was a key port on the Pacific defense front to guard against the threat of attack from Japan. This threat was well established: the Japanese army had landed in Vladivostok to intervene in the Civil War that followed the Bolshevik Revolution of 1917 in accordance with a request from the Woodrow Wilson administration, which had sent US Army forces to Siberia. The Siberian intervention ended when the Japanese forces were withdrawn in 1922, leading to the establishment of the Soviet Union. Hughes's trip to East Asia, his initial plan being derailed, thus began at this central arena of America and Japan's "undeclared war against Bolshevism" (to borrow historian David S. Foglesong's phrase).[9] At the time of his visit, the site was fraught with renewed tensions because of Japan's recent military occupation of Manchuria.

After crossing the Soviet border into Japanese-ruled Korea, Hughes found himself subjected to police surveillance. He was trailed by Japanese agents, "always a dozen or so yards behind," everywhere he went. Soon after he arrived in port in Japan proper, the police visited to inspect his papers, asking "why [he] had been in Russia, how long, and for what good reason" (*IWAIW*, 237–38). Knowing that the Japanese customs authorities "confiscate most written material coming out of the Soviet Union," he was careful not to bring with him manuscripts or photographs that might incriminate him as a radical. Hughes had sent such materials back to the United States in care of his friend and patron, Noël Sullivan.[10] These circumstances may suggest that the poet laureate of the Harlem Renaissance, arriving from the Soviet Union, was regarded as persona non grata from the outset of his stay in Japan. Despite police xenophobia, however, Hughes recalls the many Japanese people who extended their hospitality to him as being "most gracious" (*IWAIW*, 242).

Hughes was not unknown as a poet to Japanese readers and critics.[11] His picture had appeared on the front cover of a Japanese literary magazine, and in the memoir he recalls that in it, "I appeared quite Japanese, with my eyes slanting a bit" (*IWAIW*, 242; figure 4.1). As he summarily describes his stay in a letter to Sullivan a week after his arrival, he "had the grandest time imaginable in Japan": "Visited Kyoto and Nara and then came to Tokyo where the proletarian writers and the members of Tsukuji-za [*sic*] Theatre have shown me about. Seem to have seen just about everything important (for a short stay) and last night they made me an honorary member of the theatre. . . . And to go to the other extreme, at luncheon today I was guest of the Pan-Pacific Club centering in the House of Peers! So I met a few of the nobility." Hughes wound up his

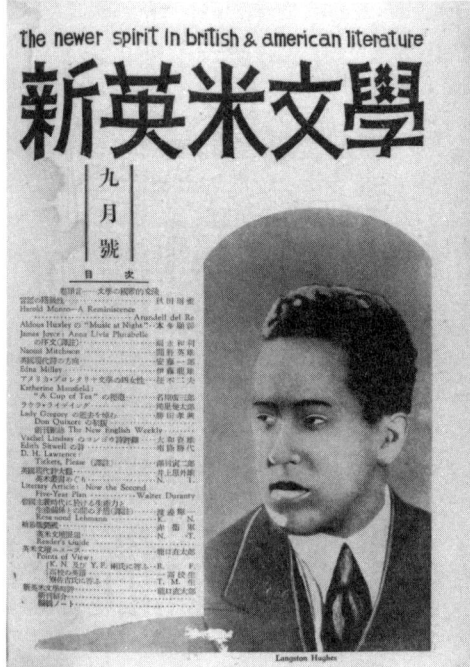

4.1. A portrait of Langston Hughes on the front cover. From the September 1932 issue of *Shin-Eibei Bungaku*. Photograph courtesy of the Museum of Modern Japanese Literature, Tokyo.

letter from Tokyo by declaring, "Over this way life is awfully exciting. You may be killed, but you'll never be bored."[12]

The poet met with warm receptions at both the Tsukiji Little Theatre and the Pan-Pacific Club in Tokyo. In an address to a luncheon at the prestigious Pan-Pacific Club, Hughes spoke on American racism and the pro-Japanese sentiments of black Americans in a manner that gratified his hosts, playing into their vanity. The following excerpt of Hughes's speech was published in an English-language daily in Japan the next day.

> I am an American, or as you can see, an American Negro, but unfortunately for me and my people, American democracy has not meant all that it has meant to the other inhabitants of my country. . . . Most of the darker peoples of the world have experienced the same sort of oppression that the American Negro has experienced, but Japan has not, because Japan has been strong against the powers of oppression and has been able to stand alone and defend herself. The American Negroes are proud of and have a feeling of sympathy and friendship for Japan. We feel it is the only large group of dark people in the world who are free and independent, and that means a lot for us psychologically, because we feel there are in the world

some dark people who are not down and oppressed. So the American Negro is glad that Japan is able to enjoy her ceremonial tea without the unwelcome intrusion of the imperial powers of the West.[13]

Perhaps Hughes was just being diplomatic, but in framing Western imperialists and the darker peoples of the world as a binary opposition of oppressor and oppressed divided along the color line, he articulates a black internationalism similar to that which George Schuyler refers to in "Japan and the Negro," as discussed in chapter 2. His assertion of the psychological importance of Japan's capacity to defend itself against invasion by Western imperialists amounted to an endorsement of Japan as a champion of the darker races, and thus the poet gave just the sort of talk that his predominantly Japanese audience at the Pan-Pacific Club would want to hear from a black American. He received a long round of applause upon concluding.

At least one member of the audience, however—the wife of a consular official of the American embassy who had been seated next to Hughes—thought that the poet had done his country a disservice (*IWAIW*, 243). In any case, it is an irony of fate that the rhetorical conformity of this speech to Japanese expectations led the Federal Bureau of Investigation (FBI) to regard it as demonstrating pan-colored identification with the Japanese on Hughes's part. Shortly after the Japanese attack on Pearl Harbor, FBI director J. Edgar Hoover was informed that during the visit of Hughes to Japan, he talked of "the alleged ill-treatment of the negroes" and predicted that "there would one day come a war in which all the colored races, black, yellow, and red, would join in the subjugation of the whites." The (female) informant who reported on the speech (who may or may not have been the wife of the American consular official—her name was blacked out in the released FBI file) claimed to have heard Hughes say that "there was a natural bond between these colored races and that their opposition to the white race should be expressed in combat." Obviously she attributed to Hughes these statements that she thought he would have made. She concluded, as quoted in a 1942 report, that "possibly HUGHES is presently engaged in subversive activities" in the United States.[14]

If the speech by Hughes in Tokyo led the informant—and the FBI—to suspect him of harboring dangerously pro-Japanese sentiments, how could the poet's stock have ostensibly fallen so abruptly in Japan that the Japanese police would label him politically undesirable so soon afterward? The actions of the police leading up to his arrest were as mysterious to

Hughes in the summer of 1933 as they may seem today. After his arrest, Hughes was astonished to learn that the Japanese police had compiled "an almost complete dossier on everything [he] had done in both Tokyo and Shanghai" and that this dossier aimed at supporting allegations that he was a Soviet spy rather than a tourist (*IWAIW*, 268).

Hughes speculates in *I Wonder as I Wander* that the police began surveilling him when he visited the Tsukiji Little Theatre. Visiting the Tsukiji was one of Hughes's first undertakings on arriving in Tokyo, and he believed that Seki Sano—a Japanese stage director in exile and a friend from Moscow who had helped him plan his trip to Tokyo—had probably written to members of the theater about his coming visit. Hughes asked a desk clerk at the Imperial Hotel where he was staying for directions to the theater. The clerk asked the poet why he wanted to see the Tsukiji, rather than the traditional Kabuki theater, which, in contrast to the Tsukiji, was a popular tourist attraction. The hotel clerk gave him directions to the Tsukiji, but Hughes suspected, as he mentions in reconstructing the course of events, that the clerk informed the police of his whereabouts: the clerk "no doubt . . . told the police where I was going," writes Hughes (*IWAIW*, 241).

Hughes's suspicion was well founded, judging from what he learned about the Tsukiji later. The Tsukiji was, in the poet's words, "Japan's only modern theatre, doing O'Neil [sic] plays, Soviet plays, and modernistic Japanese pieces in a most exciting manner."[15] Among the Soviet plays produced at the theater was Sergei Tretiakov's *Roar, China!*, a play that dramatized the arrogance of the imperialist powers in their unjust exploitation of China and that inspired the title of Hughes's poem "Roar China!" (1937).[16] Although Hughes had little inkling of the "political cloud" under which the Tsukiji lay when he asked the clerk for directions, the theater "was considered a center of left-wing activities, pacifist, and opposed to the current Japanese invasion of China." All scripts performed at the theater had to be submitted for censorship to the Metropolitan Police Board, and Hughes learned that if the actors deviated by a single word from the approved script, the "police censor" sitting at the back of the theater "had the right to ring down the curtain for the evening" (*IWAIW*, 241).

It was not simply that Hughes visited the Tsukiji (where he saw a proletarian play about "a strike of [Japanese] fishermen in feudal days") that aroused the suspicions of the Japanese police but rather that he disappeared backstage after the performance, an unlikely move for a tourist to make.[17] In Hughes's account, he went backstage in order to meet the cast, who greeted him with open arms, hailing him as "the first Negro writer to visit their theater." "It was as if Eugene O'Neill or George Bernard Shaw had walked into the theater," Hughes writes, remembering the cordial reception that he received (*IWAIW*, 241). From then on, members of the Tsukiji served as Hughes's hosts. They showed him around Tokyo and made him an honorary member of the company. Subsequently, through the acquaintances he made at Tsukiji, Hughes came to meet a circle of Japanese proletarian and left-wing writers, artists, directors, and actors who shared his intellectual views and political leanings.[18]

The Japanese police interpreted these connections as suggesting an underground network of communists, or members of the Comintern, who aimed at overthrowing the Japanese imperial government and establishing a Soviet Japan. Moreover, as I shall discuss further, Hughes fell under suspicion of being a sort of "international courier" who used the role of tourist as a cover (*IWAIW*, 266). In *I Wonder as I Wander*, the construal of Hughes's Asian travels by the Japanese police thus functions as a narrative contrapuntal to his own account of his aims, which suggests that the route the poet traveled ran perilously close to the theater of counterintelligence operations meant to block the spread of Soviet Communism into Japan by crippling the Japanese Communist Party through one mass arrest after another of members and sympathizers.

Shanghai's White Terror

The anti-Soviet police net in which Hughes became caught operated not just domestically but internationally as well, stretching as far as Shanghai, China, for which Hughes departed by ship on July 1, 1933. As biographer Faith Berry reports, "The Tokyo Metropolitan Police Board had warned the Japanese consulate in Shanghai to track [Hughes's] every move when he arrived there."[19] During his two weeks in Shanghai, Japanese intelligence agents apparently monitored his activities closely, as they had in Tokyo, compiling information that could support the case against "Spy Hughes." The question remains, however, as to why the Japanese police continued to surveil the poet with increased intensity in Shanghai. I suggest that the answer follows the status of Shanghai as a front in a cold war in Asia—that is, as a theater of an undeclared secret war against Soviet Communism in the 1930s.

Although Hughes did not detect the agents who were shadowing him, he was well aware of the presence of the Japanese in Shanghai. Upon his arrival, Shanghai looked to him "like an armed camp." Concession areas constituted the greater part of the city, including the British-ruled International Settlement and the French Concession, which defined "a color line" separating them from the Chinese and the "Negro guests." Each concession had its own jurisdiction and police force. As Hughes narrates in the memoir, "In the British area there were tall, bearded Sikhs from India. The French had imported hundreds of swarthy little Annamites to direct traffic and patrol their concession streets for them.... And there were American Marines about" (*IWAIW*, 248–49). Japanese units patrolled "in ever increasing numbers," leading foreign journalists whom Hughes met in Shanghai to predict, as he summarizes, "It won't be long until the Japs take over" (*IWAIW*, 250).

The international city of Shanghai was a haven for radical intellectuals and home to the active underground Chinese Communist Party, but it was simultaneously an environment notoriously hostile to communists and communist sympathizers. "All sorts of police" operated in the city, many focused on combating the Comintern and the Chinese left. Hughes recounts in his memoir that during his stay, "a meeting of students at the Chinese Y.M.C.A. on Szechuen Road was invaded by the British Sikh police and broken up for harboring 'radicals.'" Moreover, the "dreaded secret agents, the Blue Shirts" of the Kuomintang (KMT), the Nationalist Party that ruled much of China under Chiang Kai-shek, had earned a reputation in Shanghai as fascistic, given its members' open admiration of Mussolini, anticommunist sentiments, and use of violence (*IWAIW*, 248).[20] Under the KMT's White Terror, left-wing Chinese people lived in constant danger of assassination or midnight arrest and summary execution, while students were "imprisoned for harboring 'dangerous thoughts' against Chiang Kai-Shek" (*IWAIW*, 249). The KMT government, which concentrated its efforts on suppressing the Chinese Communist Party rather than opposing Western imperialism in China, in effect colluded with foreign powers in China in the persecution of radicals based on their shared hostility to the Comintern and Chinese (and world) revolution.

Early drafts of *I Wonder as I Wander* portray the poet as both a witness of and a participant in this cold war, which in 1930s Shanghai was indeed rather intense. In a draft of a section entitled "Shanghai Terror" that would be cut from the published 1956 version of the memoir—an omission that, as I will argue below, reflected the imperative that Hughes hide his connection with Agnes Smedley—Hughes recounts his navigation of the perilous channels of Soviet-allied internationalism in Shanghai. As he describes it, "The highly melodramatic situation that I walked into the next day in Shanghai I might have avoided had I realized the terror and tension in the Far East which the proximity of the Soviet Union, plus the undeclared Japanese-Chinese War, had created." Nonetheless, the day after he reached Shanghai, Hughes recalls telephoning the office of Harold R. Isaacs, a radical American journalist and editor of the *China Forum* (1932–1934), a newspaper serving Chinese communists. No one answered Hughes's call to the newspaper office. "No wonder!" writes Hughes, who walked over to Isaacs's apartment from his hotel and learned that Chiang Kai-shek's agents "had just wrecked [Isaacs's] office with axes the day before."[21]

According to early drafts of the memoir, Hughes had called on Isaacs at the urging of Smedley, who had left Shanghai for Russia shortly before Hughes left Moscow. He writes, "I could very well have gotten around Shanghai alone and found ways of enjoying myself. But because Agnes Smedly [*sic*] in Moscow had said I should meet Harold Isaacs, editor of the *China Forum*, according to her the brightest young American journalist in the Orient—I went to call on him."[22] Drafts of *I Wonder as I Wander* also relate that in Moscow, Smedley "had wanted to give [Hughes] a letter to Madame Sun Yat Sen in Shanghai" but that the poet had declined, in view of the turmoil in Asia.[23] Madame Sun Yat-sen (Soong Ching-ling), the young widow of the founder of the Republic of China, was known for her left-wing sympathies and unguarded criticism of Chiang Kai-shek, her brother-in-law. Nonetheless, Hughes asked Isaacs to arrange a meeting for him with her, and a week or so after Isaacs phoned Madame Sun, she "graciously invited [Hughes] to her home in the French Concession for dinner." Hughes knew that this arrangement might be "dangerous," because Madame Sun was under constant surveillance and was frequently threatened with assassination because of her politics. However, Chiang's agents could not carry out this threat, as Madame Sun—"The First Lady of China," as Hughes calls her—was too famous internationally to assassinate without great difficulty, and the meeting passed without incident. Madame Sun Yat-sen's "own car took me to my hotel," Hughes writes, adding, "Even the gangsters would hardly take a shot at her car—besides, it was bullet proof, too."[24] In the published version of *I Wonder as I Wander*, there is no mention of Isaacs's presence, and the meeting's political undertone is treated circumspectly.

A reconstruction of Hughes's sojourn in Shanghai from archival material, including drafts of *I Wonder as I Wander* and his pocket diary, suggests that Hughes made contact with others of Smedley's associates who would have been connected, whether directly or indirectly, to the Chinese Communist Party and the Comintern. Isaacs, Smedley's colleague, arranged for Hughes to meet not only with Madame Sun but also with Lu Hsin (Lu Xun), a famous modern Chinese writer, who was then under the threat of the White Terror in Shanghai.[25] Because it was unsafe to meet in public, Isaacs invited the Chinese writer to his apartment on the evening of July 5, 1933,[26] an occasion that Hughes chose to describe simply as "a private gathering" in the published version of *I Wonder as I Wander* (*IWAIW*, 256). The pocket diary that Hughes kept while in Shanghai also registers the names of leftist intellectuals and agents and their underground activities, in which Smedley and Isaacs closely collaborated. Hughes jotted down the following.

> Mao Tun—young novelist and author, "The Spring Silk Worm" . . . Is writing trilogy of development of social classes in China.
> Lu Sin [*sic*]: Gorky of China. Supervises trans. from Russian and *Japanese*. Aids young writers . . . Head L. L. Writers. . . .
> Chen Han-seng—student of rural economy . . . Am. returned student.
> Hung Shen—movie writer, Harvard man, director. Left commercialized intellectual.
> China F.—July – 20 months old. Aug. 1932, trouble, old printer's intimidated. one Chinese Printer arrested . . . Am & British Printers refused to print.
> League for Civil Rights active member and worker and Mrs. Sun. Now most workers terrorized by latest murder of Yang Chien, Pres.
> League still interested in Ruegg Case . . . Gertrude Ruegg Defense Comittie [*sic*].
> Chinese R. Aid must operate underground here. Many arrest in last 2 years. Most of work crushed.[27]

Some decoding is in order here. The "League for Civil Rights" to which Hughes refers was an organization chaired by Madame Sun in which Smedley, Isaacs, and Lu Hsin were active members.[28] At the time, the league was being terrorized by Chiang Kai-shek, whose agents assassinated its general secretary in June 1933, shortly before Hughes's arrival in Shanghai.[29] Among other campaigns, the league was involved in defending Comintern agents Paul and Gertrude Ruegg, known as Mr. and Mrs. Hilaire Noulens, who had been arrested in June 1931 in what was known as the "Ruegg Case."[30] Smedley and Isaacs had joined Madame Sun and Chen Han-seng, himself a Comintern agent,[31] on the Ruegg Defense Committee, which was working to publicize the case internationally in order to pressure the KMT to release the foreign political prisoners. The organization that Hughes refers to as "Chinese R. Aid," or the Chinese branch of International Red Aid, which was connected with the Comintern, had also mounted a campaign in support of the couple. Hughes records that this organization, under constant attack from Chiang's White Terror, which "crushed most of [its] work," had to "operate underground."

Hughes's diary also reveals his contacts with the underground literary movement in Shanghai. In the passage cited above, "L. L. Writers" refers to the League of Left-Wing Writers established in March 1930 under the direction and control of the Chinese Communist Party to promote the production of proletarian art. Lu Hsin was the head of the league. With the exception of several established writers such as Mao Tun and Hung Shen, the membership comprised young writers. In early 1931, five members of the organization (now known as "the five martyrs") were arrested by the British police in the International Settlement of Shanghai, along with other nameless Chinese Communist Party members. They were turned over to the KMT authorities in Chinese territory and slaughtered.[32] Hughes learned of this incident from Smedley in March 1931, right after it transpired, when he was in the United States. (News of the incident was also reflected in the league's appeal and manifesto in memory of the Chinese writers "butchered" by the KMT, which appeared in *New Masses* in June.)[33] Smedley wrote from Shanghai on March 13, "At the end of January, 27 Chinese Communists, among them one girl, were caught in Shanghai. They were marched to Chinese territory, graves were dug, and the soldiers ordered to bury them alive. They buried five of them alive, but the ghastliness was so terrible that even the soldiers refused to obey orders. So the officers ordered the rest shot and their bodies thrown in the grave and covered up. Two of the butchered were young writers, members of the League of Left Writers of China."[34]

The effects of the KMT's White Terror, which was as ghastly as Smedley describes, eventually extended to the *China Forum*, or the "China F." as Hughes refers to it in his diary, the newspaper edited by Isaacs. An English-language weekly printed in Shanghai but registered in the United States to avoid the Chinese censors, the *China Forum* was designed to inform its domestic and international readership on matters of importance to the Chinese communists.[35] For this reason, according to Hughes's diary, the local Shanghai KMT, as well as allied foreign authorities, obstructed its publication; according to Isaacs, even the US Department of State pressured the *China Forum* to modify its editorial stance.[36] Moreover, Chiang's agents wrecked the office of the newspaper with axes just before Hughes's visit, as described above.

To protest such civil-liberties abuses, Hughes wrote an article entitled "From Moscow to Shanghai" for the July 14, 1933, issue of the *China Forum*. In it, he offers the following scathing criticism of fascist oppression of cultural dissenters by the KMT, aided and abetted by Western imperialist powers in Shanghai: "Being a writer, naturally I am interested in how the Shanghai writers live, my fellow-workers in the craft of the word. But to my amazement, I learn that writers in Shanghai do not live—they are killed! . . . I have heard the names of the murdered writers before. See how long the list is: Hu Yeh-ping, Li Wei sen, Jou Shih, Feng Kang, and countless, nameless others. . . . Without shame the powers that be confer on young Chinese writers' bodies full of bullets—as openly as medals of honor are awarded in the West. . . . [T]he more famous they become as writers, the more surely do their names go on the death-lists of the Nanking-Shanghai militarist-imperialist dictatorship. The government of China does not like writers."[37] In contributing to the *China Forum* in this way, Hughes joined in the struggle to defend the procommunist literary front and the revolution in China (and the world).

Hughes's Chinese "fellow-workers in the craft of the word" did not fail to seek out the revolutionary writer fresh from Moscow. As Hughes relates in drafts of the memoir, "Some of the liberal writers who still dared appear in public," along with a group of journalists, gave a luncheon for him.[38] Although the final published version of *I Wonder as I Wander* tells us no more about this luncheon than that "[he] met there the young man engaged in translating [his] novel, *Not Without Laughter*, into Chinese" (*IWAIW*, 256), an account of it appeared in the Chinese literary magazine *Wen-hsueh* [Wenxue, Literature], which Lu Hsin, Mao Tun, and others launched in August 1933.[39] In a discussion during the luncheon, Hughes shared with the attendees his opinion that the best and most successful dramatic production in the Soviet Union at the time was "the latest play *Introduction* by the author of *Roar, China!*"—Sergei Tretiakov—which had been directed by Vsevolod Meyerhold. As novels in African American literature worthy of attention, Hughes cited Claude McKay's *Home to Harlem* and Walter White's *Fire in the Flint*—works of art representing the Harlem Renaissance—both of which depicted the lives of oppressed blacks, but added that both authors, once successful, had drifted away from the black masses and entered into lives of leisure. The poet predicted that US proletarian literature would not develop under American capitalism as robustly as expected; he noted that Michael "Mike" Gold and John Dos Passos were the only writers who held international status at the time and that *New Masses* was the only genuinely proletarian journal that the United States had produced.[40] Through his comments at the luncheon, Hughes supplied Chinese writers and journalists with news of the Soviet Union and of proletarian literature—just the kind of information that was vigorously suppressed in China by the KMT and would be suppressed in his memoir, as well, published in the Cold War era.

To the extent that the sojourn of Hughes in Shanghai can be reconstructed from archival materials, the route that he traveled coincided with locales associated with the Chinese Communist Party and the Comintern underground—a reality elided from the final text of *I Wonder as I Wander*. Despite the White Terror, Hughes managed to evade the calamities that befell his Chinese comrades; his extraterritorial status as a US citizen allowed him to act with relative impunity in Shanghai, where he remained beyond the reach of Chinese law. (He traveled in Asia on a US passport issued in 1931, which included a Japanese visa issued at Yokohama on June 27, 1933.)[41] However, during his two weeks in Shanghai, Japanese agents secretly tracked his movements. By the time he once again set foot on Japanese soil, the stage was set for him to be cast in the role of a spy by a Japanese police dragnet.

Mata Hari and Spy Hughes

Though Hughes's description of his encounter with the Tokyo police in *I Wonder as I Wander* has frequently been viewed as a forthright depiction of Japanese authorities' efforts to silence dissent under fascism, the poet's narrative, which unfolds like a spy thriller, imbues this view with some ambiguity, as it renders the remembered past in a manner more fictitious than factual. Particularly in the section of *I Wonder as I Wander* entitled "Spies and Spiders," as the narrative of the Japanese police pursuing suspicions that Hughes the character is a Soviet spy unfolds, Hughes the memoirist employs the 1931 "spy picture" *Mata Hari* as a subtext for evoking suspense and intrigue (*IWAIW*, 261). Given these problems of representation, "Spies and Spiders" conveys more about the memoirist writing in the 1950s than about the experiences that he is recalling.

As he describes in *I Wonder as I Wander*, Hughes sailed from Shanghai in mid-July aboard the Japanese ship *Taiyo Maru*, bound for San Francisco by way of Kobe and Yokohama. During the ship's three-day layover in Yokohama, Hughes took a train to Tokyo and once again checked in at the Imperial Hotel. By nightfall on July 23, 1933, Hughes "found [himself] back in the same pleasant room [he] had had a month before at the Imperial, with the same water lilies floating on the pond in the courtyard outside [his] window" (*IWAIW*, 261). Behind the scenes, however, his situation was assuming a wholly different aspect.

Although Hughes was perhaps unaware of how his situation had changed at the time, by introducing a screening of *Mata Hari* to the narrative of "Spies and Spiders," he invites the reader to engage in a double reading and to regard his situation not only from his perspective but also from that of the Japanese secret police. In the narrative, Hughes goes to dine at the roof garden of the Imperial Hotel, where a movie is being shown. The movie is *Mata Hari*, starring Greta Garbo, and Ramon Novarro whom Hughes had met in California (*IWAIW*, 261). Loosely based on the life of Mata Hari, an exotic dancer executed for espionage during World War I, the film follows two plot lines: Mata Hari's seduction of a young Russian officer to obtain secret documents in his possession and the efforts of the French secret police to track her down. In "Spies and Spiders," this spy picture functions to inform the reader of the suspense and intrigue unfolding around the moviegoer Hughes, an alleged spy for the Soviet Union.

During the screening of the film on the roof garden, Hughes is interrupted twice by taps on his shoulder, signaling the intermingling of the interior and exterior spy stories: "A pageboy tapped me on the shoulder politely and said I was wanted on the phone. A voice on the wire identified itself as that of a writer whom I had met previously in Tokyo, and informed me that several other Japanese writers and himself wished to honor me with a luncheon the next day so that they might see me again before I left for America" (*IWAIW*, 261).

Hughes accepts the luncheon invitation and returns to his table and the spy picture. By this time in the film, Ramon Novarro, playing the Russian officer, "[is] about to be locked in the arms of the spy, Mata Hari." As Hughes watches the intrigue approach its climax, he is once again interrupted: "Another gentle tap on my shoulder. The pageboy again. This time he said there were some gentlemen downstairs in the lobby to see me" (*IWAIW*, 261).

Hughes hesitates. He "really wanted to see how the picture about spies would turn out," but the movie "delayed so long in reaching its climax that [he] had to leave before Greta Garbo met her fate" (*IWAIW*, 261).

The suspense building around Mata Hari at the climax of the film is thus displaced onto Hughes in "Spies and Spiders," for it becomes clear that the gentlemen in the lobby are two Japanese secret agents who look like "fat spiders" and have come to entice Hughes into divulging incriminating information and perhaps to take him into custody. To ensnare Hughes in their web of intrigue, the "two portly Japanese gentlemen in European clothes" have disguised themselves as writers and have brought along a small man in a kimono, whom they introduce as "Naoshi Takunaga [sic], the famous author of *The Street Without Sun* that had been published in the United States." Tokunaga was a proletarian writer who had been recently imprisoned, as Hughes had learned while in Shanghai. Hughes says to Tokunaga, "But I thought you were in jail?" One of the disguised agents answers for the supposed writer, "He was, but is now free, and wanted so much to meet you" (*IWAIW*, 262).

The agents have succeeded in luring Hughes away from the film showing on the rooftop garden, but as he speaks with them, he grows suspicious, especially when they ask him about Mike Gold, John Dos Passos, Claude McKay, and Theodore Dreiser—"American left-wing writers"—in an effort to trick him into exposing his liaisons with a literary network of communists. He realizes that his visitors "were not writers, they were policemen pretending to be writers—except perhaps the little man in the dark kimono who [Hughes] sensed was a prisoner." When Hughes refuses to divulge any information, the writer in the kimono "smiled wanly as if to indicate he was relieved that I had found out I was the center of a police trap" (*IWAIW*, 262). Their operation having failed, the agents withdraw from the lobby, taking their bait, Tokunaga, between them. As they leave, Hughes says to Tokunaga, "I hope everything comes out all right for you," to which the latter replies in halting English, "I, too"—a closing scene evocative of male bonding that emerges between the two men, one captured and used as a decoy and the other about to be entrapped in a web of intrigue. Feeling that he has narrowly escaped the police trap, Hughes returns to his room and goes to bed "wondering how *Mata Hari* ended on the screen" (*IWAIW*, 263).

Despite the prominence of the roles that Hughes assigns to *Mata Hari* and Tokunaga in "Spies and Spiders," a chain of conflated memories problematizes his representation of both. Although Naoshi (Sunao) Tokunaga was a contemporary historical figure, he was neither a political prisoner nor in jail at the time when the poet visited Japan. Moreover, Tokunaga's novel *Taiyo no nai Machi* (The Street without Sun) was never published in English in the United States, though Hughes's characterization of it suggests the contrary.[42] Nor is there any historical evidence to support Hughes's representation of the Japanese writer whom he met in the police trap as Tokunaga. Even more problematic is a seeming slip of the pen that Hughes makes about the spy picture *Mata Hari*. After relating his encounter with Tokunaga, Hughes writes, "Pola Negri was such a beautiful spy!" (*IWAIW*, 263). This statement may lead the reader to wonder whether the movie that Hughes was watching when the police sprang their trap was *Mata Hari*, which stars Greta Garbo, or *Hotel Imperial* (L'ultimo addio), which stars Pola Negri as a chambermaid who aids an Austrian officer in defeating a Russian military spy.[43]

Regardless of whether Hughes viewed any movie on the night in question, or whether the police conducted the operation he describes, it is interesting to consider why Hughes might have recalled the movie—whichever it was—as "a spy picture" and why, in particular, he recalled it as being *Mata Hari*. Either *Mata Hari* or *Hotel Imperial* would have served equally well to add color to the narrative, as both involve Russia, spies, and romance. However, Hughes's reference to *Mata Hari* emerges as particularly evocative upon closer examination of his (inaccurate) recollection of Tokunaga as the bait in the supposed police trap that he narrowly escaped.

Given that it is historically implausible that Tokunaga played the role that Hughes describes, the reader must look elsewhere to account for both Hughes's knowledge of *The Street without Sun* and his (perhaps unconscious) urge to insert its author into the text of his spy narrative. As his research notes for *I Wonder as I Wander* reveal, Hughes did not remember the writer's name when he was drafting the manuscript. In attempting to come up with a name of a decoy writer, Hughes used the title of *The Street without Sun* as a notation. In a memo in his research notes, he types, "*INSERT*: . . . 'STREET WITHOUT SUN'—name of author," with scribbles added in the margin of the note: "Check" and "Tukonaga [sic] (Naoshi)."[44] Another memo bears related notations reading "Library-Info: . . . 'Street Without Sun' (1929) Tokunaga (Naoshi) 1899–," with the word "inserted" added.[45] The possibility exists, of course, that a Japanese agent was posing as Tokunaga in the police operation, and Hughes may have been deceived. However, it is more likely, and less speculative, to conclude that the poet's displacement (if unconscious) of Tokunaga's identity onto the person who served as bait in the police trap originated with Agnes Smedley.

It was from Smedley that Hughes learned of Tokunaga and his novel *The Street without Sun*. In 1931, the poet sent Smedley an inscribed copy of his *Not without Laughter*, a novel that a *New Masses* reviewer observed paralleled Smedley's *Daughter of Earth* (1929). In a letter that she sent Hughes in response, Smedley recommended that Hughes read Tokunaga, whose name she misspelled as "Tokagawa": "Have you read

Tokagawa's [sic] 'The Street Without Sun?' Here we have a Japanese left writer who has taken one single strike and in that [he] has shown us the entire history of the working class, wedding the deepest class consciousness with art. You have a technique of writing superior to his—but you need—as do I—his intensity of thought, his historic knowledge, his revolutionary consciousness. I have read his book only in German, but it must be in English. . . . By reading it I learned what is wrong with my book—and through it I see what is wrong with yours."[46] Thus, Hughes did indeed encounter Tokunaga but through Smedley's letter rather than in a trap that the Tokyo police set for him.

Hughes knew that Smedley worked for the Chinese Communist Party and the Comintern, and that she was closely watched as a spy, a Mata Hari, by the police. As Smedley describes in her memoir, *Battle Hymn of China*, which appeared in the summer of 1943 when she and Hughes spent time together at the Yaddo writers and artists colony in Saratoga Springs, New York,[47] the Japanese newspaper *Nichi-Nichi* of Shanghai charged her with being a member of the GPU (the Soviet secret police) and of "sleeping with military men to worm their secrets out of them." The Japanese paper declared that "this was easy" for Smedley because she was "young and beautiful and was a singer and dancer!" as Smedley recalls with amusement.[48] It is also suggestive that Smedley took the keenest interest in Hughes's arrest. When she learned of Hughes's expulsion from Japan, she wrote to him from Shanghai, asking him for an account of his interrogation in Tokyo. In particular, she wanted him to explain Japan's "charges that you admitted you were [an] 'agent.'" Smedley supplied Hughes with her "strictly confidential address," instructing him to put the address of Randall Gould, her fellow American journalist and editor of the *Shanghai Evening Post & Mercury*, on the outside of the envelope, and inside, "my initials. A. S.," an arrangement indicating that she was under police surveillance.[49] (In 1933, Gould's *Shanghai Evening Post & Mercury* carried an article featuring Hughes, then a visitor to Shanghai, quoting him as saying that he does not think Shanghai "is a very nice place" as Chinese workers are oppressed and exploited.[50]) In light of displaced memories in the text, I suggest that Hughes's compositional process and textual unconscious were haunted by Smedley and that "Spies and Spiders" may be read as a story about the poet's ensnarement in the web of intrigue that Smedley, a Mata Hari, seemed to have cast over him while in Asia (as much as one about the Tokyo police's trap, with their bait being the proletarian writer Tokunaga, whom Smedley recommended that Hughes should read). Indeed, in the McCarthy era from which the memoir emerged, Smedley was facing a charge for having spied for Soviet Russia in Asia, as I will discuss below.

The Tokyo police arrested Hughes on July 24, 1933, along with the Japanese "writer friends" who came to see him at the Imperial Hotel (*IWAIW*, 263).[51] Once they had him in custody at the Tokyo Metropolitan Police Headquarters, located across the moat from the Imperial Palace, the police interrogated him about his contacts with Sano, the Tsukiji, Madame Sun, and Isaacs. In grilling Hughes about his travels in the Soviet Union, China, and Japan, the Tokyo police revealed their deep concern with the kind of internationalism that Hughes engaged in, which they feared provided an avenue for the transmission of secret information beyond the reach of their immigration and thought-control mechanisms, because he could use his public persona as a cover to traverse state boundaries with impunity. Intent on ascertaining the nature of his Asian travels, the police questioned him about any communications that he had brought from Soviet Russia to Japan, or taken from Japan to China. Hughes recalls the police interrogation proceeding as follows.

> "How did you happen to have met Seki Sano?"
> "At Meyerhold's Theater in Moscow."
> "He did not give you letters to bring here?"
> "He did not!"
> "No one gave you messages to bring here?"
> "You flatter me," I said, "if you think I am an international courier or something. I'm not. I'm just a writer." (*IWAIW*, 266)

In the published version of *I Wonder as I Wander*, Hughes chose to omit any mention of the fact revealed in earlier drafts that notwithstanding his responses to the police, he had indeed been asked by friends in Moscow—Sano, Smedley, Tretiakov, and Si-Lan Chen—to deliver messages in Tokyo and Shanghai. Sano "wanted to give me a letter to [the] manager" of the Tsukiji, Hughes recounts. Smedley "wanted to give me a letter to Madame Sun Yat Sen in Shanghai, too." Tretiakov, who came to see Hughes off at the Moscow station and who would be executed in Stalin's 1938 purge (*IWAIW*, 197, 218), also wanted Hughes to convey a letter to Madame Sun, as did Si-Lan Chen. Hughes hastens to add, however, "With all the trouble between Japan and China in the East, I thought it best to carry no letters from anyone anywhere."[52]

In their dealings with Hughes, the police were never violent or abusive; as he describes it in his memoir, "The whole procedure was most politely done with no one raising his voice, and no show of anger or impatience when my answers led nowhere" (*IWAIW*, 269).⁵³ Nonetheless, Hughes found his treatment by the Tokyo police so disgraceful that, upon landing in San Francisco, he wrote a sharp letter of protest to the US Department of State, in which he recounts that he was detained "for more than seven hours" and that "when [he] discovered [he] was under arrest," his request to call the American consulate was refused. In this letter, Hughes describes how, at the end of the long interrogation, he was "asked to swear that [he] had brought no 'Communistic messages' into Tokio, and to allow [his] baggage to be examined for that purpose." He explains that three detectives accompanied him to his hotel, searched his baggage, read his letters, and "copied down all the names autographed on a souvenir fan which the cast of the Tsukiji Theatre had given [him]." This they designated as a "list of names." Finally the police ordered him to "go home and stay there" and to refrain from any further communication with Japanese nationals before his departure.⁵⁴ Hughes also includes these details in his memoir.

In *I Wonder as I Wander*, Hughes describes the police harassment that he encountered as extending to a fellow American citizen whom he befriended in Tokyo. After his release from the Tokyo Metropolitan Police Headquarters, Hughes goes to dinner at the Imperial Hotel, where a young man stops at his table to pay his respects. The young man, who has been "in Japan for two years, working as an industrial chemist," graduated from Hughes's alma mater, Central High School in Cleveland and ends up keeping Hughes company during his meal (*IWAIW*, 273). Hughes is at this time under surveillance by two plainclothes detectives seated at a nearby table and later he learns that the young man would subsequently be "requested to leave Japan" by the Tokyo police—presumably for speaking to Hughes (*IWAIW*, 279). For Hughes, the acme of Japan's unfair treatment of him was a made-up interview that the Tokyo police released to the press and that was published in Japan's leading newspaper, the *Tokyo Nichi-Nichi*. In his memoir, Hughes recalls with indignation that the Japanese newspaper quoted him as having said that "Japan was the destined savior of the darker races of the world, the leader of Asia, and a great stabilizing force" in China—tenets of Japanese propaganda to which he never subscribed. The newspaper, moreover, "pictured [him] . . . as praising Japan's imperialism." "This fake interview" in the *Nichi-Nichi*, writes Hughes, "seemed to me a most dastardly and contemptible thing to impose upon a visitor" (*IWAIW*, 278), one last mistreatment after many others that the Japanese police had accorded him in the summer of 1933.

From our vantage point, the made-up interview is an especially puzzling episode, for no such article appears to have been published in the *Tokyo Nichi-Nichi*, as Hughes claims. The *Nichi-Nichi* did publish two news items concerning the police interrogation of Hughes on July 25, 1933, one of which the poet read in English translation, but neither contained the interview that Hughes describes. By pointing out this discrepancy, my aim is not to suggest that Hughes fabricated the episode but rather to consider the source and extent of his knowledge of the news coverage of his expulsion in the Japanese press.

Not knowing the Japanese language, Hughes relied for his knowledge of Japanese press coverage of his case on translated newspaper clippings sent to him from Japan. The man who furnished Hughes with these clippings was Alexander Buchman, who appears anonymously in *I Wonder as I Wander* as the young graduate of Central High School whom Hughes befriended at the dinner following his interrogation. One translated article from the *Nichi-Nichi* (July 25, 1933) that Buchman sent ran under the banner headline "Colored Writer Mr. Hughes with a Certain Mission Met Advice of Exile from the Police" (Buchman also informed Hughes that this *Nichi-Nichi* article had his picture in it) and alleged that this "well known American revolutionary writer" carried "some certain 'mission'" from the Soviet Union to Japan.[55] Another article that Buchman sent to Hughes, from the *Yomiuri* (July 25, 1933), was headlined "A Red Negro Who Tried to Appeal to the Writer's Group Will Be Exiled!" The article described how the poet met with Seki Sano at the International Olympiad of Revolutionary Theatres in Moscow (organized by an affiliate of the Comintern called MORT), how Sano "handed important reports and information to him," and how the police suspected that Hughes "might divulge the information" about the Olympiad to Japanese proletarian theater organizations.[56] In a letter to Buchman dated August 21, 1933, and sent from San Francisco, Hughes complains that some of the Japanese newspapers "are as yellow in their journalism as are our worst American papers."[57]

It is not certain whether Buchman received Hughes's letter in Tokyo. On August 22, 1933, the *New York Times* and other newspapers reported, Buchman was arrested "during a police drive against 'foreign radicals and pacifists'"; he was charged with "engaging in radical propaganda" and was ordered to leave Japan immediately. Having reportedly arrived in Japan from the United States two months prior to his arrest, Buchman was accused of violating the terms of his one-month visa and, moreover, "propagating parlor bolshevism among young men and women" in Tokyo.

After his expulsion, Buchman set out on his own journey to Shanghai, where he attended the Chinese congress of the World Committee against Imperialist War, a conference "promoted and financed by the Communist International, adherence to which is a criminal offence in Japan."[58] He was one of about three hundred delegates from China and abroad (Harold Isaacs was also a delegate) who planned to attend the Anti-War Congress organized under the chairmanship of Madame Sun Yat-sen.[59] In the end, the nameless young graduate of Central High School in *I Wonder as I Wander* was not merely an "industrial chemist," as the memoir suggests; he did not live in Japan "for two years" and was not expelled simply for speaking to Hughes. The Tokyo police had cause to suspect this "friend of Langston Hughes, American Negro poet and critic" of maintaining clandestine connections to Soviet-allied organizations under the cover of tourism, much as they thought Hughes had done.[60] In his sightseeing adventure in Asia, Hughes thus did brush up against what the Tokyo police suspected to be an underground network of communists.

What emerges behind the Asian travels that Hughes recounts in *I Wonder as I Wander* is the theater of a silent war on Soviet Communism that was not confined to a national scope. Subsequent to the deportation of Hughes (and Buchman), the Tokyo police transmitted their dossier on Hughes to the Japanese consulate in Shanghai via confidential memoranda. Hughes did not know when he appealed to Washington to support his protest against Japan that the US State Department was in possession of this dossier. Upon receiving Hughes's letter of protest, the State Department sent a confidential telegram to the American embassy in Tokyo requesting a "brief statement of facts" on the Hughes case, with special instructions "*not* [to] make inquiry of Japanese authorities" (emphasis in original). The embassy wired back with the "facts" furnished to the consul general by the Tokyo Metropolitan Police Board, advising the State Department that "the action of the police seems to have been in accordance with Japanese laws and to provide no reason for representations."[61] Shortly thereafter, the State Department received a dispatch from the American consul general in Shanghai that included the Tokyo police record documenting Hughes's movements in the Far East, along with the testimony that the poet gave Japanese interrogators. This report was transmitted "from the police of the International Settlement containing information received by the police from the Japanese Consulate General."[62] In short, Hughes's dossier was transmitted in a succession of confidential memos from the Metropolitan Police Board in Tokyo, to the Japanese consulate in Shanghai, to the police of the International Settlement (where it was translated into English by the Special Branch of the SMP), to the American consulate in Shanghai, and finally to the US State Department, for shared use against Soviet Communism. In its reply to Hughes's letter, the State Department wrote that the poet's activities "apparently gave rise to a suspicion that you may have connected with some organization advocating the overthrow of the 'system of private property,' membership in which, under Japanese law, is a criminal offense punishable by severe penalties" and that the US government had no grounds for approaching their government about the matter.[63]

The Japanese police record on Hughes would remain classified until 1972 as part of the State Department's confidential file on Hughes, the "Communist negro,"[64] which it opened in 1932 while Hughes was in the Soviet Union. In the transcript of Hughes's interrogation in the Tokyo police detention room, he is quoted as saying the following:

> I am connected with the following organizations:
> International Revolutionary Writers League.
> International Revolutionary Plot Writers League.
> Authors League.
> Dramatist Guild.
> National Association for Advancement of Coloured People.
> Labourers Cultural League.
> Being a Negro I have been struggling for the emancipation of the Negros [sic] and of the oppressed masses and will continue my struggle forever. Communism aims at the emancipation of the oppressed masses but I still doubt whether or not complete freedom can be secured through the realization of communism. I do not claim to be a communist but I do not object to be regarded as a sympathizer because I sympathize with and support all Communist movements and also the oppressed people. After all I am a liberalist who is interested in communism and the struggles for the emancipation of the oppressed.[65]

In these statements to the Japanese police, Hughes explicitly acknowledged that he was a communist sympathizer, although he did not admit that he was an "agent." He insisted that the object of his visit to Shanghai in the summer of 1933 was simply "sightseeing."[66]

However, the police in the International Settlement, or more precisely the Special Branch of the SMP, which relayed the Tokyo police record to the American government, may not have accepted Hughes's tourism claim. The Special Branch, which operated, in effect, as a Far Eastern arm of MI6, the British Secret Intelligence Service, also opened a file on

Hughes. The Shanghai police file card on Hughes stated as his antecedents, "Langston Hughes is an American journalist of some repute among proletariat writers. He is at present in Moscow (10.5.34) [*sic*] where he is contributing work to various of the Moscow newspapers. He has contributed a number of articles to the organ of the International Union of Revolutionary Writers, 'International Literature' which is published in Moscow"; the card thus highlights the poet's links to the Comintern.[67] An SMP document entitled "James Langston Hughes—American Negro Intellectual" reported that Hughes was "frequently seen whilst in Shanghai" with Harold Isaacs, whom "he had never previously met," but that Isaacs's "name was given him by a mutual friend"—namely, Smedley—"whilst he was in Moscow." "There seems to be little doubt," observes the document, that "Isaacs and one or two other local hot-heads have cajoled him into saying what he has" about Shanghai, as not being a "nice place," in the aforementioned article of the *Shanghai Evening Post & Mercury*—thus suggesting the influence of the communist left in China on Hughes.[68]

In *I Wonder as I Wander*, Hughes's Asian travels end with his arrival in Hawai'i following his expulsion from Japan. Significantly, the narration of this final scene on US territory in the Pacific registers the presence of an FBI agent. When the *Taiyo Maru* steamed into Honolulu, Hughes found not only reporters awaiting him at the pier but also an "F.B.I. man," who stood some distance apart from them. Introduced by a newsman, Hughes reports that he "shook hands" with the FBI man and notes that the man subsequently "stood around while [he] repeated for Honolulu newsmen the details of [his] Tokyo police experience." Why the FBI agent turned up "to *meet*" him is not explained; in the narrative, the agent appears briefly, only to disappear without uttering a word (*IWAIW*, 278–79). Yet given that *I Wonder as I Wander* was published in the 1950s, the appearance of the FBI agent may be understood to signal to the reader that the intelligence dragnet to silence dissenters, which ensnared Hughes in its spiderlike web, had already spread across the Pacific by the 1930s.

"My World Will Not End"

Hughes's wanderlust-inspired travels through Cuba, Haiti, the Soviet Union, China, Japan, Mexico, Spain, and France in *I Wonder as I Wander* may inspire a celebratory view of their positive possibilities. However, Hughes closes the memoir, significantly, with a description of his accidental reunion with his Japanese comrade Seki Sano in Paris on New

Year's Eve, 1937. As the bells toll, the two old friends lift their glasses and toast both the entrance of the new year and the (seeming) exit of the poet's radical decade. The narrative thus draws this Japanese stage director into the poet's international orbit once again, aligning the lives of the two "fellow travelers" of color—one cast out of Japan on suspicion of being a Soviet spy and the other, as the reader learns, cast out of the Soviet Union for similar reasons.

Hughes and Sano's meeting in Paris on December 31, 1937—if it occurred—was apparently a matter of sheer chance.[69] "We were surprised to see each other," Hughes writes in the memoir. Hughes recalls that as he and Sano entered the glass-encircled winter terrace of a sidewalk café "to exchange news," Sano began to talk about his and the poet's respective expulsions from Japan: "I read a year or two ago in the Moscow papers about your being expelled from Japan. I'm sorry that happened to you in my country. But I am expelled, too. I cannot go back" (*IWAIW*, 403–4).

The reader of *I Wonder as I Wander* may assume from this exchange that Sano was in France because he had been "expelled" from Japan, as Hughes had been in 1933, and this assumption would, indeed, reflect an element of the truth. The proletarian theater activist Sano (who is also now remembered in Japan as a translator of the *Internationale*, the official anthem of international communism) had been arrested for communist sympathies three years prior to Hughes's visit to Japan. Forced to renounce his political beliefs while in custody, and paroled upon doing so, Sano fled Japan in 1931, after which he moved to the Soviet Union, via the United States, to accept an invitation to serve in Moscow as the representative of the Japanese proletarian theater league (PROT) at the International Workers' Dramatic Union. Sano settled in Moscow in November 1932, where he worked in the Meyerhold Theatre under the renowned Russian theater director Meyerhold, and actively organized the International Olympiad of Revolutionary Theatres.[70] Hughes met Sano while he was working at the Meyerhold Theatre, as noted above (*IWAIW*, 266).

Yet there is more to the story of how Sano turned up in Paris. Sano was "expelled," properly speaking, not from Japan, from which he had fled, but from the Soviet Union. As is recalled in *I Wonder as I Wander*, this Soviet-inspired exile from Japan was one of the "worldlings" whom the poet met in Moscow, "sympathetic liberals friendly to 'the Soviet experiment'—but many of them unsympathetic when they departed" (*IWAIW*, 210). It was not disillusionment, however, that led Sano to depart from the Soviet Union, leaving his Russian wife and child behind. In point of fact, Sano was ordered out of the country by Soviet authorities. When Sano says that he "cannot go back" in Hughes's account, he does not necessarily mean to Japan, for he can no longer return to the Soviet Union where he had his home and his family either (he eventually died in exile in Mexico in 1966).

By the time of Hughes's reunion with Sano in 1937, the Soviet Union was at the height of both the Stalinist purge and a wave of antifascist paranoia in response to the Anti-Comintern Pact that Japan had concluded with Nazi Germany. The Soviet government was aware of the secret supplementary protocol to the pact—thanks to its success in code breaking—according to which the pact was directed against the Soviet Union. Sano's expulsion was just one of countless actions taken in the Stalinist terror against the Japanese.[71] Virtually all Japanese in the Soviet Union, including Communist Party members and sympathizers, fell under suspicion of espionage. As *Pravda*, the news organ of the Soviet Communist Party, warned in July 1937 (a month before Sano's expulsion), Japanese residing in the Soviet Union—generally, leftist intellectuals such as Sano—were all "potentially Japanese spies" that the Japanese government planted in the country.[72] Some such resident Japanese were shot to death, or "liquidated" in the parlance of the era, while others were sent to concentration camps or prisons, and still others, like Sano, were expelled.

As a corollary, the Soviet paranoia regarding Japanese residents of the Soviet Union sparked a purge of Russian artists who were connected with the alleged spies. The case of the world-famous stage director Meyerhold was especially tragic. Early in 1938, the Meyerhold Theatre was closed down for being "alien to Soviet art," and Meyerhold himself was arrested in June 1939. The preliminary case against Meyerhold was based on a "confession" extracted under torture by the Japanese Communist Party member and stage director Ryokichi Sugimoto (also known as Yoshimasa Yoshida), who had been a colleague of Sano in Japan. Sugimoto fled Japan via Sakhalin early in 1938 to seek refuge in the Soviet Union, only to be arrested by the Soviet border police as a spy of the Japanese government. In his coerced "confession," Sugimoto named Sano as a spy, and Sano's collaborator, Meyerhold, "as an agent of Japanese intelligence who, among other terrorist activities, had been involved in plotting an assassination attempt against Stalin during a visit to his theater." The arrested Russian theater director was also tortured, made to "confess" to being a Japanese spy, and shot on February 2, 1940 (exterior to Hughes's memoir, the narrative of which ends on New Year's Day of 1938).[73]

Thus, in the moment framed by the closure of *I Wonder as I Wander*, Japan and the Soviet Union—the two Pacific Rim states—emerge as eerily resembling one another in their reactionary paranoia toward aliens traversing state boundaries, as well as in their persecutions and civil-liberty abuses to silence dissent. Ultimately, Hughes seems to find his grounding in neither of the two compass points of black internationalism—that is, neither from Japan as champion of the darker races nor even from the Soviet Union as torchbearer of proletarian liberation. Rather, "America" is the place on the globe that holds out hope as "home" for Hughes. Thus Seki Sano says to Hughes in their final encounter, "There are too many people wandering around the world now who can't go home. . . . Lots of them are in Moscow. More are in Paris—people from the Hitler countries, from the South American dictatorships, from China, from my own Japan. No exiles from America—though I wouldn't be surprised if the day didn't come." To this Hughes replies, "That's one nice thing about America. . . . I can always go home—even when I don't want to" (*IWAIW*, 404). Yet Hughes's travels in *I Wonder as I Wander* do not end with a simple gesture toward a return to America. Hughes writes the following:

> Where would I be when the next New Year came, I wondered? By then, would there be war—a major war? . . . Would civilization be destroyed? Would the world really end?
> "Not my world," I said to myself. "My world will not end." . . .
> I repeated to myself, "My world won't end."
> But how could I be so sure? I don't know.
> For a moment I wondered. (*IWAIW*, 405)

Hughes's memoir closes with the poet in Paris wandering and wondering not toward but away from home. As the memoir reaches its troubled ending, which is at once a nonending, Hughes insists, "My world will not end." *I Wonder as I Wander* thus recounts a past that has refused to end, one that continued to haunt Hughes even as he wrote the final version of the text.

I suggest that what made it so difficult for Hughes to bring his radical past to a close is the historical moment of fear and suspicion of 1950s America, when he faced a charge from a red-baiting smear campaign conducted by the American occupation in postwar Japan. The campaign was an offshoot of the Cold War project to contain the spread of Soviet Communism in Asia, which the US occupation forces had inherited, ironically, from "fascist" Japan. Over the course of this campaign, General

MacArthur and his chief of military intelligence, or G-2 Tokyo, Major General Charles A. Willoughby (whom the general described as "my lovable fascist"), issued reports on a Soviet spy ring headed by the spymaster Richard Sorge. Sorge had been operating in Shanghai and Tokyo when Hughes visited Asia in the 1930s and was eventually executed by the Japanese wartime government on November 7, 1944.[74] Confiscated prewar Japanese police files and court records that survived wartime bombing reveal that Sorge had gathered information through Hotsumi Ozaki. Ozaki was a journalist and political think-tank member in the brains trust of the Japanese government's Konoye Cabinet, and as well was a translator of Agnes Smedley's novel *Daughter of Earth*. He was hanged for treason on the same day as Sorge. Later, Willoughby and Mitsusada Yoshikawa, a Japanese procurator who investigated Sorge, testified before the House Un-American Activities Committee (HUAC) that Moscow had received word from Sorge of the planned Pearl Harbor attack beforehand, and the spy had even used his influence "to a certain extent" to direct Japanese aggression southward in the Pacific toward the United States, rather than northward toward the Soviet Union, with the end result being the attack on Pearl Harbor.[75]

A February 1949 press release on the intelligence report from Tokyo entitled "The Sorge Spy Ring: A Case Study in International Espionage in the Far East" from the Department of the Army in Washington aroused widespread controversy in the United States, not least because it characterized an American citizen, Smedley,[76] as both a member of the Sorge spy ring and a perpetrator "of the hoax that the Chinese Communists were . . . only local agrarian revolutionists" with no connections to the Soviet Union. Smedley, reportedly an "American-Soviet spy," "recruited Ozaki" for Sorge in the Shanghai phase of his ring in the early 1930s, when Sorge was posing as an American journalist named Johnson. The report also claimed that Smedley's "hoax" swayed American foreign policy on China, purportedly undermining the war against communism in Asia and ultimately enabling communism to overrun China despite America's support for Chiang Kai-shek, who would have remained America's ally in Asia. "The harm has been done," the report asserted, but the harm could be diminished "if [Smedley] is now exposed for what she is, a spy and agent of the Soviet Government."[77]

Smedley reacted vehemently to this public account of her espionage activities. She termed it a "despicable lie," pointing to the fact that the charges were based on the files of the prewar Japanese secret police, "the most discredited agency of that enemy government." Smedley threatened to sue MacArthur for libel if he waived his official immunity. In her view, the general's real end in libeling her was to "'condition the American people into allowing him' more troops and money to build Japan into a mighty military base" and thus to build up a former enemy, Japan, as an anti-Soviet bastion against Red China, because of "the defeats suffered by the Chinese Nationalist Government."[78] Confronted with Smedley's recriminations, the army in Washington admitted to a "faux pas" in making the report from Tokyo public. "A person is innocent until proven guilty," the army allowed, noting that they had insufficient proof of the accusations that they had leveled at the time when the report was issued.[79]

Smedley's defiance—and the army's retraction of their public release of the "secret" report with "quasi-apologies"—insulted Willoughby and spurred him to launch an "epic search" for further proof to authenticate the Sorge spy story.[80] With the assistance of the Central Intelligence Agency (CIA), Willoughby tracked down and procured a substantial portion of the records of the SMP prior to the communist takeover in China on October 1, 1949. The SMP files proved to be a Pandora's box, opening up "an astonishing vista on a fantastic array of Communist fronts, ancillary agencies, and the vast interlocking operations of the Third International in China."[81] Corroborating the reports from Tokyo, they revealed Smedley's underground activities and the numerous Chinese communist front organizations for which she worked, including the Noulens Defense Committee set up by the International Red Aid and the China League for Civil Rights. Moreover, the SMP records named Smedley's "red and pink associations," as Willoughby dubbed them, including those with Harold Isaacs, Lu Hsin, Mao Tun, and Langston Hughes. As discussed above, the file on Hughes that the Special Branch of the SMP opened in the early 1930s was among the records obtained by Willoughby and the CIA. Willoughby thus successfully and hostilely recovered the radical past of Hughes, or the "American Communist and staff member of the International League of Revolutionary Writers," as he calls him, from the dusty archives of Asia.[82]

The spy charges against Smedley, fueled by the Cold War red-baiting campaign, continued to be leveled even after her untimely death in May 1950 while under investigation by HUAC, and they had been extended to Hughes. In 1952, Willoughby published an innuendo-filled book entitled *Shanghai Conspiracy: The Sorge Spy Ring*, in which he quotes Hughes's poem "Goodbye Christ" (a revolutionary poem that Hughes wrote while in the Soviet Union) to demonstrate Hughes's communist sympathies. "Goodbye Christ" was a profane verse of his Soviet year that he later "dismissed ... as a regrettable error of his immature youth." Hughes—according to biographer Arnold Rampersad—practically begged the publisher E. P. Dutton not to quote his poem in Willoughby's book, but his pleas were unsuccessful.[83] Willoughby quotes the poem as epitomizing the "traitorous and corrosive quality" of "the International Union of Revolutionary Writers and its American offshoot, the League of American Writers," of which Hughes and Smedley were members. In view of this "typical sample of Hughes's poetic style," Willoughby argues, "It requires no imagination to know what would happen to the Christian churches in America if men of his ilk were ever to get the upper hand. All anyone has to do to visualize the blood bath which they would stage is to refresh one's memory about the pattern of the Soviet purges."[84] A year later, Hughes was summoned to appear before McCarthy's subcommittee.

During the Cold War smear campaign that US military intelligence launched in Tokyo, recouping the past was a political imperative. In *Shanghai Conspiracy*, the reader is presented with a Pacific-centered world map that designates the itineraries that Comintern agents, fellow travelers, and associates in the 1930s navigated from Moscow, Tokyo, and Shanghai to San Francisco and beyond. The map, printed on the front endpapers, indicates a worldwide espionage network, or what Willoughby called "the Communist 'jehad' for the subjugation of the Western world," the routes and headquarters of which suggestively overlap with Hughes's route through Asia.[85] In the published version of *I Wonder as I Wander*, Hughes largely eliminated political undertones from his black Pacific narrative, to the extent that he chose to accord Smedley only a minimal presence in the text. Nonetheless, the narrative of Hughes's framing as a Soviet spy in prewar Japan makes *I Wonder as I Wander* resonant with the historical moment at home, where McCarthyist terror had reached its height and America had begun its anticommunist war in Asia, in which Japan, the former "fascist" power, played the role of America's principal ally against a communist China. Thus, Hughes's memoir not only serves as a testimony of his encounter with a colored "Fascist country" but also offers insight into the transpacific intelligence dragnets that endeavored to silence dissenters as eerily prefiguring the international Cold War blueprint.

[5]

THE MANCHURIAN PHILOSOPHER:
W. E. B. DU BOIS IN THE EURASIAN PACIFIC

The vast struggle in the Pacific which broke out at Pearl Harbor on December 7, 1941, was merely the logical result of the events which began in Manchuria. The road to World War II is now clearly visible; it has run its terrible course from the railway tracks near Mukden to the operations of two bombers over Hiroshima and Nagasaki.
—Henry L. Stimson, *On Active Service in Peace and War* (1947)

THERE IS PERHAPS NO greater cinematic representation of the Cold War symbolism of Manchuria than *The Manchurian Candidate* (1962), a political science fiction film based on the 1959 best-selling novel of the same name by Richard Condon and starring Frank Sinatra. What this Cold War film represents, among other things, is the "terror" of Chinese communist brainwashing, for which Manchuria, a historical name given to a geographic region in Northeast Asia, stands as a potent metaphor. The film depicts how the Soviets and the Chinese Communists brainwashed American POWs during the Korean War (1950–1953), and in particular how they turned Staff Sergeant Raymond Shaw (Laurence Harvey) into a sleeper agent, or an amnesiac assassin. The brainwashing takes place in a research pavilion decorated with portraits of Joseph Stalin and Mao Tse-tung, in Manchuria, where the captured POWs are flown by helicopter. Following his conditioning in Manchuria, Shaw's chief mission in the United States is to assassinate the presidential nominee at the Republican National Convention, so that Senator John Iselin (Shaw's stepfather) is installed as US president. The red-baiting Senator Iselin, a stand-in for Senator Joseph McCarthy, is in fact a puppet—the Manchurian candidate—whose strings are pulled by his wife (Shaw's mother) who is a communist agent. In the final climactic sequence of the film, Captain Bennett Marco (Frank Sinatra), a brainwashed ex-Korean War POW himself, understands the whole story of the international communist conspiracy: that "the Soviet Union and the People's Republic of China conspired with purported

American anti-Communists, who linked themselves with fascist tendencies in American life, in order to destroy the American republic."[1]

As I have been suggesting in this study, Manchuria served as the linchpin of modern regionalism in East Asia. In the 1950s, the region gained a new geopolitical valence associated with the neologisms "the Manchurian candidate" and "brainwashing" of the popular Cold War lexicon in the United States. At the end of World War II, the regional order of the Japanese Empire had collapsed. Manchukuo,[2] the Japanese puppet state of Manchuria, was invaded by the Soviet Union on August 8, 1945, two days after the atomic bomb was dropped on Hiroshima. Manchuria immediately became a site of the civil war fought between the Chinese Communist Party (CCP), led by Mao, and the Kuomintang (KMT), the governing party of the Republic of China under Chiang Kai-shek. As historian Victor Shiu Chiang Cheng observes, Mao imagined China's "Madrid" in Manchuria. "With its political, strategic, economic, and geographical importance," Manchuria, though covered by the Sino-Soviet Treaty of August 1945 and hence in the hands of the KMT, was what Mao coveted for the Communists' expansion. In April 1946, Mao's army seized Hsinking (Changchun), the old capital of Manchukuo. This military conquest "symbolized the Communists' control of Manchuria." "The civil war in Manchuria," Cheng remarks, "foreshadowed the open general war in China over the next three years," which would end with Mao's proclaiming the establishment of the People's Republic of China in mainland China in October 1949.[3]

We now know—thanks to Bernardo Bertolucci's epic film *The Last Emperor* (1987)—that somehow the symbolic apogee of the dissolution of Manchukuo was a successful effort by the Chinese Communists to reeducate Pu Yi, the last emperor of the Ch'ing (Manchu) Dynasty and puppet emperor of Manchukuo. The opening set of the film is a train station on the Chinese-Russian border in Manchuria. The scene depicts the repatriation of a trainload of "war criminals," including the middle-aged and worn Pu Yi (John Lone), from the Soviet Union. Pu Yi, who had been captured by the invading Soviet troops at the end of World War II, is now handed over to the recently proclaimed People's Republic of China in 1950. The train brings Pu Yi home to Manchuria, which he now has to learn to call the "Northeast" (Northeast China), and to the detention center of the Fushun Bureau of Public Security, otherwise a reeducation camp. After undergoing ten years of rehabilitation as "Prisoner 981," the ex-emperor is released as a reformed citizen of Mao's China. As the prison governor (Ying Ruocheng) declares, "As a result of remolding through labor and ideological education during his captivity, he has shown that he has genuinely reformed." The final screen of the movie shows China during the Cultural Revolution in 1967. In the penultimate episode that appears exterior to Pu Yi's autobiography *From Emperor to Citizen* (1964–1965), the main source of Bertolucci's screenplay, Pu Yi comes unexpectedly upon a parade of Red Guards brandishing pictures of Mao and waving little red books. They herd before them a group of "traitors," among whom is his former prison governor made to wear a dunce cap and a chest placard reading "counter-revolutionary." Pu Yi witnesses the humiliation of the governor, his former "teacher," at the hands of the fanatical Red Guards and his being forced to "kowtow to Chairman Mao"—a command that renders Mao Communist China's emperor. *The Last Emperor* ends with scenes of a horde of modern American tourists in China in the 1980s. The tour guide, with her Klaxon emitting the notes of Yankee Doodle, leads the tourists into the Hall of Supreme Harmony, the ancient imperial throne of the Ch'ing Dynasty, where Pu Yi was crowned at age three, and announces that he died in 1967. The film thus leaves the viewer with a question as historian John K. Fairbank astutely frames: wasn't Pu Yi, the mortal representative of the puppet state Manchukuo, in the end "the world's champion puppet— first under the Ch'ing court, then under the Japanese militarists, [and] finally under the Chinese Communists"?[4]

I begin with this brief discussion of post–World War II paradigmatic cinematic representations of Manchuria because they point in the direction of a series of interrelated issues that I want to discuss in relation to W. E. B. Du Bois, the preeminent African American scholar-intellectual who is generally thought to have become a dedicated Stalinist and Maoist in the 1950s. These include the hitherto ignored experiences and responses of Du Bois to Manchukuo, the unsubstantiated rumors in the US Congress that Du Bois was a (puppet) propagandist for the Japanese imperial government, and the ambivalence at the heart of Du Bois's symbiotic sympathies both for Soviet Russia and socialism and for the Japanese Empire in pre–World War II Asia.[5] While Du Bois is known to have become a devoted admirer of Communist China in the 1950s, in the 1930s, as Gerald Horne has observed, "Du Bois, a socialist of sorts and a friend of Soviet Russia, sought to reconcile [China] with Japan as this unlikely prospect steadily slipped away in reality."[6]

Du Bois's problem indicated by Horne is succinctly described by Bill Mullen in what he considers to be the problem of "Afro-Orientalism," which Mullen defines as both emerging from and revising "Marxian analytical contributions on colonialism and imperialism." Asia played a complex role in the grand arc of Du Bois's internationalism after Japan's defeat of Tsarist Russia in 1905, and Du Bois continued to champion the ascent of Japan to power and to colonialism and imperialism. In Mullen's view, Du Bois's seemingly radical failure to oppose the Japanese Empire was partly due to the influence of the complex of events of the 1930s and was partly "fostered by selective support for Japanese nationalists in the United States," among whom was Yasuichi Hikida, "an agent of Japanese expansionism." The evolution of the political and cultural thought of Du Bois and Afro-Orientalism, however, did not end there. Indeed, argues Mullen, "it was later reflection and rumination on his Japanese 'mistake' that moved Du Bois ultimately and decidedly in the firm direction of a materialist analysis of imperialism, race, and capitalism."[7] Du Bois's encounter with the Japanese Empire thus moved him in the counter-direction of support for Mao's China, the right political objective that Du Bois attained in the end.

Compelling though Mullen's teleological narrative of interpretation is, I would like to rethink this Asian arc of Du Bois's internationalism over time by teasing out, not so much a discontinuity (and counter-direction) that is obvious, as a continuity that is more subtle but also critically important. The difficulty of seeing the mutual implications of his supports both for the Japanese Empire and for Mao's China and the Soviet Union perhaps means that many of us who work on Du Bois and Asia tend to remain caught in a prevalent (that is, post–World War II) geopolitical map of East Asia—a framework in which Manchukuo (1932–1945), once a regional linchpin and a source of international conflict, is conspicuously absent, erased as it is into the People's Republic of China (1949–). Based on Du Bois's actual travel narrative that tells a story of the now-defunct Empire of Manchukuo, this chapter proposes to examine a black Eurasian-Pacific geography that Du Bois charted.[8]

At the center of this chapter is an analysis of Du Bois's largely neglected 1936 Eurasian continental rail tour that took him from Nazi Germany via Soviet Russia to China. Du Bois landed in Manchuria as the first African American reporter to cover Manchukuo—a new colored nation on the Pacific Rim that had appeared in atlases only four years prior, with demarcated territory bordering the Soviet Union, the Republic of China, and the Empire of Japan. My primary texts in this chapter are a chapter entitled "I Gird the Globe" from Du Bois's unpublished, book-length manuscript "Russia and America," and dispatches that he sent to the *Pittsburgh Courier* from Manchuria. As with *The Last Emperor*, Du Bois's point of entry into Manchuria is a train station on the Chinese-Russian border (then the Manchukuo-Soviet border). In 1934, writing in his signature editorial "As the Crow Flies" in *Crisis*, the official organ of the National Association for the Advancement of Colored People (NAACP), Du Bois had offered his congratulations to Pu Yi on his assuming the imperial title of the Emperor Kang Teh of Manchukuo. In Du Bois's view, the coronation marked an important step toward the union of the Empire of Japan and the Empire of Manchuria, heralding a regionally integrated Asia. Du Bois writes, "Watch, colored America, with beating heart, the first fateful step toward a new united Asia. When the Emperor, Kang Teh, mounts the imperial throne and joins Japan and Manchuria in one white world–defying state."[9] However, in Du Bois's 1936 travel narrative, neither Pu Yi nor the Japanese militarists are central characters of Manchukuo. Instead, Yosuke Matsuoka, Japanese diplomat and president of the South Manchuria Railway (SMR) Company, emerges as the architect of Manchukuo. Against the backdrop of the dominant understanding of Manchukuo as a state created by Japanese militarists with Pu Yi as their puppet, Du Bois offers an alternative Manchurian narrative. My intention in the present chapter is to tap the critical potential of this Manchurian narrative that tells about the geopolitical awareness Du Bois gained when he thought he was witnessing the actualization of a new model of government for colored peoples.

Du Bois and Japanese Imperial Propaganda

Important recent theoretical work posits the centrality of Asia to Du Bois's internationalism.[10] However, a major problem surfaces when scholars consider the implications of the African American intellectual's apology for the Japanese imperium that expanded by military dominance in East Asia. As biographer David Levering Lewis has shown, Du Bois issued unnervingly pro-Japanese messages in his newspaper columns and lectures at black colleges in the 1930s.[11] As discussed below, in 1939 Du Bois's actions gave rise to rumors in the US Congress that he was a paid propagandist for the Japanese imperial government. Further, it led to his investigation by the Federal Bureau of Investigation (FBI), which opened a file on Du Bois in 1942. The FBI found no evidence that Du Bois engaged in subversive activities. Nonetheless, they placed Du Bois on a list of persons to be held in "Custodial Detention" in the event of a national emergency.[12] One document included in the file quoted Du Bois as having allegedly claimed that "in the Japanese he saw the liberation of the negroes in America, and that when the time came for them to take over the United States, they would find they would have help from the negroes in the United States"[13] when he made a speech during his stay in Japan in 1936.

There is a growing consensus among scholars of Du Bois that his defense of the Japanese Empire in the 1930s is not just an embarrassing anomaly but also a complex result of multiple factors of influence. One notorious example is Japanese propaganda operations that targeted the preeminent black intellectual. In his prize-winning biography of Du Bois, Lewis pointed out that Du Bois's circle of acquaintances included Yasuichi Hikida, an alleged Japanese agent. In Lewis's account, Hikida began his approach by making the acquaintance of Arthur Schomburg, a Harlem bibliophile, whose sponsorship enabled Hikida to infiltrate "the inner circles of the Talented Tenth" of black America. This group included, in addition to Du Bois, James Weldon Johnson, George S. Schuyler, Walter White, Claude McKay, Dorothy West, William Pickens, Rayford Logan, Claude Barnett, and Percival L. Prattis. Du Bois, according to Lewis, was "the outspoken representative of a group mind-set ideally made for Hikida's purposes" to sway black public opinion. Having established himself in this circle, Hikida drew sufficiently close to Du Bois to facilitate the Asian leg of Du Bois's tour in 1936, which included five months in Germany sponsored by the Oberlaender Trust and a journey across the Soviet Union to visit China and Japan. Hikida arranged Du Bois's stay in Japan as a quasi-state guest.[14]

Lewis's suggestion that Du Bois's trip to Japan was partly a product of Japanese "negro propaganda operations" would certainly explain why Du Bois's trip unfolded so differently from the journey that Langston Hughes undertook three years previously. As discussed in the previous chapter, the poet, arriving in Japan from Moscow in 1933, quickly fell under suspicion of being a communist "international courier" and was expelled from Japan by the Tokyo police. In contrast, the Japanese authorities treated Du Bois as an honored guest. Upon entering Japan, he found that special arrangements had been made for his lecture tour around the country. However, I would like to question this suggested relationship between Du Bois and Japan's "negro propaganda operations."

A file in Japan's national archive reveals that a detailed plan for Du Bois's stay was well in order prior to his arrival. The plan includes both official and nongovernmentally sponsored activities.

DECEMBER 11 (FRIDAY)
Morning: Arrival at Tokyo station
A.M.: A ceremonial call at the grounds of the Imperial Palace and Meiji Shrine
Noon: Luncheon at the Pan-Pacific Club
P.M.: Visits to newspaper offices
Evening: A reception hosted by the Information Department, Ministry of Foreign Affairs

DECEMBER 12 (SATURDAY)
A.M.: A visit to the Tokyo Imperial Household Museum
P.M.: A visit to the Kabuki Theatre upon the invitation of the Kokusai Bunka Shinkokai (KBS)

DECEMBER 13 (SUNDAY)
A sightseeing tour to Nikko (KBS)

DECEMBER 14 (MONDAY)
A day trip to Kamakura and Yokosuka (KBS)

DECEMBER 15 (TUESDAY)
A.M.: A visit to Tokyo Imperial University
P.M.: A visit to Waseda University
A banquet hosted by the Nippon P.E.N. Club

DECEMBER 16 (WEDNESDAY)
A.M.: Visits to department stores
P.M.: Lecture at Senshu University
A banquet hosted by KBS

DECEMBER 17 (THURSDAY)
Embark from Yokohama[15]

Among the government-sponsored activities in which Du Bois participated (not reflected on this itinerary) was a geisha party for the visiting intellectual hosted by a foreign ministry official.[16] The Ministry of the Navy, moreover, extended to Du Bois the privilege of conducting a tour of "inspection" of Japan's Combined Fleet at Yokosuka. The fleet at the time included the *Nagato*, the first battleship in the world mounted with sixteen-inch guns and the most powerful warship in the world at the time of its commissioning in 1920, as well as her sister ship *Mutsu*.[17] Both the *Nagato* and the *Mutsu* had undergone renovation and updating in the year of Du Bois's visit. In 1941, the *Nagato* began the Pacific War as the flagship of the Combined Fleet. The order to attack Pearl Harbor was issued from its decks.[18]

Among the nongovernmental organizations—cultural and educational institutions—that hosted Du Bois, the Kokusai Bunka Shinkokai (KBS; Society for International Cultural Relations) honored the black intellectual with a party at the Kabuki Theatre, as well as at a banquet presided over by "a Count who was educated at Amherst with [Calvin] Coolidge and [Dwight] Morrow," as Du Bois reports in a dispatch to the *Pittsburgh Courier* from Japan. KBS also arranged sightseeing tours for Du Bois to Nikko, Kamakura, and Yokosuka. The Pan-Pacific Club had invited Du Bois to attend its monthly luncheon (as it did Hughes), and the Nippon P.E.N. Club invited Du Bois along with two Chinese writers to its monthly dinner party. Du Bois presented lectures at a number of universities, including Tokyo Imperial University, "the largest and most noted in Japan," where he lunched with the president and "inspected" the library, in the collections of which he "found some of [his] own books."[19]

However, there is reason to doubt that he was indeed the target of Japanese "negro propaganda operations," as scholars suggest, despite the obvious privileges and courtesies accorded to Du Bois. Hikida was a clerk in the Japanese consulate in New York from 1938 to 1941 and was an employee of Japan's Foreign Office in Tokyo after 1942, during which he drafted a proposal entitled "Wartime Negro Propaganda Operations" in January 1943, as I will discuss in the epilogue. However, no official or unofficial program that could be termed "negro propaganda" targeting black Americans in general or Du Bois in particular has been shown to exist at the time of Du Bois's peacetime visit to Japan in 1936. An attempt to account for Du Bois's seeming embrace of the expanding Japanese imperium in East Asia should therefore not begin with the unsupported premise of such an influence. Let us rather begin by asking how, even in the absence of "negro propaganda operations," Japan seems to have shaped Du Bois's perceptions to elicit a response from the thinker that so deeply supported its cause.

The answer to this question lies not in Japan's interest in the ostensibly central fact of Du Bois's identity as black but rather in his status as an influential visitor from the West. It is for this reason that Du Bois's primary host in Japan was KBS.[20] Founded in 1934 under the auspices of the Foreign Ministry to coordinate Japan's cultural diplomacy, KBS was charged with making systematic use of the "soft power" of culture and values to influence foreign public opinion. Under H.I.H. Prince Takamatsu (a brother of Emperor Hirohito) as its honorary president and

Prince Fumimaro Konoye (and future prime minister of Japan) as its president, KBS counted among its advisers Japan's prime minister, minister of the imperial household, minister of foreign affairs, and minister of education, as well as "more than 130 representatives of the people" from the political, economic, social, and scholarly world who served on its body of councilors.[21] Thus, coordinated by both state and nonstate actors, KBS directed Japan's cultural diplomacy at influential statesmen, businessmen, scholars, thinkers, novelists, artists, and in particular, journalists from the West. The efforts of KBS to "enlighten" foreigners on Japanese civilization, and courtesies that it extended to them, such as free train passes, were intended to influence these people of influence to spread favorable views of Japan via lectures, radio, or books in their home countries.[22] Du Bois received a complimentary first-class train pass in Japan and was taken to see expressions and demonstrations of both Japan's ancient traditions and its modern technological achievements. These included Kabuki performances; the Shinto shrines, temples, and Buddha; and warships. These courtesies were a measure of his status as a press representative of the *Pittsburgh Courier* and a professor at Atlanta University. Notably, many of the institutions that hosted Du Bois's tour in Japan were headed by KBS councilors.[23]

Beyond the self-described objective of KBS to "introduce and encourage interest in, and study and knowledge of, Japanese culture based upon the ideal of furthering worldwide exchange of cultural relations in the cause of international peace and better understanding,"[24] Japan's exercise of soft power was imperative in the context of the diplomatic crisis that Japan faced in the early 1930s. The military occupation of Manchuria, known as the Manchurian Incident, marked a new phase of Japanese imperialism in its continental thrust. It led Japan into direct conflict with the US Open Door policy in China, affirmed as international law in the Washington Naval Conference. Subsequently, Japan withdrew from the League of Nations (in which Japan had been a charter member and one of four permanent league council members) in 1933. Japan needed new channels to influence international public opinion. KBS, founded as such a channel in 1934, was thus linked ideologically to Japan's continental advance in Manchuria. The ultimate aim of the agency, to borrow the words of historian Tomoko Akami, was "to show that Japan was a civilized and sophisticated country, and was capable of 'guiding' its puppet state" of Manchukuo.[25]

In this regard, it is noteworthy that the successive presidents of the SMR Company served on the board of councilors for KBS, and that Yosuke

Matsuoka, Japan's chief delegate to the League of Nations who pulled the nation out of the league, was installed in 1935 as president of SMR and as a KBS councilor. SMR was far more than Japan's railway company in Manchuria. Founded in 1906, the company was a giant conglomerate that propelled the development of southern Manchuria, crown jewel of the Japanese Empire. In addition to running freight and passenger services, SMR owned coal mines and wharves, and controlled diverse subsidiary corporations in Manchuria. In the railway zone under its control, SMR acted as an alternative administration to the local Chinese government, providing health care, education, and employment to Chinese as well as Japanese. It also managed schools, hospitals, libraries, museums, and a large research institute. With a president—who was Matsuoka at the time of Du Bois's visit—appointed by the Japanese government, SMR was, moreover, a quasi-state organ whose activities in Manchuria were directed "in accordance with foreign policy and national security aims."[26] After the provocation of the Manchurian Incident and the subsequent Japanese establishment of the puppet regime of Manchukuo, SMR served as the brains trust for Manchukuoan development, while also assuming management of Manchukuo's state railways.

In this light, the active role of SMR—rather than of Hikida—in the Asian leg of Du Bois's world tour emerges to demand our careful attention. As disclosed in a letter from Du Bois to Chih Meng of the China Institute in the United States, the African American intellectual had originally planned to travel from Europe across the Soviet Union "by way of the Trans-Siberian Railroad" and to proceed directly to Peiping (Peking), China, via Mukden in Manchukuo.[27] Meng, associate director of the China Institute in New York, and spokesperson for the Republic of China, had denounced Japan's establishment of Manchukuo in his book *China Speaks*, asserting that "the Chinese people have been colonizing Manchuria peacefully for centuries" and that "the Manchus in Manchuria today are somewhat in the position of Indians in the United States, except that the Manchus have been entirely assimilated into Chinese culture."[28] At the suggestion of the Japanese personnel of the SMR Company,[29] however, Du Bois altered his itinerary, adding a weeklong tour to "inspect" the new state of Manchukuo. SMR employees arranged a package tour of sorts for Du Bois along SMR's Manchurian rail lines, with accommodation provided by the Yamato Hotel chain that the company operated. SMR thus functioned in the role of unofficial publicity agent promoting Manchukuo through tourism and exercised soft power to influence international public opinion. This tour, as I shall discuss further, was a defining experience for Du Bois. It shaped his perceptions and understanding of Manchuria, becoming what we might call a black Manchurian narrative.

A Week in Manchuria

In his unpublished "Russia and America," Du Bois included a chapter entitled "I Gird the Globe" in which he relates his experiences during his Eurasian continental trip in 1936. Du Bois traveled the international trunk lines, riding the rails to national borders and traversing these borders to follow the steel rails onward. The lines he followed traced the divergent paths of the major socioeconomic systems on the continent—those of Nazi Germany, the Soviet Union, and Manchukuo. International railway links provided a connection between these divergent paths for the traveler. Through his grand tour, Du Bois came to imagine Manchuria radically as a testing ground for "some form of socialism."[30]

The new colored state of Manchukuo on the Pacific Rim, with territory bordering the Soviet Union, first appeared in atlases in 1932. Its presence redrew diplomatic relations across the Eurasian continent—a development that would have interested Du Bois, the international tourist, in 1936. While in Berlin, Du Bois was able to obtain a visa to Manchukuo through a "Manchukuo trade mission office" that had been established there as a result of a "Germany-Manchukuo trade agreement" concluded in the spring of that year.[31] This agreement, a trilateral arrangement between Germany and the economic bloc of Japan and Manchukuo (the yen bloc), amounted to Germany's "*de facto* recognition of Manchukuo" and set the stage for the Anti-Comintern Pact that Germany and Japan would conclude on November 25, 1936,[32] only days following the end of Du Bois's tour of Manchukuo. The Soviet government, meanwhile, denied Du Bois a visa to make extended stops in Soviet Russia. Du Bois recalls in his travel manuscript "I Gird the Globe" that Moscow "was not welcoming visitors, especially from the United States and en route to Japan." However, he was granted permission for "passage through to Manchuria," which he undertook on a ten-day-long ride on the Trans-Siberian Railway from Moscow to Manchouli, the station on the frontier of Manchuria (RA, 102–3).

The principal effect of the establishment of Manchukuo on international relations was to alter the balance of power in the Far East, sharply straining Japanese-Soviet relations in particular. In response to the strategic threat of Japan bringing northern Manchuria—formerly a buffer zone—under its armed control, the Soviet Union had concentrated its energies on strengthening its military forces. These were deployed along both the Manchukuo-Soviet border and the border between Manchukuo and the Mongolian People's Republic, a satellite state that the Soviet Union had established in Outer Mongolia in 1924. In his travel manuscript, Du Bois recalls the prolific military activity—"soldiers, arms, factories, all for war preparation"—that he witnessed as his train passed through Outer Mongolia and approached Manchuria. He reports feeling "the earth beneath [his] feet smoldering and quaking with the flames of coming war." However, the thinker "could not believe it" and "would not," perhaps because, in 1936, "next to Russia, Japan intrigued [him] as holding the destiny of the darker [workers in] its hands." For Du Bois, Soviet Russia was "a state seeking to replace private profit with public welfare" and the Japanese were "leaders of the world fight against white imperialism" (RA, 126–27). Du Bois's sympathies thus were divided between two states whose spheres of influence were encroaching on one another, creating an explosive situation on the continent.

Du Bois's travel manuscript records a tension-ridden border between the Mongolian People's Republic and Manchukuo at Manchouli, which he reached on November 12. When his train stopped at the "fatal border," Du Bois and his fellow travelers from Europe had to change to a different train on the Manchukuoan side, passing through both Russian and Manchukuoan customs inspections en route (RA, 128). In 1936, Manchouli was no longer the quiet frontier station on the Chinese Eastern Railway connecting Russia with China that it had been. After the establishment of the puppet state, border clashes had taken place (due to one of which Hughes had had to give up his dream of seeing the ancient city of Peking en route from Moscow [see chapter 4]). Consequently, the Soviet government decided to sell its interests in the Chinese Eastern to Manchukuo.[33] The sale of these railway interests in March 1935 represented Stalin's de facto recognition of Manchukuo. On the Manchukuoan side at Manchouli, customs officers were posted to secure the border, and entry into the country was not always guaranteed.[34] Du Bois reports that as a guest of SMR he was courteously ushered into "the stationmaster's private parlor" but that he saw an English lady struggle with a rough Manchukuo inspector who rummaged through her luggage, fingering the negatives of some films. The woman turned to Du Bois with pleading eyes and said, "For heaven's sake don't leave me" (RA, 129).

Following his account of the border crossing in "I Gird the Globe," Du Bois offers a descriptive map of Manchukuo based on his travels along the rails that crisscrossed the country. He intended to probe not only the geography but also the meaning of Manchukuo, a colored *imperium in imperio*, on his tour—its arrangement with SMR, unofficial publicity agency for the (puppet) state, notwithstanding. In his journey along the rail lines as both traveler and passenger, Du Bois traced the paths of Manchuria's coloniality and its modernity, which created contingent national and transnational forms of community in that region. Manchukuoan Manchouli served as his point of departure; he described the settlement as "a straggling town on a dusty plain, with Russian and Chinese signs" (RA, 129), and a much smaller town in proportion to its railway station than most because the station was built first and the town developed around it. Du Bois reported Harbin, the next stop, to be a thriving city that had developed with the Russian construction of the Chinese Eastern and was "the only remaining center of Czarist Russia on earth" (RA, 130).

Du Bois then describes the urban cityscape of Hsinking, which burst into sight as the train rode out of the northern desert. "The whole scene changed as if by magic," Du Bois writes. Hsinking was a crossroads of international traffic where the Chinese Eastern and SMR converged. A small riverside town only a few years before, Hsinking was in the process of growing into the capital city of Manchukuo.[35] From his room in the SMR-operated Yamato Hotel in Hsinking,[36] Du Bois saw to the right the old Chinese town, "huddled and crouching, with its strange signs and ancient insignia," and to the left, "the beginning of the new Japanese city, or the city of the new Manchoukuo, planned by the Japanese." Highlighting the differences between the Chinese and Japanese districts of the city that represented pre- and post-1932, Du Bois, whose language is encoded with what might be termed a black Orientalist or colonial discourse, justifies Manchukuo—proxy imperialism—as a modernizer in Asia. "Clearly this colonial effort of a colored nation is something to watch," Du Bois concludes (RA, 130).

Indeed, with a new SMR station as its focal point and center, Hsinking was being built according to a geometrical plan, with state-of-the-art roads radiating out from the station, and with monumental state buildings, public offices, and the palace of the emperor Pu Yi lining them in various stages of completion; "some finished, some yet building, some only projected" (RA, 130). As one historian describes it, the architecture of public buildings in the capital of Manchukuo was, characteristically, "stark but imposing modernist bodies made of reinforced concrete, topped with Chinese or Japanese-inspired ornamental roofs"—a touch of Manchukuo's "Pan-Asianism."[37] Du Bois also may have observed that Hsinking was furnished with city parks, botanical gardens, and decorative lakes, as well as a modern public hygiene system with water closets installed in all residential, commercial, and industrial buildings—the first such system in Asia. Planned and constructed as a "futuristic cityscape," the capital of Manchukuo was intended to project "the power of the colonial state as the agent of modernity," in the words of historian Louise Young.[38]

Speeding southward in "Japanese cars better than Pullmans" on SMR's streamlined super-express train, the Asia Express, Du Bois traveled to Mukden, the ancient capital of the Manchu Dynasty. In Du Bois's accurate description, the Manchus "for 267 years ruled China" until the 1911 Revolution (RA, 130). The Chinese revolution culminated in the establishment of the Republic of China and the abdication of the last Manchu emperor, Pu Yi—the same being installed twenty years later as the emperor of Manchukuo. Thus, two modern states in East Asia, the Republic of China and Manchukuo, branched off separately from the trunk line of the Chinese Empire. Du Bois found Mukden "a singular city," divided into "an ancient walled town, three hundred years old"—with a dignified palace and two royal mausoleums—and "a new Japanese city, broad and square, busy and beautiful" in the SMR zone. A war memorial had been erected in the Japanese district to commemorate the battle of Mukden in the Russo-Japanese War—a war that enabled Japan to take "her place among the Powers." Recently added to this memorial were the names of soldiers who had fallen in the Manchurian Incident,[39] in which the Japanese Kwantung Army burst from the SMR zone to occupy Manchuria, enabling the creation of Manchukuo under the (nominal) rule of Pu Yi. In reflecting on Mukden during his stay, Du Bois decided, "This is surely the place to pause and ask what is this Manchurian venture of Japan, and what does it mean?" (RA, 130–31).

His grappling with this question eventually led Du Bois to write two bold, provocative dispatches for the *Pittsburgh Courier* in which he justified Japan's Manchurian venture. He sent these dispatches, which were published in 1937, from Dairen, which was not only the final stop on his tour of inspection and the terminus of the SMR trunk line but also the location of the headquarters of SMR. In Dairen, the *Manshu Nichi-Nichi*, Manchuria's biggest SMR-affiliated newspaper, reported on Du Bois's arrival and published a photograph of the visiting dignitary.[40] Du Bois delivered a lecture on "the Problem of Race Segregation in the United States" to the SMR Club (the conference room of which was packed to overflowing with an audience of a hundred and several tens). At a dinner in the club following the lecture, Du Bois led a round-table talk on the "Future of the Black Race" and other racial matters.[41] Du Bois noticed that "graduates of several American universities were present" at this event.[42] These were most likely Japanese Americans. As historian John J. Stephan observes, Japanese Americans sometimes fled the racial tensions that afflicted them in America, the land of opportunity for whites, and sought "a multi-ethnic land of opportunity" in Manchukuo.[43] In Manchukuo, "equal treatment" among the so-called quinque racial makeup of the populace (Han Chinese, Japanese, Manchus, Mongols, and Koreans), in addition to "people of other nationalities who wish to reside permanently" within the territory, was established as a principle—though not a practice—in the declaration of the founding of the state issued in 1932.[44] Ethnic diversity was thus a defining feature of Manchukuo; there were also communities of Germans, Jews, Ukrainians, Poles, and Crimean Tartars, as well as British, American, French, and Italian expatriates, let alone White Russians. The SMR Company employed dozens of such Japanese Americans seeking a multiethnic land of opportunity in Manchukuo during its existence from 1906 to 1945.[45]

The first of the dispatches that Du Bois sent to the *Pittsburgh Courier* during this visit, captioned "Yosuke Matsuoka," describes an interview Du Bois conducted in Dairen with Matsuoka, president of SMR. Matsuoka was also a graduate of the University of Oregon in the United States. While his dispatch leaves out many details of his conversation with Matsuoka—at the time one of the best-known Japanese personages in the world, having recently pulled Japan out of the League of Nations—Du Bois's text clearly represents Matsuoka as the architect of Manchukuo. Du Bois reports that Matsuoka "ranks as a viceroy and premier," holding "the destinies of thirty millions [the inhabitants of Manchukuo] in his hands," and shouldering "the responsibility of proving to the world that colonial enterprise by a colored nation need not imply the caste, exploitation and subjection which it has always implied in the case of white Europe."[46] In the declaration of the founding of Manchukuo on March 1, 1932, the "will of thirty million people" had been offered as grounds for the establishment of the state and its secession from the Republic of China.[47]

Du Bois's symbolic coupling of Matsuoka and Manchukuo is significant, implying that Du Bois understood Japan's Manchurian venture to be a project of the SMR Company, not of Japanese militarists. Indeed Du Bois's account contains no mention either of the Chinese resistance or of the sometimes tense collaboration of Chinese local elites with the Japanese authorities.[48] Partly, this may reflect how the Japanese—rather than the Chinese—controlled the means of representation of Manchukuo that affected Du Bois while in Manchuria. In Du Bois's view, which was clearly influenced by his dialogue with Matsuoka, the prime force for "the development and independence of the colored peoples" in Manchukuo was SMR—Japan's half state-owned and half privately owned corporation that had long acted since 1906 in Manchuria as an alternative administration to the local Chinese government.[49] Because SMR worked to break down the boundaries between metropole and colony, between industry and culture, and between private capital and public welfare, the state of Manchukuo that it had helped build, albeit an *imperium in imperio*, seemed to him to disrupt the exploitative racial and social order forged between Western maritime empires and their colonies beyond oceans.

Thus, in the second of his dispatches to the *Pittsburgh Courier*, captioned "Japanese colonialism," Du Bois compares the "colonial situation" in Manchuria with "colonies in Africa and the West Indies, under white European control" in this light. He enumerates five constituent elements that make the former different from the latter: (1) "Absence of racial or color caste"; (2) "Impartial law and order"; (3) "Public control of private capital for the general welfare"; (4) "Services for health, education, city-planning, housing, consumers' co-operation and other social ends"; and (5) "The incorporation of the natives into the administration of government and social readjustment." Du Bois thus made a strong case for empire—that is, liberal empire—in East Asia. With these advantages in view, Du Bois brushes aside as "immaterial" the question of whether Manchukuo is an independent state or a colony. He then broaches what he deems "the main question," that is, "What is Japan doing for the people of Manchuria and how is she doing it? . . . Is she reducing the mass of the people to slavery and poverty? Is she stealing the land and monopolizing the natural resources?"[50]

The answer that Du Bois offers in this second *Courier* dispatch from Dairen is based on his understanding that "Japanese colonialism" in Manchuria is an integrated industrial and cultural system in which capitalism is carefully controlled for the public good. Du Bois observes,

> The people appear happy, and there is no unemployment. There is public peace and order. A lynching in Manchoukuo would be unthinkable. There are public services to improve crops, market them and increase their prices.

Manchoukuans are in the police force and the schools and public services.... The Japanese hold no absolute monopoly of the offices of the state. The new housing and new cities take account of the Chinese as well as the Japanese. There has been private investment of capital on a considerable scale; but the railroads are partially owned by the state; electricity, water, gas, telegraph and telephone are public services. The largest open cut coal mine in the world is in Manchuria.... [T]hey have schools, library, hospital, water, sewage and parks. Electricity for a large part of Manchuria is made here—a total of 130,000 kilowatts. Yet all this is not only half owned by the government, but the private employer is under strict government control and regulation.

In concluding his *Courier* dispatch, Du Bois argues that although the Manchukuo government was not "controlling capital for the benefit of the workers" as he thought it should, "neither, so far as that is concerned, is Japan. There is, however, no apparent discrimination between motherland and colony in this respect. Nowhere else in the world, to my knowledge, is this true." Du Bois suggests that the Manchurian venture aims not at unilateral dominion but at a contiguous regional community that transcends nationalism. He ends his dispatch with an affirmation of the venture, declaring that "no nation should rule a colony whose people they cannot conceive as Equals."[51]

In accordance with Du Bois's view, an anti-laissez-faire ideology was indeed at work in the state-planned and state-controlled economy in Manchukuo.[52] As Young describes, the SMR Company was staffed with Japanese leftists and Marxists who were politically marginalized at home in Japan. In Manchuria, they "tried to turn the new empire into a kind of social laboratory, a controlled environment in which to test out theories of social transformation."[53] The *Economic Construction Program of Manchukuo*, drafted by the SMR Company and issued by the Manchukuo government in 1933, stipulates that, in view of "the baneful effects which capitalism when unbridled may exert," the government of Manchukuo will "apply a certain amount of national control" and "prevent any exclusive class of people from monopolizing the natural resources and the development of industries, thus enabling all to enjoy such benefits."[54] Following the example of Soviet economic planning, SMR issued a draft proposal for the first Five-Year Industrial Development Plan for Manchukuo in October 1936, a month before Du Bois's visit, to be implemented in 1937.[55] Regarding the Soviet influence, it is also noteworthy that Hotsumi Ozaki—communist, friend, and translator of Agnes

Smedley, and informant for the Soviet spy Richard Sorge (see chapter 4)—was one of the many leftists who worked for SMR. Although Ozaki did not formally join the Research Department of SMR as a consultant until 1939, his ties with SMR dated from his Shanghai days in the late 1920s and early 1930s (when he made friends with Smedley).[56] Matsuhei Matsuo of the New York office of SMR, a staff member of the Japanese Council of the Institute of Pacific Relations, had advised Du Bois prior to his departure for Japan to communicate and meet with Ozaki in Tokyo.[57]

What lies at the heart of Du Bois's sympathy with the Manchurian venture is his affirmation of Manchukuo's socioeconomic experiment of departing from a capitalist development. In "I Gird the Globe," Du Bois demarcates four power nuclei in the world of 1936: Great Britain and Western Europe, Italy and Eastern Europe, the Union of Soviet Socialist Republics, and the Japanese Empire (RA, 132). Precisely because he looked upon Japan as "the hope of the colored world" (RA, 101), Du Bois was "curious to know just how far" Japanese imperium in Asia would "follow the western model," or alternatively, would "follow some form of socialism." For Du Bois, the future course of Asia had grave implications for the future of the darker "workers." As he toured Manchukuo, Du Bois speculated that "for historic and other reasons," the Japanese Empire in Asia would not pursue the model of the Soviet Union on the Eurasian continent but that at the same time, "there was at least equal reason for refusing the lead of Great Britain or France or the United States," that is, Western maritime empires (RA, 132). His interview with Matsuoka enabled Du Bois to envision an alternative to both the Soviet Russian and Western models—a "third way" toward which the Manchurian venture pointed.

In the most crucial passage of his travel manuscript (portions of which were published in the aforementioned dispatch captioned "Yosuke Matsuoka"), Du Bois recalls that he and Matsuoka "talked of industry, capitalism and communism." This conversation led them to share a stunning theory that, in Du Bois's account, framed Matsuoka's understanding of the Japanese Empire: "In some ways Japan [is] the most communistic of modern states." What Matsuoka had in mind, of course, was not communism as a social or political system but rather communism as a deeply rooted aspect of Japanese culture. As Du Bois reports Matsuoka to have explained it, "In Japan there had never been that strong sense of individual ownership of property that characterizes so many people[s]. There was, on the contrary, through the family and clan a strong sense of common ownership of all wealth, of willingness to give to others and sacrifice for the common good" (RA, 133). In Matsuoka's view, the Japanese—whose society was grounded in the sense of communal ownership and the common good—were morally communistic.

Embracing this idea, Du Bois "ventured boldly to add" that perhaps the Japanese could evolve, without revolution, into a state capable of replacing private profit with public welfare: "You Japanese, by your marvelous national discipline, were able without revolution to transform Japan from Feudalism to Industrialism. May it not be possible, again without revolution, and with that same discipline and sacrifice, for Japan to make that further inevitable change from private profit to public welfare?" (RA, 133).[58]

Perhaps to protect Matsuoka (the advocacy of communism—which was tantamount to endorsing the overthrow of the emperor system—was a criminal offense under Japanese law), Du Bois chose not to mention in the *Courier* dispatch that "Matsuoka expressed agreement with [him]." However, Du Bois asserts in his travel manuscript that Matsuoka did agree with him, and Du Bois concludes, "I think he was sincere" (RA, 133).

In any case, Matsuoka quite clearly restated what he said to Du Bois five years later, to Joseph Stalin. As Japan's foreign minister in 1941, Matsuoka described the common ground that Japan shared with Soviet Russia to Stalin with the resonant phrase "moral communism" in the course of concluding the Japanese-Soviet Neutrality Pact. The pact was intended to establish the partnership and ensure the mutual territorial integrity of the two states and their respective territories of Manchukuo and the Mongolian People's Republic. Stalin's de jure recognition of Manchukuo and a formation called the Eurasian Continental Bloc (discussed in the last section of this chapter) were a result. As if anticipating and endorsing this continental bloc, Du Bois describes gazing from a hill at Port Arthur out across the Yellow Sea that "Manchuria is the natural mainland of the isles of Japan" (RA, 131).[59]

In his travel manuscript, Du Bois thus comes to regard Manchukuo as a state developing through the agency of SMR toward "some form of socialism" rather than as an autarchic regional empire under Japanese militarists, functioning as a cornerstone for new regionalism in East Asia. His journey onward to the Republic of China, and in particular a luncheon meeting with a group of Chinese at the Chinese Bankers' Club in Shanghai (arranged through Chih Meng and "the American-supported University of Shanghai" [RA, 138]),[60] only strengthened Du Bois's conviction that the Manchurian venture offered hope for darker workers in

Asia. Du Bois's encounters with the elite in the Republic of China—represented at the luncheon meeting by the editor of the China Press, the secretary general of the Bank of China, the general manager of the China Publishing Company, the director of the Chinese Schools for Shanghai, and the executive secretary of the China Institute of International Relations—convinced him that they were trying to extricate themselves from the snares of European capital "by the method of establishing [their] own capitalistic control."[61] The Chinese elite, Du Bois gathered, "proposed to out-capital capital" rather than to displace capitalism (RA, 140).

The luncheon meeting also gave Du Bois a sense of the indignation that the Chinese felt toward the Japanese (they "hate Japan more than Europe when [they] have suffered more from England, France, and Germany than from Japan"), which he believed to derive partly from a Chinese sense of cultural superiority. In Du Bois's view, the Chinese felt that Japan, which they regarded as "the culture child of China," was arrogantly trying to "show China the way of life" (RA, 139–40). However, such sentiments, presupposing Japan's cultural inferiority to China, did not sway Du Bois, perhaps due to the subsequent influence of the cultural diplomacy of KBS, which fostered his appreciation of both ancient and modern Japanese civilization from the time he landed in Japan after leaving Shanghai, as we have seen. Upon returning to the United States and lecturing in Harlem "to an eager audience, which overflowed the Y.W.C.A. auditorium," Du Bois concluded that "the Japanese were creating an incredibly fine state out of the conquered territory" in Manchuria—thus assuming the role of unofficial publicity agent promoting Manchukuo in his home country as KBS may have hoped he would.[62]

The Battle of Shanghai

A major ramification of the Manchurian venture, in historical actuality, was a full-fledged war that broke out between the Republic of China and the Empire of Japan in July 1937, six months after Du Bois's return from Asia. Initially a small military clash at the Marco Polo Bridge in the suburbs of Peking, the conflict became a full-scale (though undeclared) armed conflict between the National Revolutionary Army of the Republic of China and the Imperial Japanese Army and Navy, spreading rapidly to Shanghai. The war acted as a catalyst for the formation of an anti-Japanese alliance between the KMT and the CCP, in which the Red Army became the Eighth Route Army of the National Revolutionary Army in a united Chinese front. Nonetheless, the Japanese gained control of

Shanghai after a fierce three-month battle. The rapid development of hostilities in Shanghai complicated Du Bois's black Manchurian narrative significantly.

More broadly, in the African American community, the Battle of Shanghai was represented in multiple and conflicting ways. The *New York Amsterdam News*, Harlem's leading black weekly, reported that the Sino-Japanese conflict divided public opinion. In Harlem, "a soap-boxer" on a street corner damned Japan for being "just as Fascist-minded as can be," while elsewhere "a trio of curbstone debaters" applauded Japan for showing the white world that "if they can gobble up China and everywhere else, Japan can do some gobbling, too."[63] According to another black weekly, the *Pittsburgh Courier*, the situation was "seriously argued in Aframerican gatherings." On one side, pro-Japanese blacks believed that Japan was "fighting the battle of the colored peoples of the world against a China backed by white imperialists." On the other, pro-Chinese blacks "fiercely resent[ed] Japanese aggression and the effort to destroy Chinese independence so laboriously created after twenty-six years of revolution and counter-revolution."[64]

The disparate conceptions of the Battle of Shanghai are directly reflected in the African American representations of China and Japan. On the left of the spectrum of black political thought, Langston Hughes, Richard Wright, and Paul Robeson regarded the CCP-led China as fighting an anti-imperialist war. Hughes published his poem "Roar China!" in September 1937, shortly after the outbreak of the Battle of Shanghai. Opening with a direct address, the imperative to "Roar, China! / Roar, old lion of the East!" the poem calls for resistance to Japanese and Western imperialists, for which the foreign concessions of Shanghai were the historical symbol.[65] Wright was Harlem Bureau editor of the *Daily Worker*, newspaper of the Communist Party of the United States of America (CPUSA)—a capacity in which he served for over a year from 1937 to 1938. He reported in September 1937 on a massive Harlem rally "to protest Japan's undeclared war against China." Staged by Harlem workers—"Negro, Chinese, and white"—under the auspices of the American Friends of the Chinese People and the American League against War and Fascism, the rally included as speakers black American leaders James W. Ford, organizer of the Harlem Division of the CPUSA, and Ashley L. Totten of the Brotherhood of Sleeping Car Porters.[66] Similarly, the singer-activist Robeson "openly declared his support for China in her heroic struggle against Japanese imperialism."[67] Steadfast in his support of Chinese aspirations for self-determination throughout the Sino-Japanese

War, Robeson and Liu Liang-mo, secretary of the Shanghai YMCA, would eventually release an album in the United States in 1941, entitled *Chee Lai! (Arise!)*, to aid the Chinese war of resistance. Robeson performed the title song—the future national anthem of the People's Republic of China—in English and Chinese, calling upon the Chinese masses "who refuse to be bond slaves" to "stand up and fight for liberty and true democracy." Proceeds from the sale of the album were donated to "the China Aid Council of United China Relief."[68]

During the Battle of Shanghai, the mainstream US media discourse adopted the theme of humanitarianism. The October 4, 1937, issue of *Life* magazine, founded by Henry Luce, printed images of the Japanese bombing the civilian population from the air. In one heartrending photo, which *Life* estimated was seen by 136,000,000 people around the world, a Chinese baby, wounded by a bomb, bawls pitifully amid the ruins of Shanghai's South Station, Nantao. Demonstrating the strength of public interest in the Sino-Japanese War, this famous photo was selected by US newsreaders and reproduced in *Life* early in 1938 to represent one of the top news stories of 1937.[69] In concert with such interest in the mainstream, on October 5, President Franklin D. Roosevelt gave what came to be called his "Quarantine Speech" in Chicago, calling for the international containment of aggressor nations guilty of spreading "the epidemic of world lawlessness"—thus taking a step away from the traditional US foreign policy of neutrality and nonintervention. In this speech, Roosevelt, obviously referring to Japan, described its war in criminal terms: "Without a declaration of war and without warning or justification of any kind, civilians, including vast numbers of women and children, are being ruthlessly murdered with bombs from the air."[70] In a survey conducted by the American Institute of Public Opinion (the Gallup poll) a month earlier, 43 percent had responded that they were "pro-China" as opposed to only 2 percent who were "pro-Japan." The "pro-China" figure rose to 59 percent in October.[71]

Du Bois resisted such a rising trend of public opinion. In his weekly column "Forum of Fact and Opinion," in the September 25, 1937, issue of the *Pittsburgh Courier*, he contended that "what we as American Negroes must understand is the broad outline of the whole thing, and not be unconsciously misled by the propaganda current in America."[72] In October, when Harry F. Ward, chairman of the American League against War and Fascism, wired an appeal to Du Bois to endorse the pro-China People's Congress for Democracy and Peace slated for Pittsburgh in November, Du Bois deliberately rejected it.[73] Du Bois did not accommodate himself to public opinion. Instead, in a column in the October 23 issue of the *Courier*, captioned "China and Japan," he wrote that "Japan fought China to save China from Europe, and fought Europe through China and tried to wade in blood toward Asiatic freedom. Negroes must think straight in this crisis."[74]

This seemingly proimperialist narrative of the Sino-Japanese War in Du Bois's *Courier* column has featured prominently in the scholarship as an illustration of his radical failure of vision with regard to Japanese imperialism. However, pending the eventual sublation of such narrative, I would like to here examine what Du Bois called "the broader outline of the whole thing"—an outline by which he urged African Americans to make sense of the war and make political choices relating to it. From the perspective of Du Bois, an understanding of the war requires that African Americans move beyond the facile explanations of hostilities as fascism versus antifascism, or war versus pacifism, to take a broader, better-integrated historical view of modern regionalism in East Asia. In his *Courier* column of September 25, Du Bois observes that "it would have been magnificent providence of God if Russia and China could have made common ground for the emancipation of the working classes of the world." For Du Bois, the ideal scenario would have been that after the Chinese and Russian Revolutions to end the Chinese Empire and the Tsarist Russian Empire in 1911 and 1917, respectively, a new regional order emerges based on the continental contiguity and solidarity between the Soviet Union and the Republic of China. Such a union would have been possible, according to the black thinker, because the program of Sun Yat-sen, founder of the Republic of China, was essentially "Communism; not the complete Russian line, but an extreme socialism which envisaged division of the land, control of industry, ownership of capital in heavy industry, and the welfare state" (RA, 142). If a Sino-Soviet alliance had come to pass, Du Bois claims in the same *Courier* column, "the salvation of China then would not have rested upon Japan, and two-thirds of the world would have been arrayed against the industrial imperialism of Europe." However, as Du Bois observes, "after losing her great and far-sighted leader, Sun Yatsen" (who died in 1925), the Republic of China "turned in reality toward the leadership of modern industrial imperialism as represented in China, especially by England."[75] This happened in China under "a greedy, crafty man of no ideals or integrity"—namely, Chiang Kai-shek.[76] In accordance with this outline, Du Bois concluded that Japan hence "fought Europe by attacking China, and that is the reason of the present war."[77]

From our vantage point, East Asian regionalism in 1937 was indeed marked by intersecting developments: the crisis of the centuries-old Sinocentric world in continental Asia; the crisis of the international system in maritime Asia (that had occurred on Western terms, first under the British-led treaty ports system and then under the US-defined Washington system that affirmed the Open Door policy in China); and Japan's aspiration both to be "the middle" of the Sinocentric world and to break the international Anglo-American hegemony. Du Bois seems to have understood the Battle of Shanghai in this regional context. The root of the Sino-Japanese conflict, he explained to his *Courier* readers on October 23, lay in "a mad muddle of motives." As Du Bois explains, the Republic of China "preferred to be a coolie for England" (to remain integrated in the international system based on unequal treaties) rather than to "acknowledge . . . the leadership of Japan," thereby allowing Japan, a country that had long been on the periphery of the Sinocentric world, to take the place of the "middle kingdom" in East Asia. This political choice was, as Du Bois writes, motivated by the "supercilious disdain" that the Republic of China or "young China"—a modern state that denied the imperial past but inherited from it the sense of Sinocentricism—heaped on Japan, "a parvenu." Thus, "licking the European boots," China "taught her folk that Japanese are devils." Du Bois concludes that "the straight road to world dominance of the yellow race was ruined in Asia by the same spirit that animates the 'white folks' nigger' in the United States."[78]

Remarkably, the most important context in which Du Bois understood the Battle of Shanghai was during his recent trip to Manchuria. The seemingly proimperialist narrative of the conflict in his *Courier* column of October 23 was not only informed by his interview with Matsuoka and his approval of the Manchurian venture. (Du Bois defines Japan's mission as follows in "I Gird the Globe": "Japan is called . . . to lead world revolution, and lead it with the minimum of violence and upheaval. . . . In the twentieth century she is called to save the world from the slavery to capital" [RA, 146]). The column was also a supportive response to a public statement that Matsuoka had issued from Manchuria a fortnight previously. Published in the *New York Times* on October 10, Matsuoka's statement rebutted the anti-Japanese propaganda in America that was disseminating the claim that "Japan is fighting for loot and profit." According to the president of SMR, "this fight-for-loot theory" was "an insult to plain arithmetic," let alone to Japan, as the billions of yen that Japan was spending on the war in China would clearly yield no return, and Japan knew it. "No treasure trove is in her eyes, only sacrifices upon sacrifices," declared Matsuoka, because Japan was "fighting simply for her conception of her mission in Asia," that is, to keep Asia from turning into "a crazy quilt of European colonies" and "becoming another Africa."[79] Having walked out of the League of Nations to keep Manchuria from the international control the league proposed,[80] Matsuoka in his *New York Times* statement once again took a stand before the world to defend Japan's continental expansion as an attempt to reintegrate East Asia as a contiguous regional community. In this regard, Du Bois's *Courier* column of October 23 amounted to the African American intellectual's effort to stand with Matsuoka in Manchuria across the Pacific.

When Stalin Enters

Du Bois's black Manchurian narrative endorsed Matsuoka's vision of instituting a regionally integrated Asia. It represented the African American thinker's imagined socialist internationalism encompassing Japan's Manchurian venture. A challenge to Du Bois's internationalism soon came in December 1937, however, when the Sino-Japanese War's theater shifted to Nanking, about 170 miles inland from Shanghai on China's eastern coast, and the progress of the war apparently became derailed from Japan's war aim proclaimed by Matsuoka in the *New York Times*.

On December 13, 1937, the Japanese army seized Nanking, the capital of the Republic of China under the KMT. The central episode of the Sino-Japanese War, the Nanking Massacre or Rape of Nanking as it is commonly known, that followed the fall of Nanking, is the most potent symbol of the genocidal character of the conflict. (The incident has entered the political consciousness of Americans as a genocide recently with the success of Iris Chang's bestseller *The Rape of Nanking: The Forgotten Holocaust of World War II* [1997]. Chang claimed that the death toll in Nanking far exceeded that of atomic bomb victims in Hiroshima and Nagasaki.[81]) The atrocities perpetrated in China's Nationalist capital by Japanese troops became widely known almost immediately in the United States.

Firsthand reports of the massacre appeared in the US press less than a week after the fall of Nanking, dispatched by American journalists who remained in the city during the siege and the first few days of the Japanese occupation.[82] Under the headline "Nanking Massacre Story: Japanese Troops Kill Thousands" on the front page of the *Chicago Daily News* of December 15, 1937, Archibald T. Steele reported that "Japanese brutality at Nanking is costing them a golden opportunity to win the sympathy of the Chinese population, whose friendship they claim to be seeking."[83] Arthur Menken, a newsreel cameraman for Paramount, radioed an account of the capture of Nanking to the Associated Press (AP) in which he observed that the city was strewn with hundreds of uniforms shed by Chinese soldiers "substituting civilian garb" to escape death at the hands of the Japanese. Menken wrote, "All Chinese males found with any signs of having served in the army were herded together and executed."[84]

C. Yates McDaniel, an AP correspondent, wired a firsthand account, published in the *Chicago Daily Tribune* on December 18, of a Chinese man with his hands tied, who broke away from a long line of war prisoners en route to an execution ground to beg McDaniel to save him from death. "I could do nothing," wrote the AP correspondent: "My last remembrance of Nanking: Dead Chinese, dead Chinese, dead Chinese."[85] Frank Tillman Durdin, a correspondent for the *New York Times*, reported that slaughter, looting, and rape by the Japanese had "turned Nanking into a city of terror." After the fall of the city, according to Durdin, scattered crowds of civilians, relieved that the siege was over, cheered the columns of Japanese troops marching into the city. However, their "feelings of relief and of welcome soon gave up to terror." The "barbarities" of the Japanese had the effect of creating hatred of the Japanese among the Chinese population, Durdin observed, rather than of gaining the "'cooperation' for which [the Japanese] profess to be fighting China."[86]

Moreover, contemporary magazines carried images of the Japanese atrocities that matched the eyewitness accounts. The January 10, 1938, issue of *Life* magazine included a four-picture spread of "the worst holocaust in modern history" entitled "The Japanese Conqueror Brings 'A Week of Hell' to China's Nationalist Capital of Nanking." One image presented the decapitated head of an "incorrigibly anti-Japanese" Chinese man that had been mounted on a barbed-wire barricade—frightening evidence of Japanese cruelty.[87] With anti-Japanese sentiment rapidly mounting as a result of the Japanese sinking of the US Navy gunboat *Panay* on the Yangtze River on December 12, 1937, the sympathies of Americans clearly lay with the Chinese as the media coverage of the Sino-Japanese War unfolded.

Did the prevailing mood in the mainstream US media reflect the sentiments of black America? In December and throughout the first few months of 1938, the African American press actively promoted the debate over Japan's war in China. In its editorial (January 15, 1938), the Baltimore *Afro-American* issued an equivocal endorsement of Japanese continental expansion to "set up an Asiatic 'Monroe doctrine.' " The editorial declared, "The AFRO-AMERICAN believes that Japan is fully justified." It sparked a flurry of letters to the editor and heated exchanges between its readers over the ensuing weeks.[88] The contentious nature of the Sino-Japanese conflict made it also a topic of debate for African Americans in church and literary clubs as well.[89] The African American community sought out both sides of the story—Chinese and Japanese—in attempting to understand the true import of the war.[90]

The contrast between the representations of the Sino-Japanese War in the mainstream United States and those in black America forums underscores our need to consider the social significance and political implications of the diversity of frames of reference within which African Americans in general and Du Bois in particular addressed the conflict. Having moved beyond the binarisms of fascism versus antifascism and war versus pacifism, the African American community significantly situated the war in the interaction of regional and global processes. As we have seen, Du Bois based his argument on the case of Manchuria and East Asian regionalism. William Pickens, field secretary of the NAACP and contributing editor for the Associated Negro Press, who emerged in the vanguard of advocates of the pro-Japan position in the Sino-Japanese War, argued in the context of Ethiopia and the international security system that became increasingly volatile after the Italo-Ethiopian War (1935–1936).

Indeed, on both sides of the debate, the critical lens of Ethiopia afforded black America a view of the Sino-Japanese conflict as not just a regional process but part of a global process.[91] Cyril Briggs, a black member of the CPUSA, wrote in the January 20, 1938, issue of the *Philadelphia Tribune* that he regarded the wars in East Africa and East Asia as continuous. In Briggs's account, the two wars taken together constituted a narrative of how the Japanese Empire "joined with Europe's imperialistic nations." Briggs relates that in 1935, many African Americans "eagerly turned their eyes toward the Far East in the belief that Japan would aid, in one way or another, the beleaguered East African nation" against Mussolini's fascist aggression (see chapter 2). However, "Japanese imperialism did not lift a finger to help the Ethiopian people, either materially or morally," but rather, as Briggs describes, Japan's rulers "treacherously stabbed [Ethiopia] in the back" by "extend[ing] diplomatic recognition in Italy's 'Ethiopian Empire.' " The Sino-Japanese War only brought into clearer focus what the war in Africa had revealed: that Japan's posture as the "champion" of the world's darker races was a facade.[92] Japan's recent signing of an anti-Comintern protocol with Italy and Germany on November 6, 1937, may have also offered more evidence, in Briggs's view, that Japan had joined the fascist ranks.

By contrast, in Pickens's view, published in the December 18, 1937, issue of the *Pittsburgh Courier*, it was not Japan that had "joined with Europe's imperialistic nations" in the present crisis but rather the Republic of China, in seeking Western aid and intervention by the League of Nations. Pickens observes that Haile Selassie had pursued a similar course of action in the Ethiopian crisis, only to precipitate, rather than prevent, the fall of the Ethiopian Empire. Chiang Kai-shek, Pickens asserts, "ought to send for Haile Selassie," for the Ethiopian emperor "can give him some fine points on the matter of magnanimous and altruistic help from Europe and America." Pickens writes, "These [white] nations, with their own axes to grind, kept shouting for Selassie to 'hold Mussolini!' until they could make up their minds and pass a few more resolutions. 'Hold him, Selassie! We are standing at your back!' . . . Haile stood until it was almost too late to run away with a few personal belongings." Selassie's departure for exile in England as his nation fought on cleared the way for Mussolini to proclaim the Ethiopian Italian Empire in May 1936. The lesson of the Italo-Ethiopian War for Pickens is, then, that China should "deal directly with Japan . . . and settle their own differences" and "keep those European and American Lions and Eagles and Bears [England, the United States, France, Holland, and the USSR] out of the Oriental business."[93] Chiang, advises Pickens, "had better stop waitin' on de Lord and on the white folks and deal directly with Japan, or pretty soon he will be where Haile Selassie is, cooling his heels on the Thames, or on the Seine—or on the Potomac—or more riskily still on the Moscow river."[94]

The aforementioned editorial in the January 15, 1938, issue of the Baltimore *Afro-American* captured this perception succinctly in declaring, "The Chinese have become a kind of 'Uncle Tom' of Asia." The editorial concluded that the leaders of the Republic of China "have kow-towed to the white exploiters, licked their boots and allowed themselves to become the footstools of Western conquerors." In a cartoon accompanying the editorial, a man with an old Manchu queue labeled "China" is thus depicted kowtowing to the Western members of the Pacific Community (England, the United States, Holland, and the USSR) while a soldier in uniform labeled "Japan" is, as the editorial describes, "kicking China in the pants to make it stand up straight and be a man" (figure 5.1). Yet conspicuously absent from the cartoon depicting Japan standing alone are the figures of Mussolini and Hitler, the worst enemies of black people,

5.1. "Uncle Tom in Asia," editorial cartoon. From the *Afro-American*, Baltimore edition, January 15, 1938. *Used with permission from the Afro-American Newspapers Archives and Research Center.*

with whom Japan chose to form the Anti-Comintern Pact. In trying to explain away this offensive alliance, the *Afro-American* editorial gave the following reason: "Since most of the democratic nations have their hands in China's pie, there were no other alliances for Japan to make."[95]

The Sino-Japanese War shuffled and reshuffled the partnering of nation-states across the color line in a manner that was, from a racialist perspective, unthinkable at the time of the Ethiopian crisis. China's partnering with Western powers in the Pacific Community (the United States and Great Britain) and Japan's partnering with fascist powers on continental Europe (Italy and Germany) during the Sino-Japanese War gave rise to coalitions that would eventually become the Allies and the Axis in World War II. With the Japanese attack on Pearl Harbor and America's entry into the war, the Chinese Nationalist government would issue a declaration of war on Japan on December 9, 1941, formally announcing that China, "a peace-loving nation," had been at war with Japan since 1937. The Sino-Japanese War, even as it was finally declared, was no longer simply a war between China and Japan. The declaration read, "After her long and fruitless attempt to conquer China, Japan ... has treacherously launched an attack on China's friends, the United States and Great Britain," thereby "making herself the arch enemy of justice and world peace."[96]

However, this reference in China's declaration of war to the United States and Great Britain as "friends" did not reflect a straightforward outcome of the long-term, deliberate coalition making through which the Republic of China sought victory in the Sino-Japanese War. The Soviet Union's involvement in the conflict created significant complications for both China and Japan. (Although the Soviet Union joined the Allied powers, it did not go to war against Japan in World War II until after an atomic bomb was dropped on Hiroshima, just before the end of the war.) On August 21, 1937, in the immediate wake of the outbreak of the Battle of Shanghai, the KMT government concluded the Sino-Soviet Nonaggression Pact with the Soviet Union, which provided a political basis for Stalin to supply material to Chiang Kai-shek and possibly to intervene directly in the war against Japan.[97] In response, on November 6, the Japanese imperial government signed the anti-Comintern protocol in Rome with Italy and Germany. This move increased the threat to the Soviet Union of a two-front war on its European and Far Eastern frontiers. In the Far East, in accordance with the Sino-Soviet pact, "Soviet pilots were fighting Japanese aircraft in China's skies, Soviet advisers [were] drafting military operations on Kuomintang staffs, [and] Soviet aircraft, tanks, artillery, small arms, ammunition and other military equipment [were] flowing into China in an unending stream," as historian Boris Slavinsky observed.[98] It was as if the Soviet Union and the Japanese Empire had undertaken a (proxy) war to compete for regional hegemony in East Asia. In the meantime, along both the Manchukuo-Soviet border and the border between Manchukuo and the Mongolian People's Republic, sharp military clashes between the Soviet Union and Japan were developing into the Battle of Lake Khasan (July–August 1938) and the Battle of Khalkhyn Gol or the Nomonhan Incident (May–September 1939), the latter evolving into a decisive (though undeclared) border war fought between the Soviet Union and the Mongolian People's Republic, on one side, and Japan and Manchukuo, on the other. For Du Bois, Stalin's entry into Asia's war threatened the integrity of his socialist Manchurian narrative, as I will discuss further below.

The Eurasian and the Pacific in World Geopolitics

As represented by its opponents such as black members of the CPUSA, the Japanese Empire's alliance with Hitler and Mussolini presented an antiblack pact "sealed upon the basis of predatory aims and hatred of democracy common to all three partners."[99] Yet Du Bois deliberately mapped the theme of Japan's alliance not onto antiblack race ideology but onto the modern regional system in the Pacific that had undergone a substantial change since World War I. In 1922, the Washington Naval Conference abrogated the Anglo-Japanese alliance, cornerstone of the international order in maritime Asia, and reintegrating the Pacific region instead under "US-British hegemony."[100] Du Bois contends, in his address entitled "The Meaning of Japan" delivered in black colleges in 1937, that when "the race prejudice of England and America . . . refuses Japan fellowship as an equal, she has been forced almost into the lap of Fascist Germany and Italy who represent today war, tyranny, reaction and race hate on the most dangerous scale."[101]

Not surprisingly, such criticism by Du Bois of the US-defined Washington system aroused suspicions in Congress that he was a paid propagandist for the Japanese imperial government, which had proclaimed a "New Order in East Asia" (November 1938) in defiance of the international Anglo-American hegemony. Du Bois received a letter dated February 13, 1939, from Waldo McNutt, a supporter of the NAACP's efforts to secure the passage of federal antilynching legislation. McNutt conveyed the concerns of a number of liberal members of Congress who were interested in the legislation, that Du Bois was rumored to be "receiving funds for Japanese propaganda work" in the United States. The rumor did not seem groundless, McNutt put to Du Bois, in that Du Bois's utterances regarding the Sino-Japanese War "coincided with" the propaganda of official Japanese agencies. McNutt furthermore wrote that in China, the *China Weekly Review* (a newspaper edited by American journalist James B. Powell, whom Langston Hughes met in Shanghai [see chapter 4]) had named Du Bois "a suspect in the dissemination of Japanese propaganda."[102] McNutt requested that Du Bois issue a statement indicating his "official position on the Sino-Japanese conflict" so as to put these "ugly rumors" to rest. Du Bois responded forthrightly, declaring, "I have never received a cent from Japan or from any Japanese and yet I believe in Japan." Du Bois did not falter in his belief in an East Asian regionalism, concluding, "I believe in Asia for the Asiatics and despite the hell of war and the fascism of capital, I see in Japan the best agent for this end."[103]

Du Bois also received a letter in January 1940 from Henry L. Stimson, former secretary of state, and to be installed secretary of war in July. Stimson was mobilizing public opinion in support of economic sanctions against Japan, because Japan's intention of expanding into Southeast Asia under European and American colonial rule was now clear. In February 1939, Japanese troops fighting in China had moved down to take over the island of Hainan to strengthen the blockade of the South China

Sea. In March, Japan assumed jurisdiction over the Spratly Islands that had formerly been claimed by France. The United States notified Japan in July 1939 that they would terminate the Japanese-American commercial treaty six months later. Stimson wrote that America's abrogation of the commercial treaty, which would take effect on January 26, 1940, would free the Roosevelt administration to take "prompt measures" but that such measures as the government could and would take in its foreign policy would be constrained by public opinion. As honorary chairman of the American Committee for Non-Participation in Japanese Aggression,[104] Stimson invited Du Bois to support the organization's campaign for an embargo on exports of use to the Japanese military machine. In Stimson's view, the Sino-Japanese conflict was essentially a clash of "two types of civilization," one "pacific and evolutionary" and the other "militaristic and aggressive," and the US regional policy in the Far East required a strong, independent China to ensure the stability and security of the Pacific Community, now under threat from Japanese expansion.[105] In a public reply to Stimson in his weekly column in the *New York Amsterdam News*, Du Bois voiced his suspicion—and indeed predicted correctly—that the measures short of war that Stimson was proposing for the United States would "lead to virtual and even open war with Japan," and the black thinker protested that, to achieve this end, Stimson "wishes my cooperation and support." Du Bois announced, "He will not get it."[106]

Beyond the Pacific, the Eurasian continent spanned a fault line in the shifting geopolitics of the world, providing Du Bois with another convoluted context. The diplomatic earthquake of the Nazi-Soviet Pact struck in Europe in August 1939, with aftershocks extending across the continent to the conflict in the Far East between the Soviet Union and the Japanese Empire; the latter had concluded the Anti-Comintern Pact with Germany against the Soviet Union three years previously. In a column in the *Amsterdam News* entitled "As the Crow Flies" (November 18, 1939), Du Bois responded to news of the Hitler-Stalin pact by forecasting an imminent international realignment of nation-states across the Eurasian continent. He entertained the possibility of a Nazi-Soviet-Japanese rapprochement across the continent arising from America's anti-Japan foreign policy in the Pacific area. As Du Bois writes, the United States once "broke" the Anglo-Japanese alliance in the Pacific and thereby "threw Japan into the arms of Germany and Italy" in Europe. Du Bois reasons that "analogous tactics today may bring Russia, Germany and Japan into a world-dominating position."[107]

The Nazi-Soviet-Japanese alliance across the Eurasian continent that Du Bois envisaged in his *Amsterdam News* column was precisely what Matsuoka worked to build in reality following his appointment as foreign minister of Japan in July 1940. When the news arrived that Matsuoka had been named to a new cabinet under Prince Konoye (who was also president of KBS), Du Bois welcomed the rise of the former president of the SMR Company to power. Recalling Matsuoka and Manchukuo in his *Amsterdam News* column of August 3, 1940, Du Bois wrote, "I know the Minister of Foreign Affairs of the new Konoye government of Japan. I remember the day, late in the year 1936, when he received me in his office in the capital of Manchukuo. We sat and talked together about the world and color prejudice.... That fall day in Singking [sic] we talked about democracy—that broader democracy that sees no color line. Such a democracy, said Matsuoka, only Japan could lead."[108] It would seem that Du Bois's black Manchurian narrative was moving out of the prolonged impasse precipitated by the Sino-Japanese War.

Shortly after assuming the post of foreign minister, Matsuoka proclaimed the Greater East Asia Co-Prosperity Sphere (August 1940) as a new regional system, placing a Japan-Manchukuo-China economic bloc at its core and extending to the Dutch East Indies and French Indochina in Southeast Asia.[109] The Greater East Asia Co-Prosperity Sphere was an expression of his aspiration for the Japanese Empire to be at once "the middle" in the long-established Sinocentric world in continental Asia and to challenge international Anglo-American hegemony in maritime Asia. Thereafter, Matsuoka drew up the preliminary arrangement for the Tripartite Pact with Germany and Italy to be signed in Berlin in September. This Axis Pact was a necessary step toward what Matsuoka conceived as the formation of a Eurasian Continental Bloc, comprising a Japanese-German-Italian-Soviet four-power entente as a deterrent against the international hegemony of Western maritime empires, in particular, the United States and Great Britain.[110] Based on this design, Matsuoka negotiated the Tripartite Pact and then turned to reaching an agreement with the Soviet Union.[111]

Hence, when Matsuoka departed from Manchuria by rail for Europe in March 1941—returning along the same transcontinental route taken by Du Bois in 1936—his real diplomatic mission lay in neither Germany nor Italy.[112] Ostensibly, the European tour was aimed at reaffirming the Axis alliance and demonstrating the solidarity of its partners to the world. However, the true purpose of Matsuoka's tour would be broached en route, when the train made stopovers on its outward and return journeys at the terminus of the Trans-Siberian Railway in Moscow and Matsuoka visited the Kremlin.

A striking aspect of the Matsuoka-Stalin talks in the Kremlin on March 24 and April 12, as recorded in declassified Soviet records,[113] is their resonance with the Du Bois-Matsuoka interview that took place in Dairen, Manchuria, in 1936. The records show that Matsuoka told Stalin, as mentioned above, that communism had long been practiced in Japan—as a credo that he called "moral communism"—but that this traditional aspect of Japanese society had been undermined by the "evils of capitalism." Matsuoka averred to Stalin that although "he did not agree with political and social communism," he "basically ... adhered to communism" himself and "was decisively against Anglo-Saxon capital." In view of their commonalities—despite their more substantial differences in polities: the emperor system and the single-party communist state—Matsuoka proposed that the Japanese Empire and the Soviet Union cooperate to expel the baneful influence of Anglo-Saxon capitalism from Asia.[114]

With regard to the Sino-Japanese War, Matsuoka explained to Stalin that Japan was not at war with the Chinese people, "whom Japan does not want to fight." Rather, Japan's enemy was Chiang Kai-shek, "an agent of Anglo-American capital" whom Japan was determined to fight to the end. Matsuoka maintained to Stalin that the Sino-Japanese War "must be viewed from precisely that viewpoint," a perspective from which Soviet support for Chiang (required by the Sino-Soviet Nonaggression Pact of 1937) was not "sensible." In light of world history, Matsuoka argued, Japanese-Soviet cooperation was inevitable to "wipe out the Anglo-Saxons" from Asia.[115] Evidently, Matsuoka believed that the powerful pact of the Japanese Empire and the Soviet Union would ease Japanese negotiations with Chiang's China and the United States. For Stalin, a neutral treaty with Japan meant that the Soviet Union would be saved from the danger of a two-front war on its European and Far Eastern frontiers.[116] Stalin replied that "the Russians had never been [the Anglo-Saxons'] friends, and now were perhaps not very keen to befriend them."[117] After the signature of the Japanese-Soviet Neutrality Pact (April 13, 1941), Stalin reportedly told Matsuoka that Russians were "Asiatic."[118]

The result of Matsuoka's secret negotiations in the Kremlin was the "surprise agreement" of the Japanese-Soviet Neutrality Pact. It guaranteed peaceful and friendly relations between Japan and the Soviet Union, and an accompanying declaration that pledged mutual respect for the territorial integrity and inviolability of Manchukuo and the Mongolian People's Republic. News of this sudden accord resounded throughout the world, and it was not welcomed by the Western democracies that had Pacific possessions. As the *Washington Post* reported, "The world-shaking significance of this new reaching of hands from Rome to Berlin to Tokyo to Moscow"—a Eurasian power bloc—presented momentous dangers. The *Washington Post* story presented the conclusion of the pact as follows: "Russia and Japan, long-term dueling powers of the Far East, joined in a neutrality pact today that may be as portentous as the nonaggression accord between Berlin and Moscow in 1939, which preceded the German invasion of Poland."[119] Just as the Nazi-Soviet pact safeguarded Germany's eastern front to enable its southward advancement, the story suggests, the Japanese-Soviet pact could give Japan a free hand to move southward in the Pacific.

The signing of the pact came as a psychological blow to China. For China, it represented a betrayal by the Soviet Union, which had been aiding China's war effort against Japan based on the Sino-Soviet Nonaggression Pact of 1937. American novelist Ernest Hemingway, then a war correspondent in China, predicted that Russian aid would continue even after the new Soviet pact with Japan.[120] However, according to historian Boris Slavinsky, "In mid-1941 all Soviet volunteers were recalled from China, and supply of military power to that country practically ceased."[121]

Matsuoka, as Japan's foreign minister, thus instituted two new regional systems in Asia: the Greater East Asia Co-Prosperity Sphere and the Eurasian Continental Bloc. This specter posed a "revolutionary" challenge to the old order of Western imperialists. The Japanese-Soviet Neutrality Pact, in particular, was a diplomatic triumph for Matsuoka. With his triumph, the two foundational exemplars of Du Bois's internationalism, Soviet Russia and Japan—"the fountain of socialism and the first-born of budding 'colored' world powers"—seemed to converge in their ideological and historical trajectories.[122]

The prospect of a Eurasian Continental Bloc apparently dazzled Du Bois. It was, as he put it, a "world of singular beauty with the confusing tracery of patterns but echoing our world." It lasted only for a brief moment, though, for the outbreak of the German-Soviet war shattered the idyll. In his *Amsterdam News* column of July 12, 1941, Du Bois writes in blank surprise, "Out of another world of singular beauty . . . I come back to solid earth." Du Bois tells his readers, the war "compels nearly all of us to rearrange our thoughts and forecasting." Hitler's attempt to "subdue Russia and to fight Communism with everything that Communism stands for except democracy," in Du Bois's words, left the thinker "puzzled and awhirl." Du Bois found Hitler's war even more puzzling when he pondered its implications for the destiny of Asia, as ironically the outbreak of the war seemed to link Asia's liberation from white dominance with Hitler's victory. "If the Fascists win" in Europe, Du Bois reasons, Japan would expand southward and "logically ... dominate Dutch India, British East India and Australia" to fill the power vacuum in the Pacific left by the European colonial powers, especially Great Britain, defeated by Hitler. This assumption of hegemony in Asia, however, would leave "the puzzle of the relation of Japan to Hitler and Mussolini," in Du Bois's analysis, and "eventually Japan must make a tremendous choice." Du Bois asserts that Japan "has got to realize that the new industrial revolution which has already essentially transformed the Western World which she has been imitating, must be yielded to [communism]." However, this "will be easier than it appears," Du Bois concludes, for "as Matsuoka, himself, once told me: within and essentially, Japan is already Communistic."[123]

However, Du Bois was not to see Matsuoka transform Asia into a contiguous regional community that transcends nationalism, realizing the promise of the Co-Prosperity Sphere that is "communism." A week after Du Bois's column of July 12 appeared, the Japanese foreign minister was dismissed from Konoye's cabinet, and Matsuoka's Co-Prosperity Sphere became an autarchic regional empire that Japanese militarists dreamed of as industrially strong enough to wage total war. History also proved that Japanese-Soviet cooperation—and the Eurasian Continental Bloc that it enabled—could not work as a diplomatic deterrent against the international Anglo-American hegemony in maritime Asia. The United States, fearing that the Japanese-Soviet pact would embolden Japan to advance south against the British and American assets in Asia and the Pacific, "accelerated its own war preparations against Japan and adopted an even tougher stance in its negotiations with Tokyo," setting the stage for Pearl Harbor.[124] Ironically, the geopolitical vista that appeared on the Eurasian horizon in 1941—which briefly made Du Bois's socialist Manchurian narrative seem viable in its resonance with Matsuoka's foreign diplomacy—proved to be neither a deterrent to war nor an augury of a new international (and racial) order. Rather, it precipitated the Pacific War, merging the Sino-Japanese War into the greater conflict in the Pacific theater of World War II.

―――――

In this chapter, I have delineated a black Eurasian Pacific geography that Du Bois charted and argued for the crucial—though rarely acknowledged—role that his Manchurian narrative played in it. In Du Bois's description, the communism that he imagined developing from Asia was "Marxian in its division of income according to need" but "distinctly Asiatic in its use of the vertical clan division and family tie, instead of reaction toward a new bourgeoisie along horizontal class layers" as in Europe. This communism afforded "vast hope," Du Bois writes in his travel manuscript. "With its Asiatic stress on character, on goodness, on spirit," it promised to avoid "the tendency of the Western socialistic state to freeze into bureaucracy," according to Du Bois. "Instead of socialism ever becoming a stark negation of the freedom of thought and a tyranny of action and propaganda of science and art," the black thinker posits, it might create "a great democracy of the spirit." Du Bois speculates that if the experiment had succeeded, it might have fulfilled Matsuoka's Greater East Asia Co-Prosperity Sphere; indeed, it might have "achieved a co-prosperity sphere with freedom of soul" (RA, 150–150A, 151). But the Japanese Empire was "under curious double control" (RA, 133). Eventually Japan's "headstrong leaders," writes Du Bois, "chose to apply Western imperialism to her domination of the East, and Western profit-making replaced Eastern idealism" (RA, 151).

After the Japanese Empire's capitulation in World War II, Matsuoka was judged on "Class A" charges of "crimes against peace" in the International Military Tribunal for the Far East. He died of tuberculosis before his trial was completed. Manchukuo vanished from the postwar world map; on August 8, 1945, two days after the atomic bomb was dropped on Hiroshima, the Soviet Union declared war on Japan, breaching the neutrality pact, whereupon Stalin broached the Manchurian frontier and placed Manchukuo under Soviet control.[125] Inspired by Matsuoka, Du Bois's Manchurian narrative demarcated the promise of Asian socialism that the Manchurian venture once seemed to furnish. This chapter has attempted to convey this unique power of Manchuria to exercise the imagination of the African American leftist intellectual, who would evolve into a Maoist in the 1950s.

EPILOGUE

> Asia and the United States are not separated by this great ocean; we are bound by it.... As America's first Pacific President, I promise you that this Pacific nation will strengthen and sustain our leadership in this vitally important part of the world.
> —Remarks by President Barack Obama at Suntory Hall, Tokyo, Japan, November 14, 2009.[1]

THE FEDERAL BUREAU OF INVESTIGATION (FBI) 1943 report *Survey of Racial Conditions in the United States* (*RACON*) was the result of a nationwide, yearlong investigation commissioned by its director, J. Edgar Hoover. The conclusion of the report opens with the claim that "subversive forces" were and had been at work in the African American community. The report identifies four major forces that had apparently sown "unrest and dissatisfaction." The first of these forces was the Communist Party. The second included "organizations and pseudo leaders having apparent pro-Japanese sympathies," including Marcus Garvey's Universal Negro Improvement Association. The third was homegrown civil rights organizations such as Walter White's National Association for the Advancement of Colored People (NAACP), and the fourth was the black press.[2]

This FBI list of "subversive forces" (although we may take it with a grain of salt) can be read in relation to the concurrent development of the cultures of black internationalism that I have charted in chapters 1–5. The importance that the FBI attached to a transpacific strand of black internationalism, or from its reductive view, the black-Japanese alliance for subversion, is reflected in a section entitled "Japanese Influence and Activity among the American Negroes" of the appendix to the *RACON* report. Marcus Garvey, James Weldon Johnson, and W. E. B. Du Bois are mentioned in this section. George S. Schuyler is cited in a section entitled "The Negro Press" as a writer of pro-Japanese editorials published in the *Pittsburgh Courier*, the nation's largest circulating African American newspaper. Langston Hughes appears in a section entitled "Communist Party Front Organizations and Negroes," but as discussed in chapter 4, the FBI also suspected the poet of asserting pan-racial identification with the Japanese. The specters of communist and pro-Japanese sympathies also arose together in the case of Richard Wright, a card-carrying member of the Communist Party (of which he was a member from 1934 to 1942). In 1942, the FBI received notification from the Military Intelligence Service of the War Department that Wright's text for *Twelve Million Black Voices* (1941), a photo-essay with images drawn from the files of the Farm Security Administration, contains a passage holding up the Japanese Empire as "the possible saviour of the colored races"—a sentiment that the informant found "dangerous to national welfare."[3] Thereupon, Hoover ordered the bureau's New York office to undertake an investigation of Wright as an "Internal Security—Sedition" case, which made Wright a candidate for the Security Index.[4] The irony here, and in the federal scrutiny of black authors in general, is that these reactionary post–Pearl Harbor investigations afford crucial insight into the place of narratives of the black Pacific in the social landscape of the wartime United States.

In concluding my study, I discuss briefly the role of the black Pacific narrative in World War II, which the United States fought as a two-ocean war, by examining a largely neglected aspect of Walter White's black internationalism; namely, White's "Pacific Charter." Departing from the Atlantic Charter, signed in August 1941 by US president Franklin D. Roosevelt and British prime minister Winston S. Churchill, a document that became a founding text of the United Nations, White called for a Pacific Charter. He envisioned a postwar Pacific Community that would be an alternative to the status quo in the region, which, unlike the sovereign nation-states of Europe, was composed predominantly of the colonies and territories of Western democracies.

The most important expression of black internationalism during World War II is generally acknowledged to have been the Double V campaign— "victory over fascism abroad and victory over racism at home"—of the *Pittsburgh Courier*. The paper launched the campaign in the wake of the establishment, on January 1, 1942, of the United Nations, which adopted principles of the Atlantic Charter as war aims. The Double V campaign was predicated upon the promises of self-determination and basic freedoms for all peoples enshrined in the charter. To the V symbol of a United Nations victory, the Double V campaign added another V for "victory over racism at home." Historian Brenda Gayle Plummer observes that despite the limitations of the Atlantic Charter, African Americans "expressed their agreement with the Charter's fundamental principles and their accommodation to the war through the Double-V campaign."[5]

However, the Atlantic Charter sat uneasily with White's black internationalism, which was centered on anticolonialism (which was not one of the main Allied principles) and thus went further than the Double V campaign. In biographer Kenneth Robert Janken's account, White internationalized the race issue during World War II in the context of Third World, and especially Indian, nationalism. In effect, White hitched the black freedom struggle to the anticolonial struggles of the peoples of Asia and Africa for national liberation.[6] Yet, once calls to extend the mandate of the Atlantic Charter to the Pacific context dislodged it from its narrow frame of Nazi-occupied areas in Europe, the charter posed problems for entrenched Allied interests. Churchill held the view that the principle of self-determination set forth in the charter did not apply to colonial subjects in India or other parts of the British Empire in Asia—a position that the NAACP leader challenged.

In 1942, White, who served on FDR's "Black Cabinet," pressed the White House to take a strong anticolonial position on the Indian issue. He proposed that Roosevelt call a Pacific conference equivalent to the Atlantic Conference at which Roosevelt and Churchill had negotiated the Atlantic Charter. White wanted Roosevelt to meet with leaders of India and China in order to forge a "Pacific Charter" that would "assure to all the peoples of the world that the era of white domination of colored peoples is ended."[7] Ultimately, White's vision for a postwar Pacific Community swayed neither the president nor US foreign policy in the region. The Roosevelt administration turned a blind eye to India to preserve the wartime Anglo-American unity.[8] However, White's Pacific Charter had ramifications far beyond the impact of American foreign policy, for it extended to psychological warfare.

This epilogue tells the story of White's Pacific Charter and his actual travels to and through the Pacific that charted his black Pacific geography. In calling for a postwar regionalism alternative to international Anglo-American hegemony, White's vision, as I discuss below, accorded eerily with the design for the Greater East Asia Co-Prosperity Sphere projected by the Japanese propaganda machine. Japan's hegemonic vision of Pacific Community, unlike America's vision, could link very directly to the black fantasy of a global colored empire. I construe White's black Pacific (War) as a system of "cultural exchange" with the Japanese propaganda machine and consider the predicaments and possibilities that the concept of cultural exchange held for his black internationalism.

The story of White's black Pacific begins with his tenuous relationship in the 1930s with Yasuichi Hikida, a Japanese student of the Harlem Renaissance, who became a "negro propaganda" agent for his country. The available biographical records indicate that Hikida entered the United States in 1920 and worked for seventeen years as a domestic for a white family in Bedford Hills, New York. In 1938, Hikida left this job to become a clerk in the Japanese consulate in New York, where he worked until Pearl Harbor. In the wake of the attack, he was apprehended and interned as an alien enemy.[9] As the result of an exchange of diplomatic and other personnel, Hikida was repatriated from New York on June 18, 1942, aboard a neutral Swedish ship, the *Gripsholm*.[10]

The FBI's *RACON* report identifies Hikida as having been an active Japanese agent in the United States. Hikida "possessed a large quantity of literature" concerning African Americans, which FBI officials took to be evidence that he had been "in charge of Japanese propaganda . . . for four or five years and had formally been employed by the Japanese Consulate to spread propaganda among the negroes." The FBI report notes that Hikida had a lifetime membership in the NAACP and that "in this connection," he translated *The Fire in the Flint* (1924), a novel "by Walter White, secretary of the National Association for the Advancement of Colored People, into the Japanese language." The bureau thus advanced the possibility of Japanese infiltration of White's organization.[11]

The *RACON* report reflects some elements of truth. While Hikida's social network was deeply interwoven with African American culture in Harlem, White helped to enlarge Hikida's circle of Talented Tenth acquaintances to James Weldon Johnson, former executive secretary of the NAACP. In September 1933, Hikida initiated correspondence with Johnson with a request for permission to translate into Japanese and publish Johnson's lyric "Lift Every Voice and Sing," known as the African American national anthem.[12] White personally forwarded Hikida's letter to Johnson, enclosing his own letter of introduction, in which he describes Hikida as "my very good friend" and "one of my most esteemed friends."[13] Hikida's translation (under the nom de plume Yonezo Hirayama) of White's own novel, *The Fire in the Flint*, appeared in Japan in 1935 and was reissued in 1937 with a new title, *Lynching*.

In his post–World War II autobiography, *A Man Called White* (1948),

White recalls with chagrin how he was "unwittingly and unwillingly ... utilized through the medium of *The Fire in the Flint* in Japan." According to White, in 1937, the Japanese imperial government launched "a publicity campaign" against US criticism of Japanese military operations, "pointing out that the novel pictured the kind of barbarities which were tolerated and even encouraged in the democracy which had the temerity to criticize Japan for her acts in China." White comments, "I am glad to say that I never received royalties [from the Japanese translation], for I wouldn't have liked that money,"[14] suggesting indirectly that he would not have welcomed payments from Tokyo either, though the FBI apparently suspected that he had received such payments through Hikida.

Hikida, Japan's first international student of the Harlem Renaissance, is thus remembered, to the extent that he is remembered, as a covert agent of the Japanese imperial government. Yet the shift in Hikida's career from a cultural internationalist to a nationalistic propagandist raises important questions about the role that "cultural exchange" played in forming the black Pacific Community. While it is often equated, in a celebratory manner, with internationalism and features prominently in such black Atlantic diaspora scholarship as Paul Gilroy's *Black Atlantic* and Brent Edwards's *Practice of Diaspora*, cultural exchange may be addressed critically in the black Pacific context as a problematic concept.

Hikida was able to shift seamlessly from an internationalist use of cultural exchange into intensely nationalist psychological warfare, not because cultural exchange was an intellectual veneer under which he hid his ulterior motives as a Japanese agent but because cultural exchange can itself serve as an instrument of psychological warfare shaping foreign relations. The vision that Hikida developed in the 1930s of an "Information-Research Center of Negro Race and Culture" in Tokyo to foster an understanding of African American culture among the Japanese people—a dream that he confided to Du Bois prior to the latter's departure for Japan in 1936—was readily adapted to such a use.[15] The plan centered on student, teacher, and journalist exchange programs to promote mutual understanding between African Americans and Japanese, reflecting Hikida's conviction that through exchange, individuals and groups, rather than policy makers, would develop the cultural, intellectual, and educational basis for the Pacific Community. After his return home to Japan in August 1942, Hikida worked part time for the research bureau of the Japanese Ministry of Foreign Affairs in Tokyo. In that time, he completed at least three projects: a translation of the African American author Emmett J. Scott's *American Negro in the World War* (1919);[16] "War and

Blacks," a report on the state of black America since the outbreak of the Pacific War, including analyses of public opinion and trends;[17] and most importantly for my purposes in this epilogue, a foreign policy proposal labeled "Wartime Negro Propaganda Operations."[18] The proposal aims that Hikida submitted in January 1943 were twofold: to contribute to victory in the Pacific War and to prepare for a new postvictory order in the Pacific region. Hikida's plan for achieving these dual goals centered on cultural programs for African American prisoners of war held in territories occupied by the Japanese military, or in Japan proper. Toward the goal of winning the war, he proposed that the Japanese imperial government select black POWs who were gifted in the fields of "music, literature, and speech," train them for a singing and musical corps, and use this corps to produce shortwave radio propaganda broadcasts directed at black America. Toward the second goal, Hikida proposed employing black POWs in a pilot program for postwar international student-exchange programs. He also proposed a program to educate talented POWs for postwar black leadership in the Pacific Community, believing that African Americans would play a significant role at the peace tables and in US-Japan relations after World War II. Despite the different impulses that gave rise to them, Hikida's prewar activities and his wartime and postwar plans reflect a remarkable continuity in their use of cultural exchange to establish foreign relations with black America. For Hikida, sharing with black America seemed essential to paving the way for the international relations that he envisioned in the Pacific Community. Black Americans would be not only members but also leaders, among whom graduates of his abovementioned POW program for post–World War II black leadership might feature. "Wartime Negro Propaganda Operations" ends with an appendix on "influential negro leaders to-day" which includes a list of twenty contemporary black leaders whom Hikida may also have considered to be likely future leaders. First on the list was Walter White, executive secretary of the NAACP.[19]

However, any dreams that Hikida may have had that White would support his plans for the postwar Pacific Community were not realized. Five months before Hikida's submission of "Wartime Negro Propaganda Operations" to Japan's Foreign Office—indeed, even before the repatriation ship had returned Hikida to Japanese soil—White had agreed to lend his support to the Office of War Information (OWI). Set up by the Roosevelt administration as America's wartime propaganda agency, the OWI had sought White's support soon after intercepting a Japanese broadcast to the South Seas that "manipulated a speech of Walter White's."

White had delivered the speech in question to a massive rally in Madison Square Garden in New York City organized by A. Philip Randolph as part of the March on Washington Movement. Radio Tokyo, in its South Pacific broadcast, cited White's criticism of the Atlantic Charter, presumably with the objective of discrediting both Roosevelt, an author of the charter, and the democratic system "in the eyes of the colored peoples of that area." The OWI's transcript of the broadcast reads as follows.

Tokyo to the South Seas   June 21, 1942

> STOCKHOLM: In a stirring address before an 18,000 colored audience in the Madison Square Garden in New York City, Walter White, a leading colored Negro, delivered a strong accusation against the Roosevelt administration. Urging the application of the principles of the Atlantic Charter to America's domestic problem, the colored speaker declared that before President Roosevelt attempted a racial equality among the nation, he [should] set his own house in order. White reminded his listeners that racial prejudice is still in evidence, and that the special relationship of the white and the colored people is yet to be solved.[20]

In the analysis of the OWI, the intention of the Japanese broadcaster in pointing out, via White, that the Roosevelt administration was "guilty of fostering racial inequality in the United States" was "to stir up hostility to the United States among the colored peoples" in the South Seas.[21] On August 3, 1942, Alan R. Murray, an OWI official, asked White to write a five-minute message to the Japanese for a special program entitled "Voice of Freedom" and to record it at OWI facilities in New York for broadcast via shortwave from San Francisco to Japan. Murray proposed this broadcast to White as a counter to the Japanese propaganda machine in Tokyo: "Inasmuch as the Japanese have been misquoting you at length for some time now," writes Murray, "we believe an address by you would be very effective." White agreed to do the broadcast.[22]

The message that White prepared reveals his own vision for the postwar Pacific Community. His message begins by addressing the Japanese people across the Pacific as a representative of black America: "To the people of Japan, greeting! My name is Walter White of the United States of America. I am a Negro. There are thirteen million of us in the one hundred and thirty million citizens of the United States." White then recounts the "dark, tragic history" of suffering that his race had endured in the United States, remarking on slavery, Jim Crow, lynching, and more recently, segregation in the US armed forces, "even as our country wages a bloody and expensive war for the four freedoms enunciated by President Roosevelt." After deploring these wrongs, however, White notes that they have been "played up by the Japanese propaganda machine," and "as an American Negro," he urges his Japanese audience "to throw off the spell your militarists have attempted to weave about you and to work and fight for a United Nations victory over the Axis." He reasons that Hitler's victory would inevitably lead to the "destruction" of all of the world's colored peoples—"You of the Pacific" not excepted—"whose skins are not Hitler's special kind, of white." The race prejudices of the United States and Great Britain, the Western democracies, are "bad enough," White warns, "but Hitler's will be infinitely worse." He argues furthermore that although democracy has frequently failed, "it has one great merit": in democracies, "racial, religious and other minorities can organize to fight for their place in the sun." This is precisely what African Americans are doing in the United States, White maintains, and he vows to the Japanese people that African Americans will continue their struggle to abolish discrimination against themselves in the United States and against other colored peoples abroad. "To that end," his message continues, "a steadily growing number of us are working for a Pacific Charter which will guarantee in absolute terms the four freedoms to *all* the peoples of the earth." Having thus culminated with this vision of a Pacific Charter, White's message ends with an appeal to the "men and women of Japan" for support in the creation of "a truly democratic world" in the Pacific, the only kind of world that "can give you and us, our children and our children's children freedom and peace and equal opportunity for a good life."[23]

Neither of the contrasting exchanges on the future of the Pacific Community that former friends White and Hikida prepared ever took place. Hikida's proposed cultural program for black POWs, which would have required the authorization and cooperation of the military, was apparently shelved by the Japanese foreign ministry. White ultimately refused to allow his message to be broadcast to Japan by the OWI, in protest against US foreign policy in Pacific affairs. When Roosevelt remained silent on the British arrests of Mohandas Gandhi, Jawaharlal Nehru, and other Indian nationalist leaders, in effect acquiescing to British colonial policy, White wired the OWI with the message that the "arrests leave me with nothing convincing to say [to the Japanese]."[24] White also wired Roosevelt directly to demand the president's immediate action as a mediator in India. With the turn of events in India, White wrote, "Japan won a great victory in the Pacific ... because [the Japanese] too wanted and demanded for [the] people of India the same freedom the British government is fighting to preserve for white Englishmen." American action was urgent, White insisted to Roosevelt, because "one billion brown and yellow peoples in the Pacific will without question consider ruthless treatment of Indian leaders and people typical of what white peoples will do to colored peoples if [the] United Nations win."[25]

In critiquing the Anglo-American imperial racial hegemony in Asia and calling for a Pacific Charter to supplement the Atlantic Charter, White's rhetoric accorded eerily with the Japanese propaganda machine that he denounced. Japan's own "Pacific Charter," a joint declaration of Greater East-Asiatic Nations that Japan completed with five other countries (China under the Wang Ching-wei regime, Thailand, Manchukuo, the Philippines, and Burma) on November 6, 1943, established the principles upon which the postwar Pacific order would be based. The declaration proclaimed Asia to be for Asians and pledged victory over the United States and Great Britain, nations that "have in seeking their own prosperity oppressed other nations and peoples" and "sought to satisfy their inordinate ambition of enslaving the entire region." The fifth article of the declaration set forth as an explicit aim "the abolition of racial discrimination"—an aim not specified in the text of the Atlantic Charter, which defined the goals of the Western democracies for the postwar world.[26]

After his cancellation of the OWI broadcast, White planned to write an article on the Japanese propaganda machine, drawing on OWI transcriptions of Radio Tokyo. Radio Tokyo projected the Pacific War as a war in which "England is imperialistic and the United States but a milch cow to aid Great Britain in her dastardly imperialist determination to rule the world." This narrative, White argues, pointed to "unpleasant truths" about US racial practices to substantiate itself.[27] White offered excerpts from four monitored broadcasts from Radio Tokyo to demonstrate how the Japanese conveyed this narrative:[28]

> Examples of Negro discrimination in the United States are so legion that the old superstition that in America all men are equal by the grace of God is proved untrue. (January 19, 1942)[29]
>
> When he speaks of humanity, does President Roosevelt refer only to his own white skin? Does he mean to say that in the name of common decency and humanity[,] peoples of the so-called colored races can be treacherously treated? (January 16, 1942)

> President Roosevelt warns the people against aggressors who smother free speech. What country in the world has ever been more aggressive, or treated other races with more brutality? What about Negroes, Filipinos, etc.? (January 19, 1942)[30]
>
> In southern states, the (regulation) forces Negroes to ride in *(separate) cars apart from the whites, and they are subject to *(violence) at the hands of angry and blood-thirsty whites. (April 13, 1942)[31]

In White's view, at the root of the psychological warfare being waged in the Pacific theater of World War II was a struggle over the meaning of the war, the narrative that would shape a postwar Pacific Community, and consequently "the future of mankind." White writes in his outline for the article, "Perhaps as determining a factor as guns or planes will be the sibilant hissing into a Tokyo microphone beamed at Malaya and India."[32] For the United States simply to broadcast "counter-propaganda" would not provide "convincing or effective answers." The United States must instead respond to the Japanese propaganda machine, and to the colored peoples in the Pacific, by "speedily do[ing] some housecleaning of our own" in the area of US racial-imperial practices.[33] White's message was unheard. The mainstream US journals that White approached with a proposal for the article all turned him down.[34]

As America's war with Japan entered its later stages, White increasingly perceived it to be evolving into what the Japanese propaganda machine projected it to be. In the conclusion of *A Rising Wind* (1945), White's account of an early 1944 tour of the European war theater, White drew attention to what was transpiring in the Pacific as an imperialist venture of the Western democracies. Colored peoples in the Pacific believed that "the war was being fought to restore empire to Great Britain, France, Holland, and Portugal" and that none of the Western powers would embrace the idea of relinquishing their Pacific colonial holdings after the war. Rather, the colored peoples of the Pacific viewed with foreboding "the immediate resumption of control of Hollandia and other sections of Dutch New Guinea by the Dutch, and similar action by the British in Guadalcanal and Tarawa . . . [and] the preparations being made by France to take over again control of Indo-China" as soon as the Japanese could be driven back toward their islands. The prevailing distrust of the Allies, according to White, was what "any person of normal intelligence could have foreseen." It accorded closely with the narrative of the Pacific War disseminated by the Japanese propaganda machine—a narrative "unhappily based largely on truth," and hence carrying a potent valence for the colored peoples of the Pacific. "What will America's answer be?" White asks. America, he argues, must choose one of two courses: either "revolutionize their racial concepts and practices, to abolish imperialism and grant full equality to all of its peoples, or else prepare for World War III."[35]

In December 1944, White embarked on a thirty-six-thousand-mile, island-hopping course across the Pacific theater of war in the capacity of accredited representative of the *New York Post*. White was granted authority by the commander in chief of the US Pacific Fleet headquarters to travel via Naval Air Transport Service along certain secured routes through the war zones. From Pearl Harbor, where he arrived from New York via San Francisco, White flew over to the islands dotting the ocean; Johnston Atoll, Kwajalein Atoll (the Marshall Islands), Guam, Saipan (the Mariana Islands), Leyte (the Philippines), Hollandia, Biak, and others.[36] During World War II, US forces used Pacific islands for the military tactics of island hopping and leapfrogging, building airstrips and integrating the network of military operations using aircraft. The Pacific War seemed to be drawing to a close with an Allied victory, but White's tour left him more apprehensive than ever about the ultimate meaning of the war and the future of the Pacific Community. In April 1945, White completed the four-month journey. In a report that he submitted on his Pacific trip to a meeting of the NAACP board of directors in New York (which was released to the press), White declared, "Thousands of Americans have died and billions of American dollars have been spent in the Pacific to oust the Japanese—apparently only to restore the recaptured islands to the European powers which ruled and exploited these areas and their populations before the war." The government and people of the United States, White insisted, "must wake up to what is happening in the Pacific" and make clear both to allies and enemies that America's purpose in the war is neither to restore Western maritime empires in the Pacific nor to "enslave colored peoples" under Western imperialism, "which inevitably will breed another war."[37]

When the United States ended the Pacific War with the nuclear bombings of Hiroshima and Nagasaki, it offered what seemed like a portentous answer. The bombs were carried from an airfield built on the captured island of Tinian in the South Pacific; these were to force Japan to surrender in response to what President Truman called "a rain of ruin from the air." According to a September 15, 1945, editorial in the black weekly *New York Amsterdam News*, "The Japanese surrender was drenched with US racial arrogance," and "the world's colonial thinking seems untouched."[38]

The ardent antifascist Langston Hughes wrote in his *Chicago Defender* column in January 1945, the final year of the Pacific War, "I hold no brief for Japanese fascism.... But one good thing this war has done is that it has begun to weaken the unmitigated gall of white imperialism around the world." In Hughes's view, "Japanese imperialism is just as bad as any other—except that the Japanese do not draw the color line.... Their little clash at arm[s], with the British and Americans will, I think, profoundly change the future pattern of life in Asia."[39] Hughes's reading of the Pacific War in 1945 suggests not only that the war was not simply reducible to the "good war" of democracy over fascism of normative memory (even before the war ended) but also that a vision of the future Pacific Community can reshape memories of the past as much as memories of the past shape the future. I have argued throughout this study that African American literature and letters are media that ensured then, as they continue to ensure now, the viability of radical alternative narratives of the Pacific. Although the black Pacific is primarily an idea, an imagined community forged by African American geographic imaginings, it subjected, and still subjects, the Pacific Community and its hegemonic regional order to question and challenge from its own alternative viewpoint.

After World War II, the United States replaced the British Empire as the hegemon in Asia. Interacting with, and countering, regional pressures and resistances, the United States built on a string of military bases its informal empire, which was no longer regional but global. In 1949, four years after the end of the war, White resumed his globe-trotting, joining a round-the-world tour sponsored by *America's Town Meeting of the Air*, an ABC public affairs radio program. The party visited twelve countries for the free exchange of ideas, including American-occupied Japan (figure 6.1). On this tour, White was a speaker on a program broadcast from Karachi, Pakistan, that discussed the topic of "How Can We Advance Democracy in Asia?" White proposed that "a new kind of regional organization" be formed in Asia "to exchange experiences and natural resources," putting aside "nationalist and religious differences." This "Asian union," said White, "would be a federation based upon peace instead of war." White concluded his speech by endorsing—though admitting the "grave shortcomings" of the United States—democracy under which

6.1. Walter White (with Poppy Cannon), wearing a kimono, in American-occupied Japan, in 1949. *Prints and Photographs Division, Library of Congress.*

"minorities can fight against injustice."[40] White's black "Voice of America" thus defended American democracy in a turbulent Asia at a time when the Iron and Bamboo Curtains were being erected.[41]

African American narratives of the Pacific in the Cold War era are yet to be fully recovered. However, such a recovery project would necessarily be a limited one unless it addressed the spatial paradigm shift that occurred in 1940s America, a shift that eroded any sense of hemispheric isolation and the earth's division into separate oceans and continents. The long-accepted, equator-based Mercator projection had been the standard map projection for maritime navigation since the sixteenth century, but it rapidly lost its narrative power in the wartime United States. Instead, an innovative cartography adopting an aerial perspective centered on the North Pole—popularized by the cartographic artist Richard Edes Harrison[42]—represented America's fresh world outlook, ushering in what Alan K. Henrikson has termed "air-age globalism." Air-age globalism, according to Henrikson, emerged with the surprise air attack on the US naval base at Pearl Harbor, a target presumed to be impossible because of the distance, as a "primal event." The distance was conceptually even greater in the traditional Mercator map placing Hawai'i and Japan at the extreme left and right sides respectively.[43] As one contemporary geographer noted, "We just retreated into an imaginary eastern hemisphere (a hemisphere which exists on a Mercator map but does not exist, as such, on a pole-centered air-age map)."[44] After World War II, an air-age map was adapted into a spatial context for postwar justice and durable peace. The official emblem of the United Nations, designed by the Presentation Branch of the Office of Strategic Services (America's wartime intelligence agency) and subsequently modified and approved on December 7, 1946, was "a map of the world representing an azimuthal equidistant projection centred on the North Pole, inscribed in a wreath consisting of crossed conventionalized branches of the olive tree, in gold on a field of smoke-blue with all water areas in white."[45] It mapped the postwar world—One World—centering on the North Pole, a region that did not appear at all on most versions of the Mercator projection. This codification of the postwar world, illustrating the proximity of the United States and the Soviet Union over the pole, was also adaptable to America's Cold War imaginary.

The spatial revolution, brought about by the air-age sensibility, would necessarily reframe the terrain of black internationalism. The black Pacific narrative that I have studied in this volume was primarily a product of, and active within, the interwar period marked by the rise of a Pacific Community in the 1920s and by the wartime air-age paradigm shift in the 1940s. My readings of black Pacific narratives of James Weldon Johnson, George S. Schuyler, the black Federal Theatre Project, Langston Hughes, W. E. B. Du Bois, and Walter White in the end have been undertaken to convey the power of geographic imaginings that were vitally implicated in the material process of the international and interracial ordering.

NOTES

Introduction

1. "September 11, 2001," *Washington Post*, September 12, 2001, A30.
2. Emily S. Rosenberg, *A Date Which Will Live: Pearl Harbor in American Memory* (Durham, NC: Duke University Press, 2003), 174. For an illuminating discussion of the analogy between 9/11 and Pearl Harbor, see also John W. Dower, *Cultures of War: Pearl Harbor/ Hiroshima/ 9-11/ Iraq* (New York: Norton, 2010), 3–21.
3. See, for instance, Henry Allen, "The Message in the Smoke," *Washington Post*, September 12, 2001, C01; and Joel Achenbach and William Booth, "Nation Shuts Down as It Lives Its 'Darkest Day,'" *Washington Post*, September 12, 2001, A22.
4. Dan Balz and Bob Woodward, "America's Chaotic Road to War," *Washington Post*, January 27, 2002, A01.
5. "Preacher with a Penchant for Controversy," *Washington Post*, March 15, 2008, A6.
6. Nation of Islam, "Nation of Islam Responds to the Attack on America," accessed November 22, 2010, http://www.noi.org.
7. "This Victory Alone Is Not the Change We Seek," *Washington Post*, November 5, 2008, A46.
8. Ernest J. Gaines, *The Autobiography of Miss Jane Pittman* (1971; New York: Bantam, 1972), 220.
9. Ishmael Reed, *Japanese by Spring* (1993; New York: Penguin, 1996), 136.
10. John Oliver Killens, *And Then We Heard the Thunder* (1962; Washington, DC: Howard University Press, 1983), 258–60, 328, 349.
11. John Oliver Killens, *Black Man's Burden* (1965; New York: Simon and Schuster, 1970), 121–22.
12. "A New Low in Thinking," *Chicago Defender*, September 15, 1945, 14.
13. Chester Himes, *Lonely Crusade* (1947; New York: Thunder's Mouth Press, 1986), 46.
14. Malcolm X and Alex Haley, *The Autobiography of Malcolm X* (1964; New York: Ballantine, 1992), 121.
15. George Lipsitz, "'Frantic to Join . . . the Japanese Army': Black Soldiers and Civilians Confront the Asia-Pacific War," in *Perilous Memories: The Asia-Pacific War(s)*, ed. T. Fujitani, Geoffrey M. White, and Lisa Yoneyama, 347–77 (Durham, NC: Duke University Press, 2001), 349.

16. "Concentration Camps for Japanese: Remarks of Hon. John E. Rankin of Mississippi in the House of Representatives, Monday, February 23, 1942," *Congressional Record Appendix*, 77th Cong., 2d sess. (1942), vol. 88, pt. 8: A768.

17. For illuminating discussions of the American Pacific, see, for instance, Rob Wilson, *Reimagining the American Pacific: From "South Pacific" to Bamboo Ridge and Beyond* (Durham, NC: Duke University Press, 2000); and John R. Eperjesi, *The Imperialist Imaginary: Visions of Asia and the Pacific in American Culture* (Hanover, NH: University Press of New England/Dartmouth College Press, 2005).

18. Here I borrow the concept of "imagined community" from Benedict Anderson's *Imagined Communities: Reflections on the Origin and Spread of Nationalism* (London: Verso, 1983).

19. Lawrence W. Levine, *The Unpredictable Past: Explorations in American Cultural History* (New York: Oxford University Press, 1993); see also Marc Gallicchio, ed., *The Unpredictability of the Past: Memories of the Asia-Pacific War in U.S.–East Asian Relations* (Durham, NC: Duke University Press, 2007).

20. Much excellent work has been done on connections between Asian Americans and African Americans; see, for example, Helen Heran Jun, *Race for Citizenship: Black Orientalism and Asian Uplift from Pre-Emancipation to Neoliberal America* (New York: New York University Press, 2011).

21. Pekka Korhonen, "The Pacific Age in World History," *Journal of World History* 7, no. 1 (spring 1996): 46.

22. Lanny Thompson, *Imperial Archipelago: Representation and Rule in the Insular Territories under U.S. Dominion after 1898* (Honolulu: University of Hawai'i Press, 2010), 7–8.

23. The best treatment of the Pacific Community as a modern regionalism, initiated and led by the United States, is found in Tomoko Akami, *Internationalizing the Pacific: The United States, Japan and the Institute of Pacific Relations in War and Peace, 1919–45* (London: Routledge, 2002).

24. This brief historical overview relies on Akami, *Internationalizing the Pacific*, 1–16, 33–45.

25. Susan Schulten, *The Geographical Imagination in America, 1880–1950* (Chicago: University of Chicago Press, 2001), 1.

26. Bruce Cumings, *Parallax Visions: Making Sense of American-East Asian Relations* (Durham, NC: Duke University Press, 1999), 6.

27. Brent Hayes Edwards, *The Practice of Diaspora: Literature, Translation, and the Rise of Black Internationalism* (Cambridge, MA: Harvard University Press, 2003), 3.

28. Ibid., 11, 14.

29. Michelle Ann Stephens, *Black Empire: The Masculine Global Imaginary of Caribbean Intellectuals in the United States, 1914–1962* (Durham, NC: Duke University Press, 2005), 5, 31.

30. Kate A. Baldwin, *Beyond the Color Line and the Iron Curtain: Reading Encounters between Black and Red, 1922–1963* (Durham, NC: Duke University Press, 2002), 9–10.

31. For an account of the FBI surveillance on black America, see Kenneth O'Reilly, *Black Americans: The FBI Files*, ed. David Gallen (New York: Carroll and Graf, 1994).

32. Stephens, *Black Empire*, 8, 110.

33. "Report by Special Agent P-138," New York City, October 9, 1920, in Robert A. Hill, ed., *The Marcus Garvey and Universal Negro Improvement Association Papers* (Berkeley: University of California Press, 1983–1995), 3:47; "Reports by Special Agent P-138," New York City, November 6, 1920, in Hill, *Marcus Garvey*, 3:71.

34. J. J. Hannigan, Commandant, Twelfth Naval District, to the Director, Office of Naval Intelligence, [San Francisco], December 3, 1921, in Hill, *Marcus Garvey*, 4:233–37.

35. "Japanese Racial Agitation among American Negroes," prepared by the Evaluation Section of the Counterintelligence Group, MID 291.2, Japanese, 4/15/42, 11–12, Records of Headquarters Army Service Forces, RG 160, entry 196A, box 383, National Archives and Records Administration (NARA), College Park, MD.

36. Robert A. Hill, introduction, in *The FBI's RACON: Racial Conditions in the United States during World War II*, ed. Robert A. Hill, 1–72 (Boston: Northeastern University Press, 1995), 33.

37. Ernest Allen Jr., "When Japan Was 'Champion of the Darker Races': Satokata Takahashi and the Flowering of Black Messianic Nationalism," *Black Scholar* 24, no. 1 (winter 1994): 23–24.

38. Hill, *FBI's RACON*, 513.

39. Ibid., 526, 542.

40. Quoted in Hill, introduction, 8.

41. Hill, *FBI's RACON*, 101.

42. "Japanese Racial Agitation among American Negroes," 17.

43. Killens, *And Then We Heard the Thunder*, 257.

44. For useful discussions of Japanese views of African Americans, see Hiromi Furukawa and Tetsushi Furukawa, *Nihonjin to Afurikakei Amerikajin: Nichibei kankeishi ni okeru sono Shoso* [Japanese and African Americans: Aspects in the History of Japan-U.S. Relations] (Tokyo: Akashi Shoten, 2004); and Yukiko Koshiro, "Beyond an Alliance of Color: The African American Impact on Modern Japan," in "The Afro-Asian Century," ed. Andrew F. Jones and Nikhil Pal Singh, special issue, *positions* 11, no. 1 (spring 2003): 183–215.

45. Hill, *FBI's RACON*, 512.

46. "Seized Japanese Book Reveals Propaganda for War against America," *Washington Herald*, January 15, 1934, 1.

47. Kyosuke Fukunaga, *Nichibeisen Miraiki* [Forecast of Future American Japanese War] (Tokyo: Shincho-sha, 1934), 11, 119; "Japanese Pamphlet Relates How Panama Is Blasted, Ships Lost," *Washington Herald*, January 16, 1934, 1; "Honor for Japanese Starting War on U.S. Pledged in Seized Pamphlet," *Washington Herald*, January 18, 1934, 7.

48. Hill, *FBI's RACON*, 512.

49. Mark R. Peattie, "Forecasting a Pacific War, 1912–1933: The Idea of a Conditional Japanese Victory," in *The Ambivalence of Nationalism: Modern Japan between East and West*, ed. James W. White, Michiko Umegaki, and Thomas R. H. Havens, 115–31 (Lanham, MD: University Press of America, 1990), 116.

50. Kojiro Sato, *Nichibei Senso Yume Monogatari* [A Fantasy of the Japanese–United States War] (Tokyo: Nihon Hyoron-sha, 1921), 200–202, 213–21.

51. Marcus Garvey to Emperor Yoshihito of Japan [New York, September 6, 1923], in Hill, *Marcus Garvey*, 5:442.

52. F. O. Matthiessen, *American Renaissance: Art and Expression in the Age of Emerson and Whitman* (New York: Oxford University Press, 1941), ix.

53. Hill, *FBI's RACON*, 508–9.

54. Edwards, *Practice of Diaspora*, 2.

55. Henry Louis Gates Jr., "The Trope of a New Negro and the Reconstruction of the Image of the Black," in "America Reconstructed, 1840–1940," special issue, *Representations* 24 (fall 1988): 136, 138.

56. A modern war that came to resemble a dress rehearsal for World War I, the Russo-Japanese War is sometimes called "World War Zero."

57. Korhonen, "The Pacific Age," 49. Theodore Roosevelt mediated peace negotiations between Russia and Japan that resulted in the conclusion of the Treaty of Portsmouth in New Hampshire in 1905 and was awarded a Nobel Peace Prize for this work.

58. Hill, *FBI's RACON*, 508.

59. "The Way of the World," *Colored American Magazine*, July 1905, 348.

60. James Marmaduke Boddy, "The Ethnology of the Japanese Race," *Colored American Magazine*, October 1905, 585.

61. Pauline E. Hopkins, "The Dark Races of the Twentieth Century: II, The Malay Peninsula," *Voice of the Negro* 2, no. 3 (March 1905): 191; Hopkins, "The Dark Races of the Twentieth Century: III, The Yellow Race," *Voice of the Negro* 2, no. 5 (May 1905): 333–34.

62. W. E. B. Du Bois, *The Souls of Black Folk*, in *W. E. B. Du Bois: Writings*, ed. Nathan Huggins (New York: Library of America, 1986), 372.

63. W. E. B. Du Bois, "The Color Line Belts the World," in *W. E. B. Du Bois: A Reader*, ed. David Levering Lewis (New York: Henry Holt, 1995), 42–43.

64. Lothrop Stoddard, *The Rising Tide of Color against White World-Supremacy* (1920; Honolulu: University Press of the Pacific, 2003), 43, 307–8.

65. F. Scott Fitzgerald, *The Great Gatsby* (1925; New York: Charles Scribner's Sons, 1953), 9.

66. "Villa Lewaro-on-the-Hudson, Birthplace of International League of Darker Peoples," *World Forum* 1, no. 1 (January 1919): 2–3; "Japanese Representatives Urge Fight on Race Prejudice at Waldorf Astoria," *World Forum* 1, no. 1 (January 1919): 1, both in Correspondence of the Military Intelligence Division relating to "Negro Subversion," file 10218-296 (National Archives Microfilm Publication M1440, roll 5), Records of the War Department General and Special Staff, RG 165, NARA.

67. Yuichiro Onishi, "The New Negro of the Pacific: How African Americans Forged Cross-Racial Solidarity with Japan, 1917–1922," *Journal of African American History* 92, no. 2 (spring 2007): 193.

68. For an account of the Japanese proposal for racial equality, see Naoko Shimazu, *Japan, Race and Equality: The Racial Equality Proposal of 1919* (London: Routledge, 1998). Also useful is Paul Gordon Lauren, *Power and Prejudice: The Politics and Diplomacy of Racial Discrimination*, 2nd ed. (Boulder, CO: Westview, 1996), 82–107.

69. Patrick Gallagher, *America's Aims and Asia's Aspirations* (New York: Century, 1920), 97.

70. W. E. B. Du Bois, "Opinion," *Crisis* 18 (May 1919): 11.

71. Mary Church Terrell, *A Colored Woman in a White World* (1940; North Stratford, NH: Ayer, 1998), 335, 340.

72. Hill, *FBI's RACON*, 508.

73. Dominic Lieven, *Empire: The Russian Empire and Its Rivals* (2000; New Haven, CT: Yale University Press, 2002), 6, 7.

74. Michael Hardt and Antonio Negri, *Empire* (Cambridge, MA: Harvard University Press, 2000), xii, xvi.

75. Lieven, *Empire*, xii. In the schematization of Fredric Jameson, the term "imperialism" was used between the world wars in two different (though not unrelated) contexts. In the first, "imperialism" designates "the rivalry of the various imperial and metropolitan nation-states among themselves" and, in the second, "the relationship of metropolis to colony" (Jameson, "Modernism and Imperialism," in *Nationalism, Colonialism, and Literature*, by Terry Eagleton, Fredric Jameson, and Edward W. Said, 43–66 [Minneapolis: University of Minnesota Press, 1990], 47).

76. Gerald Horne's study shows how the British Empire and its racism in Asia—bolstered by other European maritime empires—"demobilized the colonized, making them highly susceptible to Japanese racial appeals" (Horne, *Race War: White Supremacy and the Japanese Attack on the British Empire* [New York: New York University Press, 2004], viii).

77. Article 21 of the league covenant provides, "Nothing in this Covenant shall be deemed to affect the validity of international engagements, such as treaties of arbitration or regional understandings like the Monroe Doctrine, for securing the maintenance of peace."

78. See Takeshi Hamashita, "The Intra-regional System in East Asia in Modern Times," in *Network Power: Japan and Asia*, ed. Peter J. Katzenstein and Takashi Shiraishi, 113–35 (Ithaca, NY: Cornell University Press, 1997).

79. Peter J. Katzenstein and Takashi Shiraishi, "Regions in World Politics: Japan and Asia—Germany in Europe," in Katzenstein and Shiraishi, *Network Power*, 341–81, 352–53.

80. Ibid., 355.

81. Lieven, *Empire*, 293.

82. Katzenstein and Shiraishi, "Regions in World Politics," 354.

83. Shimazu, *Japan, Race and Equality*, 172.

84. "Japan and the Race Issue," *Messenger*, May–June 1919, 6–7, in Correspondence of the Military Intelligence Division relating to "Negro Subversion," file 10218-296, RG 165, NARA.

85. Barbara Foley, *Spectres of 1919: Class and Nation in the Making of the New Negro* (Urbana: University of Illinois Press, 2003), 105.

86. James Weldon Johnson, "Views and Reviews: Little Japan," *New York Age*, May 24, 1919, 4. For Johnson, the Great War just ended was a consequence of inter-imperialist rivalry, and he considered the incidental rebukes the great powers directed at one another on "moral" issues of colonial injustice to be mere "hypocrisy" (James

Weldon Johnson, "Views and Reviews: The Shantung Grant," *New York Age*, July 26, 1919, 4).

87. Johnson, "Views and Reviews: Little Japan," 4.

88. Schulten, *Geographical Imagination*, 1.

89. By the same token, the black Pacific narrative should not be confused with stories of African American encounter with Japan or China as told in such pioneering scholarship as Allen, "When Japan Was 'Champion'"; Reginald Kearney, *African American Views of the Japanese: Solidarity or Sedition?* (Albany: State University of New York Press, 1998); and Marc Gallicchio, *The African American Encounter with Japan and China: Black Internationalism in Asia, 1895–1945* (Chapel Hill: University of North Carolina Press, 2000).

90. Bill V. Mullen, *Afro-Orientalism* (Minneapolis: University of Minnesota Press, 2004), xv.

91. Marshall G. S. Hodgson, *Rethinking World History: Essays on Europe, Islam, and World History* (Cambridge: Cambridge University Press, 1993), 5.

92. Nella Larsen, *Passing* (1929; Mineola, NY: Dover, 2004), 91.

Chapter 1. The Cartography of the Black Pacific: James Weldon Johnson's Along This Way

1. James Weldon Johnson to Grace Nail Johnson, on board SS *President Pierce*, October 16, 1929, box 41, folder 32, James Weldon Johnson and Grace Nail Johnson Papers, Yale Collection of American Literature, Beinecke Rare Book and Manuscript Library, Yale University, New Haven, CT (hereafter cited as JWJ Papers).

2. Biographer Eugene Levy depicts Johnson on this journey as essentially a vacationer (Levy, *James Weldon Johnson: Black Leader, Black Voice* [Chicago: University of Chicago Press, 1973], 289–90). Given the ignominious demise of the IPR, which was disbanded in 1961 after being demonized in 1950s Cold War America as a communist front organization, Levy's failure to ascribe significance to the organization in his 1973 study of Johnson may come as no great surprise.

3. The most thorough treatment of the IPR is found in Akami, *Internationalizing the Pacific*.

4. Shimazu, *Japan, Race and Equality*, 172.

5. Institute of Pacific Relations, *Problems of the Pacific, 1929: Proceedings of the Third Conference of the Institute of Pacific Relations, Nara and Kyoto, Japan, October 23 to November 9, 1929*, ed. J. B. Condliffe (Chicago: University of Chicago Press, 1930), 660.

6. "Report of Informal Discussions Bearing on Problems of the Pacific," box A-1, folder 1, Institute of Pacific Relations Records, Manuscripts in the Department of Archives and Manuscripts at the University of Hawai'i at Manoa, Honolulu (hereafter cited as IPR Records).

7. "Opening Address by Dr. Inazo Nitobe at Institute of Pacific Relations Conference at Kyoto," *Osaka Mainichi & the Tokyo Nichi Nichi*, October 29, 1929, 4.

8. "Suggested Copy for Tentative Printed Statement: A Pan-Pacific Institute," box A-1, folder 1, IPR Records.

9. Box B-4, folder 5, IPR Records.

10. James Weldon Johnson, *Along This Way: The Autobiography of James Weldon Johnson* (1933; New York: Da Capo Press, 2000), 393. Further references are to this edition and will be cited parenthetically as *ATW*.

11. Edward C. Carter to James Weldon Johnson, August 7, 1929; Carter to Johnson, August 8, 1929, box 10, folder 231, JWJ Papers.

12. Johnson's belated appointment to the American delegation complicated his travel arrangements. Upon Johnson's acceptance of the appointment, Carter wrote Arthur B. Spingarn requesting the permission of the board of the NAACP for Johnson to leave his duties in time to depart for the conference on the *Empress of Asia*, which was to sail on October 3 from Vancouver (Edward C. Carter to Arthur B. Spingarn, August 14, 1929, box 10, folder 231, JWJ Papers). This done, Carter hurriedly embarked for Japan by way of Europe and Siberia. Left behind, Johnson soon found things running awry. He attempted to make steamship reservations through the American Council of the IPR, but by the time he became a delegate, the *Empress of Asia* was fully booked. American Council, in the absence of Carter, asked Johnson to contact the American Mail Line directly ("Memorandum for Mr. Johnson," August 21, 1929, box 10, folder 231, JWJ Papers). A week later, Johnson managed to book passage on the SS *President Pierce* sailing from Seattle and sent his itinerary to Tokyo (James Weldon Johnson to Soichi Saito, August 28, 1929, box 10, folder 229, JWJ Papers). This done, Johnson telegraphed his wife on September 3 to request that she send him snapshots of himself to be used as passport photographs (James Weldon Johnson to Grace Nail Johnson, telegram, September 3, 1929, box 41, folder 31, JWJ Papers). On September 30, feeling "blue and lonely," Johnson left Grand Central Station in New York for Seattle (James Weldon Johnson to Grace Nail Johnson, October 1, 1929, box 41, folder 31, JWJ Papers).

13. "Minutes: Joint Meeting of Executive and Delegates Committees," New York City, April 14, 1927, box A-1, folder 5, IPR Records.

14. "Conference of American Members of Kyoto Conference," New York City, May 26–27, 1929; "Summary of Discussion . . . May 27, 1929: RE. Widening the Racial Basis of the American Group at the Kyoto Conference," 151–151A, box B-2, folder 19, IPR Records.

15. "J. Weldon Johnson Goes to Conference in Japan," *New York Age*, October 5, 1929, 1; "N.A.A.C.P. Secretary Off to Japan," *Afro-American*, October 5, 1929, 1.

16. *Tokyo Asahi Shimbun*, October 19, 1929, evening edition, 2.

17. "Professor Heads Italian Engineers Here for Congress:. . . Negro Leader Arrives; Association for Advancement of Colored People's Delegate Going to Kyoto," *Japan Advertiser*, October 19, 1929, 1, 3; "More Delegates Here for Parley: President Pierce Arrives from Seattle with Many Passengers," *Japan Times & Mail*, October 19, 1929, 1.

18. "Delegates to Engineering Congress and Pacific Conference Arrive at Yokohama: President Pierce Brings . . . Negro Leader . . . to Japan," *Osaka Mainichi & the Tokyo Nichi Nichi*, October 19, 1929, 2.

19. James Weldon Johnson to Grace Nail Johnson, Imperial Hotel of Tokyo, October 19, 1929, box 41, folder 32, JWJ Papers.

20. "Chrysanthemum Garden Party Held after Three Year Lapse," *Japan Advertiser*, November 13, 1929, 1.

21. Koshiro, "Beyond an Alliance," 187.
22. "Chrysanthemum Garden Party," 1. This scene, described in Johnson's autobiography, "fascinated" black critic William Stanley Braithwaite. Braithwaite, reviewer of *Along This Way* in the monthly magazine *Opportunity* in 1933, wrote, "Did one, as one read Mr. Johnson's simple, but impressive, description of the affair and the picture of the arrival of the Imperial family and court upon the scene, feel some magic by which the spectacle was transformed into an allegory of the Past and Future, of Time and Race? If an allegory is evoked did it fuse the spirit of the dark people who had mastered with the dark people who were rising to a mastery of their own? And the framework to hold the allegory, the fact that both dark peoples had been freed of a bondage but a few years apart!" (Braithwaite, "*Along This Way*: A Review of the Autobiography of James Weldon Johnson," *Opportunity* 11, no. 12 [December 1933]: 377, 378). Most likely alluding to the Meiji Restoration (1868) that marked the end of the Japanese system of feudalism, Braithwaite viewed it as comparable to the emancipation of African American slaves in the United States in 1863, thus linking the destinies of the two dark peoples, blacks and Japanese.
23. Johnson, "Views and Reviews: Little Japan," 4.
24. Japan Society, "Annual Dinner in Honor of His Excellency Viscount Ishii, Imperial Japanese Ambassador, and Viscountess Ishii," Scrapbooks of Clippings and Miscellaneous Ephemera about James Weldon Johnson and His Books, *Along This Way* II, Beinecke Rare Book and Manuscript Library, Yale University; "Ishii Looks to End of Race Prejudice," *New York Times*, March 15, 1919, 8.
25. Johnson, "Views and Reviews: Little Japan," 4.
26. "Nihonjin no Mune e Kokujin no Kokoro o" [The Black Soul to the Japanese Heart], *Tokyo Asahi Shimbun*, October 19, 1929, evening edition, 2. My translation.
27. James Weldon Johnson to Grace Nail Johnson, Kyoto Hotel, October 27–29, 1929, box 41, folder 32, JWJ Papers.
28. Ibid.
29. J. Merle Davis, speech, quoted in *Japan Advertiser*, October 29, 1929, 3.
30. "Opening Address by Dr. Inazo Nitobe," 4.
31. "Address of Premier Hamaguchi," *Osaka Mainichi & the Tokyo Nichi Nichi*, October 29, 1929, 1.
32. Herbert Hoover, telegram, box B-3, folder 1, IPR Records; "President Hoover's Message Is Read by U.S. Chief Delegate," *Osaka Mainichi & the Tokyo Nichi Nichi*, October 29, 1929, 1.
33. See "Report of Round Table No. 2," box B-3, folder 8; "Report of Round Table No. 3," box B-3, folder 14; and "Report of Round Table No. 2," box B-4, folder 2, IPR Records.
34. "Report of Round Table No. 2," box B-4, folder 2, IPR Records.
35. Johnson to Grace Nail, October 27–29, 1929.
36. "Institute of Pacific Relations: Informal Conference," box B-2, folder 21, IPR Records.
37. James Weldon Johnson to Grace Nail Johnson, Kyoto Hotel, November 4, 1929, box 41, folder 32, JWJ Papers.
38. During a stop in Hawai'i en route home from Japan, Johnson gave an address

at a luncheon for the visiting members of the American Council of the IPR. Viewing the problems of the Pacific as "a member of an inner American group, a nation within the nation," Johnson addressed "one factor deeply imbedded and tremendously charged emotionally, which has hardly yet come to the surface," that is, "the factor of inter-racial feeling" ("Kyoto Meet to Have Far Flung Effect," *Honolulu Advertiser*, November 22, 1929, 6). As he recalls in *Along This Way*, his speech chilled the audience, but he "had never made a less popular or a better speech in [his] life" (*ATW*, 405).

39. David Levering Lewis, *When Harlem Was in Vogue* (1981; New York: Penguin, 1997), 147.

40. Ibid., 148, 147.

41. Harold Norman Denny, *Dollars for Bullets: The Story of American Rule in Nicaragua* (New York: Dial Press, 1929), 7, 118.

42. See, for instance, Donald C. Hodges, *Intellectual Foundations of the Nicaraguan Revolution* (Austin: University of Texas Press, 1986), 107–58.

43. Karl Bermann, *Under the Big Stick: Nicaragua and the United States since 1848* (Boston: South End Press, 1986), vii.

44. Richard Millett, *Guardians of the Dynasty* (Maryknoll, NY: Orbis Books, 1977), 117.

45. For instance, in *Along This Way*, Johnson counsels Commander Terhune, who was tormented by a sense of guilt for his men's shooting and killing of an innocent Nicaraguan boy, that "under the circumstances," he should not "assume the guilt personally" (*ATW*, 287).

46. William E. Gibbs, "James Weldon Johnson: A Black Perspective on 'Big Stick' Diplomacy," *Diplomatic History* 8, no. 4 (fall 1984): 345.

47. "N.A.A.C.P. Secretary Testifies on U.S. Imperialism before Senate Committee," February 27, 1925, part 11, series B, reel 9, frame 506, *Papers of the NAACP*, Library of Congress, Washington, DC.

48. "Would Curb Officials," *New York Times*, February 26, 1925, 3.

49. Smedley D. Butler, "America's Armed Forces," *Common Sense* 4, no. 11 (November 1935): 8.

50. Gibbs, "James Weldon Johnson," 346.

51. For insightful hemispheric readings of James Weldon Johnson, see Harilaos Stecopoulos, "Up from Empire: James Weldon Johnson, Latin America, and the Jim Crow South," in *Imagining Our Americas: Toward a Transnational Frame*, ed. Sandhya Shukla and Heidi Tinsman, 34–62 (Durham, NC: Duke University Press, 2007); and Amanda M. Page, "The Ever-Expanding South: James Weldon Johnson and the Rhetoric of the Global Color Line," *Southern Quarterly* 46, no. 3 (spring 2009): 26–46.

52. "Japanese Attacks Policies of United States in Pamphlets Broadcast in Latin America," *New York Times*, November 23, 1932, 1.

53. "South Americans Stress Tokyo Reply," *New York Times*, December 27, 1931, 22.

54. "Preserving Foreign Policies," *New York Age*, January 28, 1933, 4.

55. Perhaps a brief explanation is in order here. A major point in dispute was the Japanese stationing of troops (known as the Kwantung Army) along the Japanese-owned South Manchuria Railway, which the Japanese group justified by maintaining

that Manchuria was "Japan's first line of defence" against Russia/the Soviet Union (Institute of Pacific Relations, *Problems of the Pacific*, 171). As a result of victory in the Russo-Japanese War and the treaty of Portsmouth, Japan had been granted the Russian lease on the southernmost section of the South Manchuria branch of the Chinese Eastern Railway, founding the South Manchuria Railway Company in 1906. Dr. Shuhsi Hsu, a Chinese delegate, launched a series of attacks on Japan's imperialism, arguing that "China was paying more than [its] share of benefits, economic or otherwise, accruing from Japan's control of South Manchuria" ("Matsuoka Tells Japan's Relation to Manchuria," *Japan Times & Mail*, November 6, 1929, 1). In rebuttal, Yosuke Matsuoka raised the issue of the cost Japan had paid in taking control of Manchuria from Russia in the Russo-Japanese War before returning it to China. By Matsuoka's account, the war cost Japan "100,000 men, and 2 billion yen, which, plus interest, reached a total of six billion yen"—a sacrifice that Matsuoka claimed Japan made for China ("Joint Meeting of All Round Tables [November 5, 1929]," box B-3, folder 14, IPR Records). Matsuoka also ventured his opinion that if Japan, during the war, had known of the secret Sino-Russian treaty of alliance entered into in 1896, Japan would have annexed Manchuria outright after the war. "No nation," said Matsuoka, "would have said a word about it," and "we would not have had the Manchurian Question to discuss at this Conference today (great laughter)" (Matsuoka, *An Address on Manchuria, Its Past and Present, and Reply to Prof. Shuhsi-Hsu's Criticisms and Observations: Third Biennial Conference, Institute of Pacific Relations* [Kyoto, 1929], 24).

56. Matsuoka, *An Address on Manchuria*, 23.

57. See 793.94/3437a: Telegram, the Secretary of State to the Ambassador in Japan (Forbes), January 7, 1932, in US Department of State, *Papers Relating to the Foreign Relations of the United States, Japan: 1931–1941* (Washington, DC: Government Printing Office, 1943), 1:76.

58. On Stimson and Manchuria, see Henry L. Stimson, *The Far Eastern Crisis* (New York: Harper and Brothers, 1936); and Armin Rappaport, *Henry L. Stimson and Japan, 1931–33* (Chicago: University of Chicago Press, 1963).

59. "Text of Stimson's Address Here on Pact of Paris," *New York Times*, August 9, 1932, 2.

60. "Report of Round Table No. 2," box B-4, folder 2, IPR Records.

61. "Japan Tells League It Cannot Stop Her," *New York Times*, December 9, 1932, 1.

62. League of Nations, delegation from Japan, *Japan's Case in the Sino-Japanese Dispute as Presented before the Special Session of the Assembly of the League of Nations* (Geneva: Author, 1933), 40; see also "Japan Tells League It Cannot Stop Her," 4.

63. Rollin Kirby, "Oh, Yes They Can!" Cartoon Drawings, Prints and Photographs Division, Library of Congress, Washington, DC.

64. Rollin Kirby, "A Treaty Is a Treaty, My Friend," Cartoon Drawings, Prints and Photographs Division, Library of Congress, Washington, DC.

65. "Matsuoka Jeered by London Crowd," *New York Times*, March 12, 1933, 18.

66. "Matsuoka Arrives," *New York Times*, March 25, 1933, 1, 9.

67. Sandra Wilson, *The Manchurian Crisis and Japanese Society, 1931–33* (Lon-

don: Routledge, 2002), 96. According to David J. Lu, because Matsuoka wanted Japan to remain in the League of Nations, his dramatic exit from the assembly was "a moment of defeat, not of victory or glory," though this performance transformed him into Japan's national hero (Lu, *Agony of Choice: Matsuoka Yōsuke and the Rise and Fall of the Japanese Empire, 1880–1946* [Lanham, MD: Lexington Books, 2002], 93).

68. "Matsuoka Arrives," 9.

69. Rollin Kirby, "His St. Helena," Cartoon Drawings, Prints and Photographs Division, Library of Congress, Washington, DC.

70. David Levering Lewis, *W. E. B. Du Bois: The Fight for Equality and the American Century, 1919–1963* (New York: Henry Holt, 2000), 391.

71. "Not China vs. Japan but Japan vs. Anybody," *Chicago Defender*, February 6, 1932, 13.

72. "The Case for Japan," *Afro-American*, January 15, 1938, 4; "Uncle Tom in Asia," editorial cartoon, *Afro-American*, January 15, 1938, 4.

73. Lewis, *W. E. B. Du Bois*, 392.

74. W. E. B. Du Bois, "As the Crow Flies," *Crisis* 38 (December 1931): 412.

75. Du Bois, "As the Crow Flies," *Crisis* 39 (April 1932): 116.

76. William N. Jones, "Day by Day: A Typhoon Rises in the Far East," *Afro-American*, February 6, 1932, 6.

77. During this occupation, Stimson also disarmed Nicaraguan troops and established a new military force, the National Guard (which would give rise to the Somoza dictatorship), under US supervision. On Stimson's work in Nicaragua and his vision of the US imperial project in the Caribbean, see David F. Schmitz, *Henry L. Stimson: The First Wise Man* (Wilmington, DE: SR Books, 2001), 47–61.

78. William Pickens, "Reflections: Japanese Make History," *New York Amsterdam News*, February 17, 1932, 8.

79. W. E. B. Du Bois, "The Wide, Wide World: Muddle," *New York Amsterdam News*, November 25, 1931, 8; W. E. B. Du Bois, "World Much More Logical than It Used to Be in Spite of the Unusual Muddle of Politics," *Philadelphia Tribune*, November 26, 1931, 9. Reminding readers that "Japan didn't raise the roof when our marines annexed Hawaii, Haiti and Nicaragua, and stole the Panama Canal site from Columbia," the *Afro-American* also dubbed Uncle Sam the "big meddler" who "boss[es] everything in the world" ("The Big Meddler in China," *Afro-American*, February 6, 1932, 6).

80. "The Naughty Japanee," *Crisis* 40 (December 1933): 281. Similarly, an editorial in the *Philadelphia Tribune*, an African American newspaper, observed, "One recalls that neither the League nor any one else has ever said anything to the United States that it was bound to respect, about sending troops to 'protect its interests,'" to Haiti and Nicaragua. But when Japan sent troops to "protect its interests," continued the editorial sarcastically, "the whole civilized world goes into a football huddle," claiming, "Japan cannot be allowed to do that, oh no, that right is reserved for the United States, or possibly Great Britain, in her Indian trouble—but never Japan" ("If America Had Interests in Manchuria," *Philadelphia Tribune*, November 5, 1931, 16).

81. R. O. Berg, cartoon, *Crisis* 39 (August 1932): 246.

82. Du Bois, "The Wide, Wide World," 8; Du Bois, "World Much More Logical," 9.

83. William Pickens, "Reflections: 'White Supremacy' Is Dead," *New York Amsterdam News*, March 9, 1932, 8.

84. Pickens, "Reflections: Japanese Make History," 9. These comments clearly show that in the early 1930s American blacks were producing alternative readings of the Manchurian Incident. However, not all black papers identified Japan's militarism as a blow against white supremacy. Sounding an alarm against the "sentimental appeal" of a coalition of nonwhite races "as pictured by some Negro speakers," the *New York Age* reasoned that "foreign alliances, entangling or otherwise based on color, have no part in the Negro's constructive program of the present." As the *Age* saw it, "[White and colored Americans] have a community of interests. . . . Together they will sink or swim" ("Interracial Relationships," *New York Age*, July 2, 1932, 4).

85. William N. Jones, "Day by Day: Japan Again Thumbs Nose," *Afro-American*, November 26, 1932, 14.

86. William Pickens, "Reflections: 'Wrong-Horse Harry' Again!" *New York Amsterdam News*, February 3, 1932, 8.

87. W. E. B. Du Bois, "Postscript: Listen, Japan and China," *Crisis* 40 (January 1933): 20.

88. Johnson, "Views and Reviews: The Shantung Grant," 4.

89. George Lipsitz points out, "The African American encounter with Japan has been especially fraught with contradictions. In their zeal to identify with a 'non-White' nation whose successes might rebuke Eurocentric claims about White supremacy, Blacks have often overlooked, condoned, and even embraced elements of Japanese fascism and imperialism" (Lipsitz, "Frantic to Join," 350). If in slightly different terms, Marc Gallicchio endorses this view, arguing that although many black activists enlisted in the left-liberal coalition against racism and colonialism, "there was no shortage of black internationalists willing to apologize for Japan" (Gallicchio, *African American Encounter*, 4).

90. A similar view had been voiced in 1929 by Harold Norman Denny: "The real motives for America's interposition . . . have been far deeper. . . . They are rooted in the basic strategy of America's national defense, which hinges on the canal, and are bolstered when necessary by America's one principle of foreign policy, the Monroe Doctrine" (Denny, *Dollars for Bullets*, 12–13).

91. Korhonen, "The Pacific Age," 53–54.

92. George T. Weitzel, *American Policy in Nicaragua* (Washington, DC: Government Printing Office, 1916), 9–10. The letter, however, was not known to exist until two years after the United States actually drove Zelaya from power. Furthermore, there is no evidence that Washington ever seriously believed that the Japanese would build a rival canal (Denny, *Dollars for Bullets*, 35; Bermann, *Under the Big Stick*, 150).

93. "Nicaragua Shows Hostility to US," *New York Times*, May 18, 1909, 2.

94. To read the string of events that composes a black Pacific narrative in *Along This Way* as historically causative—rather than as narrative memory—is to miss the literary function of the genre of autobiography. Andreas Huyssen writes, "The past is not simply there in memory, but it must be articulated to become memory. The fissure that opens up between experiencing an event and remembering it in representation is

unavoidable. Rather than lamenting or ignoring it, this split should be understood as a powerful stimulant for cultural and artistic creativity" (Huyssen, *Twilight Memories: Marking Time in a Culture of Amnesia* [New York: Routledge, 1995], 3).

95. I thank Bill Mullen for helping me to think about Johnson's infatuation with state power.

96. James Weldon Johnson to Grace Nail Johnson, Corinto, November 16, 1912, box 41, folder 23, JWJ Papers.

97. Here we may say that Johnson is reenacting what Mary Louise Pratt terms a "contact zone," which Kay Anderson and Susan J. Smith define as "emotionally heightened spaces." Created in colonial contexts, spaces of cross-cultural encounter are where lives, of colonizer and colonized alike, are lived through intensities of emotion (Anderson and Smith, "Editorial: Emotional Geographies," *Transactions of the Institute of British Geographers* 26, no. 1 [March 2001]: 8).

98. Katzenstein and Shiraishi, "Regions in World Politics," 354.

99. Edgar Snow, *Far Eastern Front* (London: Jarrolds, 1934), 268–69. The New York edition of *Far Eastern Front* was published in 1933.

100. For an analysis of black transnational engagement and the nation-state, see Brian Russell Roberts, *Artistic Ambassadors: Literary and International Representation of the New Negro Era* (Charlottesville: University of Virginia Press, 2013).

Chapter 2. Colored Empires in the 1930s: Black Internationalism, the US Black Press, and George S. Schuyler

1. Brenda Gayle Plummer, *Rising Wind: Black Americans and U.S. Foreign Affairs, 1935–1960* (Chapel Hill: University of North Carolina Press, 1996), 80.

2. Penny M. Von Eschen, *Race against Empire: Black Americans and Anticolonialism, 1937–1957* (Ithaca, NY: Cornell University Press, 1997), 11.

3. The Ethiopian emperor's name is also spelled Haile Sellassie.

4. George S. Schuyler, *Black Empire*, edited by Robert A. Hill and R. Kent Rasmussen (Boston: Northeastern University Press, 1991). All references to *Black Empire* are to this edition and will be cited parenthetically in the text as *BE*.

5. Andrew Buni, *Robert L. Vann of the "Pittsburgh Courier": Politics and Black Journalism* (Pittsburgh: University of Pittsburgh Press, 1974), 224, 257.

6. Roi Ottley, *"New World A-Coming": Inside Black America* (Boston: Houghton Mifflin, 1943), 109. The most thorough treatment of the African American response to the Italo-Ethiopian crisis is found in William R. Scott, *The Sons of Sheba's Race: African-Americans and the Italo-Ethiopian War, 1935–1941* (Bloomington: Indiana University Press, 1993); also useful is Joseph E. Harris, *African-American Reactions to War in Ethiopia, 1936–1941* (Baton Rouge: Louisiana State University Press, 1994).

7. Mark Naison, *Communists in Harlem during the Depression* (Urbana: University of Illinois Press, 1983), 138.

8. Langston Hughes, "Call of Ethiopia," in *The Collected Poems of Langston Hughes*, ed. Arnold Rampersad (New York: Vintage, 1994), 184.

9. Robert A. Hill, introduction, in *Ethiopian Stories*, by George S. Schuyler, 1–50 (Boston: Northeastern University Press, 1994), 14.

10. George S. Schuyler, "Views and Reviews," *Pittsburgh Courier*, July 27, 1935, 10.

11. Schuyler, "Views and Reviews," August 17, 1935, 10.

12. Schuyler, "Views and Reviews," July 27, 1935, 10.

13. In an unsigned editorial, Schuyler writes, "That Italy can defeat Ethiopia is a foregone conclusion if no country actively aids the African empire" ([George S. Schuyler], "Ethiopia Girds for Battle," *Pittsburgh Courier*, July 27, 1935, 10).

14. "Another World War Threatens as Japan Talks," *Pittsburgh Courier*, July 27, 1935, 1, 4.

15. Ibid., 4.

16. "'Civilizing' Ethiopia," *New York Age*, August 3, 1935, 6.

17. "Another World War Threatens," 4.

18. "Rome Press Turns Attack on Japan," *New York Times*, July 23, 1935, 12.

19. "Japanese Embassy Guarded," *New York Times*, July 23, 1935, 12.

20. "Rome Press Turns," 12.

21. "Japanese Embassy Guarded," 12; see also "Attacks on Japan Continue," *New York Times*, July 24, 1935, 8.

22. Arden Brizan Lester Taylor (Nationalist Negro Movement) to the Ministry of Foreign Affairs of Japan, telegram, August 9, 1935, frame 0503, Ref. B02031218800, Japan Center for Asian Historical Records (JACAR), National Archives of Japan, Tokyo.

23. "Japan Prepares to Aid Ethiopia," *Indianapolis Recorder*, July 13, 1935, 1; "Ethiopian, Italian Armies Face Each Other in Africa . . . Hostilities Expected Any Minute as Emperor Turns to Japan," *Chicago Defender*, July 13, 1935, 1; "Japanese Hit at Mussolini," *New York Amsterdam News*, July 20, 1935, 1; "Japanese Scored by Italians: Attitude of Tokyo Called Hostile," *New York Age*, July 27, 1935, 1; "Japan Looms as Bar to Italy," *Chicago Defender*, July 27, 1935, 1.

24. The capital of Ethiopia is variably spelled Addis Abeba or Addis Ababa. I use the latter spelling, which has been more commonly employed in English-speaking countries.

25. "Japan Arming Ethiopia," *Pittsburgh Courier*, August 10, 1935, 1. For a useful discussion of Ethio-Japanese relations during the Ethiopian crisis, see J. Calvitt Clarke III, *Alliance of the Colored Peoples: Ethiopia and Japan before World War II* (Woodbridge, UK: James Currey, 2011), 78–147.

26. Wilbert L. Holloway, "Tough Going," cartoon, *Pittsburgh Courier*, August 10, 1935, 10.

27. "Is Ethiopia Stretching Forth Her Hand?" *Chicago Defender*, July 20, 1935, 10.

28. "Troops Mass for War!" *Chicago Defender*, July 13, 1935, 1.

29. "Is Ethiopia Stretching Forth Her Hand?" 10.

30. Even the mainstream newspapers in the United States reported on Japanese military aid to Ethiopia. See, for instance, "Haile Selassie Pleased by U.S. Hope for Peace:. . . Arms Contract with Japan Reported," *Washington Post*, August 6, 1935, 3; "Selassie Faces East in Search of War Sinews," *Washington Post*, August 9, 1935, 3; and "Ethiopia May Seek Arms from Japan," *New York Times*, August 9, 1935, 8.

31. "Japanese Remember Shattered Romance," *Chicago Defender*, July 13, 1935, 1.

32. Harold G. Marcus, *Haile Sellassie I: The Formative Years, 1892–1936* (1987; Lawrenceville, NJ: Red Sea Press, 1995), 200n46.

33. Some black American intellectuals, as well, read Ethiopia and Japan in analogous terms. For George Padmore, the points of similarity between Ethiopia and Japan included their both being "among the oldest empires in the world"; their both being "the first non-European peoples since the Haitian Revolution to defeat the white race at arms"; and last but not least, their both "knowing that all other colored people are under the yoke of white imperialist domination" and hence their both being "very suspicious of the white man" (Padmore, "Ethiopia Today: The Making of a Modern State," in *Negro: An Anthology*, ed. Nancy Cunard, 386–92 [1934; New York: Continuum, 2002], 386). J. A. Rogers traces the moments of origination of "a unifying consciousness" of the darker peoples back to two comparable events: "black Ethiopia's defeat of white Italy in 1896, and colored Japan's victory over white Russia in 1905"; according to Rogers, there was a racial theory of some currency that "the Ethiopians are Asiatics" (Rogers, *The Real Facts about Ethiopia* [1936; Baltimore: Black Classic Press, 1982], 2, 7).

34. Harold G. Marcus, *A History of Ethiopia*, updated ed. (Berkeley: University of California Press, 2002), 134. On Ethiopian "Japanizers," see Addis Hiwet, *Ethiopia: From Autocracy to Revolution* (London: Review of African Political Economy, 1975), 68–77.

35. Herui Wolde Selassie, *Dai-Nihon* [Greater Japan], trans. Oreste Vaccari and Enko Vaccari (Tokyo: Eibumpo Tsuron Hakkojo, 1934), 26, 29–30; Clarke, *Alliance of the Colored Peoples*, 42.

36. Marcus, *Haile Sellassie I*, 200n46.

37. Selassie, *Dai-Nihon*.

38. Richard Albert Bradshaw, "Japan and European Colonialism in Africa, 1800–1937" (PhD diss., Ohio University, 1992), 314–15.

39. On the planned marriage, see Kazuhiro Yamada, *Masukaru no Hanayome* [The Bride of Maskal] (Tokyo: Asahi Shimbun-sha, 1998), 108–44; Clarke, *Alliance of the Colored Peoples*, 83–87.

40. Yotaro Sugimura to Koki Hirota (Foreign Minister), December 14, 1934, frame 0010, Ref. B02031217400, JACAR. My translation.

41. O. Tanin and E. Yohan, *When Japan Goes to War* (New York: Vanguard Press, 1936), 14.

42. Schuyler, "Views and Reviews," February 3, 1934, 10. Many African American weeklies reported and editorialized on this potential Ethio-Japanese matrimony. See, for instance, J. A. Rogers, "Abyssinian-Japanese Alliance Unites World's Oldest Families," *Philadelphia Tribune*, January 25, 1934, 2; "Abyssinian Prince Reported Seeking Japanese Bride," *New York Age*, January 27, 1934, 1; "Japanese Girl Announces Her Engagement to African Prince," *Chicago Defender*, January 27, 1934, 1; "New Ties of Blood," *Chicago Defender*, January 27, 1934, 14; "Wedding May Join Japan and Abyssinia," *Afro-American*, January 27, 1934, 3; and "Abyssinian Prince to Wed Japanese Girl," *Chicago Defender*, February 17, 1934, 1.

43. See "Italy Scotches African Prince's Plan to Take Japanese Bride," *Washington Post*, April 3, 1934, 1; Kendall Foss, "Japan's 'Conquest' of Ethiopia Halts at Il Duce's Frown," *Washington Post*, April 8, 1934, B1; "Abyssinian Ends Troth to Japanese," *New York Times*, April 3, 1934, 11. Araya Abeba later revealed that it was not Italy

but France that intervened to cancel the marriage (Yamada, *Masukaru no Hanayome*, 230).

44. Haile Sellassie, *My Life and Ethiopia's Progress, 1892–1937: The Autobiography of Emperor Haile Sellassie I*, trans. Edward Ullendorff (1976; Chicago: Research Associates School Times Publications and Frontline Distribution International, 1999), 208–9.

45. "'Holy War': A Trade War," *New York Age*, September 22, 1934, 6.

46. "Watching Hailie [sic] Selassie," *Chicago Defender*, September 22, 1934, 14.

47. J. A. Rogers, "Italy over Abyssinia," *Crisis* 42 (February 1935): 38.

48. George Padmore, "Ethiopia and World Politics," *Crisis* 42 (May 1935): 157.

49. Quoted in S. K. B. Asante, *Pan-African Protest: West Africa and the Italo-Ethiopian Crisis, 1934–1941* (London: Longman, 1977), 41.

50. Scott, *Sons of Sheba's Race*, 125.

51. J. Calvitt Clarke III, "Italo-Soviet Military Cooperation in the 1930s," in *Girding for Battle: The Arms Trade in a Global Perspective, 1815–1940*, ed. Donald J. Stoker Jr. and Jonathan A. Grant, 177–99 (Westport, CT: Praeger, 2003), 180–83.

52. Schuyler makes a sardonic treatment of "anticolonial violence," an example that Caribbean-born Frantz Fanon would endorse in *The Wretched of the Earth*. In Fanon's discussion of the process of decolonization, violence is inevitable and necessary. For Fanon, there is no transition from the socially constructed Manichean world of black and white that is colonialism; rather, there is only substitution, and violence is the only means to break down the colonial machinery: "If the last shall be first, this will only come to pass after a murderous and decisive struggle between the two protagonists," that is, colonizer and colonized. The production of violence for Fanon is the "work" through which colonized people liberate themselves from the passivity of the "thing," the product of work for which they have been condemned to labor. On the collective level, the practice of violence unifies a people on a national (and sometimes a racial) basis, as it "introduces into each man's consciousness the ideas of a common cause." Such solidarity alone can overcome the regionalism and tribalism that colonialism not only circumscribes but also exploits, dividing the colonial world into "compartments" in which each of the colonized, conditioned to "stay in his place, and not to go beyond certain limits," is imprisoned (Fanon, *The Wretched of the Earth*, trans. Constance Farrington [New York: Grove Press, 1963], 37, 51–52, 93–94).

53. For a discussion of Schuyler's fantasy of black fascism, see Mark Christian Thompson, *Black Fascisms: African American Literature and Culture between the Wars* (Charlottesville: University of Virginia Press, 2007), 72–86.

54. Kali Tal, "'That Just Kills Me': Black Militant Near-Future Fiction," *Social Text* 20, no. 2 (summer 2002): 67, 80.

55. James C. Scott, *Domination and the Arts of Resistance: Hidden Transcripts* (New Haven, CT: Yale University Press, 1990), 4, 37–38.

56. Tal, "That Just Kills Me," 79.

57. In *Black Empire*, the BI encounters the only opposition in Africa from the black officials in Sierra Leone who "were generally more loyal to the British imperialists than King George VI," a monarch (*BE*, 99).

58. George S. Schuyler, *Black and Conservative: The Autobiography of George S. Schuyler* (New Rochelle, NY: Arlington House, 1966), 248.

59. George S. Schuyler, "The Rise of the Black Internationale," *Crisis* 45 (August 1938): 256, 277.

60. Ottley, *"New World,"* 104.

61. Henry Louis Gates Jr., "A Fragmented Man: George Schuyler and the Claims of Race," *New York Times Book Review*, September 20, 1992, 42.

62. Nation of Islam, "A Brief History on the Origin of the Nation of Islam in America," accessed April 3, 2012, http://www.noi.org.

63. Karl Evanzz, *The Messenger: The Rise and Fall of Elijah Muhammad* (1999; New York: Vintage, 2001), 119.

64. FBI headquarters file on Elijah Muhammad; quoted in Evanzz, *Messenger*, 106.

65. John Edgar Hoover, "Memorandum for the Attorney General: RE: Robert O. Jordan," February 19, 1942, 1, Records of the Office of War Information, RG 208, entry 5, box 3, NARA; Hill, *FBI's RACON*, 186.

66. "Second Garvey Asks for United Black World," *New York Amsterdam News*, November 9, 1935, 2.

67. Robert O. Jordan to the Ministry of Foreign Affairs of Japan, May 12, 1936, frame 0396, Ref. B02031221000, JACAR.

68. Robert O. Jordan to Hachiro Arita (Foreign Minister), November 18, 1936, frame 0422, Ref. B02031216000, JACAR.

69. Ottley, *"New World,"* 336.

70. "Four Face Court in Sedition Plot," *New York Times*, December 15, 1942, 16.

71. Hoover, "Memorandum for the Attorney General," 3.

72. "Revenge All Planned by Harlem Fuehrer," *New York Times*, September 16, 1942, 16; "Trial Bares Dream of a Harlem Nazi," *New York Times*, December 16, 1942, 11.

73. "Five Who Urged Revolt in Harlem and Aid to Japanese Are Indicted," *New York Times*, September 15, 1942, 1.

74. George S. Schuyler, "Japan and the Negro," 3 installments, box 8, folder 10, Schuyler Family Papers: George S. Schuyler: Writings, Schomburg Center for Research in Black Culture, New York.

75. Schuyler, "Japan and the Negro," 2nd installment, 4.

76. See Jeffrey B. Ferguson, *The Sage of Sugar Hill: George S. Schuyler and the Harlem Renaissance* (New Haven, CT: Yale University Press, 2005), 27, 262–63n51; and Hill, *FBI's RACON*, 438–42.

77. "Guests at Dinner" list, scrapbook, vol. 16, microfilm reel 6, George S. Schuyler Papers, Special Collections Research Center, Syracuse University Library, Syracuse, NY (hereafter cited as Schuyler Papers/SU).

78. "Sino-Jap Dispute Explained to Harlemites," *New York Amsterdam News*, February 5, 1938, 4.

79. Schuyler, "Japan and the Negro," 1st installment, 1; Schuyler, "Japan and the Negro," 2nd installment, 1.

80. Ira F. Lewis to George S. Schuyler, December 29, 1937, box 1, folder 2, Schuyler Papers/SU.

81. [George S. Schuyler], "The World This Week," *Pittsburgh Courier*, December 11, 1937, 11.

82. Schuyler, "Japan and the Negro," 3rd installment, 1; Schuyler, "Japan and the Negro," 2nd installment, 3.

83. Schuyler, "Japan and the Negro," 1st installment, 3; Schuyler, "Japan and the Negro," 2nd installment, 4; Schuyler, "Japan and the Negro," 1st installment, 4; Schuyler, "Japan and the Negro," 2nd installment, 4; Schuyler, "Japan and the Negro," 3rd installment, 4.

84. John Cullen Gruesser, *Black on Black: Twentieth-Century African American Writing about Africa* (Lexington: University Press of Kentucky, 2000), 111, 116.

85. W. E. B. Du Bois, "Forum of Fact and Opinion," *Pittsburgh Courier*, October 23, 1937, 11.

86. W. E. B. Du Bois, "Inter-Racial Implications of the Ethiopian Crisis: A Negro View," *Foreign Affairs* 14, no. 1 (October 1935): 85, 89.

87. Du Bois, "Forum of Fact and Opinion," October 23, 1937, 11.

88. Schuyler, "Rise of the Black Internationale," 275.

89. Schuyler, "Japan and the Negro," 1st installment, 4.

90. Schuyler, "Rise of the Black Internationale," 275, 277.

91. Ira F. Lewis to George S. Schuyler, November 22, 1937, box 1, folder 2, Schuyler Papers/SU.

92. Lewis to Schuyler, December 29, 1937. Even after Pearl Harbor, it would seem that Lewis remained favorably disposed to Japan as he claimed in a *Courier* editorial: "The Japanese now are enemies of the United States, and are necessarily enemies of all Negro Americans. But between the Japanese and the Chinese, the Negroes much prefer the Japanese. The Chinese are the worst 'Uncle Toms' and stooges that the white man has ever had" (Ira F. Lewis, "The World This Week," *Pittsburgh Courier*, March 28, 1942, 1). An examiner in the Office of Censorship noted that "the paragraph ... is a studied attempt to cast a slur upon the CHINESE, an ally of ours, and at the same time accord left-handed praise to the JAPANESE, our enemy" ("National Censorship" record, *Pittsburgh Courier*, March 28, 1942, Records of the Office of Censorship, RG 216, entry 1, box 550, NARA).

93. Roman Freiherr von Procházka, *Abyssinia: The Powder Barrel* (London: British International News Agency, [1936]), 1, 54.

94. "The Fake 'Ethiopians,'" *New York Amsterdam Star-News*, October 3, 1942, 6.

95. Hill, *FBI's RACON*, 187, 198. The *RACON* cites both Ethiopian organizations under the heading "Pro-Japanese Activities among the Negroes" in New York (ibid., 185–88).

Chapter 3. *The Swing and the Sword in the Black* Mikados:
An Afro-Japanese Nexus in the US (White) Pacific Imagination

1. By "racechange," Susan Gubar means "the traversing of race boundaries, racial imitation or impersonation, cross-racial mimicry or mutability, white posing as black or black passing as white, pan-racial mutuality" (Gubar, *Racechanges: White Skin, Black Face in American Culture* [New York: Oxford University Press, 1997], 5).

2. A Japanese opera singer, Tamaki Miura, won international acclaim for her performances in the role of the *Madame Butterfly* heroine Cho-Cho-San in Europe and America in the 1910s, with cultural resonances that critic Mari Yoshihara signifi-

cantly examines. See Yoshihara, *Musicians from a Different Shore: Asians and Asian Americans in Classical Music* (Philadelphia: Temple University Press, 2007), 23–33.

3. Ralph Teatsorth, "Mikado Is Staged for 1st Time Here," *Nippon Times*, August 13, 1946, 2.

4. Ian Bradley, ed., *The Complete Annotated Gilbert and Sullivan* (Oxford: Oxford University Press, 1996), 554.

5. W. A. Darlington, *The World of Gilbert and Sullivan* (1951; Freeport, NY: Books for Libraries Press, 1970), 113.

6. For an account of the exhibition, see Yoshihiro Kurata, *1885-nen Rondon Nihonjin-mura* [The Japanese Village in London, 1885] (Tokyo: Asahi Shimbun-sha, 1983).

7. Leslie Baily, *The Gilbert and Sullivan Book* (London: Spring Books, 1952), 269.

8. Lieven, *Empire*, 8.

9. On Anglo-Japanese court diplomacy in this period, see Antony Best, "Race, Monarchy, and the Anglo-Japanese Alliance, 1902–1922," *Social Science Japan Journal* 9, no. 2 (October 2006): 171–86.

10. "Comic Opera Diplomacy," *New York Times*, June 9, 1907, C4.

11. "The Lord Chamberlain and 'The Mikado,'" *Times*, May 6, 1907, 11.

12. Baily, *Gilbert and Sullivan Book*, 417.

13. "The Lord Chamberlain and 'The Mikado,'" *Times*, May 17, 1907, 11.

14. "The Lord Chamberlain and 'The Mikado,'" *Times*, May 9, 1907, 3; "The Lord Chamberlain and 'The Mikado,'" *Times*, May 7, 1907, 12.

15. Quoted in Sidney Dark and Rowland Grey, *W. S. Gilbert: His Life and Letters* (London: Methuen, [1923]), 101.

16. Quoted in ibid.

17. G. K. Chesterton, *The Illustrated London News, 1905–1907*, ed. Lawrence J. Clipper, vol. 27 of *The Collected Works of G. K. Chesterton* (San Francisco: Ignatius Press, 1986), 448.

18. Ibid., 470–72.

19. Gayden Wren, *A Most Ingenious Paradox: The Art of Gilbert and Sullivan* (New York: Oxford University Press, 2001), 165.

20. Harvard Sitkoff, *A New Deal for Blacks: The Emergence of Civil Rights as a National Issue; The Depression Decade*, 30th anniversary ed. (New York: Oxford University Press, 2009), 63–76.

21. Lauren Rebecca Sklaroff, *Black Culture and the New Deal: The Quest for Civil Rights in the Roosevelt Era* (Chapel Hill: University of North Carolina Press, 2009), 1, 9.

22. The most thorough treatment of the black Federal Theatre is found in Rena Fraden, *Blueprints for a Black Federal Theatre, 1935–1939* (New York: Cambridge University Press, 1994).

23. John Houseman, *Run-through: A Memoir by John Houseman* (New York: Simon and Schuster, 1972), 185, 190, 205.

24. Hallie Flanagan, *Arena: The History of the Federal Theatre* (New York: Benjamin Blom, 1965), 147; Vanita Marian Vactor, "A History of the Chicago Federal Theatre Project Negro Unit: 1935–1939" (PhD diss., New York University, 1998), 181.

25. Alain Locke, "Broadway and the Negro Drama," *Theatre Arts* 25, no. 10 (October 1941): 748.

26. Charles Washburn, "The Great Bojangles," in *Michael Todd's Hot Mikado with Bill Robinson*, souvenir program, New York World's Fair, Hall of Music, 1939, "Hot Mikado" file, Theatre Collection, Free Library of Philadelphia (hereafter cited as "Hot Mikado"/FLP).

27. "Berlin Heard First 'Mikado' to be Jazzed Up," newspaper clipping, "Swing Mikado" file, Theatre Collection, Free Library of Philadelphia (hereafter cited as "Swing Mikado"/FLP).

28. "'The Mikado': Screen and Swing Versions," *Pic*, March 21, 1939, clipping, Production Report, *The Mikado*, Federal Theatre Project Collection, Library of Congress, Washington, DC (hereafter cited as FTP Collection).

29. Allen Woll, *Black Musical Theatre: From "Coontown" to "Dreamgirls"* (Baton Rouge: Louisiana State University Press, 1989), 183; "Theatre: Show Business," *Time*, May 8, 1939, 54.

30. Burns Mantle, "Labor Stage Adds 'Red Mikado' to Its 'Pins and Needles,'" *Daily News* (New York), April 21, 1939, reel 16, Collection of Newspaper Clippings of Dramatic Criticisms, Billy Rose Theatre Collection, New York Public Library for the Performing Arts, New York (hereafter cited as Clippings/NYPL); Stanley Green, *Ring Bells! Sing Songs! Broadway Musicals of the 1930's* (New York: Galahad Books, 1971), 153.

31. Bradley, *Complete Annotated Gilbert and Sullivan*, 555. Enthusiasm for the opera was such that the post office department in Washington assigned the name Mikado Township to a town in Michigan after rejecting the locally requested name of Bruceville (Walter Romig, *Michigan Place Names* [Detroit: Wayne State University Press, 1986], 368). After the Japanese attack on Pearl Harbor, the residents of Mikado Township in Michigan found the name of their town so repugnant that they nearly succeeded in renaming it (Naoki Inose, *Mikado no Shozo* [Portrait of the Mikado] [Tokyo: Shogakukan, 2005], 358–68).

32. See, for instance, Josephine Lee, *The Japan of Pure Invention: Gilbert and Sullivan's "The Mikado"* (Minneapolis: University of Minnesota Press, 2010), 83–120.

33. Interestingly, however, Graham did not obtain credit for the adaptation, for as historian Gerald Horne remarks, "her superiors within the project left the impression that they had been solely responsible for its success" (Horne, *Race Woman: The Lives of Shirley Graham Du Bois* [New York: New York University Press, 2000], 80).

34. Vactor, "A History," 165–67; Patrice S. Sales, "*Swing Mikado*: Exemplar of the Struggle for the Black Stage Image through Music and Dance" (Master's thesis, Indiana University, 1993), 79–80.

35. Bernard Simon, "He Had a Lot of Negroes Handy, So He Heated Up Sullivan Music," newspaper clipping, "Swing Mikado"/FLP.

36. Stephanie Leigh Batiste, *Darkening Mirrors: Imperial Representation in Depression-Era African American Performance* (Durham, NC: Duke University Press, 2011), 151–53.

37. Clive Rickabaugh, Notes on Set Design, Production Report, *The Mikado*, FTP Collection.

38. Cecil Smith, "Negro Players Stage 'Mikado' in Swing Style," *Chicago Daily Tribune*, September 26, 1938, 13.

39. [John Pratt], Costume Notes, Production Report, *The Mikado*, FTP Collection.

40. John Hobart, "'The Swing Mikado' Makes Hit: 'De Punishment Fits De Crime,'" *San Francisco Chronicle*, June 16, 1939, Clippings: *The Swing Mikado*, Billy Rose Theatre Collection, New York Public Library (hereafter cited as *Swing Mikado*/NYPL).

41. Brooks Atkinson, "Swinging 'The Mikado,'" *New York Times*, March 12, 1939, 150.

42. Smith, "Negro Players," 13.

43. Hubert Odishaw, "New Version of 'Mikado' Has Harlem-Congo Swing," review of *The Swing Mikado*, *Daily Northwestern*, October 4, 1938, Production Report, *The Mikado*, FTP Collection.

44. Lloyd Lewis, "Mikado Malayed," review of *The Swing Mikado*, *Chicago Daily News*, September 26, 1938, Production Report, *The Mikado*, FTP Collection.

45. Gail Borden, "Negro Unit Jazzes Up Opera 'Mikado,'" review of *The Swing Mikado*, *Chicago Daily Times*, September 26, 1938, Production Report, *The Mikado*, FTP Collection.

46. Burns Mantle, "Swinging Swing to Stage a Great Boon to Colored Actors," *Daily News* (New York), March 23, 1939, *Swing Mikado*/NYPL.

47. Batiste, *Darkening Mirrors*, 162.

48. "Sarongs Replace Kimonos in 'The Swing Mikado,'" newspaper clipping, "Swing Mikado"/FLP.

49. "The Theatre: Of Thee I Swing," *Wall Street Journal*, March 3, 1939, 11.

50. Sidney B. Whipple, [title unknown], *New York World-Telegram*, March 2, 1939, *Swing Mikado*/NYPL.

51. "The Jitterbug's 'Mikado,'" *New York Times*, March 4, 1939, 14. The phrase "apologetic statesm[e]n of a compromising kind" in the *Times* editorial refers to a line in the Lord High Executioner's "little list" song in *The Mikado*.

52. Jonathan G. Utley, *Going to War with Japan, 1937–1941* (New York: Fordham University Press, 2005), 44.

53. Richard Watts Jr., "The Theaters: Sepia Savoy," *New York Herald Tribune*, March 2, 1939, reel 16, Clippings/NYPL.

54. Richard Watts Jr., "Richard Watts, Jr.—Swings 'The Mikado' and Mr. Fay's Vaudeville," *Washington Post*, March 12, 1939, A3.

55. Shannon Steen, *Racial Geometries of the Black Atlantic, Asian Pacific and American Theatre* (Basingstoke, UK: Palgrave Macmillan, 2010), 162–63. To see *The Swing Mikado* as an attractive political dream, however, one must assume that the performers who profess themselves to be Japanese are "happy black Americans" loyal to the nation and in its service. Hence, the political dream of the cross-racial mutability of African Americans and Japanese that the Federal Theatre furnished in *The Swing Mikado* was portentously susceptible to resignification and subversion, even as the imagery of African Americans could and did swing reflexively between the two poles, the harmless and the threatening in the (white) American imagination.

56. For an account of the competition between *The Swing Mikado* and *The Hot Mikado*, see Stephen M. Vallillo, "The Battle of the Black *Mikados*," *Black American Literature Forum* 16, no. 4 (winter 1982): 153–57.

57. Jim Haskins and N. R. Mitgang, *Mr. Bojangles: The Biography of Bill Robinson* (New York: William Morrow, 1988), 214.

58. Brooks Atkinson, "The Play: Bill Robinson Trapping Out the Title Role in 'The Hot Mikado' at the Broadhurst Theatre," *New York Times*, March 24, 1939, 26.

59. Haskins and Mitgang, *Mr. Bojangles*, 251.

60. Drama critic John Mason Brown, however, saw an image of the United States in this flag: "The stars-and-stripes are somehow stylized to represent Fujiyama" (Brown, "Bill Robinson Appears in 'The Hot Mikado,'" *New York Post*, March 24, 1939, reel 15, Clippings/NYPL).

61. Robert Coleman, "Todd's 'Hot Mikado': A Sizzling Platter for Jitterbugs," *Daily Mirror* (New York), March 24, 1939, reel 15, Clippings/NYPL.

62. "The Hot Mikado," cartoon caption, "Hot Mikado"/FLP.

63. Will B. Johnstone, "Swing Explodes 'Mikado' Myth: Gilbert-Sullivan Boom in Colored Versions," *New York World-Telegram*, April 8, 1939, Clippings: *The Hot Mikado*, Billy Rose Theatre Collection, New York Public Library (hereafter cited as Hot Mikado/NYPL).

64. Burns Mantle, "'The Hot Mikado' Burns Up All the Colored Show Records," *Daily News* (New York), March 24, 1939, reel 15, Clippings/NYPL; "New Play in Manhattan," *Time*, April 3, 1939, 23.

65. John Anderson, "Bill Robinson Steams Up 'The Hot Mikado,'" *New York Journal-American*, March 24, 1939, reel 15, Clippings/NYPL.

66. Gilbert and Sullivan, *The Mikado*, in Bradley, *Complete Annotated Gilbert and Sullivan*, 621. Further references to *The Mikado* are to this edition and will be cited parenthetically in the text.

67. Bradley, *Complete Annotated Gilbert and Sullivan*, 620.

68. Ibid., 572, 622.

69. Russell Rhodes, "A More Humane Mikado Never Did in Japan Exist, Believe Us," *New York Herald Tribune*, April 16, 1939, Hot Mikado/NYPL; "Bojangles Finds the Mikado a Mighty Nice Character," *New York Post*, April 15, 1939, Hot Mikado/NYPL.

70. Washburn, "Great Bojangles."

71. Brown, "Bill Robinson."

72. For the FTP's script changes, see Batiste, *Darkening Mirrors*, 136–37.

73. "Topical Lyrics Heard in 'Hot Mikado' by Dave Greggory and William Tracy," in *Michael Todd's Hot Mikado*.

74. Ibid.

75. "'The Hot Mikado' and Bill Robinson Move to the Fair," *New York Post*, June 23, 1939, Hot Mikado/NYPL.

76. John Mason Brown, "Spying on Gotham: 'Hot Mikado' Is Really Hot—It Outswings 'Swing Mikado,'" newspaper clipping, "Hot Mikado"/FLP.

77. "The Hot Mikado," *Variety*, reel 15, Clippings/NYPL; Coleman, "Todd's 'Hot Mikado.'"

78. Brown, "Spying on Gotham."

79. "Hot Mikado," *Variety*.

80. Cecil Jensen, "Hot Mikado," editorial cartoon, *Chicago Daily News*, January 29, 1940, 10.

81. Hiroshi Ashino to Paul Scott Mowrer, January 30, 1940, frame 0517; Mowrer to Ashino, February 1, 1940, frame 0519; Hiroshi Ashino to Hachiro Arita (Foreign Minister), February 2, 1940, frame 0514, Ref. B02030592500, JACAR.

82. In some places, performances of *The Mikado* were cancelled ("War Causes Closing of 'Mikado' Production," *New York Times*, December 9, 1941, 47). In places where performances were held, the opening lyrics were altered from "We are gentlemen of Japan" to "We are gangsters of Japan" (Nelson B. Bell, "Gilbert and Sullivan Opera Co., Scores Rousingly in 'Mikado,'" *Washington Post*, December 16, 1941, 26). Moreover, parodies of *The Mikado* were created after Pearl Harbor such as "The End of the Mikado," featuring Yankie-Poo (instead of Nanki-Poo), as a US Marine ("'End of Mikado' Is New Title for Famed Operetta," *Chicago Daily Tribune*, March 22, 1942, W7).

83. On *Treasury Star Parade*, see J. Fred MacDonald, "Government Propaganda in Commercial Radio: The Case of Treasury Star Parade, 1942–1943," *Journal of Popular Culture* 12, no. 2 (fall 1978): 285–304.

84. Neal Hopkins, "A Lesson in Japanese," in *The Treasury Star Parade*, ed. William A. Bacher, 351–65 (1942; Ann Arbor: University of Michigan Library, 2006), 355–56, 358, 359.

85. "Texts of the Statements on Japan," *New York Times*, April 22, 1943, 4.

86. Edwin Marcus, editorial cartoon, *New York Times*, April 25, 1943, E11.

87. In a letter to Archibald MacLeish, Moss expresses his concern about Japanese activities among black Americans. He writes, "We have strong evidences of Japanese agents working among the Negro people. For example, the persistent argument that springs up in barber shops, street corners etc. the argument that—'Japan is the friend of the colored races'—'What Japan is doing should be an inspiration to the darker races.' . . . There can be no question as to where this poison stems from. And while its full strength will never act on the Negro people. It can and will, unless we counter attack it, do a great deal of harm" (Carlton Moss to Archibald MacLeish, [received February 18, 1942], Records of the Office of War Information, RG 208, entry 5, box 3, NARA).

88. "The Negro Looks at the War," May 19, 1942, planned and summarized by the Extensive Surveys Division, Bureau of Intelligence, Office of Facts and Figures, 4, Records of the Office of Government Reports, RG 44, entry 164, box 1797, NARA.

89. Charles A. Siepmann (Office of Facts and Figures) to Sherman Dryer (Chicago University), June 8, 1942, Records of the Office of War Information, RG 208, entry 5, box 3, NARA.

90. The survey also brought to light an important variable affecting African Americans' perceptions of Japan: educational differences, the effects of which the researchers found "striking." In both groups, "the more educated appeared to be more kindly disposed to Japanese rule than the less educated." The study also asserted, "It is a fact . . . that the Japanese, through such propaganda agencies as the South Manchuria Railway, have been reaching the better educated Negroes through personal contact and through the mail" ("The Negro Looks at the War," 5). This assertion was not

baseless: the South Manchuria Railway Company, as I discuss in chapter 5, hosted W. E. B. Du Bois in his 1936 tour across Manchuria.

91. "News of the Screen: Of Local Origin," *New York Times*, June 2, 1943, 21.

92. Jeanine Basinger, *The World War II Combat Film: Anatomy of a Genre* (New York: Columbia University Press, 1986), 60.

93. Ibid., 58.

94. Brian Locke, "Strange Fruit: White, Black, and Asian in the World War II Combat Film *Bataan*," *Journal of Popular Film and Television* 36, no. 1 (spring 2008): 15–17.

Chapter 4. "Spies and Spiders": Langston Hughes and the Transpacific Intelligence Dragnet

1. Baldwin, *Beyond the Color Line*, 2, 16.

2. For discussions of the left-influenced poetry of Hughes, see James Edward Smethurst, *The New Red Negro: The Literary Left and African American Poetry, 1930–1946* (New York: Oxford University Press, 1999), 93–115; and Anthony Dawahare, *Nationalism, Marxism, and African American Literature between the Wars: A New Pandora's Box* (Jackson: University Press of Mississippi, 2003), 92–110.

3. It is interesting to note as context that there was a faction in the African American group who saw the Soviet-Japan animosity as a factor that led to the scrapping of the film. As Mark Solomon observes, Theodore Poston and Henry Lee Moon of the *New York Amsterdam News*, who were among the group, accused the Soviet authorities that withdrew support for the project of "caving in to 'the forces of race prejudice' in the United States, because they feared Japanese advances in Manchuria and were courting Washington to gain diplomatic recognition as a counterweight to the Japanese" (Solomon, *The Cry Was Unity: Communists and African Americans, 1917–1936* [Jackson: University Press of Mississippi, 1998], 176).

4. "J. L. Hughes Will Depart after Questioning as to Communism," *New York Times*, July 25, 1933, 7; "American Negro Poet Deported by Japan as Red," *Chicago Daily Tribune*, July 25, 1933, 3; "American Writer Questioned . . . as Red Suspect," *Japan Times & Mail*, July 26, 1933, 2; "Japan Ousts Negro for 'Red' Leanings," *Atlanta Constitution*, July 26, 1933, 4; "Hughes Refused Entry in Japan as 'Red,'" *Honolulu Advertiser*, August 4, 1933, 2. African American newspapers also reported Hughes's deportation; see "Langston Hughes Driven Out Japan" (*Chicago Defender*, July 29, 1933, 1) and "U.S. Author Ousted by Japanese" (*Pittsburgh Courier*, July 29, 1933, 7).

5. Langston Hughes, *I Wonder as I Wander: An Autobiographical Journey* (New York: Hill and Wang, 1993), 277. Further references are to this edition and will be cited parenthetically as *IWAIW*.

6. "Negro Author Is Tossed Out by Japanese," *Honolulu Star-Bulletin*, August 3, 1933, 1.

7. Ideologically, it seems reasonable to postulate, at least provisionally, that in the imagination of the black communist left, the two modes of black internationalism I have discussed—one allied with the Japanese Empire and the other with the Soviet Union—were mutually exclusive, to the extent that fascism and democracy were irreconcilable (though, of course, those African American intellectuals allied with Japan did so on the basis not of fascism but of race). In the realm of political life, it further-

more affected the careers of black Communist Party members, as illustrated in the case of Trinidadian journalist George Padmore, a CPUSA member who was "expelled" from the Comintern in 1934. As executive secretary of the Comintern-sponsored International Trade Union Committee of Negro Workers and editor-in-chief of its official organ, the *Negro Worker* (which published Hughes's "Goodbye Christ" in 1932), Padmore commanded wide respect. Nonetheless, he was removed from his prominent positions by his black comrades because he accepted "the Japanese Imperialist propaganda that the Mikado is the guardian of the 'darker races,' that his conquest of Korea, Formosa, Manchuria, and North China (all 'darker races') are 'for their own good,' and that the road to liberation of the Negroes, lies through race war of these 'darker races' against the whites," as Earl Browder, general secretary of the CPUSA, explained in the NAACP's *Crisis* magazine in 1935 ("Earl Browder Replies," *Crisis* 42 [December 1935]: 372).

8. On the creations of the Special Far Eastern Army and the Pacific Fleet, see John J. Stephan, *The Russian Far East: A History* (Stanford, CA: Stanford University Press, 1994), 180–88.

9. David S. Foglesong, *America's Secret War against Bolshevism: U.S. Intervention in the Russian Civil War, 1917–1920* (Chapel Hill: University of North Carolina Press, 1995), 5.

10. Langston Hughes to Noël Sullivan, Trans-Siberian Express, June 12, 1933, box 40, Noël Sullivan Papers, Bancroft Library, University of California, Berkeley.

11. See Tadatoshi Saito, "Langston Hughes in Japan," *Journal: Faculty of Humanities* (Japan Women's University) 47 (1997): 1–13.

12. Langston Hughes to Noël Sullivan, Imperial Hotel of Tokyo, June 30, 1933, box 40, Noël Sullivan Papers.

13. "Tea Cult Described as an Aid to Grace:... Langston Hughes, Noted Negro Poet, Also Speaks and Says His People Are Oppressed," *Japan Advertiser*, July 1, 1933, 3. See also "Portion of a Speech by Langston Hughes before the Pan-Pacific Club of Tokyo, June 30, 1933," box 479, folder 11917, Langston Hughes Papers, Yale Collection of American Literature, Beinecke Rare Book and Manuscript Library, Yale University, New Haven, CT (hereafter cited as Hughes Papers/YU).

14. R. P. Hood (Special Agent in Charge) to J. Edgar Hoover, Los Angeles, February 7, 1942, Langston Hughes, FBI file 100-151-39.

15. Hughes to Sullivan, June 30, 1933.

16. Xiaobing Tang, "Echoes of *Roar, China!* On Vision and Voice in Modern Chinese Art," *positions* 14, no. 2 (fall 2006): 485.

17. The play was Sakae Kubo's *Goryokaku Kessho*.

18. Hughes recorded in the pocket diary the following names of leading Japanese proletarian theater activists and writers: Korea Senda, Tomoyoshi Murayama (a Japan Communist Party member who was then in jail), Mikio Osawa, Sakae Kubo, and S. (Seikichi) Fujimori (Langston Hughes, pocket diary: kept while in China and Japan, [1933], Papers of Langston Hughes, Huntington Library, San Marino, CA [hereafter cited as Hughes Papers/HL]).

19. Faith Berry, *Langston Hughes: Before and beyond Harlem* (Westport, CT: Lawrence Hill, 1983), 193.

20. For the Blue Shirts and fascism, see Lloyd E. Eastman, *The Abortive Revolution: China under Nationalist Rule, 1927–1937* (Cambridge, MA: Harvard University Press, 1974), 31–84.

21. "I Wonder as I Wander," draft, 519, box 307, folder 5014, Hughes Papers/YU; see also "I Wonder as I Wander," draft, 519, box 306, folder 5013, Hughes Papers/YU.

22. Ibid.

23. Ibid., 510; see also "I Wonder as I Wander," draft, 508–9, box 306, folder 5013, Hughes Papers/YU.

24. "I Wonder as I Wander," draft, 521–22, box 307, folder 5014, Hughes Papers/YU; see also "I Wonder as I Wander," draft, 520–21, box 306, folder 5013, Hughes Papers/YU.

25. In the spelling of Chinese names, I use the Wade-Giles system, which Hughes employed. Isaacs also introduced Hughes to others of his acquaintance, including James B. Powell, American editor of the *China Weekly Review* ("I Wonder as I Wander," draft, 522, box 307, folder 5014, Hughes Papers/YU).

26. Shen Pengnian, "Lu Xun Huijian Xiushi Jiqi Beiwu Shijian" [The Meeting between Lu Xun and Hughes and the Incident of Lu Being Falsely Accused], *Shaoxing Lu Xun Yanjiu* 27 (July 2005): 125–26.

27. Hughes, pocket diary, Hughes Papers/HL.

28. On the League for Civil Rights, see Israel Epstein, *Woman in World History: Life and Times of Soong Ching Ling (Mme. Sun Yatsen)* (Beijing: New World Press, 1993), 277–85.

29. See "Yang Chien Murdered!" *China Forum*, June 19, 1933, 9.

30. For an account of the Ruegg case, see Epstein, *Woman in World History*, 264–69.

31. Ruth Price, *The Lives of Agnes Smedley* (New York: Oxford University Press, 2005), 181.

32. The history of the League of Left-Wing Writers finds its most thorough treatment in Wong Wang-chi, *Politics and Literature in Shanghai: The Chinese League of Left-Wing Writers, 1930–1936* (Manchester, UK: Manchester University Press, 1991). On the "five martyrs," see Hsia Tsi-an, *The Gate of Darkness: Studies on the Leftist Literary Movement in China* (Seattle: University of Washington Press, 1968), 163–233.

33. See Left Writers' League of China, "A Letter to the World: An Appeal from the Writers of China," *New Masses*, June 1931, 14–15.

34. Agnes Smedley to Langston Hughes, Shanghai, March 13, 1931, box 147, folder 2735, Hughes Papers/YU.

35. On the *China Forum*, see Harold R. Isaacs, *Re-Encounters in China: Notes of a Journey in a Time Capsule* (Armonk, NY: M. E. Sharpe, 1985), 13–26.

36. "State Department Threatens Forum," *China Forum*, July 30, 1932, 1, 4.

37. Langston Hughes, "From Moscow to Shanghai," *China Forum*, July 14, 1933, 5.

38. "I Wonder as I Wander," draft, 540, box 307, folder 5014, Hughes Papers/YU; see also "I Wonder as I Wander," draft, 540, box 306, folder 5013, Hughes Papers/YU.

39. See Wu Shi, "Xiushi Zai Zhongguo" [Hughes in China], *Wenxue* 1, no. 2 (August 1933): 254–58.

40. Ibid., 258.

41. Shanghai Municipal Police, "James Langston Hughes—American Negro Intellectual," 1, Records of the Central Intelligence Agency, RG 263, box 40, file D-5127 (Microfilm series M-1750, roll 16), NARA.

42. See Yoshio Kubota, *Tokunaga Sunao ron* [A Study on Sunao Tokunaga] (Tokyo: Gogatsu Shobo, 1977), 193–94.

43. Hughes may have conflated the movies because of the linguistic association of *Hotel Imperial* and the Imperial Hotel, where Hughes supposedly watched the movie. The University of Missouri Press edition of *I Wonder as I Wander* changes "Greta Garbo" to "Pola Negri" throughout, as typographical errors.

44. Research note, box 304, folder 4997, Hughes Papers/YU.

45. Research note, box 304, folder 4996, Hughes Papers/YU.

46. Agnes Smedley to Langston Hughes, Shanghai, March 14, 1931, box 147, folder 2735, Hughes Papers/YU.

47. Langston Hughes to Arna Bontemps, August 31, 1943, in Langston Hughes, *Arna Bontemps–Langston Hughes Letters, 1925–1967*, ed. Charles H. Nichols (New York: Paragon House, 1990), 140.

48. Agnes Smedley, *Battle Hymn of China* (New York: Knopf, 1943), 97.

49. Agnes Smedley to Langston Hughes, Shanghai, October 31, 1934, Hughes Papers/HL.

50. "Famous American Negro Poet Says Shanghai Not Nice Place," *Shanghai Evening Post & Mercury*, July 19, 1933, clipping, in Records of the Central Intelligence Agency, RG 263, box 40, file D-5127 (Microfilm series M-1750, roll 16), NARA.

51. Among the arrested "writer friends" were Seikichi Fujimori, Tsuyoshi Kimura, and Kaku Arai (Itaru Nii) ("U.S. Writer Denies Charges Made Here: Langston Hughes Leaves Japan, Having Seen Little Because of Police Questioning," *Japan Advertiser*, July 26, 1933, 3). Shortly after Hughes's expulsion, Kimura published a journal article claiming that Hughes was falsely accused of red intrigue. Kimura concludes his article by wondering if the police would be preventing Agnes Smedley from visiting Japan (Tsuyoshi Kimura, "Kokujin shijin Hyuzu kun" [Mr. Hughes, A Black Poet], *Kaizo* 15, no. 9 [September 1933]: 91).

52. "I Wonder as I Wander," draft, 510, box 307, folder 5014, Hughes Papers/YU; see also "I Wonder as I Wander," draft, 508–9, box 306, folder 5013, Hughes Papers/YU.

53. Hughes may or may not have expected worse, given his knowledge that the Japanese police had ruthlessly brutalized communists in detention. Earlier drafts of Hughes's memoir relate that five months before his detention, Takiji Kobayashi, an underground Communist Party member and a famed proletarian writer "whose *Crab Fishing Boat* had been translated into several languages, was found dead in the Tokyo jail, beaten to death by the police" ("I Wonder as I Wander," draft, 568, box 307, folder 5014, Hughes Papers/YU; see also "I Wonder as I Wander," draft, 567, box 306, folder 5013, Hughes Papers/YU).

54. Langston Hughes to US Department of State, San Francisco, August 30, 1933, box 157, folder 2907, Hughes Papers/YU.

55. Alex Buchman to Langston Hughes, Tokyo, July 24, 1933, box 36, folder 630, Hughes Papers/YU; the article appeared in *Tokyo Nichi-Nichi*, July 25, 1933, evening edition, 2.

56. Buchman to Hughes, July 24, 1933; the article appeared in *Yomiuri*, July 25, 1933, evening edition, 2.

57. Langston Hughes to Alex Buchman, San Francisco, August 21, 1933, box 36, folder 630, Hughes Papers/YU.

58. "American 'Radical' Ordered from Japan," *Christian Science Monitor*, August 24, 1933, 3; "Tokyo Police Oust American Pacifist: Alexander Buchman Is Suspected of Radical Activity on Way to Shanghai Anti-War Parley," *New York Times*, August 23, 1933, 11; "Japanese Order American Youth to Quit Country," *Chicago Daily Tribune*, August 23, 1933, 12. The *Chicago Daily Tribune* reported, "For the second time in a month an American has been told to leave Japan because of his alleged communist activities.... Last month Langston Hughes, a colored writer, was ordered to depart."

59. For an account of the Anti-War Congress held in Shanghai on September 30, 1933, see Epstein, *Woman in World History*, 291–96. According to Isaacs's *China Forum*, fifty-five delegates met, despite the suppression of the KMT and foreign authorities in the International Settlement and the French Concession in Shanghai; the conclave took place, in secret ("Anti-War Congress Takes Place despite Kuomintang-Imperialist Ban," *China Forum*, October 4, 1933, 3–4).

60. "Japan Deports Anti-War Congress Delegates," August 23, 1933, newspaper clipping, Records of the Central Intelligence Agency, RG 263, entry Murphy Papers China, box 15, NARA. On Alexander Buchman, see Suzi Weissman, "Alex Buchman: The Last Survivor of Trotsky," *Critique* 32, no. 1 (April 2004): 151–62.

61. Secretary of State (Cordell Hull) to American Embassy in Tokyo (Joseph C. Grew), confidential telegram, September 14, 1933; American Embassy to Secretary of State, confidential telegram, September 15, 1933, Records of Foreign Service Posts of the Department of State, RG 84, Diplomatic Posts: Japan, volume 869, NARA.

62. Edwin S. Cunningham (American Consul General, Shanghai) to Secretary of State, dispatch, August 28, 1933, General Records of the Department of State, RG 59, box 4507, 800.00B Langston Hughes, NARA.

63. Stanley K. Hornbeck, Chief of Division of Far Eastern Affairs, Department of State, to Langston Hughes, September 25, 1933, box 157, folder 2907, Hughes Papers/YU.

64. Embassy of the United States of America, London, to Secretary of State, memorandum, May 29, 1933, RG 59, box 4507, 800.00B Langston Hughes, NARA.

65. S. 2. Special Branch of the Shanghai Municipal Police, "Movements of James Langston Hughes, American Nigger Writer, in Japan," August 21, 1933, a copy enclosed in Cunningham to Secretary of State, RG 59, box 4507, 800.00B Langston Hughes, NARA.

66. Ibid.

67. Shanghai Municipal Police file card on Langston Hughes, Records of the Central Intelligence Agency, RG 263, entry Shanghai Police Files, box 5, NARA.

68. "James Langston Hughes—American Negro Intellectual," 2.

69. Hughes had written previously about the New Year's Eve that he spent with Sano in Paris, in his column "Here to Yonder" in the *Chicago Defender* in 1945

(Langston Hughes, "Here to Yonder: New Years I've Known," *Chicago Defender*, December 29, 1945, 12).

70. Michiko Tanaka, "Seki Sano and Popular Political and Social Theatre in Latin America," *Latin American Theatre Review* 27, no. 2 (spring 1994): 55–56.

71. On the Japanese victims of the Stalinist purge, see Tetsuro Kato, "The Japanese Victims of Stalinist Terror in the USSR," *Hitotsubashi Journal of Social Studies* 32, no. 1 (July 2000): 1–13; and Tetsuro Kato, *Mosukuwa de Shukuseisareta Nihonjin* [The Japanese Purged in Moscow] (Tokyo: Aoki Shoten, 1994).

72. Quoted in Kato, "Japanese Victims," 12; Kato, *Mosukuwa*, 294–96.

73. "Meyerhold Ousted from Soviet Stage," *New York Times*, January 9, 1938, 40; Edward Braun, "Vsevolod Meyerhold: The Final Act," in *Enemies of the People: The Destruction of Soviet Literary, Theater, and Film Arts in the 1930s*, ed. Katherine Bliss Eaton, 145–62 (Evanston, IL: Northwestern University Press, 2002), 152.

74. Arriving in Yokohama on September 6, 1933 (shortly after Hughes was expelled from the same port), Sorge began operating in Japan undercover as a Nazi journalist. On Richard Sorge, see Robert Whymant, *Stalin's Spy: Richard Sorge and the Tokyo Espionage Ring* (London: I. B. Tauris, 1996).

75. US Congress, House, *Hearings on American Aspects of the Richard Sorge Spy Case (Based on Testimony of Mitsusada Yoshikawa and Maj. Gen. Charles A. Willoughby): Hearings before the Committee on Un-American Activities, House of Representatives, Eighty-Second Congress, First Session, August 9, 22, and 23, 1951* (Washington, DC: Government Printing Office, 1951), 1139, 1172. See also John D. Morris, "Soviet Knew Ahead of Tokyo War Plan: Japanese Investigator Asserts Spy Told Russians of Attack Two Months in Advance," *New York Times*, August 10, 1951, 1, 3.

76. For an account of the espionage charges leveled against Smedley by General MacArthur, see Price, *Lives of Agnes Smedley*, chaps. 17–18. Price claims that Smedley was indeed guilty of the charges.

77. "The Sorge Spy Ring: A Case Study in International Espionage in the Far East," report, *Congressional Record Appendix*, 81st Cong., 1st sess. (1949), vol. 95, pt. 12: A707.

78. "Spy Charge Denied by Miss Smedley," *New York Times*, February 11, 1949, 4; "Army Admits Spy Faux Pas: No Proof on Agnes Smedley," *New York Times*, February 19, 1949, 6.

79. "Army Admits Spy Faux Pas," 1.

80. "Officer Welcomes Suit on Spy Report: U.S. Intelligence Chief in Tokyo Waives Immunity to Face Action by Agnes Smedley," *New York Times*, February 22, 1949, 11; Charles A. Willoughby, *Shanghai Conspiracy: The Sorge Spy Ring* (New York: Dutton, 1952), 247, 271.

81. Willoughby, *Shanghai Conspiracy*, 273–74.

82. "Willoughby Exhibit No. 40: Smedley and Associates: 1918–48," document, in U.S. Congress, *Hearings on Richard Sorge*, 1222, 1223.

83. Arnold Rampersad, *The Life of Langston Hughes*, 2nd ed. (New York: Oxford University Press, 2002), 2:4, 197.

84. Willoughby, *Shanghai Conspiracy*, 254–56, 298–99. Willoughby also cited Hughes's poem "Goodbye Christ" when he testified before the House Un-American Activities Committee in August 1951 (U.S. Congress, *Hearings on Richard Sorge*, 1231).

85. Willoughby, *Shanghai Conspiracy*, 275.

Chapter 5. The Manchurian Philosopher: W. E. B. Du Bois in the Eurasian Pacific

1. Greil Marcus, *The Manchurian Candidate* (London: British Film Institute, 2002), 62.

2. The state established in Manchuria was also spelled Manchoukuo.

3. Victor Shiu Chiang Cheng, "Imagining China's Madrid in Manchuria: The Communist Military Strategy at the Onset of the Chinese Civil War, 1945–1946," *Modern China* 31, no. 1 (January 2005): 77, 94, 103.

4. John K. Fairbank, "Born Too Late," in *Bertolucci's "The Last Emperor": Multiple Takes*, ed. Bruce H. Sklarew et al., 203–11 (Detroit: Wayne State University Press, 1998), 203.

5. As Arnold Rampersad observes, "Two concerns dominated [Du Bois's] analyses of international events in the 1930s and 1940s: the success of socialism, objectified in the fate of the USSR, and the rise of the darker races out of colonialism or, in the case of Japan, to the height of international power" (Rampersad, *The Art and Imagination of W. E. B. Du Bois* [Cambridge, MA: Harvard University Press, 1976], 225). In the phrasing of Francis L. Broderick, Du Bois's assessments of world powers were based on two criteria—"their sympathy for colored colonial peoples and their aversion to capitalism"—which resulted in his championing of Soviet Russia and Japan (Broderick, *W. E. B. DuBois: Negro Leader in a Time of Crisis* [Stanford, CA: Stanford University Press, 1959], 196).

6. Horne, *Race War*, 110.

7. Mullen, *Afro-Orientalism*, xvii, xxxvii, xxxviii.

8. While Du Bois's 1928 novel *Dark Princess* is a prime example of "Afro-Orientalism" that stresses Afro-Asian solidarity, I am interested in rethinking black internationalism by linking it less to ideology and more to travel.

9. Du Bois, "As the Crow Flies," *Crisis* 41 (April 1934): 93. El Salvador was the first country in the Americas to recognize Manchukuo diplomatically, and the Dominican Republic also extended recognition.

10. See, for instance, Mullen, *Afro-Orientalism*; and Yuichiro Onishi, *Transpacific Antiracism: Afro-Asian Solidarity in Twentieth-Century Black America, Japan, and Okinawa* (New York: New York University Press, 2013).

11. Lewis, *W. E. B. Du Bois*, 392, 419.

12. Report, Atlanta, Georgia, November 12, 1942, 1, William E. B. Du Bois, FBI file 100-99729; O'Reilly, *Black Americans*, 83.

13. Report, New York City, May 1, 1942, 1, FBI file 100-99729.

14. Lewis, *W. E. B. Du Bois*, 390–91, 392.

15. Travel itinerary, in "No. 5741, December 12, 1936, Visit of Professor Du Bois," Adjutant, Ministry of Navy, Ref. C05034825300, JACAR. My translation.

16. Du Bois, "Forum of Fact and Opinion," *Pittsburgh Courier*, March 13, 1937, 15; W. E. B. Du Bois, *Newspaper Columns by W. E. B. Du Bois*, ed. Herbert Aptheker (White Plains, NY: Kraus-Thomson Organization, 1986), 1:180.

17. "No. 5741, December 12, 1936, Visit of Professor Du Bois." KBS requested permission for Du Bois to inspect the navy's battleship at Yokosuka.

18. Mark Stille, *Imperial Japanese Navy Battleships, 1941–45* (Oxford, UK: Osprey, 2008), 31–32, 34.

19. Du Bois, "Forum of Fact and Opinion," March 20, 1937, 10; Du Bois, *Newspaper Columns*, 1:181–82. The "count" mentioned in Du Bois's dispatch was probably Count Ayske Kabayama, chairman of the board of directors of KBS and member of the House of Peers.

20. KBS did not "invite" Du Bois to Japan, though it significantly facilitated his planned visit. In 1936, KBS was "contemplat[ing]" extending an invitation to Zona Gale Breese, winner of the 1921 Pulitzer Prize, to visit Japan. She was indeed invited and visited Japan in the spring of 1937 ("Distinguished Visitors," *K.B.S. Quarterly* 3, nos. 1–4 [April 1937–March 1938]: 3).

21. "The Kokusai Bunka Shinkokai since Its Establishment," *K.B.S. Quarterly* 1, no. 1 (April–June 1935): 4. On KBS, see also *Kokusai Bunka Shinkokai (The Society for International Cultural Relations): Prospectus and Scheme* (Tokyo: Kokusai Bunka Shinkokai, 1934); and Atsushi Shibasaki, *Kindai Nihon to Kokusai Bunka Koryu: Kokusai Bunka Shinkokai no Sosetsu to Tenkai* [International Cultural Relations and Modern Japan: History of Kokusai Bunka Shinkokai, 1934–1945] (Tokyo: Yushindo, 1999). The cultural activities of KBS included the production of films, lantern slides, gramophone records, and photographs; exchanges of professors and students; exhibitions; the establishment of contacts with overseas organizations; and the arrangement and sponsorship of visits by distinguished foreign guests. KBS also established the Japan Institute (1938–1941) in New York.

22. "Kokusai Bunka Shinkokai Jigyo Hokoku: Kokusai Bunka Jigyo no 7 ka nen" [Report on the Seven-Year Work of KBS's International Cultural Activities] (December 1940), 26, KBS Activities Collection, Japan Foundation Information Center Library, Tokyo (hereafter cited as KBS Collection).

23. "Kokusai Bunka Shinkokai Yakuin Meibo" [KBS: Directors, Advisers, Councilors List, as of September 1, 1936], KBS Collection. KBS's councilors included the director of the information department of the Foreign Office (which gave Du Bois a geisha party); the president of the Tokyo Pan-Pacific Club (which invited him to its monthly luncheon); the director of the Tokyo Imperial Household Museum (which he visited); the presidents of Tokyo Imperial University and Waseda University (at each of which he lectured); the director of the Tokyo Imperial University Library (which he inspected); the chairman of the board of directors of the *Osaka Mainichi*, a major newspaper company (at the hall of which he gave a lecture entitled "Message to Japan"); the executive director of Japan Broadcasting Corporation, Japan's national public broadcasting organization (which mentioned Du Bois's arrival in Japan "twice in nationwide radio hookups"); the mayor of Osaka (who "officially" received him); the vice minister of railways in the Japanese government (which provided him a free rail pass); the president of Nippon Yusen Kaisha (which provided passage on its ship

Tatsuta Maru when he left Japan); and others (Du Bois, "Forum of Fact and Opinion," March 13, 1937, 11; Du Bois, *Newspaper Columns*, 1:179).

24. "Purpose," *K.B.S. Quarterly* 1, no. 1 (April–June 1935): v.

25. Tomoko Akami, "The Emergence of International Public Opinion and the Origins of Public Diplomacy in Japan in the Inter-War Period," *Hague Journal of Diplomacy* 3, no. 2 (September 2008): 120.

26. Ramon H. Myers, "Japanese Imperialism in Manchuria: The South Manchuria Railway Company, 1906–1933," in *The Japanese Informal Empire in China, 1895–1937*, ed. Peter Duus, Ramon H. Myers, and Mark R. Peattie, 101–32 (Princeton, NJ: Princeton University Press, 1989), 119.

27. W. E. B. Du Bois to Chih Meng, May 15, 1936, reel 45, frame 494, Papers of W. E. B. Du Bois (microfilm), University of Massachusetts, Amherst, MA (hereafter cited as Du Bois Papers).

28. Chih Meng, *China Speaks: On the Conflict between China and Japan* (New York: Macmillan, 1932), 4–5.

29. M.[Matsuhei] Matsuo to W. E. B. Du Bois, June 4, 1936, reel 46, frames 129–30; Y.[Yoshiyasu] Kumazawa to W. E. B. Du Bois, July 29, 1936, reel 45, frame 946, Du Bois Papers. As a result of this change in itinerary, Du Bois reached Peking from the port of Dairen by steam, rather than from Mukden by rail.

30. W. E. B. Du Bois, "Russia and America: An Interpretation," draft manuscript, 132, reel 85, Du Bois Papers. All subsequent references to the work are cited as RA in the text. Page numbers for "Russia and America" are cited as they appear in the manuscript.

31. M. Matsuo to W. E. B. Du Bois, September 22, 1936, reel 46, frame 131, Du Bois Papers.

32. William C. Kirby, *Germany and Republican China* (Stanford, CA: Stanford University Press, 1984), 143–44.

33. For an account of border tension between the Soviet Union and Manchukuo, see Robert T. Pollard, "Russo-Japanese Tension," *Annals of the American Academy of Political and Social Science* 175 (September 1934): 101–9.

34. All foreign travelers through Manchukuo were required to obtain visas at the passport office in the compound of Manchouli station.

35. On the city planning of Hsinking, see Akira Koshizawa, *Manshukoku no Shuto Keikaku* [Planning of Manchukuo's Capital] (Tokyo: Nihon Keizai Hyoron-sha, 1988); and Qinghua Guo, "Changchun: Unfinished Capital Planning of Manzhouguo, 1932–42," *Urban History* 31, no. 1 (May 2004): 100–117.

36. Du Bois notes that the Yamato Hotel at Hsinking was once "a Russian club . . . amid ancient acacias" (RA, 130), but he has probably confused the two Yamato hotels—both owned by SMR—at Harbin and at Hsinking.

37. Eri Hotta, *Pan-Asianism and Japan's War, 1931–1945* (New York: Palgrave Macmillan, 2007), 116.

38. Louise Young, *Japan's Total Empire: Manchuria and the Culture of Wartime Imperialism* (Berkeley: University of California Press, 1998), 250.

39. South Manchuria Railway Company, *Illustrated Guide Book for Travelling in Manchoukuo with Sketch Map* (Dairen, Manchukuo: Author, 1934), 45.

40. "Senman-nin 'Kokujin no Jifu': Dyuboisu hakase Sakuya Rairen" [Father of Ten Million Blacks: Dr. Du Bois Arrived at Dairen Last Night], *Manshu Nichi-Nichi*, November 18, 1936, 7.

41. "Kokujin no Jifu, Sakuya Koenkai" [Father of Blacks Lectured Last Night], *Manshu Nichi-Nichi*, November 19, 1936, 7.

42. Du Bois, "Forum of Fact and Opinion," February 13, 1937, 15; Du Bois, *Newspaper Columns*, 1:168.

43. John J. Stephan, "Hijacked by Utopia: American Nikkei in Manchuria," *Amerasia Journal* 23, no. 3 (winter 1997–1998): 3.

44. "Manshukoku Kenkoku Sengen" [Declaration of Founding of Manchukuo], March 1, 1932, frame 0021, Ref. B02030709100, JACAR.

45. Stephan, "Hijacked by Utopia," 2, 15.

46. Du Bois, "Forum of Fact and Opinion," February 13, 1937, 7; Du Bois, *Newspaper Columns*, 1:166; RA, 132.

47. "Manshukoku Kenkoku Sengen" [Declaration of Founding of Manchukuo], frame 0021.

48. For an analysis of the competing resistant nationalist and collaborative accommodationist discourses that developed on the Japanese Empire in Manchuria, see Rana Mitter, "Evil Empire? Competing Constructions of Japanese Imperialism in Manchuria, 1928–1937," in *Imperial Japan and National Identities in Asia, 1895–1945*, ed. Li Narangoa and Robert Cribb, 146–68 (London: RoutledgeCurzon, 2003).

49. Du Bois, "Forum of Fact and Opinion," February 13, 1937, 7; Du Bois, *Newspaper Columns*, 1:167; RA, 132.

50. Du Bois, "Forum of Fact and Opinion," February 13, 1937, 7; Du Bois, *Newspaper Columns*, 1:167.

51. Du Bois, "Forum of Fact and Opinion," February 13, 1937, 7, 15; Du Bois, *Newspaper Columns*, 1:167–68.

52. See Katsuji Nakagane, "Manchukuo and Economic Development," in Duus, Myers, and Peattie, *Japanese Informal Empire in China*, 141–46.

53. Young, *Japan's Total Empire*, 291.

54. Manchukuo, *Economic Construction Program of Manchukuo* (New York: New York Office of the South Manchuria Railway Company, 1933), 4.

55. Nagaharu Yasuo, "Manchukuo's New Economic Policy," *Pacific Affairs* 11, no. 3 (September 1938): 326.

56. Yoshio Miyanishi, *Mantetsu Chosa-bu to Ozaki Hotsumi* [The Research Department of the South Manchuria Railway Company and Hotsumi Ozaki] (Tokyo: Aki Shobo, 1983), 10, 17.

57. Matsuo to Du Bois, September 22, 1936.

58. See also Du Bois, "Forum of Fact and Opinion," February 13, 1937, 7; Du Bois, *Newspaper Columns*, 1:167.

59. See also Du Bois, "Forum of Fact and Opinion," February 13, 1937, 7; Du Bois, *Newspaper Columns*, 1:166.

60. Chih Meng to W. E. B. Du Bois, September 10, 1936, reel 45, frame 495; see also Poeliu Dai to W. E. B. Du Bois, November 27, 1936, reel 45, frame 496, Du Bois Papers.

61. Du Bois, "Forum of Fact and Opinion," February 27, 1937, 15; Du Bois, *Newspaper Columns*, 1:174.

62. Roy Wilkins, "Watchtower," *New York Amsterdam News*, January 30, 1937, 12.

63. "Weekly Topics: Japan Gets Both Cheers and Boos," *New York Amsterdam News*, September 4, 1937, 14.

64. [George S. Schuyler], "The Far East and Us," *Pittsburgh Courier*, October 30, 1937, 10.

65. Hughes, "Roar China!" in *Collected Poems*, 198.

66. Richard Wright, "Big Harlem Rally for China Tonight," *Daily Worker*, September 27, 1937, 4. In 1941, Wright applied to cover the Sino-Japanese War as a foreign correspondent for the Associated Negro Press (ANP). Wright sought this assignment out of envy of Ernest Hemingway, who had recently visited Chungking, the wartime capital of China's Nationalist government, as a correspondent for the New York leftist newspaper *PM*, along with his wife Martha Gellhorn, a war correspondent for *Collier's* magazine (Hazel Rowley, *Richard Wright: The Life and Times* [New York: Henry Holt, 2001], 235). Wright wanted "to see how men and women of color are living in other parts of the world" and became determined to go to the Far East (Richard Wright to Claude A. Barnett, March 4, 1941, box 93, folder 1187, Richard Wright Papers, Yale Collection of American Literature, Beinecke Rare Book and Manuscript Library, Yale University, New Haven, CT). However, Wright's application to the State Department for a passport to travel to China and the Soviet Union as a reporter for the ANP was denied (R. B. Shipley, Passport Division, to Richard Wright, June 24, 1941, box 107, folder 1645, Richard Wright Papers).

67. "Robeson to Help Chinese in War," *Pittsburgh Courier*, November 27, 1937, 1; "Paul Robeson Aiding China against Japan," *Chicago Defender*, November 27, 1937, 24.

68. *Chee Lai! (Arise!): Songs of New China* (New York: Keynote Recordings, 1941), 5.

69. "The Camera Overseas: 136,000,000 People See This Picture of Shanghai's South Station," *Life*, October 4, 1937, 102; "Ten Best News Stories of 1937 Are Picked by the Newsreaders," *Life*, January 3, 1938, 13.

70. Franklin D. Roosevelt, "Quarantine" Speech at Chicago, in *The Public Papers and Addresses of Franklin D. Roosevelt, 1937* (New York: Macmillan, 1941), 407, 410.

71. George H. Gallup, *The Gallup Poll: Public Opinion, 1935–1971* (New York: Random House, 1972), 1:69, 72.

72. Du Bois, "Forum of Fact and Opinion," September 25, 1937, 11; Du Bois, *Newspaper Columns*, 1:240.

73. Harry F. Ward to W. E. B. Du Bois, October 7, 1937; Du Bois to Ward, October 7, 1937, in W. E. B. Du Bois, *The Correspondence of W. E. B. Du Bois*, ed. Herbert Aptheker (Amherst: University of Massachusetts Press, 1973–1978), 2:147.

74. Du Bois, "Forum of Fact and Opinion," October 23, 1937, 11; Du Bois, *Newspaper Columns*, 1:245.

75. Du Bois, "Forum of Fact and Opinion," September 25, 1937, 11; Du Bois, *Newspaper Columns*, 1:240–41.

76. RA, 142. As Manning Marable observes, "Du Bois had been quite critical of the regime of Chiang Kai-Shek since 1928, primarily because of Chiang's anti-Marxist policies" (Marable, *W. E. B. Du Bois: Black Radical Democrat*, updated ed. [Boulder, CO: Paradigm, 2005], 156).

77. Du Bois, "Forum of Fact and Opinion," September 25, 1937, 11; Du Bois, *Newspaper Columns*, 1:241.

78. Du Bois, "Forum of Fact and Opinion," October 23, 1937, 11; Du Bois, *Newspaper Columns*, 1:245.

79. Yosuke Matsuoka, "A Knockout Blow Held Aim of Japan," *New York Times*, October 10, 1937, 12.

80. The league had proposed establishing international control of Manchuria. In speaking against this proposal, Matsuoka, Japan's chief delegate, asked rhetorically, "What justification is there for such an attempt on the part of the League of Nations? I cannot see. Would the American people agree to such control over the Panama Canal Zone? Would the British people permit it over Egypt?" (League of Nations, *Japan's Case*, 60).

81. Iris Chang, *The Rape of Nanking: The Forgotten Holocaust of World War II* (1997; London: Penguin, 1998), 6.

82. On the American journalists who witnessed the massacre, see Takashi Yoshida, *The Making of the "Rape of Nanking": History and Memory in Japan, China, and the United States* (New York: Oxford University Press, 2006), 38–39.

83. A. T. Steele, "Nanking Massacre Story: Japanese Troops Kill Thousands," *Chicago Daily News*, December 15, 1937, 1.

84. Arthur Menken, "Witness Tells Nanking Horror as Chinese Flee," *Chicago Daily Tribune*, December 17, 1937, 4.

85. C. Yates McDaniel, "Nanking Horror Described in Diary of War Reporter," *Chicago Daily Tribune*, December 18, 1937, 8.

86. F. Tillman Durdin, "All Captives Slain: Civilians Also Killed as the Japanese Spread Terror in Nanking," *New York Times*, December 18, 1937, 1; F. Tillman Durdin, "Japanese Atrocities Marked Fall of Nanking after Chinese Command Fled," *New York Times*, January 9, 1938, 38. In addition to reports by US journalists, *Manchester Guardian* correspondent Harold John Timperley's stories became available to the American public in 1938 (H. J. Timperley, *Japanese Terror in China* [New York: Modern Age Books, 1938]). Timperley's manuscripts were successfully smuggled out of China with the help of Alexander Buchman, a friend of Langston Hughes (see chapter 4), who worked at the Chinese-financed Trans-Pacific News Agency that transmitted images and dispatches from China to news organizations throughout the world (Weissman, "Alex Buchman," 155).

87. "The Camera Overseas: The Japanese Conqueror Brings 'A Week of Hell' to China's Nationalist Capital of Nanking," *Life*, January 10, 1938, 51. Later in the year 1938, *Look* magazine carried shocking photos under the title "Killing for Fun!" which captured Japanese soldiers executing Chinese prisoners of war by bayonet and live burial. One picture showed a boy about to be beheaded "because he stepped on a telephone wire" ("Killing for Fun!" *Look*, November 22, 1938, 55).

88. "The Case for Japan," 4. A number of readers reacted negatively (see, for example, John Chen Tome, "Chinese Differs with Editorial on Japanese," *Afro-American*, January 22, 1938, 4; H. Baker, "Raps China Editorial," *Afro-American*, January 22, 1938, 4; and Louis W. Hann, "Dislikes Editorial," *Afro-American*, February 26, 1938, 4). Exchange and debate also took place in the *Philadelphia Tribune*, following Robert W. Bagnall's editorial (see Bagnall, "Bagnall: Sino-Japanese Situation," *Philadelphia Tribune*, November 25, 1937, 4; Bilal Farook, "Wants Japanese to Dominate China," *Philadelphia Tribune*, December 9, 1937, 4; A. White, "Sino-Japanese War Is Fascism vs. Communism," *Philadelphia Tribune*, December 23, 1937, 4; and Bilal Farook, "Masses Treated Same under All Systems," *Philadelphia Tribune*, January 6, 1938, 4).

89. See, for instance, "Discuss Japanese in Chinese Intervention," *New York Amsterdam News*, March 19, 1938, 11; "Discussed Japs in China," *New York Amsterdam News*, April 9, 1938, 10; and "Brooklyn Debaters Meet Lincoln," *Afro-American*, April 9, 1938. 14.

90. See, for instance, "City-Wide Forum Hears America Is Headed for World Struggle," *Afro-American*, October 16, 1937, 22; "Sino-Jap Dispute Explained to Harlemites," *New York Amsterdam News*, February 5, 1938, 4; and Kaju Nakamura, "The Situation in the Far East—An Analysis," *New York Age*, April 16, 1938, 1–2. Du Bois arranged for Kiichi Miyake, a professor at Tokyo Imperial University and one of his KBS acquaintances, to give a talk on the Sino-Japanese War at Atlanta University in March 1938 (W. E. B. Du Bois to Yasuichi Hikida, March 11, 1938, reel 48, frame 1166; Kiichi Miyake to Du Bois, March 15, 1938, reel 49, frame 282, Du Bois Papers). The issue of propaganda in the China-Japan conflict is complex, for propaganda emanated from both Japan and China; see William E. Daugherty, "China's Official Publicity in the United States," *Public Opinion Quarterly* 6, no. 1 (spring 1942): 70–86.

91. That the Italo-Ethiopian War was one of the most important points of reference in the African American community is reflected by the invitation of Malaku E. Bayen, "representative of Emperor Haile Selassie" and founder of the Ethiopian World Federation in New York, to attend a debate on the Sino-Japanese conflict at the Dunbar Literary Club of Harlem in January 1938 ("Discuss Japan," *New York Amsterdam News*, January 29, 1938, 2).

92. Cyril Briggs, "Japan Proves Not to Be 'The Hope Darker Races,'" *Philadelphia Tribune*, January 20, 1938, 2.

93. William Pickens, "Dean William Pickens Writes on Japan—'Masters of the Orient,'" *Pittsburgh Courier*, December 18, 1937, 14.

94. "The Week's Editorial," *Afro-American*, December 18, 1937, 1.

95. "The Case for Japan," 4.

96. "China Declares War on the Axis Powers: Declaration of War on Japan," *Contemporary China* 1, no. 15 (December 15, 1951): 1.

97. On Sino-Soviet relations, see John W. Garver, "Chiang Kai-shek's Quest for Soviet Entry into the Sino-Japanese War," *Political Science Quarterly* 102, no. 2 (summer 1987): 295–316.

98. Boris Slavinsky, *The Japanese–Soviet Neutrality Pact: A Diplomatic History, 1941–1945*, trans. Geoffrey Jukes (London: RoutledgeCurzon, 2004), 16.

99. Communist Party of the United States of America, *Is Japan the Champion of the Colored Races? The Negro's Stake in Democracy* (New York: Workers Library, 1938), 17.

100. Bruce Cumings, "Japan and Northeast Asia into the Twenty-first Century," in Katzenstein and Shiraishi, *Network Power*, 136–68, 146–47.

101. W. E. B. Du Bois, "The Meaning of Japan," speech, Morehouse College, Atlanta, GA, March 12, 1937, and Dillard University, New Orleans, LA, June 2, 1937, reel 80, frame 660, Du Bois Papers.

102. The *China Weekly Review* reported on a rumor circulating in China that Du Bois, "who recently toured the Orient, had expressed pro-Japanese sympathies" ("Serious Racial Element in the Sino-Japanese Struggle," *China Weekly Review*, December 10, 1938, 32).

103. Waldo McNutt to W. E. B. Du Bois, February 13, 1939; Du Bois to McNutt, February 25, 1939, in Du Bois, *Correspondence of W. E. B. Du Bois*, 2:184–85.

104. For an account of the committee, see Donald J. Friedman, *The Road from Isolation: The Campaign of the American Committee for Non-Participation in Japanese Aggression, 1938–1941* (Cambridge, MA: East Asian Research Center, Harvard University, 1968).

105. Henry L. Stimson to W. E. B. Du Bois, January 24, 1940, in Du Bois, *Correspondence of W. E. B. Du Bois*, 2:205.

106. Du Bois, "As the Crow Flies," *New York Amsterdam News*, February 24, 1940, 14; Du Bois, *Newspaper Columns*, 1:287.

107. Du Bois, "As the Crow Flies," *New York Amsterdam News*, November 18, 1939, 14; Du Bois, *Newspaper Columns*, 1:271.

108. Du Bois, "As the Crow Flies," *New York Amsterdam News*, August 3, 1940, 10. This column on Matsuoka is reprinted erroneously under the date of March 30, 1940, in Du Bois, *Newspaper Columns*, 1:292.

109. See Yosuke Matsuoka, "Proclamation of the Greater East Asia Co-Prosperity Sphere," in *Japan's Greater East Asia Co-Prosperity Sphere in World War II: Selected Readings and Documents*, ed. Joyce C. Lebra, 71–72 (Kuala Lumpur, Malaysia: Oxford University Press, 1975).

110. On Matsuoka and the Eurasian Continental Bloc, see Chihiro Hosoya, "The Japanese–Soviet Neutrality Pact," trans. Peter A. Berton, in *The Fateful Choice: Japan's Advance into Southeast Asia, 1939–1941*, ed. James William Morley, 13–114 (New York: Columbia University Press, 1980), 44–85; and Yukiko Koshiro, "Eurasian Eclipse: Japan's End Game in World War II," *American Historical Review* 109, no. 2 (April 2004): 420–23.

111. Slavinsky, *Japanese–Soviet Neutrality Pact*, 7. Also, it is worth noting that Matsuoka's pro-Axis attitude did not entail anti-Semitism, although that charge has been leveled against him. As biographer David J. Lu notes, Matsuoka launched a rescue operation through SMR to render assistance to Jewish refugees from Nazi persecution. The operation provided refugees with shelter, visas for travel, passage to the United States and South America, or settlement in Manchuria and Shanghai (Lu, *Agony of Choice*, 135–36).

112. In Rome, American modernist poet Ezra Pound welcomed Matsuoka in a letter to the foreign minister, in which he wrote, "No occidental decently aware of"

the qualities of Japanese civilization could be "infected with anti-japanese [sic] propaganda." In this letter, Pound also raised a proposal for peace directly with Matsuoka: "Men like myself would cheerfully give you Guam for a few sound films" of Noh drama (Ezra Pound to Yosuke Matsuoka, March 29, 1941, in Sanehide Kodama, ed., *Ezra Pound and Japan: Letters and Essays* [Redding Ridge, CT: Black Swan Books, 1987], 249).

113. The details of the Matsuoka-Stalin talks that transpired in the Kremlin on March 24 and April 12 were slow to emerge. Although an account of the first conversation as Matsuoka described it to Hitler was found in confiscated German Foreign Ministry files immediately after the war, and was in the hands of the Allied prosecutors in the Nuremberg and Tokyo Trials, official Soviet records of the conversations remained classified in the Russian Foreign Ministry archives until December 1994. The declassified records were fully brought into the public domain by Slavinsky's *Japanese–Soviet Neutrality Pact*.

114. "Record of Conversation of Comrade I. V. Stalin with Minister of Foreign Affairs of Japan Matsuoka, 24 March 1941," and "Record of Conversation between Comrade J. V. Stalin and Foreign Minister of Japan Matsuoka, 12 April 1941," Russian Federation Foreign Ministry, quoted in Slavinsky, *Japanese–Soviet Neutrality Pact*, 37, 49.

115. Ibid.

116. Hosoya, "Japanese–Soviet Neutrality Pact," 79, 80–81.

117. "Record of Conversation of Comrade I.V. Stalin with Minister of Foreign Affairs of Japan Matsuoka, 24 March 1941," in Slavinsky, *Japanese–Soviet Neutrality Pact*, 37.

118. Otto D. Tolischus, "Victor's Welcome Given to Matsuoka," *New York Times*, April 23, 1941, 7; "Japan: Matsuoka Home with a Head," *Time*, May 5, 1941, 30; "Japan's Foreign Minister Does Grand Tour of Axis," *Life*, May 5, 1941, 40. According to John W. Dower, America's Cold War rhetoric of the Russians as an "Asian" people, the menace from the East, originated in this reported exchange (Dower, *War without Mercy: Race and Power in the Pacific War* [New York: Pantheon, 1986], 364n16). According to Yukiko Koshiro, in prewar Japan, the recasting of the Russians as Asians posed no problems; "the lesser 'whiteness' of the Russians facilitated their inclusion in Japan's pan-Asianist rhetoric" (Koshiro, "Eurasian Eclipse," 423).

119. "Accord Frees Tokyo's Hands in East, Soviet's in Europe," *Washington Post*, April 14, 1941, 1.

120. Ernest Hemingway, "Russia Still Aids China, despite Neutrality Pact with Japan," *Washington Post*, June 10, 1941, 1. For an account of Hemingway's trip to China as war correspondent, see Peter Moreira, *Hemingway on the China Front: His WWII Spy Mission with Martha Gellhorn* (Washington, DC: Potomac Books, 2006).

121. Slavinsky, *Japanese–Soviet Neutrality Pact*, 60.

122. Broderick, *W. E. B. DuBois*, 193.

123. Du Bois, "As the Crow Flies," *New York Amsterdam Star-News*, July 12, 1941, 1, 14; Du Bois, *Newspaper Columns*, 1:376.

124. Hosoya, "Japanese–Soviet Neutrality Pact," 85.

125. George S. Schuyler attributed the surprise attack of the Soviet Union on Manchukuo to the US dropping of the atomic bomb in Hiroshima. He editorialized in his *Pittsburgh Courier* column, "The dropping of the atom bomb did more than slaughter Japanese workers and their families. It spurred Russia to belatedly declare war on her erstwhile Japanese allies so that she would not be left out in the cold when the time came for distributing the Far Eastern swag" (Schuyler, "Views and Reviews," *Pittsburgh Courier*, August 18, 1945, 7).

Epilogue

1. The White House, "Remarks by President Barack Obama at Suntory Hall," accessed November 19, 2012, http://www.whitehouse.gov.

2. Hill, *FBI's RACON*, 406–7, 409, 411.

3. Military Intelligence Service to J. Edgar Hoover, November 2, 1942, Richard Nathaniel Wright, FBI file 100-157464.

4. J. Edgar Hoover to SAC (Special Agent in Charge), New York, December 9, 1942, FBI file 100-157464; Natalie Robins, *Alien Ink: The FBI's War on Freedom of Expression* (1992; New Brunswick, NJ: Rutgers University Press, 1993), 285. It is interesting to note that Wright similarly depicts Bigger Thomas, a working-class black youth living in Chicago's South Side ghetto, as having pro-Japanese sympathies (Wright, *Native Son* [1940; New York: HarperPerennial, 1998], 115; "How 'Bigger' Was Born," in *Native Son*, 440).

5. Plummer, *Rising Wind*, 123.

6. Kenneth Robert Janken, *Walter White: Mr. NAACP* (2003; Chapel Hill: University of North Carolina Press, 2006), 277, 279–80.

7. Walter White to Franklin D. Roosevelt, May 4, 1942, group II, box A320, folder 1, Records of the National Association for the Advancement of Colored People, Manuscript Division, Library of Congress, Washington, DC (hereafter cited as NAACP Records).

8. Gary R. Hess, *America Encounters India, 1941–1947* (Baltimore: Johns Hopkins Press, 1971), 82.

9. Hill, *FBI's RACON*, 194, 509.

10. See "Japan-U.S. Exchange Ships," frame 0381, Ref. B05014041100, JACAR.

11. Hill, *FBI's RACON*, 509–10.

12. Yasuichi Hikida to James Weldon Johnson, September 26, 1933, box 9, folder 206, JWJ Papers. In his letter, Hikida shared with Johnson a vision of Japan welcoming black athletes to the Olympic Games, which Japan was slated to host in 1940 (but which were cancelled as Japan was bogged down in its war with China), with the singing of this anthem.

13. Walter White to James Weldon Johnson, September 25, 1933, box 24, folder 542, JWJ Papers.

14. Walter White, *A Man Called White: The Autobiography of Walter White* (1948; Athens: University of Georgia Press, 1995), 69.

15. Yasuichi Hikida to W. E. B. Du Bois, April 24, 1936, reel 45, frame 1047; Hikida to Du Bois, [October 15, 1936], reel 45, frame 1059, Du Bois Papers.

16. Yasuichi Hikida, *Beikoku Kokujin to Dai ichiji Taisen* [Black Americans and World War I], February 1943, Ref. B04013211300, JACAR.

17. Yasuichi Hikida, "Senso to Kokujin" [War and Blacks], October 1942, Ref. B04013211200, JACAR.

18. Yasuichi Hikida, "Senji Kokujin Kosaku" [Wartime Negro Propaganda Operations], January 1943, Ref. B02032466100, JACAR.

19. Ibid., frames 0211, 0212, 0223. Other African American leaders listed include A. Philip Randolph, Mary McLeod Bethune, Channing H. Tobias, William Pickens, Rayford W. Logan, Adam Clayton Powell, Mordecai Johnson, and W. E. B. Du Bois.

20. "Axis Propaganda Intended to Undermine Relations between Whites and Negroes," July 21, 1942, 5–6, Records of the Office of Government Reports, RG 44, entry 171, box 1849, NARA.

21. Ibid. For a discussion of the Japanese "negro propaganda" broadcasts, see Masaharu Sato and Barak Kushner, "'Negro Propaganda Operations': Japan's Short-Wave Radio Broadcasts for World War II Black Americans," *Historical Journal of Film, Radio and Television* 19, no. 1 (March 1999): 5–26.

22. Alan R. Murray to Walter White, August 3, 1942; White to Murray, August 5, 1942, group II, box A320, folder 2, NAACP Records.

23. Walter White, "To the People of Japan, Greetings!" [August 1942], 1–3, group II, box A320, folder 2, NAACP Records.

24. Walter White to Alan P. Murray, telegram, August 10, 1942, group II, box A320, folder 2, NAACP Records.

25. Walter White to Franklin D. Roosevelt, telegram, August 10, 1942, group II, box A320, folder 2, NAACP Records.

26. Greater East Asia Congress, *Addresses before the Assembly of Greater East-Asiatic Nations, Tokyo, November 1943* (Tokyo: Ministry of Greater East-Asiatic Affairs, 1943), 63–65. White's vision of the Pacific Charter, and that underlying the framing of the joint declaration, however, were less convergent than they appeared to be. The fifth article of the joint declaration concerns not so much the Western principle of "equality" as the Japanese principle of "proper place," that is, "the nations of the world have each its proper place" (ibid., 63).

27. Walter White, "Outline of Article on Axis Propaganda on Racial Issue" [1942], 2, group II, box A79, folder 9, NAACP Records; a copy of the outline is also found in Walter White to Robert P. Patterson (Under Secretary of War), September 14, 1942, Records of the Office of the Secretary of War, RG 107, entry 143, box 52, NARA.

28. White's quotations of Radio Tokyo in the outline for his proposed article are most likely from "Axis Propaganda on the Negro for the Intelligence Survey on the 'Harlem Negro,'" May 9, 1942, Records of the Office of Government Reports, RG 44, entry 171, box 1849, NARA.

29. White, "Outline of Article," 4.

30. Ibid., 5.

31. Ibid., 5–6.

32. Ibid., 1.

33. Ibid., 7–8.

34. See Stuart Rose (*Saturday Evening Post*) to Walter White, September 10, 1942; Rose to White, October 1, 1942, group II, box A80, folder 1; William A. H. Birnie (*American Magazine*) to Walter White, October 22, 1942, group II, box A79, folder 9; and Editorial Offices *(Life* magazine) to Walter White, January 28, 1943, group II, box A79, folder 9, NAACP Records.

35. Walter White, *A Rising Wind* (Garden City, NY: Double Day, Doran, 1945), 147, 153, 154.

36. Commander in Chief, US Pacific Fleet and Pacific Ocean Areas, to Walter White, travel authority, December 22, 1944, box 24, folder 222; White, memo (a list of visited places), box 24, folder 222, Walter Francis White and Poppy Cannon White Papers, Yale Collection of American Literature, Beinecke Rare Book and Manuscript Library, Yale University, New Haven, CT.

37. "Walter White Warns U.S. Must Wake Up to Happenings in Pacific: Restoration of Colonial Systems Will Lead to World War III," press release, April 12, 1945, group II, box A611, folder 3, NAACP Records.

38. "Has American Learned?" *New York Amsterdam News*, September 15, 1945, 6.

39. Langston Hughes, "Here to Yonder," *Chicago Defender*, January 27, 1945, 10.

40. *Bulletin of America's Town Meeting of the Air* 15, no. 19 (September 6, 1949): 13.

41. The geopolitical map of Asia was entirely being redrawn. The onset of the Cold War—the establishing of the Democratic People's Republic (North Korea) in 1948, and of the People's Republic of China in 1949 that triggered the "who lost China?" debate in the United States, and the Korean War in 1950–1953—marked a watershed for regional dissolution in East Asia. The United States was building America's "defense perimeter" in the Pacific that (in Secretary of State Dean Acheson's 1950 definition) connected the Aleutians, the Japanese archipelago, Okinawa, and the Philippines.

42. On Richard Edes Harrison, see Schulten, *Geographical Imagination*, 214–26.

43. Alan K. Henrikson, "The Map as an 'Idea': The Role of Cartographic Imagery during the Second World War," *American Cartographer* 2, no. 1 (April 1975): 19–20.

44. George T. Renner, "7 Realities about Japan," *Clearing House* 17, no. 8 (April 1943): 488.

45. United Nations, "UN Flag and Emblem," last updated December 30, 2013. http://www.un.org.

BIBLIOGRAPHY

Archives
Bancroft Library, University of California, Berkeley
    Noël Sullivan Papers
Beinecke Rare Book and Manuscript Library, Yale University, New Haven
    Langston Hughes Papers
    James Weldon Johnson and Grace Nail Johnson Papers
    Walter Francis White and Poppy Cannon White Papers
    Richard Wright Papers
Federal Bureau of Investigation
    William E. B. Du Bois, file number 100-99729
    Langston Hughes, file number 100-151-39
    Richard Nathaniel Wright, file number 100-157464
Free Library of Philadelphia
    Theatre Collection
Huntington Library, San Marino, CA
    Papers of Langston Hughes
Japan Center for Asian Historical Records, National Archives of Japan, Tokyo
Japan Foundation Information Center Library, Tokyo
    KBS Activities Collection
Library of Congress, Washington, DC
    Federal Theatre Project Collection
    Papers of the NAACP (Frederick, MD: University Publications of America, [c1982]–) (microfilm)
    Records of the National Association for the Advancement of Colored People
National Archives and Records Administration, College Park, MD
    RG 44, Records of the Office of Government Reports
    RG 59, General Records of the Department of State
    RG 84, Records of Foreign Service Posts of the Department of State
    RG 107, Records of the Office of the Secretary of War
    RG 160, Records of Headquarters Army Service Forces
    RG 165, Records of the War Department General and Special Staffs
    RG 208, Records of the Office of War Information
    RG 216, Records of the Office of Censorship
    RG 263, Records of the Central Intelligence Agency

New York Public Library for the Performing Arts
    Billy Rose Theatre Collection
Schomburg Center for Research in Black Culture, New York
    Schuyler Family Papers: George S. Schuyler
Syracuse University Library, Syracuse
    George S. Schuyler Papers
University of Hawai'i at Manoa, Honolulu
    Institute of Pacific Relations Records
University of Massachusetts, Amherst, MA
    Papers of W. E. B. Du Bois, 1803 (1877–1963) to 1979. Microfilm ed. Sanford, NC: Microfilming Corporation of America, c1980. Ann Arbor: University Microfilms International.

Newspapers and Periodicals
    Afro-American (Baltimore)
    Bulletin of America's Town Meeting of the Air
    Chicago Daily News
    Chicago Daily Tribune
    Chicago Defender
    China Forum
    China Weekly Review
    Colored American Magazine
    Crisis
    Daily Worker
    Honolulu Advertiser
    Honolulu Star-Bulletin
    Indianapolis Recorder
    Japan Advertiser
    Japan Times & Mail
    K.B.S. Quarterly
    Life
    Look
    Manshu Nichi-Nichi
    New York Age
    New York Amsterdam News
    New York Amsterdam Star-News
    New York Times
    Nippon Times
    The Osaka Mainichi & the Tokyo Nichi Nichi
    Philadelphia Tribune
    Pittsburgh Courier
    Time
    Times (London)
    Tokyo Asahi Shimbun
    Tokyo Nichi-Nichi Shimbun

Voice of the Negro
Wall Street Journal
Washington Herald
Washington Post
Yomiuri Shimbun

Books and Articles

Akami, Tomoko. "The Emergence of International Public Opinion and the Origins of Public Diplomacy in Japan in the Inter-War Period." *Hague Journal of Diplomacy* 3, no. 2 (September 2008): 99–128.

———. *Internationalizing the Pacific: The United States, Japan and the Institute of Pacific Relations in War and Peace, 1919–45*. London: Routledge, 2002.

Allen, Ernest, Jr. "When Japan Was 'Champion of the Darker Races': Satokata Takahashi and the Flowering of Black Messianic Nationalism." *Black Scholar* 24, no. 1 (winter 1994): 23–46.

Anderson, Benedict. *Imagined Communities: Reflections on the Origin and Spread of Nationalism*. London: Verso, 1983.

Anderson, Kay, and Susan J. Smith. "Editorial: Emotional Geographies." *Transactions of the Institute of British Geographers* 26, no. 1 (March 2001): 7–10.

Asante, S. K. B. *Pan-African Protest: West Africa and the Italo-Ethiopian Crisis, 1934–1941*. London: Longman, 1977.

Baily, Leslie. *The Gilbert and Sullivan Book*. London: Spring Books, 1952.

Baldwin, Kate A. *Beyond the Color Line and the Iron Curtain: Reading Encounters between Black and Red, 1922–1963*. Durham, NC: Duke University Press, 2002.

Basinger, Jeanine. *The World War II Combat Film: Anatomy of a Genre*. New York: Columbia University Press, 1986.

Batiste, Stephanie Leigh. *Darkening Mirrors: Imperial Representation in Depression-Era African American Performance*. Durham, NC: Duke University Press, 2011.

Bermann, Karl. *Under the Big Stick: Nicaragua and the United States since 1848*. Boston: South End Press, 1986.

Berry, Faith. *Langston Hughes: Before and beyond Harlem*. Westport, CT: Lawrence Hill, 1983.

Best, Antony. "Race, Monarchy, and the Anglo-Japanese Alliance, 1902–1922." *Social Science Japan Journal* 9, no. 2 (October 2006): 171–86.

Bradley, Ian, ed. *The Complete Annotated Gilbert and Sullivan*. Oxford: Oxford University Press, 1996.

Bradshaw, Richard Albert. "Japan and European Colonialism in Africa, 1800–1937." PhD diss., Ohio University, 1992.

Braithwaite, William Stanley. "*Along This Way*: A Review of the Autobiography of James Weldon Johnson." *Opportunity* 11, no. 12 (December 1933): 376–78.

Braun, Edward. "Vsevolod Meyerhold: The Final Act." In *Enemies of the People: The Destruction of Soviet Literary, Theater, and Film Arts in the 1930s*, edited by Katherine Bliss Eaton, 145–62. Evanston, IL: Northwestern University Press, 2002.

Broderick, Francis L. *W. E. B. DuBois: Negro Leader in a Time of Crisis.* Stanford, CA: Stanford University Press, 1959.

Buni, Andrew. *Robert L. Vann of the "Pittsburgh Courier": Politics and Black Journalism.* Pittsburgh: University of Pittsburgh Press, 1974.

Butler, Smedley D. "America's Armed Forces." *Common Sense* 4, no. 11 (November 1935): 8–12.

Chang, Iris. *The Rape of Nanking: The Forgotten Holocaust of World War II.* London: Penguin, 1998. First published 1997 by Basic Books.

Chee Lai! (Arise!): Songs of New China. New York: Keynote Recordings, 1941.

Cheng, Victor Shiu Chiang. "Imagining China's Madrid in Manchuria: The Communist Military Strategy at the Onset of the Chinese Civil War, 1945–1946." *Modern China* 31, no. 1 (January 2005): 72–114.

Chesterton, G. K. *The Illustrated London News, 1905–1907.* Edited by Lawrence J. Clipper. Vol. 27 of *The Collected Works of G. K. Chesterton.* San Francisco: Ignatius Press, 1986.

"China Declares War on the Axis Powers: Declaration of War on Japan." *Contemporary China* 1, no. 15 (December 15, 1951): 1.

Clarke, J. Calvitt, III. *Alliance of the Colored Peoples: Ethiopia and Japan before World War II.* Woodbridge, UK: James Currey, 2011.

———. "Italo-Soviet Military Cooperation in the 1930s." In *Girding for Battle: The Arms Trade in a Global Perspective, 1815–1940*, edited by Donald J. Stoker Jr. and Jonathan A. Grant, 177–99. Westport, CT: Praeger, 2003.

Communist Party of the United States of America. *Is Japan the Champion of the Colored Races? The Negro's Stake in Democracy.* New York: Workers Library, 1938.

Cumings, Bruce. "Japan and Northeast Asia into the Twenty-first Century." In Katzenstein and Shiraishi, *Network Power*, 136–68.

———. *Parallax Visions: Making Sense of American-East Asian Relations.* Durham, NC: Duke University Press, 1999.

Dark, Sidney, and Rowland Grey. *W. S. Gilbert: His Life and Letters.* London: Methuen, [1923].

Darlington, W. A. *The World of Gilbert and Sullivan.* Freeport, NY: Books for Libraries Press, 1970. First published 1951 by Peter Nevill.

Daugherty, William E. "China's Official Publicity in the United States." *Public Opinion Quarterly* 6, no. 1 (spring 1942): 70–86.

Dawahare, Anthony. *Nationalism, Marxism, and African American Literature between the Wars: A New Pandora's Box.* Jackson: University Press of Mississippi, 2003.

Denny, Harold Norman. *Dollars for Bullets: The Story of American Rule in Nicaragua.* New York: Dial Press, 1929.

Dower, John W. *Cultures of War: Pearl Harbor/ Hiroshima/ 9-11/ Iraq.* New York: Norton, 2010.

———. *War without Mercy: Race and Power in the Pacific War*. New York: Pantheon, 1986.

Du Bois, W. E. B. "The Color Line Belts the World." In *W. E. B. Du Bois: A Reader*, edited by David Levering Lewis, 42–43. New York: Henry Holt, 1995.

———. *The Correspondence of W. E. B. Du Bois*. Edited by Herbert Aptheker. 3 vols. Amherst: University of Massachusetts Press, 1973–1978.

———. "Inter-Racial Implications of the Ethiopian Crisis: A Negro View." *Foreign Affairs* 14, no. 1 (October 1935): 82–92.

———. *Newspaper Columns by W. E. B. Du Bois*. Edited by Herbert Aptheker. 2 vols. White Plains, NY: Kraus-Thomson Organization, 1986.

———. *The Souls of Black Folk*. In *W. E. B. Du Bois: Writings*, edited by Nathan Huggins, 357–547. New York: Library of America, 1986.

Duus, Peter, Ramon H. Myers, and Mark R. Peattie, eds. *The Japanese Informal Empire in China, 1895–1937*. Princeton, NJ: Princeton University Press, 1989.

Eastman, Lloyd E. *The Abortive Revolution: China under Nationalist Rule, 1927–1937*. Cambridge, MA: Harvard University Press, 1974.

Edwards, Brent Hayes. *The Practice of Diaspora: Literature, Translation, and the Rise of Black Internationalism*. Cambridge, MA: Harvard University Press, 2003.

Eperjesi, John R. *The Imperialist Imaginary: Visions of Asia and the Pacific in American Culture*. Hanover, NH: University Press of New England/ Dartmouth College Press, 2005.

Epstein, Israel. *Woman in World History: Life and Times of Soong Ching Ling (Mme. Sun Yatsen)*. Beijing: New World Press, 1993.

Evanzz, Karl. *The Messenger: The Rise and Fall of Elijah Muhammad*. New York: Vintage, 2001. First published 1999 by Pantheon.

Fairbank, John K. "Born Too Late." In *Bertolucci's "The Last Emperor": Multiple Takes*, edited by Bruce H. Sklarew et al., 203–11. Detroit: Wayne State University Press, 1998.

Fanon, Frantz. *The Wretched of the Earth*. Translated by Constance Farrington. New York: Grove Press, 1963.

Ferguson, Jeffrey B. *The Sage of Sugar Hill: George S. Schuyler and the Harlem Renaissance*. New Haven, CT: Yale University Press, 2005.

Fitzgerald, F. Scott. *The Great Gatsby*. 1925. New York: Charles Scribner's Sons, 1953.

Flanagan, Hallie. *Arena: The History of the Federal Theatre*. New York: Benjamin Blom, 1965.

Foglesong, David S. *America's Secret War against Bolshevism: U.S. Intervention in the Russian Civil War, 1917–1920*. Chapel Hill: University of North Carolina Press, 1995.

Foley, Barbara. *Spectres of 1919: Class and Nation in the Making of the New Negro*. Urbana: University of Illinois Press, 2003.

Fraden, Rena. *Blueprints for a Black Federal Theatre, 1935–1939*. New York: Cambridge University Press, 1994.

Friedman, Donald J. *The Road from Isolation: The Campaign of the American Committee for Non-Participation in Japanese Aggression, 1938–1941.* Cambridge, MA: East Asian Research Center, Harvard University, 1968.

Fukunaga, Kyosuke. *Nichibeisen Miraiki* [Forecast of Future American Japanese War]. Tokyo: Shincho-sha, 1934.

Furukawa, Hiromi, and Tetsushi Furukawa. *Nihonjin to Afurikakei Amerikajin: Nichibei kankeishi ni okeru sono Shoso* [Japanese and African Americans: Aspects in the History of Japan-U.S. Relations]. Tokyo: Akashi Shoten, 2004.

Gaines, Ernest J. *The Autobiography of Miss Jane Pittman.* 1971. New York: Bantam, 1972.

Gallagher, Patrick. *America's Aims and Asia's Aspirations.* New York: Century, 1920.

Gallicchio, Marc. *The African American Encounter with Japan and China: Black Internationalism in Asia, 1895–1945.* Chapel Hill: University of North Carolina Press, 2000.

———, ed. *The Unpredictability of the Past: Memories of the Asia-Pacific War in U.S.–East Asian Relations.* Durham, NC: Duke University Press, 2007.

Gallup, George H. *The Gallup Poll: Public Opinion, 1935–1971.* 3 vols. New York: Random House, 1972.

Garver, John W. "Chiang Kai-shek's Quest for Soviet Entry into the Sino-Japanese War." *Political Science Quarterly* 102, no. 2 (summer 1987): 295–316.

Gates, Henry Louis, Jr. "A Fragmented Man: George Schuyler and the Claims of Race." *New York Times Book Review,* September 20, 1992, 31, 42–43.

———. "The Trope of a New Negro and the Reconstruction of the Image of the Black." In "America Reconstructed, 1840–1940," special issue, *Representations* 24 (fall 1988): 129–55.

Gibbs, William E. "James Weldon Johnson: A Black Perspective on 'Big Stick' Diplomacy." *Diplomatic History* 8, no. 4 (fall 1984): 329–47.

Gilroy, Paul. *The Black Atlantic: Modernity and Double Consciousness.* Cambridge, MA: Harvard University Press, 1993.

Greater East Asia Congress. *Addresses before the Assembly of Greater East-Asiatic Nations, Tokyo, November 1943.* Tokyo: Ministry of Greater East-Asiatic Affairs, 1943.

Green, Stanley. *Ring Bells! Sing Songs! Broadway Musicals of the 1930's.* New York: Galahad Books, 1971.

Gruesser, John Cullen. *Black on Black: Twentieth-Century African American Writing about Africa.* Lexington: University Press of Kentucky, 2000.

Gubar, Susan. *Racechanges: White Skin, Black Face in American Culture.* New York: Oxford University Press, 1997.

Guo, Qinghua. "Changchun: Unfinished Capital Planning of Manzhouguo, 1932–42." *Urban History* 31, no. 1 (May 2004): 100–117.

Hamashita, Takeshi. "The Intra-regional System in East Asia in Modern Times." In Katzenstein and Shiraishi, *Network Power,* 113–35.

Hardt, Michael, and Antonio Negri. *Empire.* Cambridge, MA: Harvard University Press, 2000.

Harris, Joseph E. *African-American Reactions to War in Ethiopia, 1936–1941*. Baton Rouge: Louisiana State University Press, 1994.

Haskins, Jim, and N. R. Mitgang. *Mr. Bojangles: The Biography of Bill Robinson*. New York: William Morrow, 1988.

Henrikson, Alan K. "The Map as an 'Idea': The Role of Cartographic Imagery during the Second World War." *American Cartographer* 2, no. 1 (April 1975): 19–53.

Hess, Gary R. *America Encounters India, 1941–1947*. Baltimore: Johns Hopkins Press, 1971.

Hill, Robert A., ed. *The FBI's RACON: Racial Conditions in the United States during World War II*. Boston: Northeastern University Press, 1995.

———, ed. *The Marcus Garvey and Universal Negro Improvement Association Papers*. 10 vols. Berkeley: University of California Press, 1983–1995.

Himes, Chester. *Lonely Crusade*. 1947. New York: Thunder's Mouth Press, 1986.

Hiwet, Addis. *Ethiopia: From Autocracy to Revolution*. London: Review of African Political Economy, 1975.

Hodges, Donald C. *Intellectual Foundations of the Nicaraguan Revolution*. Austin: University of Texas Press, 1986.

Hodgson, Marshall G. S. *Rethinking World History: Essays on Europe, Islam, and World History*. Cambridge: Cambridge University Press, 1993.

Hopkins, Neal. "A Lesson in Japanese." In *The Treasury Star Parade*, edited by William A. Bacher, 351–65. 1942. Ann Arbor: University of Michigan Library, 2006.

Hopkins, Pauline E. "The Dark Races of the Twentieth Century: II, The Malay Peninsula." *Voice of the Negro* 2, no. 3 (March 1905): 187–91.

———. "The Dark Races of the Twentieth Century: III, The Yellow Race." *Voice of the Negro* 2, no. 5 (May 1905): 330–35.

Horne, Gerald. *Race War: White Supremacy and the Japanese Attack on the British Empire*. New York: New York University Press, 2004.

———. *Race Woman: The Lives of Shirley Graham Du Bois*. New York: New York University Press, 2000.

Hosoya, Chihiro. "The Japanese–Soviet Neutrality Pact." Translated by Peter A. Berton. In *The Fateful Choice: Japan's Advance into Southeast Asia, 1939–1941*, edited by James William Morley, 13–114. New York: Columbia University Press, 1980.

Hotta, Eri. *Pan-Asianism and Japan's War, 1931–1945*. New York: Palgrave Macmillan, 2007.

Houseman, John. *Run-through: A Memoir by John Houseman*. New York: Simon and Schuster, 1972.

Hsia Tsi-an. *The Gate of Darkness: Studies on the Leftist Literary Movement in China*. Seattle: University of Washington Press, 1968.

Hughes, Langston. *Arna Bontemps–Langston Hughes Letters, 1925–1967*. Edited by Charles H. Nichols. New York: Paragon House, 1990.

———. *The Collected Poems of Langston Hughes*. Edited by Arnold Rampersad. New York: Vintage, 1994.

———. *I Wonder as I Wander: An Autobiographical Journey*. 1956. New York: Hill and Wang, 1993.

———. *I Wonder as I Wander: An Autobiographical Journey*. Edited by Joseph McLaren. Vol. 14 of *The Collected Works of Langston Hughes*. Columbia: University of Missouri Press, 2003.

Huyssen, Andreas. *Twilight Memories: Marking Time in a Culture of Amnesia*. New York: Routledge, 1995.

Inose, Naoki. *Mikado no Shozo* [Portrait of the Mikado]. Tokyo: Shogakukan, 2005.

Institute of Pacific Relations. *Problems of the Pacific, 1929: Proceedings of the Third Conference of the Institute of Pacific Relations, Nara and Kyoto, Japan, October 23 to November 9, 1929*. Edited by J. B. Condliffe. Chicago: University of Chicago Press, 1930.

Isaacs, Harold R. *Re-Encounters in China: Notes of a Journey in a Time Capsule*. Armonk, NY: M. E. Sharpe, 1985.

Jameson, Fredric. "Modernism and Imperialism." In *Nationalism, Colonialism, and Literature*, by Terry Eagleton, Fredric Jameson, and Edward W. Said, 43–66. Minneapolis: University of Minnesota Press, 1990.

Janken, Kenneth Robert. *Walter White: Mr. NAACP*. Chapel Hill: University of North Carolina Press, 2006. First published 2003 by New Press.

Johnson, James Weldon. *Along This Way: The Autobiography of James Weldon Johnson*. 1933. New York: Da Capo Press, 2000.

———. *The Autobiography of an Ex-Coloured Man*. 1912. New York: Vingate, 1989.

Jun, Helen Heran. *Race for Citizenship: Black Orientalism and Asian Uplift from Pre-Emancipation to Neoliberal America*. New York: New York University Press, 2011.

Kato, Tetsuro. "The Japanese Victims of Stalinist Terror in the USSR." *Hitotsubashi Journal of Social Studies* 32, no. 1 (July 2000): 1–13.

———. *Mosukuwa de Shukuseisareta Nihonjin* [The Japanese Purged in Moscow]. Tokyo: Aoki Shoten, 1994.

Katzenstein, Peter J., and Takashi Shiraishi. "Regions in World Politics: Japan and Asia—Germany in Europe." In Katzenstein and Shiraishi, *Network Power*, 341–81.

———, eds. *Network Power: Japan and Asia*. Ithaca, NY: Cornell University Press, 1997.

Kearney, Reginald. *African American Views of the Japanese: Solidarity or Sedition?* Albany: State University of New York Press, 1998.

Killens, John Oliver. *And Then We Heard the Thunder*. 1962. Washington, DC: Howard University Press, 1983.

———. *Black Man's Burden*. 1965. New York: Simon and Schuster, 1970.

Kimura, Tsuyoshi. "Kokujin shijin Hyuzu kun" [Mr. Hughes, A Black Poet]. *Kaizo* 15, no. 9 (September 1933): 90–91.

Kirby, William C. *Germany and Republican China*. Stanford, CA: Stanford University Press, 1984.

Kodama, Sanehide, ed. *Ezra Pound and Japan: Letters and Essays*. Redding Ridge, CT: Black Swan Books, 1987.

Kokusai Bunka Shinkokai (The Society for International Cultural Relations): Prospectus and Scheme. Tokyo: Kokusai Bunka Shinkokai, 1934.

Korhonen, Pekka. "The Pacific Age in World History." *Journal of World History* 7, no. 1 (spring 1996): 41–70.

Koshiro, Yukiko. "Beyond an Alliance of Color: The African American Impact on Modern Japan." In "The Afro-Asian Century," edited by Andrew F. Jones and Nikhil Pal Singh, special issue, *positions* 11, no. 1 (spring 2003): 183–215.

———. "Eurasian Eclipse: Japan's End Game in World War II." *American Historical Review* 109, no. 2 (April 2004): 417–44.

Koshizawa, Akira. *Manshukoku no Shuto Keikaku* [Planning of Manchukuo's Capital]. Tokyo: Nihon Keizai Hyoron-sha, 1988.

Kubota, Yoshio. *Tokunaga Sunao ron* [A Study on Sunao Tokunaga]. Tokyo: Gogatsu Shobo, 1977.

Kurata, Yoshihiro. *1885-nen Rondon Nihonjin-mura* [The Japanese Village in London, 1885]. Tokyo: Asahi Shimbun-sha, 1983.

Larsen, Nella. *Passing*. 1929. Mineola, NY: Dover, 2004.

Lauren, Paul Gordon. *Power and Prejudice: The Politics and Diplomacy of Racial Discrimination*. 2nd ed. Boulder, CO: Westview, 1996.

League of Nations, delegation from Japan. *Japan's Case in the Sino-Japanese Dispute as Presented before the Special Session of the Assembly of the League of Nations*. Geneva: Author, 1933.

Lee, Josephine. *The Japan of Pure Invention: Gilbert and Sullivan's "The Mikado."* Minneapolis: University of Minnesota Press, 2010.

Left Writers' League of China. "A Letter to the World: An Appeal from the Writers of China." *New Masses*, June 1931, 14–15.

Levine, Lawrence W. *The Unpredictable Past: Explorations in American Cultural History*. New York: Oxford University Press, 1993.

Levy, Eugene. *James Weldon Johnson: Black Leader, Black Voice*. Chicago: University of Chicago Press, 1973.

Lewis, David Levering. *W. E. B. Du Bois: The Fight for Equality and the American Century, 1919–1963*. New York: Henry Holt, 2000.

———. *When Harlem Was in Vogue*. New York: Penguin, 1997. First published 1981 by Knopf.

Lieven, Dominic. *Empire: The Russian Empire and Its Rivals*. New Haven, CT: Yale University Press, 2002. First published 2000 by John Murray.

Lipsitz, George. "'Frantic to Join . . . the Japanese Army': Black Soldiers and Civilians Confront the Asia-Pacific War." In *Perilous Memories: The Asia-Pacific War(s)*, edited by T. Fujitani, Geoffrey M. White, and Lisa Yoneyama, 347–77. Durham, NC: Duke University Press, 2001.

Locke, Alain. "Broadway and the Negro Drama." *Theatre Arts* 25, no. 10 (October 1941): 745–50.

Locke, Brian. "Strange Fruit: White, Black, and Asian in the World War II Combat Film *Bataan*." *Journal of Popular Film and Television* 36, no. 1 (spring 2008): 9–20.

Lu, David J. *Agony of Choice: Matsuoka Yōsuke and the Rise and Fall of the Japanese Empire, 1880–1946.* Lanham, MD: Lexington Books, 2002.

MacDonald, J. Fred. "Government Propaganda in Commercial Radio: The Case of Treasury Star Parade, 1942–1943." *Journal of Popular Culture* 12, no. 2 (fall 1978): 285–304.

Malcolm X and Alex Haley. *The Autobiography of Malcolm X.* 1964. New York: Ballantine, 1992.

Manchukuo. *Economic Construction Program of Manchukuo.* New York: New York Office of the South Manchuria Railway Company, 1933.

Marable, Manning. *W. E. B. Du Bois: Black Radical Democrat.* Updated ed. Boulder, CO: Paradigm, 2005.

Marcus, Greil. *The Manchurian Candidate.* London: British Film Institute, 2002.

Marcus, Harold G. *Haile Sellassie I: The Formative Years, 1892–1936.* Lawrenceville, NJ: Red Sea Press, 1995. First published 1987 by University of California Press.

———. *A History of Ethiopia.* Updated ed. Berkeley: University of California Press, 2002.

Matsuoka, Yosuke. *An Address on Manchuria, Its Past and Present, and Reply to Prof. Shuhsi-Hsu's Criticisms and Observations: Third Biennial Conference, Institute of Pacific Relations.* Kyoto, 1929.

———. "Proclamation of the Greater East Asia Co-Prosperity Sphere." In *Japan's Greater East Asia Co-Prosperity Sphere in World War II: Selected Readings and Documents*, edited by Joyce C. Lebra, 71–72. Kuala Lumpur, Malaysia: Oxford University Press, 1975.

Matthiessen, F. O. *American Renaissance: Art and Expression in the Age of Emerson and Whitman.* New York: Oxford University Press, 1941.

Meng, Chih. *China Speaks: On the Conflict between China and Japan.* New York: Macmillan, 1932.

Millett, Richard. *Guardians of the Dynasty.* Maryknoll, NY: Orbis Books, 1977.

Mitter, Rana. "Evil Empire? Competing Constructions of Japanese Imperialism in Manchuria, 1928–1937." In *Imperial Japan and National Identities in Asia, 1895–1945*, edited by Li Narangoa and Robert Cribb, 146–68. London: RoutledgeCurzon, 2003.

Miyanishi, Yoshio. *Mantetsu Chosa-bu to Ozaki Hotsumi* [The Research Department of the South Manchuria Railway Company and Hotsumi Ozaki]. Tokyo: Aki Shobo, 1983.

Moreira, Peter. *Hemingway on the China Front: His WWII Spy Mission with Martha Gellhorn.* Washington, DC: Potomac Books, 2006.

Mullen, Bill V. *Afro-Orientalism.* Minneapolis: University of Minnesota Press, 2004.

Myers, Ramon H. "Japanese Imperialism in Manchuria: The South Manchuria Railway Company, 1906–1933." In Duus, Myers, and Peattie, *The Japanese Informal Empire in China*, 101–32.
Naison, Mark. *Communists in Harlem during the Depression*. Urbana: University of Illinois Press, 1983.
Nakagane, Katsuji. "Manchukuo and Economic Development." In Duus, Myers, and Peattie, *The Japanese Informal Empire in China*, 133–57.
Nation of Islam. "A Brief History on the Origin of the Nation of Islam in America." Accessed April 3, 2012. http://www.noi.org.
———. "Nation of Islam Responds to the Attack on America." Accessed November 22, 2010. http://www.noi.org.
Onishi, Yuichiro. "The New Negro of the Pacific: How African Americans Forged Cross-Racial Solidarity with Japan, 1917–1922." *Journal of African American History* 92, no. 2 (spring 2007): 191–213.
———. *Transpacific Antiracism: Afro-Asian Solidarity in Twentieth-Century Black America, Japan, and Okinawa*. New York: New York University Press, 2013.
O'Reilly, Kenneth. *Black Americans: The FBI Files*. Edited by David Gallen. New York: Carroll and Graf, 1994.
Ottley, Roi, *"New World A-Coming": Inside Black America*. Boston: Houghton Mifflin, 1943.
Padmore, George. "Ethiopia Today: The Making of a Modern State." In *Negro: An Anthology*, edited by Nancy Cunard, 386–92. 1934. New York: Continuum, 2002.
Page, Amanda M. "The Ever-Expanding South: James Weldon Johnson and the Rhetoric of the Global Color Line." *Southern Quarterly* 46, no. 3 (spring 2009): 26–46.
Peattie, Mark R. "Forecasting a Pacific War, 1912–1933: The Idea of a Conditional Japanese Victory." In *The Ambivalence of Nationalism: Modern Japan between East and West*, edited by James W. White, Michiko Umegaki, and Thomas R. H. Havens, 115–31. Lanham, MD: University Press of America, 1990.
Plummer, Brenda Gayle. *Rising Wind: Black Americans and U.S. Foreign Affairs, 1935–1960*. Chapel Hill: University of North Carolina Press, 1996.
Pollard, Robert T. "Russo-Japanese Tension." *Annals of the American Academy of Political and Social Science* 175 (September 1934): 101–9.
Price, Ruth. *The Lives of Agnes Smedley*. New York: Oxford University Press, 2005.
Procházka, Roman Freiherr von. *Abyssinia: The Powder Barrel*. London: British International News Agency, [1936].
Rampersad, Arnold. *The Art and Imagination of W. E. B. Du Bois*. Cambridge, MA: Harvard University Press, 1976.
———. *The Life of Langston Hughes*. 2 vols. 2nd ed. New York: Oxford University Press, 2002.
Rappaport, Armin. *Henry L. Stimson and Japan, 1931–33*. Chicago: University of Chicago Press, 1963.

Reed, Ishmael. *Japanese by Spring*. 1993. New York: Penguin, 1996.
Renner, George T. "7 Realities about Japan." *Clearing House* 17, no. 8 (April 1943): 488.
Roberts, Brian Russell. *Artistic Ambassadors: Literary and International Representation of the New Negro Era*. Charlottesville: University of Virginia Press, 2013.
Robins, Natalie. *Alien Ink: The FBI's War on Freedom of Expression*. New Brunswick, NJ: Rutgers University Press, 1993. First published 1992 by William Morrow.
Rogers, J. A. *The Real Facts about Ethiopia*. 1936. Baltimore: Black Classic Press, 1982.
Romig, Walter. *Michigan Place Names*. Detroit: Wayne State University Press, 1986.
Roosevelt, Franklin D. *The Public Papers and Addresses of Franklin D. Roosevelt, 1937*. New York: Macmillan, 1941.
Rosenberg, Emily S. *A Date Which Will Live: Pearl Harbor in American Memory*. Durham, NC: Duke University Press, 2003.
Rowley, Hazel. *Richard Wright: The Life and Times*. New York: Henry Holt, 2001.
Saito, Tadatoshi. "Langston Hughes in Japan." *Journal: Faculty of Humanities* (Japan Women's University) 47 (1997): 1–13.
Sales, Patrice S. "*Swing Mikado*: Exemplar of the Struggle for the Black Stage Image through Music and Dance." Master's thesis, Indiana University, 1993.
Sato, Kojiro. *Nichibei Senso Yume Monogatari* [A Fantasy of the Japanese–United States War]. Tokyo: Nihon Hyoron-sha, 1921.
Sato, Masaharu, and Barak Kushner. "'Negro Propaganda Operations': Japan's Short-Wave Radio Broadcasts for World War II Black Americans." *Historical Journal of Film, Radio and Television* 19, no. 1 (March 1999): 5–26.
Schmitz, David F. *Henry L. Stimson: The First Wise Man*. Wilmington, DE: SR Books, 2001.
Schulten, Susan. *The Geographical Imagination in America, 1880–1950*. Chicago: University of Chicago Press, 2001.
Schuyler, George S. *Black and Conservative: The Autobiography of George S. Schuyler*. New Rochelle, NY: Arlington House, 1966.
———. *Black Empire*. Edited by Robert A. Hill and R. Kent Rasmussen. Boston: Northeastern University Press, 1991.
———. *Ethiopian Stories*. Edited by Robert A. Hill. Boston: Northeastern University Press, 1994.
Scott, James C. *Domination and the Arts of Resistance: Hidden Transcripts*. New Haven, CT: Yale University Press, 1990.
Scott, William R. *The Sons of Sheba's Race: African-Americans and the Italo-Ethiopian War, 1935–1941*. Bloomington: Indiana University Press, 1993.
Selassie, Herui Wolde. *Dai-Nihon* [Greater Japan]. Translated by Oreste Vaccari and Enko Vaccari. Tokyo: Eibumpo Tsuron Hakkojo, 1934.
Sellassie, Haile. *My Life and Ethiopia's Progress, 1892–1937: The Autobiography of Emperor Haile Sellassie I*. Translated by Edward Ullendorff. Chicago:

Research Associates School Times Publications and Frontline Distribution International, 1999. First published 1976 by Oxford University Press.

Shen Pengnian. "Lu Xun Huijian Xiushi Jiqi Beiwu Shijian" [The Meeting between Lu Xun and Hughes and the Incident of Lu Being Falsely Accused]. *Shaoxing Lu Xun Yanjiu* 27 (July 2005): 119–26.

Shibasaki, Atsushi. *Kindai Nihon to Kokusai Bunka Koryu: Kokusai Bunka Shinkokai no Sosetsu to Tenkai* [International Cultural Relations and Modern Japan: History of Kokusai Bunka Shinkokai, 1934–1945]. Tokyo: Yushin-do, 1999.

Shimazu, Naoko. *Japan, Race and Equality: The Racial Equality Proposal of 1919*. London: Routledge, 1998.

Sitkoff, Harvard. *A New Deal for Blacks: The Emergence of Civil Rights as a National Issue; The Depression Decade*. 30th anniversary ed. New York: Oxford University Press, 2009.

Sklaroff, Lauren Rebecca. *Black Culture and the New Deal: The Quest for Civil Rights in the Roosevelt Era*. Chapel Hill: University of North Carolina Press, 2009.

Slavinsky, Boris. *The Japanese–Soviet Neutrality Pact: A Diplomatic History, 1941–1945*. Translated by Geoffrey Jukes. London: RoutledgeCurzon, 2004.

Smedley, Agnes. *Battle Hymn of China*. New York: Knopf, 1943.

Smethurst, James Edward. *The New Red Negro: The Literary Left and African American Poetry, 1930–1946*. New York: Oxford University Press, 1999.

Snow, Edgar. *Far Eastern Front*. London: Jarrolds, 1934.

Solomon, Mark. *The Cry Was Unity: Communists and African Americans, 1917–1936*. Jackson: University Press of Mississippi, 1998.

"The Sorge Spy Ring: A Case Study in International Espionage in the Far East." Report. *Congressional Record Appendix*. 81st Cong., 1st sess., 1949. Vol. 95, pt. 12: A705–23.

South Manchuria Railway Company. *Illustrated Guide Book for Travelling in Manchoukuo with Sketch Map*. Dairen, Manchukuo: Author, 1934.

Stecopoulos, Harilaos. "Up from Empire: James Weldon Johnson, Latin America, and the Jim Crow South." In *Imagining Our Americas: Toward a Transnational Frame*, edited by Sandhya Shukla and Heidi Tinsman, 34–62. Durham, NC: Duke University Press, 2007.

Steen, Shannon. *Racial Geometries of the Black Atlantic, Asian Pacific and American Theatre*. Basingstoke, UK: Palgrave Macmillan, 2010.

Stephan, John J. "Hijacked by Utopia: American Nikkei in Manchuria." *Amerasia Journal* 23, no. 3 (winter 1997–1998): 1–42.

———. *The Russian Far East: A History*. Stanford, CA: Stanford University Press, 1994.

Stephens, Michelle Ann. *Black Empire: The Masculine Global Imaginary of Caribbean Intellectuals in the United States, 1914–1962*. Durham, NC: Duke University Press, 2005.

Stille, Mark. *Imperial Japanese Navy Battleships, 1941–45*. Oxford, UK: Osprey, 2008.

Stimson, Henry L. *The Far Eastern Crisis.* New York: Harper and Brothers, 1936.
———. *On Active Service in Peace and War.* New York: Harper, 1947.
Stoddard, Lothrop. *The Rising Tide of Color against White World–Supremacy.* 1920. Honolulu: University Press of the Pacific, 2003.
Tal, Kali. "'That Just Kills Me': Black Militant Near-Future Fiction." *Social Text* 20, no. 2 (summer 2002): 65–91.
Tanaka, Michiko. "Seki Sano and Popular Political and Social Theatre in Latin America." *Latin American Theatre Review* 27, no. 2 (spring 1994): 53–69.
Tang, Xiaobing. "Echoes of *Roar, China!* On Vision and Voice in Modern Chinese Art." *positions* 14, no. 2 (fall 2006): 467–94.
Tanin, O., and E. Yohan. *When Japan Goes to War.* New York: Vanguard Press, 1936.
Terrell, Mary Church. *A Colored Woman in a White World.* 1940. North Stratford, NH: Ayer, 1998.
Thompson, Lanny. *Imperial Archipelago: Representation and Rule in the Insular Territories under U.S. Dominion after 1898.* Honolulu: University of Hawai'i Press, 2010.
Thompson, Mark Christian. *Black Fascisms: African American Literature and Culture between the Wars.* Charlottesville: University of Virginia Press, 2007.
Timperley, H. J. *Japanese Terror in China.* New York: Modern Age Books, 1938.
United Nations. "UN Flag and Emblem." Last updated December 30, 2013. http://www.un.org.
US Congress, House. *Hearings on American Aspects of the Richard Sorge Spy Case (Based on Testimony of Mitsusada Yoshikawa and Maj. Gen. Charles A. Willoughby): Hearings before the Committee on Un-American Activities, House of Representatives, Eighty-Second Congress, First Session, August 9, 22, and 23, 1951.* Washington, DC: Government Printing Office, 1951.
US Department of State. *Papers Relating to the Foreign Relations of the United States, Japan: 1931–1941.* 2 vols. Washington, DC: Government Printing Office, 1943.
Utley, Jonathan G. *Going to War with Japan, 1937–1941.* New York: Fordham University Press, 2005.
Vactor, Vanita Marian. "A History of the Chicago Federal Theatre Project Negro Unit: 1935–1939." PhD diss., New York University, 1998.
Vallillo, Stephen M. "The Battle of the Black *Mikados*." *Black American Literature Forum* 16, no. 4 (winter 1982): 153–57.
Von Eschen, Penny M. *Race against Empire: Black Americans and Anticolonialism, 1937–1957.* Ithaca, NY: Cornell University Press, 1997.
Weissman, Suzi. "Alex Buchman: The Last Survivor of Trotsky." *Critique* 32, no. 1 (April 2004): 151–62.
Weitzel, George T. *American Policy in Nicaragua.* Washington, DC: Government Printing Office, 1916.
White, Walter. *A Man Called White: The Autobiography of Walter White.* 1948. Athens: University of Georgia Press, 1995.
———. *A Rising Wind.* Garden City, NY: Double Day, Doran, 1945.

Whymant, Robert. *Stalin's Spy: Richard Sorge and the Tokyo Espionage Ring.* London: I. B. Tauris, 1996.
Willoughby, Charles A. *Shanghai Conspiracy: The Sorge Spy Ring.* New York: Dutton, 1952.
Wilson, Rob. *Reimagining the American Pacific: From "South Pacific" to Bamboo Ridge and Beyond.* Durham, NC: Duke University Press, 2000.
Wilson, Sandra. *The Manchurian Crisis and Japanese Society, 1931–33.* London: Routledge, 2002.
Woll, Allen. *Black Musical Theatre: From "Coontown" to "Dreamgirls."* Baton Rouge: Louisiana State University Press, 1989.
Wong Wang-chi. *Politics and Literature in Shanghai: The Chinese League of Left-Wing Writers, 1930–1936.* Manchester, UK: Manchester University Press, 1991.
Wren, Gayden. *A Most Ingenious Paradox: The Art of Gilbert and Sullivan.* New York: Oxford University Press, 2001.
Wright, Richard. *Native Son.* 1940. New York: HarperPerennial, 1998.
Wu Shi. "Xiushi Zai Zhongguo" [Hughes in China]. *Wenxue* 1, no. 2 (August 1933): 254–58.
Yamada, Kazuhiro. *Masukaru no Hanayome* [The Bride of Maskal]. Tokyo: Asahi Shimbun-sha, 1998.
Yasuo, Nagaharu. "Manchukuo's New Economic Policy." *Pacific Affairs* 11, no. 3 (September 1938): 323–37.
Yoshida, Takashi. *The Making of the "Rape of Nanking": History and Memory in Japan, China, and the United States.* New York: Oxford University Press, 2006.
Yoshihara, Mari. *Musicians from a Different Shore: Asians and Asian Americans in Classical Music.* Philadelphia: Temple University Press, 2007.
Young, Louise. *Japan's Total Empire: Manchuria and the Culture of Wartime Imperialism.* Berkeley: University of California Press, 1998.

INDEX

Note: Page numbers with "n" or "nn" indicate notes. The note number is displayed after the page number.

Adowa, Battle of (1896), 69
Afro-Orientalism, 27, 150–51, 228n8
Akami, Tomoko, 9, 156
Allen, Ernest Jr., 14
Along This Way (Johnson), 26, 28–29, 33; IPR and, 33–40; Manchuria and, 45, 51, 56; Nicaragua and, 40–43, 53–54
American Committee for Non-Participation in Japanese Aggression, 179
American Friends of the Chinese People, 168
American League against War and Fascism, 168–69
American Renaissance, 16
Anderson, Kay, 211n97
Anti-Comintern Pact (1936), 143, 158, 175, 177, 179
anti-Semitism, 235n111
Anti-War Congress, 139, 226n59
Araya Abeba, 66–67, 84, 213n43
Arnaz, Desi, 114
"As the Crow Flies" (Du Bois), 152, 179
Atkinson, Brooks, 98
Atlantic Charter, 186–87, 193
Autobiography of an Ex-Coloured Man, The (Johnson), 32
Axis (Tripartite) Pact, 180

Back-to-Africa movement, 12
Baldwin, Kate, 11–12, 116–17

Barnett, Claude, 153
Bataan (film), 113–15
Batiste, Stephanie Leigh, 96, 98–99, 112
Bayen, Malaku E., 84, 234n91
Berry, Faith, 125
Bertolucci, Bernardo, 149–50
"Black Atlantic," 11–12, 14, 116
Black Empire (Schuyler), 29, 58–60; Ethiopia and, 60, 74–76; Japan and, 80–85; narrative of, 70–76; as satire, 80–85; Soviet Union analogy, 71–73; violence in, 72–74
"Black Internationale," 59–60, 65, 71, 76
Black internationalism: generally, 9–17, 198; Harlem Renaissance and, 16–17; of Hughes, 116–17, 123, 144; of Johnson, 26, 28, 44; of Schuyler, 29, 58–59, 70, 74, 76–79, 83, 85; of White, 31, 185–88
Black nationalism, 7, 11–12, 222n7
Black Star Line Steamship Company, 12–13
Boddy, James Marmaduke, 19
Braithwaite, William Stanley, 206n22
Breese, Zona Gale, 229n20
Briggs, Cyril, 174–75
British Secret Intelligence Service (MI6), 140–41
Broderick, Francis L., 228n5
Broekman, David, 111

Brooks, Samuel I., 60. *See also* Schuyler, George S.
Brotherhood of Liberty for the Black People of America, 14
Brown, John Mason, 105–6, 108, 220n60
Buchman, Alexander, 138–39, 233n86
Bureau of Motion Pictures, 113
Bush, George W., 2
Butler, Gen. Lee, 14
Butler, Smedley D., 40–42

"Call of Ethiopia" (Hughes), 61
Capra, Frank, 112
Carter, Edward C., 34, 205n12
"Caucasian Problem, The" (Schuyler), 116
Central Intelligence Agency (CIA), 146
Chang, Iris, 172
Chen, Si-Lan, 136
Chesterton, G. K., 91–92
Chiang Kai-shek, 126–29, 145, 170, 175, 177, 181
China: Boxer Rebellion (1900), 8; colonialism in, 8, 23; Communist Party, 126, 128–29, 131, 135, 149, 167–68; Cultural Revolution, 150; as empire, 23; founding of People's Republic of China (1949), 149, 239n41; Hughes and, 125–31; IPR and, 37, 39; Kuomintang, 126, 129–30, 149, 167, 177, 226n59; League of Nations and, 175; Revolution of 1911, 24, 161, 170; White Terror (Shanghai), 125–31. *See also* Manchuria
"China and Japan" (Du Bois), 170
China Institute, 157
China League for Civil Rights, 146
Chinese Eastern Railway, 24, 120
Churchill, Winston S., 186–87
Cohn, Roy, 119
Cold War, 144–47, 204n2
Coleman, Robert, 103
colonialism, 8, 23, 163–64

"Color Line Belts the World, The" (Du Bois), 19
Comic Opera Diplomacy, 88–92
Communist International (Comintern), 11, 22, 71, 117, 125–26, 128–29, 135, 141
Communist Party of the United States of America, 117, 168, 185–86
concept of empire, 22–23
Condon, Richard, 148
Cooper, Ann Nixon, 3

Dark Princess (Du Bois), 228n8
Denny, Harold Norman, 210n90
Dewey, Thomas E., 94
Diaz, Adolfo, 40, 48
diverse ideals regarding "Black Pacific" narrative, 22
Dodo, Masao, 79
Doolittle raid, 111
Dos Passos, John, 130, 133
Double V campaign, 2, 186–87
Dower, John W., 236n118
D'Oyly Carte, Richard, 95
D'Oyly Carte Opera Company, 94, 104–5
Dreiser, Theodore, 133
Du Bois, W. E. B., 27, 30, 148–52, 183–84, 189, 198; on colonialism, 163–64; on empire, 163; Ethiopia and, 81; FBI and, 152–53, 185; geopolitics and, 177–83; vs. Hughes, 153; Japan and, 21, 48–50, 81–83, 152–58; Manchuria and, 30, 158–67; Marxism of, 164, 183–84; Matsuoka and, 30, 162, 165–66, 171–72, 180–84; in NAACP, 48, 152; on Russo-Japanese War, 19–20; Soviet Union and, 116, 159
Durdin, Frank Tillman, 173
Dutton, E. P., 147

Economic Construction Program of Manchukuo (SMR), 164
Edwards, Brent Hayes, 11, 17, 189
Edward VII (King of Great Britain and Northern Ireland), 90

Emerson, Ralph Waldo, 16
emotional geography of empire, 65–70
Engels, Friedrich, 73
Epps, Wesley, 113–15
Erwin, David D., 14
Ethiopia: Du Bois and, 81; FDR and, 60; League of Nations and, 69–70; relations with Japan, 62–70, 79–80, 84, 212n30; Schuyler and, 29, 60–65, 68–70, 212n13; White and, 60, 70
Ethiopian Pacific Movement, 14, 76–78
Ethiopian World Federation, 59, 84, 234n91
Eurasian Continental Bloc, 166, 180, 182–83
Evanzz, Karl, 77

Fairbank, John K., 150
Fanon, Frantz, 214n52
Fard, Wallace D., 77
Farrakhan, Louis, 2–3, 6
Federal Bureau of Investigation (FBI), 12–17, 84; Du Bois and, 152–53, 185; Garvey and, 12–14, 16; Hughes and, 123–24, 141, 186; Nation of Islam and, 77; *RACON report*, 13–15, 17–18, 20–22, 185, 188–89; Schuyler and, 79, 185
Federal Theatre Project, 27, 29–30, 86–87, 92–93, 198. See also *Swing Mikado, The* (adaptation)
Fire in the Flint, The (White), 130, 188–89
First Sino-Japanese War (1894–1895), 23
Fisk University, 56
Fitzgerald, F. Scott, 20
Five Power Treaty, 24
Foley, Barbara, 25
Ford, James W., 117, 168
"Forum of Fact and Opinion" (Du Bois), 81, 169
Four Power Treaty, 24
Fraction, Edward, 98, 105
French Concession (Shanghai), 126, 226n59

Fujimori, Seikichi, 225n51
Fukunaga, Kyosuke, 15
Fushimi Sadanaru (Prince of Japan), 91

Gaines, Ernest J., 3
Gandhi, Mohandas, 192
Garbo, Greta, 132, 134
Garvey, Marcus, 11–14, 16, 20, 78, 81, 83, 185
Gates, Henry Louis Jr., 18, 77
Geneva Convention, 111
Gibbs, William E., 41–42
Gilbert, William S., 29–30, 86, 88–89, 91–96, 99, 101, 103–7, 111
Gilroy, Paul, 11, 14, 189
Goebbels, Joseph, 107
Gold, Michael, 130, 133
"Goodbye Christ" (Hughes), 117, 146–47
"Good Morning Revolution" (Hughes), 117
Gordon, Mittie Maud Lena, 14
Gould, Randall, 135
Graham, Shirley, 93, 95
Greater East Asia Co-Prosperity Sphere, 24, 83, 180, 182, 184, 187
Gruesser, John Cullen, 81, 83
Gubar, Susan, 216n1

Haile Selassie I (Emperor of Ethiopia), 59, 66, 68–69, 70, 75, 78, 175
Hamaguchi, Osachi, 38
Harding, Warren G., 9
Hardt, Michael, 22
"Harlemperor," 103, 109. See also *Hot Mikado, The* (adaptation); Robinson, Bill "Bojangles"
Harlem Renaissance, 7, 11–12, 14, 94; Black internationalism and, 16–17; "Black Pacific" narrative and, 9; female writers in, 27; gays in, 27–28; Hikida and, 188–89; Hughes in, 121, 130; Johnson in, 32; Schuyler in, 58
Harrington, Francis Clark, 94
Harrison, Richard Edes, 197
Hart, Stokely Delmar, 14

Haskins, Jim, 103
Havier, J. Alex, 115
Hawthorne, Nathaniel, 16
Hay, John, 8, 45
Hemingway, Ernest, 182, 232n66
Henrikson, Alan K., 197
Herriot, Eduard, 50
Herui Wolde Selassie, Blatengeta, 66
Hikida, Yasuichi, 79, 151, 153, 155, 157, 188–90, 193, 237n12
Hill, Robert A., 13, 60–61, 71, 82
Himes, Chester, 5
Hirohito (Emperor of Japan), 36, 66, 99, 108–9, 111
Hiroshima bombing, 2, 4–5, 149, 172, 184, 195
Hitler, Adolf, 107, 118, 174–75, 177, 179, 182–83, 192
Hodgson, Marshall G.S., 27
homolosine equal-area projection, 9–10
Hoover, Herbert, 38, 40
Hoover, J. Edgar, 94, 123, 185
Hopkins, Harry, 94
Hopkins, Pauline E., 19
Horne, Gerald, 150, 203n76, 218n33
Horton, Asadata Dafora, 93
Hotel Imperial (film), 134
Hot Mikado, The (adaptation), 29, 87–88, 94; in cartoons, 110; Japanese signification in, 98–102; political themes in, 106–7; production of, 102–4; retribution theme in, 104–6; vs. *The Swing Mikado*, 106
House Un-American Activities Committee, 145–46
Hsu, Shuhsi, 44
Hughes, Langston, 27, 30, 93, 178, 198; arrest of in Japan, 136–39; on Battle of Shanghai, 168; Black internationalism of, 116–17, 123, 144; China and, 125–31; Cold War and, 144–47; vs. Du Bois, 153; Ethiopia and, 60–61; FBI and, 123–24, 141, 186; in Harlem Renaissance, 121, 130; on imperialism, 196; Japan and, 118–25, 131–41; Japanese surveillance of, 121, 123–25, 131–36, 139–41; McCarthyism and, 144–47; photograph, 122; Sano and, 141–44; in Shanghai, 125–31; Soviet Union and, 11, 116–18; on World War II, 196. See also *I Wonder as I Wander*
Hung Shen, 129
Hurston, Zora Neale, 27–28, 93
Huyssen, Andreas, 210n94

"I Gird the Globe" (Du Bois), 30, 151–52, 158–60, 165
ILDP (International League of Darker Peoples), 20–21, 25
imagined community, "Black Pacific" as, 6–7, 12, 26, 47–48, 196, 200n18
"imperial archipelago," 8
imperialism, 203n75; concept of, 22, 24–25; Du Bois on, 19–20; Hughes on, 126, 137, 151, 156, 159–60, 168, 170, 174, 184; IPR and, 39–40; Johnson on, 29, 39–43, 47–48, 50–56; Schuyler on, 58–59, 62, 65, 68, 70–71, 76, 80; in *The Swing Mikado*, 87, 98–100; White on, 195–96
Institute of Pacific Relations (IPR): African Americans in, 34–36, 38–39; American Council, 34–35; Central America and, 34; Cold War and, 204n2; imperialism and, 39–40; Johnson in, 33–40, 205n12, 206n38; "Pacific Community" and, 9, 33–34
International Ladies' Garment Workers' Union, 94
International League of Darker Peoples (ILDP), 20–21, 25
International League of Revolutionary Writers, 146
International Military Tribunal for the Far East, 184
International Red Aid, 128–29, 146
International Settlement (Shanghai), 126, 129, 139–40, 226n59
International Union of Revolutionary Writers, 141

International Workers' Dramatic Union, 142
Irwin, Wallace, 37
Isaacs, Harold R., 127–29, 136, 141, 146
Ishii, Kikujiro, 37
I Wonder as I Wander (Hughes), 30, 118–19; fictionalized portions, 131–36; Japan and, 120, 125, 131–41; Mata Hari analogy in, 131–36; McCarthyism and, 147; Sano and, 141–44; White Terror and, 125–31

Jameson, Fredric, 203n75
Janken, Kenneth Robert, 187
Japan: aggressive foreign policy of, 100–101; Communist Party, 125; conquest of Manchuria by, 43–51, 120–21, 156, 161; Du Bois and, 21, 48–50, 81–83, 152–58; as empire, 23, 90–91; Hughes and, 118–25, 131–41; IPR and, 37; Johnson and, 33, 35–39; Kwantung Army, 45–46, 207n55; League of Nations, 20, 44, 96–97, 156–57, 162, 172; Meiji Constitution (1889), 66; Nicaragua and, 51–53; relations with Ethiopia, 62–70, 79–80, 84, 212n30; Schuyler and, 79–85; Treaty of Versailles, 20; White and, 79. *See also* Manchuria
"Japan and the Negro" (Schuyler), 79–80
Japanese people: African American attitudes toward, 112–13, 210n89, 221n90; attitudes toward African Americans, 201n44; depiction in film, 110–15; internment of, 6; signification in *The Hot Mikado,* 107–9; signification in *The Mikado,* 88–92; signification in *The Swing Mikado,* 98–100; in Soviet Union, 141–44; viewed as Black, 19–20
"Japanese Racial Agitation among American Negroes" (MID), 13–15
Japanese–Soviet Neutrality Pact (1941), 166, 181–82
Japan Society, 36–37

Jesus, 46
Johnson, James Weldon, 27, 28–29, 33, 153, 188, 198; *Along This Way* [see *Along This Way* (Johnson)]; Black internationalism of, 26, 28, 44; on empire, 25–26; FBI and, 185; in Harlem Renaissance, 32; in IPR, 33–40, 205n12, 206n38; Japan and, 33, 35–39; League of Nations and, 37; Manchuria and, 40, 45, 51, 56; Matsuoka and, 53; in NAACP, 33, 37, 41–42, 56, 60; Nicaragua and, 26, 28–29, 33, 40–43, 50–57; on World War I, 203n86
Jones, William N., 48, 50
Jordan, Robert O. (aka Leonard Robert Jordan), 14, 77–78, 80

Kabayama, Ayske, 229n19
Karson, Nat, 103
Kato, Kanji, 15
Kellogg-Briand Pact, 45–46
Killens, John Oliver, 3–5, 15
Kimura, Tsuyoshi, 225n51
Knox, Frank, 78
Kobayashi, Takiji, 225n53
Kokusai Bunka Shinkokai (KBS), 155–57, 167, 229n21, 229n22
Konoye, Fumimaro, 100, 156, 180, 183
Korean War, 148
Korhonen, Pekka, 18, 52
Kuroda, Masako, 66–67, 84
Kuroiwa, Shuroku, 21

LaGuardia, Fiorello Henry, 94
Larsen, Nella, 27
Last Emperor, The (film), 149–50
League of Left-Wing Writers, 129
League of Nations, 21–26; China and, 175; Ethiopia and, 69–70; internationalism and, 11; Japan and, 20, 44, 96–97, 156–57, 162, 172; Johnson and, 37; Manchuria and, 46–47, 120, 233n80; Monroe Doctrine, 203n77; Pacific and, 9, 33–34

League of Struggle for Negro Rights, 117
Levine, Lawrence W., 7
Levy, Eugene, 204n2
Lewis, David Levering, 39, 47, 152–53
Lewis, Ira F., 83, 216n92
Lieven, Dominic, 22–23
"Lift Every Voice and Sing" (Johnson), 188
Lincoln, Abraham, 92
Lipsitz, George, 6, 210n89
Litvinov, Maxim, 70
Liu Liang-mo, 169
Locke, Alain, 94
Locke, Brian, 114–15
Logan, Rayford, 153
London, Jack, 18
Loomis, Charles F., 35
Lord Chamberlain, 90
Louis, Joe, 106–7
Lu, David J., 208n67, 235n111
Luce, Henry, 169
Lu Hsin (Lu Xun), 128–30, 146

MacArthur, Douglas, 118–19, 144–46
MacDonald, Ramsay, 50
MacLeish, Archibald, 112, 221n87
Mahan, Alfred Thayer, 8
Makino, Nobuaki, 21
Malcolm X, 2, 6
Man Called White, A (White), 188–89
Manchuria: African American opinion on Japanese conquest of, 47–51, 210n84; in cartoons, 50; Du Bois and, 30, 158–67; Japanese conquest of, 43–51, 120–21, 156, 161; Johnson and, 40, 45, 51, 56; League of Nations and, 46–47, 120, 233n80; vs. Nicaragua, 26, 43–45; Schuyler and, 237n125; Soviet Union and, 149, 158–59
Manchurian Candidate, The (film), 148–49
Manifest Destiny, 47
Mantle, Burns, 98

Mao Tse-tung, 148–51
Mao Tun, 129–30, 146
mapping of Pacific, 7–9
Marable, Manning, 233n76
March, Frederic, 110–11
March on Washington Movement, 191
Marcus, Harold G., 66
Marxism, 23, 116, 164, 183–84
Mata Hari, 132
Mata Hari (film), 131–34
Matsuo, Matsuhei, 165, 171–72
Matsuoka, Yosuke, 235n112; on anti-Semitism, 235n111; Du Bois and, 30, 162, 165–66, 171–72, 180–84; Johnson and, 53; League of Nations and, 208n67; Manchuria and, 44–47, 152, 156–57; on Second Sino-Japanese War, 181; Stalin and, 166, 181, 236n113
Matthiessen, F. O., 16
McCarthy, Joseph, 118–19, 147
McCarthyism, 30, 118–19, 135–36, 147
McDaniel, C. Yates, 173
McKay, Claude, 11, 116, 130, 133, 153
McNutt, Waldo, 178
Melville, Herman, 8, 16
Meng, Chih, 157
Menken, Arthur, 173
Mercator projection, 9, 27, 197–98
Meyerhold, Vsevolod, 130, 142–43
Meyerhold Theatre, 142–43
MI6 (British Secret Intelligence Service), 140–41
MID (Military Intelligence Division), 13–17
Mikado, The (Gilbert and Sullivan), 29–30, 86–87; adaptations of, 94–96; Japanese signification in, 88–92; as satire of British society, 88–92; during World War II, 110–15, 221n82
Military Intelligence Division (MID), 13–17
Military Intelligence Service, 186
Miller, Doris, 1–2, 112
Ministry of Foreign Affairs (Japan), 17

Minturn, Harry, 95–96
Mitgang, N. R., 103
Miura, Tamaki, 216n2
Miyake, Kiichi, 234n90
Monroe Doctrine, 8, 23, 26, 33, 38, 40, 46, 203n77
Moon, Henry Lee, 222n3
Moss, Carlton, 221n87
Muhammad, Elijah, 14, 77, 79–80
Mullen, Bill V., 27, 150–51
Murray, Alan R., 191
Mussolini, Benito, 59, 61, 63–67, 69–71, 78, 126, 174–75, 177

Nagasaki bombing, 2, 4, 195
Nail, Grace, 36
"Nanking Massacre" (1937), 172–73
National Association for the Advancement of Colored People (NAACP), 195; Du Bois in, 48, 152; FBI and, 185; Johnson in, 33, 37, 41–42, 56; White in, 60, 70, 79, 113, 190
Nation of Islam, 2, 6, 14, 76–77
Nazi-Soviet Pact (1939), 179, 182
Negri, Antonio, 22
Negri, Pola, 134
Nehru, Jawaharlal, 192
New Deal, 29, 86–88, 92–95, 98, 106, 110
"New Negro" movement, 17–18
"New Order in East Asia," 100, 178
Nicaragua: Japan and, 51–53; Johnson and, 26, 28–29, 33, 40–43, 50–57; vs. Manchuria, 26, 43–45; Stimson and, 209n77
Nii, Itaru, 225n51
9/11 attacks, 1–4, 6
Nine Power Treaty, 24
Nippon Club, 79
Nitobe, Inazo, 37–38
North Korea, 239n41
Not without Laughter (Hughes), 130
Noulens Defense Committee, 146
Novarro, Ramon, 132
Nugent, Richard Bruce, 27–28

Obama, Barack, 2–3, 185
Office of Facts and Figures, 17, 112
Office of Naval Intelligence, 13, 16
Office of War Information, 17, 113, 190–93
O'Neill, Eugene, 124–25
Onishi, Yuichiro, 21
"Open Door" policy, 8, 24, 45, 100, 109, 156
Orientalism, 27
Ottley, Roi, 76–77
Owen, Chandler, 25
Ozaki, Hotsumi, 145, 164–65

"Pacific Age," 8
"Pacific Charter" (White), 31, 186–87, 192–93, 238n26
"Pacific Community," 9, 17–26, 33–34, 186–96, 198, 200n23
Pacific Movement of the Eastern World, 14
Padmore, George, 58, 69, 213n33, 222n7
Pan-Africanism, 7, 11
Panama Canal, 8, 52
Pan-Asianism, 160–61
Pan-Pacific Club, 121–23, 155
Paris Peace Conference (1919), 17, 20, 21–23, 25
Peace Movement of Ethiopia, 14, 76
Pearl Harbor attack, 1–4, 14, 109–12, 115, 145, 155, 175
Peattie, Mark R., 16
People's Congress for Democracy and Peace, 169
Perry, Matthew, 8
Phelps, G. S., 35
Pickens, William, 47–48, 153, 174–75
Plummer, Brenda Gayle, 58–59, 186–87
Poston, Theodore, 222n3
Pound, Ezra, 235n112
Powell, James B., 178
Pratt, John, 97
Pratt, Mary Louise, 211n97
Prattis, Percival L., 153

Procházka, Baron Roman, 83–84
Puccini, Giacomo, 88
Pu Yi, 45–46, 149–50, 152, 160

Qaeda, 2

RACON report, 13–15, 17–18, 20–22, 185, 188–89
Radio Tokyo, 193–94, 238n28
Rampersad, Arnold, 147, 228n5
Randolph, A. Philip, 20–21, 25, 191
Rankin, John E., 6
"Rape of Nanking" (1937), 172–73
Rasmussen, R. Kent, 60–61, 71, 82
Reed, Ishmael, 1, 4
Rickabaugh, Clive, 96–97
Rising Wind, A (White), 194
"Roar China!" (Hughes), 124, 168
Robeson, Paul, 116, 168–69
Robinson, Bill "Bojangles," 29–30, 87–88, 94, 102–9
Rogers, J. A., 69
Roosevelt, Eleanor, 94
Roosevelt, Franklin D., 1, 4; on Battle of Shanghai, 169; "Black Cabinet," 187; "Black Pacific" narrative and, 78; Ethiopia and, 60; The Hot Mikado and, 88, 106–7, 109; The Swing Mikado and, 92–93; White and, 186–87, 190–93; in World War II, 111–12, 115
Roosevelt, Theodore, 8, 18, 23, 32–33, 202n57
Roosevelt Corollary, 33, 38, 40
Rosenberg, Emily S., 2
Rosenberg, Ethel, 119
Rosenberg, Julius, 119
Ruegg, Gertrude, 128
Ruegg, Paul, 128
Ruegg Defense Committee, 128
"Russia and America" (Du Bois), 151–52, 158
Russo-Japanese War (1904–1905), 17–20, 24, 45, 90, 161, 202n56

Said, Edward, 27
Sano, Seki, 124, 136, 138, 141–44
Sato, Kojiro, 16
Schomburg, Arthur, 79, 153
Schulten, Susan, 26
Schuyler, George S., 27, 29, 58–60, 116, 153, 198; Black internationalism of, 29, 58–59, 70, 74, 76–79, 83, 85; Ethiopia and, 29, 60–65, 68–70, 212n13; FBI and, 79, 185; in Harlem Renaissance, 58; Japan and, 79–85; Manchuria and, 237n125; on Second Sino-Japanese War, 81–83; on violence, 214n52. See also Black Empire
Scott, Emmett, J., 189
Scott, James C., 74
Scribner's Magazine, 18
Second Italo-Ethiopian War (1935–1936), 29, 58–59, 64, 70, 77, 81, 174, 234n91
Second Sino-Japanese War (1937–1945): generally, 79; African American attitudes toward, 173–77; Battle of Shanghai, 167–72; Matsuoka on, 181; "Rape of Nanking," 172–77; Schuyler on, 81–83
Shakespeare, William, 90–91, 93
Shanghai, Battle of (1937), 167–72, 177
Shanghai Municipal Police, 17, 119, 139–41, 146
Shaw, George Bernard, 125
Shimazu, Naoko, 24
Sinatra, Frank, 148
Sino-Soviet Treaty (1945), 149
Sklaroff, Lauren Rebecca, 93
Slavinsky, Boris, 177, 182
Smedley, Agnes, 126–29, 134–36, 141, 145–46, 164–65, 227n76
Smith, Susan J., 211n97
SMR (South Manchuria Railway Company), 30, 152, 156–57, 159–65, 207n55, 221n90
Snow, Edgar, 56
Solomon, Mark, 222n3
Soong Ching-ling. See Sun Yat-sen, Madame

Sorge, Richard, 119, 145, 165, 227n74
Souls of Black Folk (Du Bois), 19
Southerland, William H. H., 40–41
South Manchuria Railway Company (SMR), 30, 152, 156–57, 159–65, 207n55, 221n90
Soviet Union: Communist Party, 143; Du Bois and, 117, 159; Japanese people in, 141–44; Manchuria and, 149, 158–59; in Pacific, 116–17; Russian Revolution (1917), 24, 121, 170; Sano and, 141–44; Stalinist purge, 143
Spanish-American War (1898), 7–8
Spingarn, Arthur B., 205n12
Spratly Islands, 179
Stalin, Joseph, 148, 166, 177, 179, 181, 236n113
State Department, 17, 40, 111, 129, 137, 139–40, 232n66
Steele, Archibald T., 172–73
Steen, Shannon, 101–2
Stephan, John J., 162
Stephens, Michelle Ann, 11–13
Stewart, James R., 14
Stimson, Henry L., 45–46, 48, 50, 78, 148, 178–79, 209n77
Stimson Doctrine, 45
Stoddard, Lothrop, 20
Sugimoto, Ryokichi, 143
Sugimura, Yotaro, 62–63, 67
Sullivan, Arthur, 29–30, 86, 88–89, 93–96, 103–7, 111
Sullivan, Noël, 121
Sun Yat-sen, 170
Sun Yat-sen, Madame, 127–28, 136, 139
Survey of Racial Conditions in the United States (FBI), 13–15, 17–18, 20–22, 185, 188–89
Swing Mikado, The (adaptation), 29–30, 86–88; historical background, 92–94; vs. *The Hot Mikado*, 106; Japanese signification in, 98–102; photograph, 97; political themes in, 219n55; production of, 95–98; reviews of, 98–102; World War II and, 114–15

Taft, William Howard, 41
Takamatsu (Prince of Japan), 155
Tal, Kali, 74
Tanin, O., 67–68
Taylor, Robert, 113
Temple, Shirley, 102
Terhune, Warren J., 40, 207n45
Terrell, Mary Church, 21
Thompson, Lanny, 8, 86
Thoreau, Henry David, 16
Tijerino, Toribio, 54–56
Timperley, Harold John, 233n86
Todd, Michael, 94, 102
Tokunaga, Naoshi (Sunao), 133–35
Tokyo Imperial University, 155
Totten, Ashley L., 168
Trans-Siberian Railway, 24, 120, 158
Treasury Department, 110
Treaty of Portsmouth (1905), 202n57
Treaty of Versailles (1919), 20, 24, 33
Tretiakov, Sergei, 124, 130, 136
Tripartite (Axis) Pact, 180
Truman, Harry, 195
Tsukiji Little Theatre, 122–25, 136
Tsurumi, Yusuke, 38

United Nations, 186, 198
Universal Negro Improvement Association (UNIA), 13–14, 185

Vann, Robert L., 80
Victor Emmanuel III (King of Italy), 70, 78
Von Eschen, Penny M., 59, 84

Walker, Madam C. J., 20–21
Walker, Margaret, 93
Walker, Robert, 114
Ward, Harry F., 169
Ward, Theodore, 93
Warden, Gentry, 95–96
War Department, 112, 186
Washington, Booker T., 18–19
Washington Naval Conference (1921–1922), 9, 45, 156, 178

"Washington system," 24, 100, 101, 171, 178
Watts, Richard Jr., 101
Welles, Orson, 93
West, Dorothy, 153
Westphalian system, 23
Whipple, Sidney B., 99
White, Walter, 27, 130, 153, 198; Black internationalism of, 31, 185–88; Ethiopia and, 60, 70; FDR and, 186–87, 190–93; Hikida and, 188–90, 193; Japan and, 79; in NAACP, 60, 70, 79, 113, 190; Office of War Information and, 190–93; "Pacific Charter," 31, 186–87, 192–93, 238n26; "Pacific Community," 186–96; photograph, 197; Radio Tokyo and, 193–94, 238n28; on World War II, 188–96
White Terror (Shanghai), 125–31
Whitman, Walt, 16
Williams, John A., 72
Willoughby, Charles A., 145–47
Wilson, Sandra, 47
Wilson, Woodrow, 21, 121

Woll, Allen, 94
Works Progress Administration, 86, 93–94, 100–101
World Engineering Congress, 36
World War I, 203n86
World War II: African American concept of as race war, 77–79; depiction of Japan in film, 110–15; FDR in, 111–12, 115; Hughes on, 196; *The Mikado* during, 110–15, 221n82; *The Swing Mikado* and, 114–15; White on, 188–96
Wright, Jeremiah, 2–4
Wright, Richard, 93, 168, 186, 232n66, 237n4

Yohan, E., 67–68
Yoshida, Yoshimasa. *See* Sugimoto, Ryokichi
Yoshihara, Mari, 216n2
Yoshihito (Emperor of Japan), 16
Yoshikawa, Mitsusada, 145

Zelaya, José Santos, 41, 51–52, 210n92